SCOTLAND
BEFORE
THE INDUSTRIAL
REVOLUTION

Longman Economic and Social History of Britain

General Editor: J.V. Beckett
Professor of English Regional History, University of Nottingham

This new seven-volume series will become a standard recommendation for students and other readers in search of an authoritative but readable introduction to the economic and social history of Britain from the Norman Conquest to the present day.

Distinctive features will be the commitment to a genuinely British approach, especially from the Union onwards; the openness to new ideas and new approaches; the effective use of instances and examples to animate theory; and a concern with both regional unity and regional diversity, to highlight the development of a national economy and a national consciousness.

The first volume to be published is:

SCOTLAND BEFORE THE INDUSTRIAL REVOLUTION
An Economic and Social History, c1050–c1750
Ian D. Whyte

SCOTLAND

BEFORE
THE INDUSTRIAL
REVOLUTION

An Economic and Social History
c1050–c1750

IAN D. WHYTE

LONGMAN
London and New York

Longman Group Limited
Longman House, Burnt Mill,
Harlow, Essex CM20 2JE, England
and Associated Companies throughout the world

*Published in the United States of America
by Longman Publishing, New York*

First published 1995

ISBN 0 582 05090 1 CSD
ISBN 0 582 05091 X PPR

British Library Cataloguing-in-Publication Data

A catalogue record for this book is available from the British Library

Library of Congress Cataloging-in-Publication Data

Whyte, Ian (Ian D.)
Scotland before the Industrial Revolution: an economic and social history, c1500–c1750 / Ian
D. Whyte.
    p.   cm. -- (Longman economic and social history of Britain)
Includes bibliographical references and index.
ISBN 0-582-05090-1 (CSD). -- ISBN 0-582-05091-X (pbk.)
1. Scotland--Economic conditions. 2. Scotland--Social conditions.
I. Title. II. Series.
HC257.S4W48   1995
330.9411--dc20
                                                                                    94-35109
                                                                                        CIP

Set by 7 in 10/13pt ITC Garamond Light
Produced by Longman Singapore Publishers (Pte) Ltd.
Printed in Singapore

CONTENTS

CONTENTS

LIST OF MAPS

LIST OF TABLES

PREFACE

1969 saw the publication of T.C. Smout's *A History of the Scottish People 1560–1830*,[1] a landmark in the social and economic history of Scotland which, in reviewing what was already known, pointed out many new directions for historians. In the last 25 years there has been a veritable explosion of research and scholarship in what had previously been a neglected field. Whole new areas of study relating to pre-industrial Scotland have been opened up or reappraised including agriculture, urban development, social structure, demography, crime, witchcraft, wages and prices, diet and literacy. This research has generated new questions about Scotland's past and led to the exploitation of an ever wider variety of sources. It has also featured the adoption of theoretical approaches drawn not only from history but also from other disciplines including anthropology, economics, geography and sociology.

The purpose of this book is to review Scotland's economic and social history from early medieval times to the eve of the Industrial Revolution in the light of recent research. The problems of compressing into a single volume the development of a country with up to a million inhabitants over 700 years have been considerable. Of necessity I have had to be selective and I have been unable to do full justice to a number of important themes. Although I have tried to highlight new work on medieval Scotland, coverage is weighted towards the last 250 years or so of my period. Bearing in mind that this book forms part of a series on the economic and social history of Britain, this has enabled me to emphasise the growing integration which occurred between Scotland and England from the sixteenth century onwards.

In the past Scottish history has often been introverted and parochial. Stress has been laid on the distinctiveness of Scotland's society and institutions rather than on drawing meaningful parallels and contrasts with neighbouring countries. The effect of this has been to marginalise Scottish history in European terms by making its concerns seem peripheral to mainstream scholarship. Historians south of the Border have often been equally guilty of

1. T.C. Smout, *A History of the Scottish People 1560–1830* (London 1969).

parochialism by ignoring Scotland. Much so-called 'British' history is still English history with barely a cursory glance at the 'Celtic periphery'. An aim of this book is to try to present the development of Scotland in broad terms emphasising similarities and differences with neighbouring countries.

In a sense this book has been some 25 years in the making for it reflects my own attempts to understand and explain the workings of Scotland's society and economy in the past. Along this path I have received stimulus and encouragement, directly and indirectly, from a great many people. Among those who have been most influential I would like to record my gratitude to Ian Adams, Bob Dodgshon, Gordon Donaldson, Tom Devine, Sandy Fenton, Rab Houston, Michael Lynch, Rowy Mitchison, Ian Morrison, Christopher Smout and Graeme Whittington. Although their ideas and those of many other scholars have influenced the way I have written this book its shortcomings are entirely my own responsibility.

For

Kathy, Rebecca and Ruth

CHAPTER 1

THE MAKING OF
MEDIEVAL SCOTLAND

'Till Birnam Wood do come to Dunsinane...' In 1054 an event occurred which, thanks to Shakespeare, has become the most celebrated popular image of early-medieval Scotland. King Edward of England ordered Siward, Earl of Northumbria, to invade Scotland and drive out the usurper Macbeth so that his protégé Malcolm, in his view the rightful heir to the kingdom, could be installed. In a battle at Dunsinnan Hill, near the ancient royal centre of Scone, Macbeth was defeated. The accession of Malcolm III has been seen as a turning-point in Scotland's history. Brought up at the English court he later married Margaret, sister of the Saxon prince Edgar. Their marriage has been seen as marking the start of a reorientation of Scottish society in which English and continental influences were prominent. Three of their sons, Edgar, Alexander I and David I, were successively kings of Scotland. Under all of them, but especially under David, the introduction of Anglo-Norman influences was accelerated. The accession of Malcolm III provides a suitable point from which to begin a survey of the economic and social development of medieval Scotland. About the same time – possibly in 1057 – Thorfinn, Earl of Orkney died. His reign marked the apex of Norse power in northern and western Scotland. His death heralded the start of a decline in Norse influence which allowed the medieval kingdom of Scotland to expand to its full territorial limits.

Malcolm's accession was more complex than Shakespeare's compelling but simplified image. The victory at Dunsinnan was only a partial one. For Macbeth was not killed. He retreated beyond the mountain barrier, known as the Mounth, which pinches the coastal plain of eastern Scotland into a narrow pass north of Stonehaven. For another four years Malcolm ruled only Lothian and Strathclyde. When Macbeth was finally defeated and killed in 1057, at Lumphanan beyond the River Dee, his supporters set up his stepson, Lulach, in his place. It was not until the following year, after Lulach was killed, that Malcolm truly became king of Scots.

Although Malcolm can be seen as the king who began the reorganisation of Scottish society along Anglo-Norman lines, it was Macbeth who, at Dunsinnan, strengthened his army with a force of Norman mercenaries. The tenacity of support for Macbeth north of the Mounth following his initial defeat indicates that far from being the usurper of popular history he may have had a legitimate claim to the throne. He had been mormaer (great steward) of the province of Moray, in earlier times a kingdom in its own right. Behind his bid for the throne lay rivalry between different lineages which extended back for centuries. These tensions may have been superimposed on a north–south division of power across the Mounth which can be traced back to Roman times.

A focus on the accession of Malcolm III encourages us to look forward to the social and economic changes which occurred in twelfth- and thirteenth-century Scotland, yet on probing deeper into the events of 1054–58 we are also drawn back into Scotland's pre-medieval past and into a consideration of important elements of continuity in Scottish society. A starting date of around 1050 is a convenient but arbitrary benchmark and we need to consider Scotland's society and economy in earlier centuries as a foundation on which to build. The introduction of Anglo-Norman feudalism in the twelfth and thirteenth centuries was superimposed on, and integrated with, frameworks of social structures, territorial units and settlement patterns whose origins take us far back beyond the reign of Malcolm III. Historians now emphasise the period from the ninth to the eleventh centuries as one of consolidation within the Scottish kingdom. In seeking the origins of the structures of medieval Scottish society, as they start to become evident with more detailed documentation in the twelfth century, we need to go back beyond the dynasty founded by Kenneth mac Alpin in the mid-ninth century. In doing so we enter a period for which surviving documentary sources are limited, laconic and usually ambiguous. To fill in more of the picture we need to turn to evidence provided by archaeologists and place-name specialists. The information they provide is equally difficult to interpret and sometimes conflicts with what we know from historical sources. Therein lies much of the fascination and the frustration behind the search for the origins of medieval Scotland.

A MULTIPLICITY OF PEOPLES

An unwary reader who ventures into the history of the area we now know as Scotland between the fifth and eleventh centuries is liable to emerge bewildered by the multiplicity of peoples involved – Picts, Scots, Britons, Northumbrians, Norse, Danes, Cumbrians, Gall-Gaedhil – and the complexity of their political relations. Presented baldly, much of the known history of this period appears as a tale of campaigns mounted by outlandishly named warlords for obscure reasons, punctuated by battles and sieges in uncertain locations. There is plenty of scope for theorising on the basis of limited evidence concerning how these peoples became integrated into what was to become the kingdom of Scotland. Nowhere is this more evident than in ideas about the Picts.

Most of what we know about the Picts comes second-hand from records produced by other peoples. As a result Pictish history has been written largely by deduction. This helps explain why they are such a mystery and why differences between them and the other peoples of early-historic North Britain have been emphasised rather than similarities. A tendency to see the Picts as a problem or a curiosity has led to their contribution to the making of medieval Scotland being marginalised. Only in recent years have the Picts been rediscovered as a Celtic people and their role reassessed. The origins of the Picts are uncertain. 'Picti', a nickname meaning 'painted people', is first recorded by a Roman author in AD297. A century earlier the tribes of eastern Scotland north of the Forth had coalesced into two major groups, the Caledonii and the Maeatae, their territories probably separated by the Mounth. Gradual consolidation under over-kings in northern and southern Pictland and the development of a single monarchy ruling the whole of Pictland emerges only indirectly and indistinctly from the sources. Nevertheless, this process provided the foundations for the later Scottish kingdom. Pictland remained a remarkably stable unit. The Picts beat off the Northumbrian threat to their southern frontier and it was only with the settlement of the Norsemen in the Northern and Western Isles that they were forced to cede territory.

Three elements of Pictish distinctiveness have been emphasised by scholars. First was their use of a different P-Celtic language from that spoken by the Britons of southern Scotland, as well as the existence of an earlier pre-Indo-European tongue, thought by some to have been the language used in Scotland before the arrival of the Celts. Next was a matrilineal system of succession to kingship unique within Britain. This was also thought to have had ancient non-Indo-European origins. Finally, more tangible but no less enigmatic, were the Pictish symbol stones. Recently the reality of the first two of these hallmarks of Pictish individuality has been questioned.[1] Doubt has been cast on the survival of a pre-Celtic language among the Picts, the evidence for which was a limited number of unintelligible ogam inscriptions. Place-name studies have shown that a number of name elements were shared between the Picts and the Britons south of the Forth suggesting that linguistic differences between them may have been less than once suggested. Increasing evidence of intermarriage between the royal houses of Pictland, Strathclyde and Dalriada indicate that linguistic barriers between them were not insuperable.

The existence among the Picts of a markedly different system of succession to the kingship has also been challenged and the evidence – principally a list of Pictish kings – re-interpreted. The matrilineal argument was largely based on the fact that while brother sometimes succeeded brother, son did not follow father until the very end of the Pictish period. This was thought to indicate that the right to kingship was vested in the sons of a royal mother and that in the next generation it passed to the sons of their sisters. These king lists have been assumed to chronicle a single dynasty of kings succeeding through a matrilineal system. It has, however, been suggested that they refer to an over-kingship which was open to claimants from a number of

1. A.P. Smyth, *Warlords and Holy Men: Scotland AD 80–1000* (London 1984), pp. 36–83.

lineages ruling sub-kingdoms, similar to contemporary systems elsewhere in the Celtic world.[2] Under such circumstances it would have been almost impossible for a son to succeed his father in the kingship. Interpreting the evidence so as to draw parallels between the Picts and neighbouring societies seems more realistic than adopting a theory which places them in a unique category.

To the west of Pictland were the Scots. Migrating from Ireland they established the kingdom of Dalriada around AD500. From an initial base in Cowal, Dalriada expanded to include most of later Argyll. The boundary between Pictland and Dalriada was Drumalbyn, the main West Highland watershed. How far the influence of Dalriada had spread northwards towards Skye and the Outer Hebrides before the arrival of the Norse is not clear. Although speaking a different version of Celtic from the Picts the Scots shared a similar society based on tribal kingdoms controlled by warrior kings and their war bands. Within Dalriada three main lineages occupying distinctive territories can be recognised; the Cenel nGabrain in Kintyre, Cowal and mid-Argyll, as well as Arran, Bute and Jura, the Cenel Loairn in Lorn, Ardnamurchan and probably Mull and Tiree, and the smaller, less important Cenel Oengusa based on Islay. Each lineage had its own ruler and the kings of the two more powerful ones competed for the over-kingship of Dalriada.

South of the Forth and Clyde were other Celtic peoples who can be termed Britons. In the Lothians the kingdom of Gododdin was overrun by the Northumbrians during the seventh century. In the west was the kingdom of Strathclyde, with one of its major centres on Dumbarton Rock. The Strathclyde Britons have, like the Picts, been underrated in the past because most of the surviving sources that refer to them were generated elsewhere. Strathclyde was powerful enough to keep the Scots in check and possibly at times to impose kings on southern Pictland. Until their fortress on Dumbarton Rock was besieged and captured by the Norse in 870 the military strength of Strathclyde remained considerable.

In south-west Scotland the political structure is less clear. In post-Roman times the British kingdom of Rheged extended north of the Solway and may have included most of Galloway. This region was to become a cultural melting-pot. Place names indicate an influx of settlers from Ireland roughly contemporary with the foundation of Dalriada, and a later phase of Gaelic immigration, perhaps from Dalriada itself around 800. There was an infiltration of Anglians into Dumfries-shire in the early eighth century, a later wave of Norse and Norse-Gaelic incomers from the west and north, and a Danish element from the south. In the early tenth century the sub-kings of Strathclyde pushed southwards into Cumbria annexing the Solway Lowlands and the Eden Valley. What languages the inhabitants of Galloway spoke at any time, which culture they identified with and whose leadership they accepted is something of a puzzle.

What we know of the political history of the Picts, Scots and Britons tends

2. Ibid.

to emphasise the differences between them but their similarity as Celtic peoples should not be forgotten. In terms of material culture and social structures they had an essential unity which was to persist for centuries. Against them impinged two different groups, the Angles of Northumbria and the Scandinavians. In the seventh century the Anglian kingdom of Northumbria expanded northwards through the Merse and into Lothian. British strongholds at Edinburgh and Stirling may have fallen in 638 and 642. Only a little later the dynastic takeover of Rheged gave the Anglians an entry into Galloway. The Northumbrians pushed beyond the Forth in 658 and for a brief period dominated southern Pictland. In 685 at Nechtansmere near Dunnichen in Angus, an Anglian army was defeated and its leader, King Ecgfrith, killed. The frontier between Pictland and Northumbria then seems to have been pushed back to the Lothians, possibly marked by the line of the Pentland ('Pictland') Hills but Northumbrian influence in East Lothian and the Merse persisted for three centuries.

To what extent the Anglian occupation of south-east Scotland involved a takeover of existing settlements and territorial units by an incoming aristocracy, or was accompanied by a substantial influx of population has been debated. That estates and their centres were transferred as going concerns is suggested by the site at Doon Hill above Dunbar where a timber hall belonging to a British landholder was destroyed and replaced by an Anglian one. By Ecgfrith's reign Dunbar itself was a Northumbrian royal centre but the name suggests that it had originally been a British stronghold. The distribution of places whose names contain Anglian elements suggests an initial zone of occupation in the Merse and then East Lothian. This was followed by an intensification of settlement in these areas and penetration up the valleys of the Tweed and its tributaries. Anglian names are scarcer in Midlothian and rare in West Lothian, suggesting that the Northumbrians' occupation west of the River Almond was short-lived. In the Tweed basin British landholders may have remained in possession of the upland areas. Fragments of linear earthworks like the 20 kilometre Catrail may be the remains of territorial divisions between Anglians and British.

In the north the Viking age opened abruptly, as elsewhere in Britain, with a series of raids in the 790s including one on Iona in 795. There is no indication that permanent settlement in the Northern Isles preceded or accompanied these first raids. Any occupation is likely to have involved 'ness-taking', the temporary fortification of promontories by raiding bands. Permanent settlement of the Northern and Western Isles was under way during the first half of the ninth century and around 870 the establishment of the Earldom of Orkney gave the new arrivals some political coherence. The Norse takeover of the Northern Isles was once thought to have wiped out the indigenous population. Recent excavations have suggested that there was a greater mixing of Norse and Pictish cultures. The Norsemen brought their own styles of houses, weapons and ornaments but adopted other elements of the local material culture. Even if a substantial element of the Pictish population did survive their language was submerged fairly quickly. In the

Western Isles the preponderance of Norse names for settlements alongside a predominance of Gaelic ones for topographical features may hint at the survival of a subjugated Celtic stratum in the population doing much of the menial work such as herding livestock and cutting peat.

Further south Pictland, Dalriada and Strathclyde all suffered from Norse raids and invasions. Olaf, Norse king of Dublin, devastated Pictland in 866 and appears to have occupied part of the kingdom for some time before going on, in 870, to destroy the British citadel on Dumbarton Rock. Norse pressure may have pushed the Scots eastwards and led to Kenneth mac Alpin's takeover of Pictland. By the end of the tenth century the Earldom of Orkney had expanded to become a major power under Earl Sigurd and his son Earl Thorfinn. At its peak the earldom controlled the Northern Isles, the Western Isles as far south as the Isle of Man, substantial areas of Caithness and possibly some of the West Highland mainland as well.

Place-name scholars have worked out a sequence which appears to reflect various phases in the expansion and consolidation of Norse settlement. Primary settlement on the best land in the Northern Isles was followed by the infilling of less favourable sites and an expansion into new areas. In the Northern Isles, where the Norn dialect continued to be spoken for centuries, modern place names are overwhelmingly of Norse derivation but in the Western Isles there was a resurgence of Gaelic speech and culture by the twelfth century. In the Hebrides the adaptation of Norse words by Gaelic speakers distorts Scandinavian place names. Despite this, indications are that the initial Norse settlement in the Outer Hebrides was dense. There are no indications of any Celtic place names that have survived from before the Norse settlement and in Lewis out of 126 settlement names 99 are pure Scandinavian in origin and another nine partly so.

In the north Scandinavian settlement names occur on the mainland as far south as the Black Isle. Norse settlement in the Western Isles seems to have been fairly dense as far south as Islay and then to have tailed off. The ratio of Norse to Gaelic place names falls from around 1:2 on Islay to 1:8 on Arran. On the West Highland mainland Norse settlement names are rare but topographic elements such as 'dale', a valley, are widespread. It has been suggested that such names delimit a Norse sphere of influence beyond the area of direct settlement, or that Scandinavian settlers in the islands may have used the mainland valleys as summer pastures for their herds. On the other hand it would have required a lot of influence to cause the inhabitants of an area to accept new names for major landscapes feature like valleys, so that it is possible that the Norse had some permanent presence here. In south-west Scotland the place-name evidence suggests a complex mixture of peoples with a movement of Danish speakers from the northern Danelaw bringing settlement names ending in -byr (a farmstead) as well as an influx of Gall-Gaedhil, people with a mixed Norse/Gaelic background, giving rise to Norse place names with a Celtic word order. Small clusters of places and isolated settlements with Scandinavian names in parts of eastern Scotland may indicate pockets of Scandinavian settlement.

THE CREATION OF ALBA

The earliest date in Scottish history which every schoolchild north of the Border was once expected to remember was 843, the union of Pictland and Dalriada (or, as it was often termed, the Picts and Scots), under Kenneth mac Alpin. As with the downfall of Macbeth, neither the date nor its significance as a watershed in Scottish history is as clear-cut as was once believed. The events and the circumstances which helped determine them are uncertain. The end of the Picts as a separate people, as a result of Kenneth's takeover, is as obscure as their origins.

Around 840, Kenneth mac Alpin, an upstart from a fairly undistinguished lineage, became King of Dalriada. Between about 843 and 847 he took over the Pictish throne and brought the two kingdoms under his rule. Within two or three generations the distinctive elements of Pictish culture seem to disappear and the Picts vanish from history. There is evidence of a large-scale penetration of Gaelic influences into eastern Scotland after Kenneth's takeover and later sources suggest that there was a substantial migration of population from west to east as well. Later medieval traditions claim that Kenneth secured his position by the treacherous slaughter of Pictish nobles. Whether or not this was true, Gaelic influences seem to have spread rapidly through Pictland under Kenneth and his successors. Even if there was no large-scale migration of Scots into Pictland a takeover of territorial units by Dalriadan nobles is likely. It may have been in this context that bilingual place names with Pictish and Gaelic elements, like many 'pit' names, were coined.

On closer examination Kenneth's takeover seems less epoch-making. Pictland and Dalriada had been growing closer for a considerable time and many processes thought to have been set in motion by him and his successors can be seen at work in earlier centuries. Pictish relations with Dalriada and Strathclyde from the seventh to the mid-ninth centuries were complex. At times the Picts were able to dominate their neighbours. Some historians have considered that Pictish domination of Dalriada lasted for considerable periods during the later eighth and early ninth centuries. Yet by 768 a king of Dalriada was invading the heart of Pictland and at other times both Strathclyde and Dalriada were able to impose kings on Pictland. Gradually, among the murky history of raid and counter-raid one can see the kingdoms of Dalriada, Strathclyde and Pictland coming closer together. Two seventh-century Pictish kings were linked with the ruling house of Strathclyde while Kenneth was not the first king to reign over both Dalriada and Pictland. It may have been sheer chance that the unification of both countries under a single dynasty came under Kenneth rather than one of his immediate predecessors. Increasing intermarriage, at least at the higher levels of society, is likely to have spread Gaelic influences in Pictland long before Kenneth's takeover. Constantine I who reigned from 789 to 820, and Oengus (820–34) had ruled Pictland and Dalriada from Forteviot in Strathearn, suggesting a steady infiltration of Scots into Pictland, perhaps under Norse pressure, some decades before Kenneth's coup.

While Norse pressure on Dalriada may have encouraged the Scots to look eastwards Kenneth's takeover seems to have been an opportunistic reaction to a major defeat of the Picts by the Norsemen in 839. The dynasty of Fortriu, which had ruled Pictland with increasing authority, was ended with the death of Eoganan (836–9), and many Pictish nobles were killed. This created a vacuum which Kenneth filled, perhaps with Norse assistance. Seen in broader perspective Kenneth appears less of a key figure; much of his fame seems retrospective, based on the dynasty that he founded rather than his own achievements. His reign was neither particularly long or peaceful. It took him several years to establish his rule over the whole of Pictland and his degree of control north of the Mounth is debatable. His reign does not seem to have been marked by major institutional innovations or cultural achievements.

Kenneth's reign was followed by a phase of consolidation during which the peoples of Pictland, Dalriada and eventually Strathclyde were brought together, especially under the long reigns of Constantine II (900–43), Kenneth II (971–95) and Malcolm II (1005–34). Under Kenneth's successors the focus of the kingdom was firmly established in east-central Scotland. Although the rulers of the united kingdoms were buried on Iona the royal inauguration site was moved from Dunadd to Scone which became the principal centre of power in the new kingdom. In dynastic terms, however, the line established by Kenneth was not particularly stable. Direct patrilineal succession had not been established and several reigns were short, terminated abruptly by murder. Grandsons, cousins and sometimes brothers succeeded rather than sons as the kingship rotated between different segments of the royal family. There appears to have been a deep-rooted feud between the two main branches of the dynasty which only ended with the accession of Malcolm III.

Despite dynastic instability, between the mid-ninth century and the reign of Macbeth the amalgamated Pictish and Dalriadan kingdoms gradually fused into the Kingdom of Alba or Scotia under leaders who became known as kings of Scots. This contrasts with the disunity of England south of the Humber and with the numerous tribal kingdoms of Ireland. By the end of the eighth century Strathclyde had become a client kingdom of Alba. Its native line of kings died out around the end of the 880s. Between 900 and 1018 the kings of Alba maintained Strathclyde as a sub-kingdom which was usually granted to their designated heir, a process which helped to integrate Strathclyde into the rest of the kingdom. This custom continued in a modified form into the late eleventh century. Alba expanded southwards against Northumbria to take first Lothian and then the Merse. King Edgar of Wessex finally conceded the Scottish occupation of Lothian in 973. In 1018 Malcolm IIs victory at the Battle of Carham confirmed the Scottish hold on the Merse and established a frontier along the Tweed. For a time it looked as though Scottish expansion would continue to the Tees. The situation in the north was less clear-cut. It is not certain how much control the kings of Alba had over the far north on the borders of the Norse sphere of influence. Even further south in Moray they may only have ruled on sufferance. During the tenth century three kings of Alba were killed fighting in the north and the mormaers of Moray were still referred to as kings into the eleventh century.

KINGSHIP AND SOCIETY

Picts, Scots and Britons shared a social structure based on tribal kingship with an aristocratic warrior elite society in which wealth was counted in cattle. Within this tribal society men were bound to chief or king. But the sources only give us tantalising glimpses of social structures and relationships. As in Ireland many apparent conflicts may have been ritualised raids to collect tribute from recalcitrant vassals. The survival of the poem by Aneirin about the Gododdin, telling of a British attempt to check the northward advance of the Angles by attacking their camp at Catterick, reminds us of the importance of heroic exploits in this warrior society even if many forays were mere cattle raids.

We have a clearer picture of Irish society in the early historic period than for Scotland because the documentation is far better. As long as it is remembered that society in Dalriada, and even more so in Pictland and Strathclyde, was probably not an exact counterpart, the broad outlines of Irish society provide a framework against which we can compare the Scottish evidence. Celtic society appears as tribal but hierarchical with high kings, over-kings, tribal kings, nobles, freemen and commoners bound together in a complex structure of political authority and alliegiance. Kingship was, in theory, hereditary but among those men who were lawfully eligible the succession may sometimes have been determined by election. A system of tanistry in which a successor was designated during the king's lifetime was in use. The importance of kinship in conferring eligibility for kingship helps to explain the emphasis which was placed on genealogy.

The fact that the Pictish king lists show that direct succession from father to son was virtually unknown until the very end of the Pictish period does not necessarily indicate the existence of a matrilineal system. It could have resulted in part from the imposition of kings on Pictland from Dalriada and Strathclyde. It is also possible that the lists refer to an over-kingship open to candidates from a number of tribal kingdoms within Pictland rather than a single dynasty succeeding through a matrilineal system. It seems likely that there were two tribal confederations among the Picts, north and south of the Mounth, with an over-king and tribal kings in each region and, at a later stage, a king ruling over both provinces. In Ireland (and probably Dalriada) a four-generation pyramid of male lineage, the derbfine, existed within which all the male descendants of a king down to great grandsons were eligible for kingship. The Scots appear to have had a king for each of the three main lineages and an over-king. Until the mid-seventh century the over-king was drawn from the largest and most powerful lineage, the Cenel nGabrain, but then they were displaced by the Cenel Loairn in the late seventh century before staging a comeback less than a century later.

The dynasty established by Kenneth mac Alpin seems to have had a succession which alternated between two major branches, so that son might succeed father but with a member of the other dynasty in between. This was an improvement on earlier systems in which the succession was open to competition from or rotated around the families of several tribal leaders. Nevertheless, by the end of the tenth century it was causing problems, leading to a series of assassinations by impatient successors. Kenneth II appears to have persuaded his magnates to agree to a new system of succession within one family.

Society was cemented by clientship, a series of contractual and carefully defined reciprocal relationships between people of different rank involving mutual benefits and obligations. Clientship helped to give security to people at lower levels of society while defining the status and position of those higher up. Early Irish laws recognised two forms of clientship: base and free. Base clients, usually of lower status, rendered food, military service and hospitality in return for protection and land. Free clients were usually men of noble status whose duties included acting as companions to their leader. Below the nobility it is not clear to what extent there may have been a stratum of independent farmers in Pictish, British or Scottish society which can be equated with the Anglo-Saxon ceorl (freeman). It has been suggested that the ordinary tillers of the soil were bondmen but there is also likely to have been a slave group below them. Churchmen and craftsmen stood outside this hierarchy but could be slotted into it at levels appropriate to their status. The upper levels of society maintained their position by a combination of kinship and wealth, power being measured in terms of numbers of cattle and clients.

Such societies might appear simple in structure. However, the survival of the Senchus fer nAlban, a later copy of what was probably a seventh-century document, shows that Dalriada had a surprisingly sophisticated system for raising tribute and military service from units which may have represented the households of freemen. Every 20 'houses' had to provide the manpower for two seven-bench boats. Much of this manpower must have come from bondmen dependent on the free householders. No evidence of a comparable system survives for Pictland but references to a Pictish navy makes it likely that one existed. In Orkney, a series of ounceland districts, originally areas from which an ounce of money had to be paid, formed the basis of the taxation system into post-medieval times. Although introduced by the Norse there are indications that it was based on an earlier Pictish system.

The smaller tribal kingdoms within Pictland gradually lost their status and autonomy. From the early tenth century we hear of mormaers or 'great stewards' in charge of provinces. Whether they were tribal rulers transformed into provincial administrators or new officials created under the impact of the Viking threat is not clear but as mormaers had something of the status of kings the former seems more likely. In the case of Moray, as we have seen, the transition from tribal king to mormaer was not complete by the early eleventh century. North of the Forth there were perhaps a dozen mormaers. Below them was a more numerous gentry group, the thanes, comparable to those in Northumbria and Strathclyde, administering shires within which they held estates.

In the Northern Isles the mass of Norse society was composed of independent farmers divided into bonders (ordinary freemen) and those with the superior rank of 'hold'. In Orkney the power of the earls may have inhibited the development of a strong chieftain class until the time of Earl Thorfinn. The bonders were free in legal terms and when they acted in concert they were sometimes able to negotiate with the earl regarding the tenure of their lands and the burdens placed on them. In particular, they sought to protect their distinctive odal tenure, under which land was held inalienably within families. Place-name evidence from Tingwall in Orkney through Dingwall to Tinwald in Dumfries-shire indicates the existence of a series of thing sites or assembly places, the foci of administrative and judicial districts. The southern part of the Western Isles may have sent representatives to the assembly at Tynwald in the Isle of Man. Evidence for a regular structure of local thing assemblies is strongest in Shetland. In Orkney the system appears to have been centralised by the earls at Tingwall and then Kirkwall. The Law Thing Holm in Shetland, site of the central assembly, was still being used for legal transactions in the sixteenth century. In late-medieval times the Council of the Isles met at a similar site near Finlaggan on Islay, almost certainly another ancient assembly site, probably one of many scattered through the Norse dominated Hebrides.

SETTLEMENT, TERRITORY AND ECONOMY

Our knowledge of settlement patterns in early-historic Scotland, and the degree to which they continued into medieval times, is scanty and mostly indirect. Archaeological excavation has concentrated on high-status sites representing the upper levels of the settlement hierarchy. The most characteristic type of high-status centre among the Britons, Picts and Scots was a defensive work with ramparts encircling a hill or cutting off a promontory. Such sites appear to have been the descendants, in a slightly different social context, of large Iron Age hillforts like Traprain Law and Eildon Hill North. The early-historic fortified sites that replaced them were characteristically smaller in area and often utilised rocky sites with stronger natural defences. Alcock[3] has suggested that some time between the first and sixth centuries AD there was a change in society which was reflected in a move in the unit of defence from the tribe as a whole to chiefs and their warbands. This was accompanied by the abandonment of large hillforts like Traprain and the development of smaller citadels like Dunadd, Dundurn, and Dumbarton Rock. The change may only have involved relocation over a short distance, sometimes from an inland to a coastal site. The fort on Traprain Law

3. L. Alcock, *Economy, Society and Warfare among the Britons and Saxons* (Cardiff 1987).

may have been replaced by a stronghold at Dunbar while the citadel on Dumbarton Rock may have been the successor to a larger fort at Carman a few kilometres inland.

Sites of this type are found throughout Dalriada, Pictland and the British kingdoms of southern Scotland suggesting a basic similarity in social structures and patterns of authority. The vertical distinction between the citadels and lower enclosures may have been accompanied by a hierarchical and functional contrast between inner areas occupied by tribal leaders and outer zones accommodating retainers and used for industrial activities. While such centres were, as we know from both historical and archaeological evidence, sometimes attacked and besieged they should be considered less as fortresses and more as defended homesteads sufficiently grand to house, often only temporarily, a king with his warband. Sites like Dunadd and Dumbarton have been described as the 'capitals' of early-historic kingdoms, but this concept is anachronistic at a time when kings were almost certainly peripatetic, moving round a circuit of royal centres to which tribute was brought. Forts like Dunadd can be seen as places to which tribute from the local population was first brought and then consumed by local rulers. Periodic visits to centres in different parts of his territory allowed a king to discharge administrative and legal functions, distribute largesse and display hospitality. Consumption of tribute was a visible sign that it was being paid, helping to define the relationships between rulers and their clients. Within a kingdom a number of centres may have been used regularly by peripatetic over-kings. In Dalriada royal use of Dunadd, Dunollie and less certainly forts at Tarbert, Loch Fyne and Dunaverty is recorded and other centres are likely to have existed. Similar patterns may have been repeated on a smaller scale among tribal kings though where the territory was smaller the existence of a single permanently occupied tribal centre is likely.

Dunadd may nevertheless have had special functions which enhanced its importance. Rock carvings near the summit of the citadel, including a deep-cut footprint, have been associated with inauguration rituals in which new kings were symbolically married to their kingdoms. Dunadd may have been the inauguration centre for the over-kings of Dalriada for it stands close to the probable boundary between the territories of the two most powerful lineages, the Cenel nGabrain and the Cenel Loairn. A similar carved footprint near Dunaverty may mark an inauguration site for tribal kings of the Cenel nGabrain. Such customs were not confined to Dalriada and a rock-cut seat at the summit of the Pictish fort at Dundurn in Strathearn may have had a similar function.[4]

Not all high-status centres, particularly in the south and east, were as prominent and durable as nuclear forts. South of the Forth timber halls defended by wooden palisades, similar to the complex that has been excavated at Yeavering, were used by the Northumbrians and the Britons. At

4. L. Alcock, *PSAS*, 119, 189–226.

Doon Hill near Dunbar a timber hall 23 metres long dating from the second half of the sixth century was replaced by a seventh-century Anglian hall. At Sprouston near Kelso aerial photography has revealed the outlines of what may have been another hall complex. Recent excavation of a coastal promontory site near Coldingham has uncovered two palisades, possibly marking a British fort succeeded by an Anglian one on a site which was later re-used as a Northumbrian monastery.[5] Rectangular timber halls remained in use into medieval times. At Courthill in Ayrshire a hall of this type was burnt to make way for an Anglo-Norman motte, probably in the early twelfth century.

The Pictish royal centre at Forteviot has recently been investigated by Alcock.[6] The site is a gravel river terrace above the River Earn and a tributary. Indications are that the foundations of stone-built structures, possibly the remains of a palace from Pictish times or the reign of Malcolm III, have been removed by river erosion. A richly sculptured stone found in the stream-bed may have formed part of an arch in a royal church or chapel, possibly from the period of Kenneth mac Alpin. Crop marks around the modern village may indicate an early Christian cemetery. They also pick out a range of prehistoric ritual monuments which suggests that this site was venerated well before Pictish times. In this Forteviot appears as a Scottish counterpart of the Irish royal centre at Tara.

When we turn to lower levels in the settlement hierarchy evidence is most abundant for northern and western Scotland. Here later disturbance by intensive cultivation has been less than in the Lowlands. In the West Highlands the commonest type of settlement from early historic times is the dun, a small, thick-walled stone fort. Although the origins of duns lie in pre-Roman times five of the 11 examples which have been excavated in Argyll have provided signs of occupation during early historic times. The percentage of duns occupied in post-Roman times may have been higher than this figure suggests for dating has been largely determined by distinctive imported items which may not have filtered down to every site.

Duns can be visualised as fortified homesteads housing family-sized groups of relatively high status. The largest must have required a substantial labour force for their construction suggesting that their occupants had considerable power locally. They were probably similar in function to the ring forts of Ireland. There may also be parallels with medieval Scottish tower houses. As landscape features duns have often, like tower houses, been considered in isolation rather than as centres from which surrounding territories were controlled. Closer examination shows that some duns are surrounded by enclosures and what may be the sites of hut platforms. We can perhaps see them as foci for undefended nucleated settlements of dependent farmers.

Another type of settlement which may have been comparable in function and status with duns was the crannog, a lake-dwelling constructed on an artificial island. Although their use in Scotland extends from the Bronze Age

5. L. Alcock, *PSAS*, 116, 255–80.
6. L. Alcock, *PSAS*, 122, 215–89.

to medieval times, in Ireland crannogs seem to have become especially popular from the seventh century AD and a number of Scottish examples are known to have been occupied at around the same period though crannogs continued to be used in the Highlands into the sixteenth century. It is hard to imagine such seemingly damp and inconveniently located sites as being occupied by high-status families. We have, however, the example of the royal crannog at Lagore in Ireland, while Scottish sites like Loch Glashan in Argyll have produced a similar range of imported pottery, glass and jewellery to nuclear forts. The construction of crannogs rather than duns may have been related to local topography. In Islay for example crannogs are common in the north west of the island where few duns occur. Here there are many small lochs suitable for crannog construction but a lack of the type of sites associated elsewhere with duns.

We are still a long way from identifying the settlements of the bulk of the population. In Ireland it has been suggested that ring forts were accompanied by undefended nucleated settlements of bondmen, the ancestors of later clachans. A similar pattern may be envisaged for the West Highlands. The ubiquitous remains of deserted clachan settlements there have generally been considered to date from the later eighteenth and early nineteenth centuries. Nevertheless, the remains at some sites suggest several phases of development and it is possible that the origins of some of these may reach back into medieval times or earlier.

Excavation has provided a clearer picture of early-medieval settlement in the Norse-dominated Northern Isles. At Jarlshof continuity of occupation is emphasised by a sequence of building extending from the Bronze Age to post-medieval times. At Buckquoy in Orkney the contrast between Pictish and Norse housing styles is particularly clear. Here three successive Pictish buildings spanned the seventh and early eighth centuries. Two cellular houses with rounded central chambers surrounded by smaller cells were overlain by a more advanced figure-of-eight house with a large oval chamber and a smaller circular one attached. After 50 years or so a rectangular Norse farmstead was constructed on the same site. The first Norse houses at Jarlshof had separate byres (cowsheds) but later ones were true long houses with house and byre integrated. The byres were paved for ease of cleaning while the living areas had beaten earth floors to retain the heat of the fire. Finds of the tips of ards or light ploughs at Jarlshof indicate that the Norse economy had an arable element as well as a pastoral one. The proportions of animal bones at Buckquoy show little difference between the Pictish and Norse phases of settlement (50 per cent cattle, 30 per cent sheep, 20 per cent pig). Sea-birds also formed a useful source of food while the stone bases of haystacks at Underhoull in Shetland emphasise the importance of winter fodder. That the value of fertile land might outweigh the benefits of access to the sea is shown by the inland location of some high-status centres like Birsay in Orkney and Tingwall in Shetland. Fish do not seem to have been a dominant element in the diet of the Norse inhabitants of excavated settlements but was nevertheless more important to them at Buckquoy than to their Pictish predecessors. There is some evidence, however, from Jarlshof and Underhoull that fishing became more important after the initial Norse settlement, perhaps as the population grew.

Settlements existed within territorial frameworks whose structures come down to us faintly in documents from the twelfth and thirteenth centuries and which were important in determining the pattern of lordship and landholding in medieval Scotland. The system was structured to allow a landowning elite to exploit the land by means of peasants or bondmen. The feudal baronies of medieval Scotland were direct successors, in terms of scale and functions, of these earlier units. As in other parts of Britain territorial organisation involved 'multiple estates'. These existed throughout Scotland but the former homogeneity of the system is obscured by variations in terminology between different regions.

Multiple estates normally had a caput or central settlement where the lord's court, his demesne, and possibly a royal residence were located and to which rents in produce were brought. Within them there may have been freemen under a thane or administrator and a series of settlements occupied by bondmen whose status and obligations were clearly defined. An important element of multiple estates was an area of common grazing shared between the inhabitants. As commonties these survived as enduring features into the eighteenth and even the nineteenth century. The officer who administered a multiple estate for the king was responsible for maintaining law, organising military services within the estate, seeing that payments in produce and hospitality (cain and conveth) – were discharged, and looking after the king's residence if one existed. Cain rents still appear as miscellaneous small payments of livestock and produce in many estate rentals until the eighteenth century.

In south-east Scotland multiple estates survived into the twelfth century as shires, held from the king by ministerial tenants known as thanes. North of the Forth similar units were called thanages. Around 70 have been identified, mostly located in lowland areas but with some in the valleys of the Tay and Spey occupying mainly upland country. This suggests that thanages worked best in lowland arable areas with relatively small units that facilitated the collection of food renders and the discharge of services. Thanages varied greatly in size. There has been speculation as to whether they were once established as roughly similar-sized units and were later subject to amalgamation and sub-division, or whether they were initially created on an ad hoc basis as different-sized units. Thanages were administered by an official known as a thane and sometimes mair or toiseach. The location of the former estate caput (centre) sometimes survives in the place name 'thaneston'. Most thanages also had a kirkton with a church and its endowed land.

In Orkney a similar framework appears as the huseby system. The Earls of Orkney established a series of administrative or huseby farms and districts for the collection of food renders and other taxes and the organisation of a naval levy. This was modelled on a system which is said to have been introduced into western Norway in the time of Rognvald, the first Earl of Orkney, who may have brought it to the Northern Isles. Evidence for multiple estates is weakest in the West Highlands but many district names which survive to the present day, such as Ardnamurchan, Moidart and Morvern, may preserve a memory of their former existence. Equally in south-west Scotland districts like Annandale, Cunningham and Nithsdale, seen as discrete units in the twelfth century, may originally have been multiple estates.

Some multiple estates were parish sized and, indeed, developed into ecclesiastical parishes. Others were considerably larger. During the twelfth and thirteenth century some shires became the nucleus of larger sheriffdoms bearing the same name. The extent of the old shire of Berwick is given in a charter of 1095. Most of its dependent settlements were scattered within a radius of half a dozen miles of Berwick itself with another group further up the Tweed but the sheriffdom of Berwickshire was a far larger unit. The original shires of Haddington, Edinburgh, Linlithgow and Stirling were expanded into sheriffdoms in a similar way. Edinburghshire's boundaries to east and west are likely to have been the Rivers Esk and Almond, the same as the later sheriffdom, but the shire did not extend nearly as far south as the later sheriffdom. In the case of Clackmannan and Kinross, which survived into modern times as counties, the transfer from shire to sheriffdom was direct.

The fact that multiple estates in eastern Scotland are described in terms derived from Northumbria is no longer considered as an indication that the system originated under Anglian rule. Early-medieval Scottish monarchs merely applied Northumbrian terminology to an existing system. Barrow[7] has demonstrated that some shires can be traced back to the seventh century and there is no reason to suppose that they were not then already long-established. North of the Forth it is probably significant that many thanages focused on places whose names contain Pictish elements. This may indicate that they pre-date the spread of Gaelic into Pictland from the mid-ninth century. Although the huseby system appears to have been introduced to Orkney and possibly Shetland at a later date it may have been superimposed on existing Pictish administrative divisions.

The economy over much of Scotland at this time appears to have been one of mixed farming rather than the nomadic pastoralism of the 'footloose Celtic cowboys' that was once suggested. The importance of the arable element in Pictland is shown by the ways in which settlements containing the Pictish element 'pit', (a share of land or a farm), are linked to areas of well-drained soils suitable for cultivation. Pit names, which often have Gaelic personal names as suffixes, are thought to date from the ninth and tenth centuries when Gaelic-speaking Scots were settling in Pictland. In the West Highlands the locations of crannogs, duns and royal centres like Dunadd are also related to pockets of well-drained fertile land. Traces of field systems or ridge cultivation which are likely to be contemporary with the occupation of such

7. G.W.S. Barrow, *The Kingdom of the Scots* (London 1973), pp. 7–63.

settlements have yet to be securely identified. In most cases they have probably been obliterated by later cultivation. Finds of wheat, oats and barley from Dunadd, and oats and barley at Dundurn, along with the more frequent discovery of querns, confirm the importance of cereal cultivation.

Within such an economy craftsmen were supported at two levels. At a local scale, perhaps associated with sites like the smaller duns, were artisans working iron, wood, and leather, making pottery and weaving cloth. At a more sophisticated level specialist metal workers – jewellers and armourers – were linked with high-status centres. To what extent such craftsmen were peripatetic or were based more permanently at places enjoying royal and monastic patronage is uncertain but it is likely that local rulers would have exerted as much control as possible over the makers of prestige goods in order to enhance their position. The existence of separate communities of specialist metal workers is suggested by excavations at the small fortified site of Mote of Mark in Galloway. Here a wealth of raw materials and debris of jewellery was discovered in a context which suggests a purely industrial site rather than an unusually small royal stronghold with a resident jeweller. There is ample historical evidence that in early-historic times smiths were regarded with awe and superstition; this, and their importance in exchange systems as producers of prestige goods, may help explain their segregation.

The economies of the kingdoms of early-historic Scotland operated without the use of coins but were by no means closed. Finds of pottery imported from northern or western Gaul as kitchenware or tableware, fragments of glass which probably originated in the Rhineland and remains of amphorae from the Mediterranean point to more distant contacts. Some of these imports could have been adjuncts to more perishable cargoes such as casks of Gaulish wine for use in both ecclesiastical and secular contexts. The imports seem to reflect genuine trading contacts rather than gifts between rulers and are likely to have been carefully controlled by kings. One can only guess at the nature of the return cargoes; furs, hides and wool perhaps, and possibly slaves.

THE SPREAD OF CHRISTIANITY

Christianity seems to have entered Scotland by three routes; via Galloway, from Ireland and through Northumbria. The different streams sometimes coalesced and sometimes clashed. There seems to have been an early Christian colony in south-west Scotland in the immediate post-Roman period. The fifth-century saint Ninian seems to have come to this group as a minister rather than a missionary. The seat of his diocese, Candida Casa, has been identified with Whithorn but may have been shifted to Kirkmadrine in the Rhinns of Galloway by c500. Ninian has also been credited with converting the Picts but if so his influence must have been confined to the margins of southern Pictland around the Forth-Clyde isthmus. By c600 Ninian's successors had spread Christianity from Galloway throughout southern

Scotland. Kentigern, who died in 612, became the first bishop of Strathclyde, based on Govan or Glasgow, while early Christian inscribed stones at Yarrow and near Kirkliston indicate the existence of Christian communities in the south east by the late fifth or early sixth century. The structure of the early Christian church in this region down to the seventh century may have been diocesan with episcopal centres at Whithorn, Glasgow and possibly Abercorn, Old Melrose and Stobo. The Northumbrians may already have been converted when they moved into the Merse and Lothian. No Anglian place names in south-east Scotland have connotations of pre-Christian worship and no pagan burials have been found. Under Northumbrian rule a number of monastic sites were established, some at old episcopal centres like Abercorn, and Old Melrose, others in new locations such as Coldingham and Tyninghame.

In 563 another major influence arrived from Ireland in the person of Columba. Again he was not a missionary; the Scots of Dalriada were probably already at least partially Christian. From 565, when he set up a monastery on Iona, most of his work involved ministering to the inhabitants of Dalriada. He made more than one trip into Pictland and met Bridei, king of the northern Picts but none of his biographers claim that he converted Bridei or many of his people, or that he founded any monasteries in Pictland. Nevertheless, his contacts paved the way for later missionary work. In Dalriada his followers established a number of monasteries including ones on Tiree, Skye and beside Loch Awe. Within a century of Columba's death a chain of monasteries extended to the Moray Firth and Lindisfarne had been founded by Aidan in 635 or 636. This led to the revival of Christianity in Northumbria where the merging of Celtic monasticism with Northumbrian wealth produced some of the finest manuscript illumination and sculpture in early-Christian Europe.

Columba's fame has overshadowed contemporaries like Comgall and Brendan who founded monasteries on Tiree and the Garvellach islands, Moluag who established a community on Lismore, and Donnan who was killed when his monastery on Eigg was destroyed, presumably by Picts, in 617. Christianity pushed into Pictland from the north and west in the mid and later seventh century while missionaries worked their way northwards through Southern Pictland. Following the Synod of Whitby in 663 the influence of Iona over the church of Northumbria was removed and Roman rather than Celtic forms of worship became normal in south-east Scotland. In the early eighth century, the Pictish king Nechtan sent for Northumbrian craftsmen to build a stone church in the Roman style in Pictland. The church at Restenneth in Angus is considered to have been the one referred to but others may have been built as well. Many Class II and III symbol stones may have served as preaching sites. The relative scarcity of these monuments south and west of the Tay, close to the royal centre of Forteviot, may indicate a greater density of early churches in this district.

Following Nechtan's reforms the church in Pictland was strongly influenced by Northumbria. An episcopal centre appeared at Abernethy by the early eighth century. Others may have been set up at the same time. After Kenneth mac Alpin's takeover contact with the Columban church was renewed although elements of the Northumbrian reforms survived to give a distinctive character to the church in the former Pictish heartland into the twelfth century. Among the monastic sites established in Pictland by the mid-ninth century was one at Kilrymond (St Andrews) which housed relics of St Andrew which may have been brought from Byzantium, and Dunkeld which may have been the site of an earlier Columban monastery. A system of dioceses may have been established around these and other centres but they are less clear than those south of the Forth where diocesan boundaries are likely to have been fitted to existing secular divisions of Northumbria and Strathclyde.

In the early ninth century most of the monks on Iona retreated to Ireland because of Viking raids rather than following the Scottish kings to Forteviot. This marked the start of a lessening of influence of the western church in Alba. Although the Vikings were notorious as pillagers of monasteries there are indications that in the Northern Isles Christian worship and some monastic communities may have continued under Norse rule and that Christianity may have been accepted by some Norse settlers long before their supposed conversion under the influence of Olaf Tryggvason around 995. In Orkney the re-use of early religious sites by Norse churches implies some continuity although the real organisation of the church in Orkney dates from the time of Earl Thorfinn who established a bishopric based on a large new church at Birsay.

In the ninth century a movement towards reform and a stricter observance of celibacy and other rules by the clergy spread from Ireland. New communities of culdees (servants of God) were established at a number of sites in eastern Scotland. Although we know the locations and something of the history of many early monastic sites it is not clear how widespread and well developed was the organisation of the Church by the eleventh century. Many churches undoubtedly existed. Some, like the group of churches in East Lothian dedicated to Saint Baldred, may have been established by holy men. Others were built by secular landowners. A pattern of large parishes served by bodies of clergy operating from minister churches with dependent chapels and open-air preaching sites continued into the twelfth century. Surviving churches from the early eleventh century and before are few. Ones like Restenneth and St Rule's at St Andrews reflect Northumbrian links while Irish influences are suggested by the round towers at Abernethy and Brechin. An early link between churches and shire centres has been suggested by Barrow[8] on the basis of place names containing the element 'eccles'. In southern Scotland at least, churches may have been deliberately founded shire by shire. In Orkney the distribution of early Norse chapels relates closely to the ounceland divisions suggesting that while many of them may have been established by individual landowners there was an element of central direction by the earls.

8. Ibid., pp. 60–4.

In the early ninth century, before the start of Norse settlement, the political situation in north Britain had changed only in detail for centuries. North of the Forth the Picts faced the Scots across the spine of Drumalbyn. Northumbria dominated the south east, British Strathclyde the south west. By the eleventh century the picture had changed. Pictland and Dalriada had merged to form Alba or Scotia, absorbed Strathclyde and driven its southern frontier to the Tweed and beyond. The Norse had established a powerful presence in the Northern and Western Isles which was to influence these regions for centuries. The kingdom of Scotland had taken on something resembling its medieval shape. At a smaller scale, regional differences, such as the distinctiveness of Galloway, were already apparent. If underlying continuity in social structures and territorial frameworks was evident changes were at hand which were to have a major impact in shaping the society and economy of medieval Scotland.

CHAPTER 2

THE INTRODUCTION OF ANGLO-NORMAN FEUDALISM

The Norman Conquest in 1066 imposed feudalism over most of England at a stroke. In Scotland, it arrived peacefully through the deliberate policies of Scottish kings. It was imported in a fully-developed form but unlike England its introduction was gradual and its geographical impact piecemeal. Feudalism was a system under which all land belonged to the king and was held from him by vassals in return for precisely specified obligations the most important of which, initially, were military in character. Major vassals in turn granted or sub-infeudated their lands in turn to lesser men. The spread of feudalism produced major alterations in the social and economic organisation of Scotland but many of its attributes are now considered less revolutionary than was once thought. In theory feudalism contrasted strongly with the tribal, kinship-based structure of Celtic society. In practice, however, many aspects of eleventh-century Scottish society, notably tenure, food renders and military service, were already essentially feudal. It is doubtful if, at the lower end of the social scale, the bulk of the population noticed much difference with the transition from Celtic to feudal lordship. Nevertheless, any feudal elements in pre-twelfth-century Scottish society were structured only within individual earldoms and lordships. From the twelfth century onwards these were increasingly integrated into a single all-embracing framework. Its lack of a kinship basis also allowed Scottish kings to use feudalism to make major changes in patterns of landholding. Malcolm III and Queen Margaret are sometimes considered to have introduced feudalism to Scotland. Certainly they were receptive to English and continental influences but the scale of their innovations was limited. The English who came to Scotland during their reign appear to have been a handful of court followers rather than a wave of settlers. Malcolm's, and especially Margaret's, greatest legacy was an indirect one; the influence they exerted on their sons. Yet there is also little evidence of significant Anglo-Norman influence in Scotland during the reigns of Edgar and Alexander I. It was David I (1124–53), only a boy at the time of his parents' death, who was the real innovator. Changes before his reign were limited and their impact has been over-emphasised.

THE SPREAD OF FEUDALISM

In the twelfth and thirteenth centuries the spread of feudalism played a key role in the consolidation and extension of royal power in Scotland, particularly in the west and north. Between the reign of Kenneth mac Alpin and the twelfth century the centre of gravity of the Scottish kingdom shifted decisively eastwards and southwards. During the twelfth and thirteenth centuries the area of effective royal control included most of southern Scotland (apart from Galloway) and the east-coast Lowlands as far as Moray. To the north and west were areas, including the heartland of Dalriada, which were rarely visited by Scottish kings and where royal control was, at best, uncertain. Ross and Moray were centres of periodic rebellion while Galloway retained a strongly individual identity. William I was too involved in clashes with England to give full attention to the northern and western parts of his realm. His successor, Alexander II, was able to deal more effectively with Galloway and then from the 1240s with the West Highlands, a process which was continued under Alexander III.

Although the earldom of Orkney ensured continuing Norse domination in the Northern Isles their power in the Hebrides weakened during the twelfth century leading to a Gaelic resurgence and the forging of new links with Ireland. Lack of firm control by Norway in the Hebrides led to rivalry and conflict among the warrior aristocracy there. Of these mid-twelfth century warlords Somerled, lord or king of Argyll, was the most powerful. He built up an empire which extended from Kintyre to the Outer Hebrides holding some of his territories from the king of Norway and other lands from the king of Scots. On Somerled's death in 1164 his lands were divided among his four sons who each founded powerful families. One of these, the MacRorys, styled themselves Lords of the Isles. When their line died out in the fourteenth century the title went to the MacDonalds, descended from another of Somerled's sons. Scottish expansionist policies in the Isles brought a reaction from Norway in 1261 with an invasion led by King Haakon. Checked at Largs the Norsemen retreated and Haakon died in Orkney soon afterwards. His son Magnus, more pragmatic, negotiated the Treaty of Perth in 1266 under which Scotland acquired the Western Isles (but not Orkney and Shetland) in return for a cash payment.

Although the Anglo-Norman era in Scottish history can be considered as spanning the two centuries between the accession of Edgar in 1094 or 1097 and the outbreak of the Wars of Independence in 1296 the key phases of innovation occurred under David I (1124–53), Malcolm IV (1153–65) and William I (1165–1214). David had been brought up at the English court, a member of the royal household and a close friend of Henry I. His marriage in 1113 or 1114 to the Countess Maud de Senlis, the richest widow in England, brought him the Honour of Huntingdon, a huge block of estates in central England, making him one of the greatest English magnates. He had seen the efficiency of feudalism in action and had noted how its military structure could support royal authority. It is not surprising then that he began to apply new ideas to the large area of south-east Scotland which had been granted to him by his elder brother Edgar and was grudgingly confirmed by Alexander I. This area he controlled from around 1107, long before he succeeded to the throne of Scotland.

The reality of power in medieval Scotland was that monarchs relied on personal loyalties to rule effectively rather than administrative structures. A successful king needed a strong group of supporters through which he could consolidate, strengthen and extend his rule. David's success lay in his ability to link his ambitions with those of incoming Anglo-Norman knights and churchmen, a new nobility of service and ecclesiastical hierarchy ready to enforce the king's will to their mutual benefit. David established a unified system of control based on feudal lordships and sheriffdoms over southern Scotland (except Galloway) and began the feudal settlement of lowland Moray. His successors, Malcolm IV and William I, built on these foundations extending their power into the south west, the west and the north. The earldoms, still in the hands of Celtic families, were areas where support for the crown was often half-hearted. To counter this Malcolm and William strengthened their power base in eastern Scotland and spread their influence by feudal grants to Anglo-Normans while at the same time trying to bring the earls into a closer, more personal relationship with the crown.

At the very start of his reign David I began granting large blocks of royal demesne to Anglo-Norman incomers in return for knights' service. His reign saw the minting of Scotland's first coinage, the introduction of burghs, motte and bailey castles, and sheriffdoms. Parallel with this went changes in the organisation of the church including the creation of an effective system of dioceses and parishes and the establishment of continental monastic orders. Each new element was important in itself but taken together they reinforced one another and formed a powerful integrated system through which royal power was increased. However, their introduction and spread was gradual and the full impact of Anglo-Norman feudalism was not felt until well after David's reign. David did not, for instance, found any new religious houses north of the Forth. Most of his innovations were concentrated in south-eastern Scotland, the area that he had controlled before his accession. Even here it took decades for the newly established monastic orders to complete their initial building programmes and organise the efficient running of their new estates.

Although David and his successors managed to change their relationship with some of the native earls to feudal ones, the most distinctive feature of the spread of feudalism was its close association with the settlement of immigrant Anglo-Norman landholders, some recruited from England others from Normandy, Brittany and Flanders. Their settlement in Scotland was part of the energetic outburst which carried Norman organisation and military skills from Ireland to the Mediterranean. The Anglo-Normans, Barrow[1]

1. G.W.S. Barrow, *Kingship and Unity 1000–1306* (London 1981).

suggests, formed a bridge between the Celtic kingdom of Malcolm Canmore and the Scotland which successfully waged war against Edward I, II and III. Seen from this perspective they were the men who dragged Scotland into the Middle Ages. But though their achievement remains impressive they may have received too much credit for transforming Scotland.

The focus of this chapter on innovation and change should not obscure the importance of continuity in medieval Scottish society. It was not a case of Celtic traditions and institutions being replaced by Norman ones so much as the two blending and interacting. Scottish kings in the twelfth and thirteenth centuries, even David I the most prolific of innovators, were careful to strike a balance between continuity and change. Many developments, such as the spread of the parish system, involved standardising and improving existing structures which had previously developed in a piecemeal manner. William I was the most pro-Norman of these monarchs but his successor, Alexander II, redressed the balance by encouraging the native aristocracy, promoting Gaelic culture and venerating Celtic saints. The re-absorption of Galloway and later the West Highlands into the kingdom also encouraged a resurgence of Celtic influences. Alexander III, at his inauguration in 1249, inherited a kingdom that had been significantly altered by feudalism but the basic features of the ceremony were all derived from Scotland's Celtic past and symbolised the continuity which underlay the changes of the twelfth and early thirteenth centuries.

Scotland was nevertheless a land of opportunity for ambitious younger sons of Norman families who had little hope of a substantial inheritance at home. Few of the Anglo-Normans who came to Scotland were men of power and substance. It was already common for elder sons to inherit their father's lands in Normandy and for younger ones to seek their fortune in England. The process was repeated for Scotland with cadet branches of many families established in England moving north. Sometimes they did spectacularly better than their stay-at-home elder brothers. The classic example is Walter, third son of Alan, a Breton knight. Walter's eldest brother inherited the family's estate near Dol in Brittany. The second son received most of the lands that Alan had acquired in England. Walter took service with David I around 1136, receiving a huge lordship in western Scotland and becoming king's steward, an office which gave the title to the later dynasty of Scottish kings.

The origins of a number of Anglo-Norman immigrants to Scotland in the reign of David I can be traced to the Honour of Huntingdon which David's successors continued to hold into the late thirteenth century. Some families seem to have come direct from Normandy though with only an incidental connection with the Honour. The Bruces took their name from the village of Brix in Normandy, the de Morvilles from a settlement a few kilometres away. In the reigns of Malcolm IV and William I newcomers came from a much wider area. Within England Somerset and Yorkshire were fruitful recruiting areas but despite the speculations of genealogists, the origins of many new families are not known.

The pattern of feudal landholding varied geographically and over time. In the Lothians and the Merse fiefs were generally small; a single village and its territory was a frequent grant. Many of these units were shires held by thanes which, when they came into the hands of the crown, were granted to Anglo-Norman tenants. In the south east fiefs rarely encompassed more than a couple of villages though some holdings, like that of the de Morvilles which encompassed most of Lauderdale, were larger. In western and south-western Scotland, where royal control was less certain, David I created larger lordships. Annandale, some 200,000 acres, was given to Robert de Brus for the servive of 10 knights. It was one of the earliest feudal grants dating from the start of David's reign in 1124 but several other grants like Cunningham to Hugh de Morville, Liddesdale to Ranulf de Soules and Renfrew with part of Kyle to Walter the Steward were equally impressive. Within their huge territories the new nobles sub-infeudated land to their followers creating a distinct colonial settler class of smaller Anglo-Norman landholders, often owing only a fraction of a knight's service. They were linked to each other by a common background, culture and language and closely tied to their feudal lord. David's successors were less willing to give out huge tracts of land for the service of several knights; single, half and even quarter knights' fees were normal while sub-infeudation greatly increased the number of fiefs held for fractions of a knight's service.

Under David I a start was made on feudalising the north with grants in Moray. During the reign of Malcolm IV feudal grants were extended into the western Lowlands on a large scale and began to penetrate the south west. Upper Clydesdale was occupied by groups of Flemings. Their settlement is evident today in a series of mottes linked with settlements whose names incorporate the personal names of the Flemish immigrants; Lamington (Lambin), Roberton (Robert), Symington (Simon), Thankerton (Tancard) and Wiston (Wice). The largest settlement, Biggar, was the caput of Baldred who may have brought in and planted the other Flemings. Their lands came partly from the church and partly from native landholders. By the time William I succeeded in 1165 most of southern Scotland had been feudalised. Anglo-Norman landholders were also strongly established in Fife, Angus, Gowrie and the Mearns. Most of the fiefs here were relatively small, often based on earlier thanages. Under William, a new wave of large 'frontier' lordships was created in the North East, Moray and even beyond the Great Glen, establishing a feudal aristocracy powerful enough to balance the influence of the native earls.

Stringer's[2] study of Earl David of Huntingdon, William's younger brother, shows how royal control was extended. Sometime between 1178 and 1182 David was granted the earldom of Lennox, an area of strategic importance where royal authority had previously been limited. This can be seen as part of a plan by William to increase his influence over the south-west Highlands. It was linked with the expansion of the Stewarts' power from their original feudal base on the south side of the Clyde estuary. David's grant of Lennox

2. K.J. Stringer, *Earl David of Huntingdon 1152–1219* (Edinburgh 1985).

and the new Stewart fief of Bute represented a front-line defence and a springboard for further expansion. By, or during, the 1190s David gave up the earldom of Lennox, presumably at William's request. It was returned to its native mormaers but on the basis of a new, closer relationship with the crown. David had initiated the development of Lennox as a feudal lordship on the frontiers of royal control and the native earls continued the process, sub-infeudating land to Anglo-Norman barons whose mottes can still be seen today. By the mid-thirteenth century a new sheriffdom centred on a new castle and burgh at Dumbarton had been established in Lennox. Secular control was augmented by the spread of ecclesiastical organisation through the area. By the 1250s Lennox was fully integrated into the normal government of Scotland.

David was subsequently awarded another frontier lordship, Garioch, in north-east Scotland, a compact 100-square-mile block of country straddling routes from the south to Moray and the north, situated between the great celtic earldoms of Buchan and Mar. Garioch was the first of a new series of extensive lordships to be created north of the Mounth. Prior to William's grant of Garioch to his brother royal influence in the north east had been limited. David's infeftment started the process of broadening the base of royal power in the region. The caput of the new lordship was at Inverurie where the prominent motte and adjacent burgh are a tangible reminder of the impact of feudalism.

There has been debate concerning the extent to which large feudal lordships were created from pre-existing landholding units, a theory favoured by Barrow[3] for south-west Scotland or whether, as Stringer[4] suggests, these large feudal grants were new, carefully constructed creations, custom-built to enhance their strategic and military role. For feudal colonisation north of the Mounth deliberate strategic considerations seem to have been important. David's lordship appears to have been a newly created unit, assembled by using existing thanages as building blocks, rather than an ancient territory.

Eventually Anglo-Normans were settled in feudal lordships and over most of Scotland south of the Forth. North of the Forth Fife, the lower Tay valley, Angus and the Mearns were heavily affected by feudal settlement as were parts of the north east, Moray and the valleys of the eastern Highlands. The western Highlands were affected much less by feudalism than other parts of Scotland. Certainly the region was not planted with Normans. It has been argued that almost the whole of Scotland was feudalised during the twelfth and thirteenth centuries though with varying degrees of completeness but for the western Highlands this is probably the wrong emphasis. In this area it was more the case that, rather than being brought within a feudal system, the native aristocracy adopted and adapted those elements of feudalism which helped support their traditional authority including, in the thirteenth and fourteenth centuries, an impressive range of stone castles.

3. G.W.S. Barrow, *The Anglo-Norman Era in Scottish History* (Oxford 1980).
4. Stringer, *Earl David*, pp. 65–7.

FEUDALISM AND SOCIETY

The social impact of feudalism and Anglo-Norman settlement is far from clear. The incomers brought only limited numbers of retainers and servants rather than large numbers of peasant settlers. In Galloway, where much Anglo-Norman settlement was direct from neighbouring Cumbria, the occurrence of several 'Ingliston' place names associated with mottes suggests that the numbers of immigrants were small and their settlement largely confined to estate caputs. In some cases the newcomers were granted existing settlements which they re-named. Elsewhere their arrival encouraged the foundation of new settlements and the intake of land from the waste. Overall, however, there was probably little displacement of the peasantry. Most of the fiefs granted to the immigrants were taken from land which had been royal demesne or which had come into royal hands by various means. This process sometimes had a makeshift appearance. In some cases scattered blocks and parcels of land in several parishes were combined to make up a knight's fee. When the tenure of shires and thanages came up for renewal they were not sometimes granted back to the native families who had held them but were given to outsiders. Nevertheless, while Norman lords were influential at court the native aristocracy continued to dominate extensive areas. Elsewhere many smaller landholders must have found themselves under the lordship of an incomer and bound to accept a new type of relationship based on knight service. In areas where Anglo-Norman settlement was dense, however, changes in the pattern of landholding must have been considerable particularly where huge new lordships were granted out and extensive sub-infeudation to vassals was undertaken.

The economic impact of the Norman settlement may not have been great. Although the creation of feudal fiefs encouraged the expansion of settlement and cultivation in some areas the normal pattern appears to have been for Anglo-Normans to take over existing shires or thanages with their dependent townships. There is no evidence to suggest that sweeping innovations in the economic organisation of rural society were introduced. In the great lordships like Garioch a new level of estate administration was created but in many cases the thanes may have continued to operate, collecting rents and renders under the supervision of Norman stewards. The initial contrast between the Celtic aristocracy and the immigrants was gradually reduced through intermarriage. The Comyns became the first Norman family to acquire an earldom in this way around 1212. By 1286 five of the ancient earldoms were in the hands of Norman families. The power of the ancient earldoms remained unchanged though. The earls still retained responsibility for mustering the common army of Scotland. The long-established requirement to fight in the common army remained separate and distinct from knight service.

In social terms feudalism had little impact at the level of the peasantry although the Anglo-Normans undoubtedly encouraged the spread of the use of English and the retreat of Gaelic over Lowland Scotland. The renders peasants made to their feudal lords in produce, livestock, demesne cultivation and carriage work were similar to those which had been required in pre-feudal shires and thanages. At a higher level the granting of knights' fees and fractions of them was the foundation of the class of lairds which began to emerge in the fifteenth century. Many families which later became prominent, including ones which eventually rose into the ranks of the nobility, traced their origins to Anglo-Normans who came to Scotland as followers of greater lords. Hugh de Morville, David I's Constable, brought from Normandy the ancestors of the Sinclairs, the Haigs and the Maules. By the thirteenth century grants of land for tiny fractions of a knight's fee – a 24th and even a 32nd – were becoming common. In practice there was a distinction between the holders of entire knights' fees (or by the thirteenth century sometimes a half and a quarter) and those with smaller fractions. The former group enjoyed full baronial jurisdiction while the other did not.

At a lower social level, early monastic records such as those of Coldingham Priory provide some information on peasant tenure. On the Priory's lands in the Merse the cultivators of the soil were catagorised as cottars, bond tenants, husbandmen and free tenants. At the lowest level cottars owed mainly labour services. Occupiers of bond land were unfree, with servile status. Husbandmen paid rents mostly in money with some services, as did free tenants, the distinction between them not being very clear.

It is easy to consider feudalism, once introduced to Scotland, as an unchanging set of relationships but feudalism evolved through the twelfth century into the thirteenth even as it continued to spread. The castle became a home, the ethos of knighthood became more exaulted, fiefs became hereditary possessions rather than rewards. William's long reign marks the peak of feudalism in its classic military form. After this elements of feudalism merged increasingly with Celtic practices and customs to form a distinctively Scottish brand of feudalism, one that was to exert a strong and continuing influence on society throughout our period. During the reigns of Alexander II and III the purely military aspects of feudalism declined in the Lowlands. Serfdom also faded, having virtually disappeared by the fourteenth century. The more rapid disappearance of serfdom compared with England has sometimes been seen by the Scots as a matter of congratulation, an indication that society north of the Border was 'free' at a relatively early date. But the broader structures of feudalism that bound society together were more enduring. Anyone familiar with seventeenth-century estate records with their baron courts, thirlage to mill and smithy, rents in kind, labour services on the mains, carriage work and peat cutting for the laird can have little doubt that feudalism in a wider sense flourished long after the demise of serfdom. Nor was the decline of serfdom entirely to the advantage of the peasantry for it loosened the hereditary bond between peasant families and the land they worked. Comments of fifteenth- and sixteenth-century writers like John Major on widespread insecurity of tenure may have been exaggerated but there is little doubt that short leases and year-to-year tenancies were normal on many late-medieval estates and that whatever the *de facto* situation under paternalistic estate management the legal security enjoyed by most tenants was limited.

THE CROWN AND THE NOBILITY

In medieval Scotland, unlike England, territorial influence was concentrated in the hands of a limited number of magnates whose lands were usually grouped in compact blocks. In England many of the great fiefs were fragmented making them harder to organise as administrative and judicial units, especially with the crown extending its power. In Scotland, where royal bureaucracy was much less developed, the crown depended far more on the magnates to rule effectively and the great fiefs and lordships remained important as administrative units. In Angevin England royal power expanded and magnate power declined. In twelfth- and thirteenth-century Scotland both grew in step forming a close-knit partnership where kings had sufficient power and resources to reward magnates but not necessarily enough to overawe them.

Interpretations of the relationship between the crown and the nobility in thirteenth-century Scotland have been re-evaluated in recent years, as they have been for late-medieval times. Instead of stressing conflict and confrontation, the emphasis is now on co-operation.[5] Traditional views of the medieval Scottish nobility have been coloured by the bias of medieval chroniclers who, concentrating on the development of Scotland as an independent kingdom, tended to favour the interests of the monarchy. They portrayed the nobility as violent and factious, needing taming by strong kings like Alexander III. This tendency to emphasise crisis and conflict needs to be offset by a more balanced view of the nobility. Their concerns were to advance their families and extend their influence by good marriages and of royal patronage. In a country where state bureaucracy was less developed than in contemporary England there were more plums, including posts as sheriff and justiciar, with which to reward nobles. A combination of well-chosen marriages and royal patronage lay behind the rise of the Comyns and their supporters to a dominant position in Scottish society in the mid-thirteenth century. The alliance between Alexander III and the Comyns allowed the crown to extend its influence in the north and west while at the same time binding the Comyns to the monarchy by powerful ties of self-interest.

Anglo-Normans in Scotland maintained contact with their English relatives. Through grants and marriages a number of families came to hold land in both countries. The granting of lands in England to Scottish religious houses and vice versa also demonstrates that the Border was not a barrier to contact and landownership. For 200 years or so the Norman world was a flexible and

5. Stringer, *Earl David.*

fluid one in which the holding of lands and other activities were not unduly hampered by national boundaries. The period of nearly 80 years of peace between Scotland and England before 1296 was particularly favourable for the development of cross-Border landholding. Only at the end of the thirteenth century did the outbreak of war and the resulting rise of nationalist feeling make such links increasingly difficult to maintain. Eventually families were forced to decide on which side of the Border their allegiance lay.

Cross-border estates were not unique to Scotland and England. Cross-Channel, Anglo-Welsh and Anglo-Irish landholding was also common. But until Stringer's recent study[6] the scale and importance of Anglo-Scottish landholding had been underestimated. The tendency to focus on the crisis periods of Anglo-Scottish relationships in the later twelfth and later thirteenth century rather than the long periods of peace between made such landholding appear ephemeral and of little significance. By the reign of Alexander III, however, the pattern of Anglo-Scottish landownership was complex ranging from the crown down to quite modest estates.

Such estates were uncommon in the twelfth century. The Anglo-Normans who settled in Scotland under David I were mostly men with little or no patrimony in England. Intermarriage between landed families in Scotland and England soon began to alter this situation as even native Scottish earls started to acquire land south of the Border. On the eve of the Wars of Independence Anglo-Scottish magnates controlled land in nearly every English shire and Scottish sheriffdom. When it is appreciated that between c1170 and 1296 eight of the 15 chamberlains of Scotland, 12 of the 17 Justiciars of Lothian and five of the 12 Justiciars of Scotia held estates in England, as well as nine of the 13 earldoms between c1200 and 1296, the influence of this group becomes apparent. Clearly the outbreak of war interrupted a process of steady integration into a single Anglo-Scottish aristocracy.

David I's Honour of Huntingdon, which remained in the hands of his successors until the late thirteenth century, exhibits cross-Border landownership at the highest level. Hugh de Morville, originally a landless knight from the Cotentin peninsula, was granted a sizable fief in the Honour of Huntingdon by David I, a position which he consolidated by a good marriage. As Constable of Scotland he did even better receiving the lordships of Lauderdale and Cunningham. His success in Scotland did not lead to the neglect of his English estates though and his son Richard acquired by marriage extensive estates in the West Riding of Yorkshire. Until the family died out at the end of the twelfth century the de Morvilles ran their lands, widely scattered over two countries, as a single carefully managed lordship. When the male line of the de Morvilles died out the bulk of their lands passed to Roland, lord of Galloway, who had married a sister of the last male de Morville. The amalgamated de Morville/Galloway estate formed an even larger trans-Border holding.

6. Stringer, *Earl David*, pp. 117–211.

The balance of landholding varied from one family to another; some held estates which were evenly balanced between the two countries while in other cases holdings were concentrated in one country or the other. Scottish families which held relatively small portions of land in England worked hard to retain and develop them. Even after the outbreak of war they relinquished them with reluctance. The existence of such a substantial block of landowners with interests in both countries must have been a major force encouraging peaceful relations and economic, as well as social, links. It was only the succession crisis in Scotland combined with the unresolved question of the constitutional relationship with England which severed them.

The nobles – 13 earls and 25 barons – who swore in 1284 to uphold the succession of Margaret of Norway were an interesting group emphasising the diversity of Scotland's aristocracy at the end of the thirteenth century. Most of the earldoms were still held by ancient Celtic families but some had passed into Norman control. Anglo-Norman families like the Comyns and the Stewarts had risen through a combination of shrewd marriages and royal service. The success of other families, like the Bruces and Balliols, less close to the crown, related mainly to the acquisition of territory through marriage. Some new families like the Frasers, Morays and St Clairs had risen mainly through royal service but this group also included native families like the MacDonalds which had supported royal campaigns in the West Highlands. Despite their diversity, however, they were united in their appreciation of the advantages of co-operating with the crown.

THE TRANSFORMATION OF THE CHURCH

During the twelfth and thirteenth centuries the organisation of the Scottish church was radically altered and its hierarchy became more clearly defined. In the process it was brought more closely into line with religious practice in Western Europe and many of its distinctive Celtic elements were removed or toned down. David I rationalised and extended the system of dioceses. The pattern of diocese in the mid-twelfth century was complex. Some dioceses were already ancient reflecting the activities of the early-Christian church and the political frameworks within which it had operated. Whithorn diocese, still under the authority of York, was directly descended from the eighth-century Northumbrian diocese, which in turn reflected the even earlier see of Ninian. Its boundaries coincided with the political unit of semi-independent Galloway. The limits of the diocese of Glasgow were effectively those of the ancient kingdom of Strathclyde and went back to the time of St Kentigern. Others in eastern Scotland, like Dunblane, Dunkeld and St Andrews were centred on Pictish monastic sites. They had probably developed as diocesan centres from the mid-ninth century. They were characterised by a piecemeal intermingling of territories, each with many widely scattered detached churches reflecting endowments to their monastic centres or early missionary work.

Other dioceses were new, established by the crown during the twelfth century to help give the northern and western fringes of the kingdom greater cohesion. Argyll, Caithness, Moray and Ross were created in this way. The two dioceses of the Western and Northern Isles were still subject to Norwegian authority. Diocesan centres in Scotland were normally long-established religious sites, providing further evidence of continuity, and there was little effort to move them to nearby expanding towns as in England, with the possible exception of Aberdeen which may have been moved from Mortlach.

Although some dioceses had formerly been vacant for long periods, during the twelfth and thirteenth centuries appointments became more regular and bishops began to provide their sees with the necessary fabric and administrative organisation. Diocesan centres became fixed with the building of cathedrals. As throughout Western Europe, this was the great age of cathedral building. Some cathedrals were large and impressive like St Andrews, others smaller but still dignified like Dunblane and Dunkeld. The mid-thirteenth century was the busiest phase of construction, a time when considerable resources were also going into building abbeys and priories. At St Andrews the late eleventh-century cathedral of St Rule was replaced by a far grander one founded in the 1160s but not formerly dedicated until the early fourteenth century. At Glasgow the present cathedral, the most complete example from medieval Scotland, was built in the thirteenth century replacing two successive twelfth-century ones on the same restricted, awkward site. St Andrews and Glasgow, the two wealthiest dioceses, were the first to have a full chapter of clergy but the others soon followed. The clergy were secular for the most part but at St Andrews the cathedral was served by Augustinian canons and at Whithorn by Premonstratensians.

Tidying up and extending the system of dioceses as well as providing them with cathedrals and bodies of clergy was a major achievement. Of greater significance for the ordinary population, however, was the establishment of a network of parishes served by hundreds of stone churches and chapels. There were probably already a great many churches and chapels in existence by the time of Malcolm and Margaret. Some had been established by monasteries, some by individual holy men and many others had been built on episcopal estates and by lay landowners. There are indications that at least some Anglo-Normans were required to build and endow churches within their new fiefs. The sites of many of these churches went back to the early days of Christianity. Their organisation was often of the minster type, especially in southern Scotland where Northumbrian influence was strong, with resident bodies of secular clergy serving extensive districts. North of the Forth many groups of Culdees had, by the twelfth century, effectively become secular colleges of priests similar to the clergy serving the minsters further south. This system was gradually modified as more and more landowners built their own churches and chapels and provided priests to serve them, reducing the need for large central churches.

David I systematised the provision of endowments for churches by requiring the payment of teinds (tithes). In the process he created a national parochial framework. Many churches had been endowed with land by their founders but the teinds of crops, livestock and animal products were of far greater value. Once everyone was required to pay teinds to their local church, parishes soon became constituted as legal and territorial units with boundaries rapidly fixed and demarcated. Many parishes were established using the boundaries of ancient shires and thanages. Others were created around new Anglo-Norman fiefs. Again continuity and change were intermingled. The network of nearly 1,000 parishes which resulted, almost complete by the end of the twelfth century, is substantially the one which survives today. Some large parishes were split during medieval times as dependent chapels achieved parochial status. However, this meant a loss of teinds to the parent church and was generally resisted. After David I's enactment concerning teinds the creation of a new parish became a deliberate act rather than a chance development. With the spread of the practice of granting the revenues of parishes to ecclesiastical corporations it became easier to split appropriated parishes as there was no loss of revenue to the owner. The number of new parishes created began to rise again in the thirteenth century after a burst of appropriations at the end of the twelfth but this did not significantly modify the overall pattern. Even after the Reformation the changes which were made to the medieval parochial system were fairly minor.

From the mid-twelfth century the revenues of many parish churches became appropriated by religious institutions; by dioceses to support their cathedrals and chapters, by monasteries and by nunneries. At first the Cistercians resisted this trend for receiving the teinds of parishes was against the rule of their order. But by the end of the twelfth century they too were appropriating parish revenues. Even so, Scotland's 11 Cistercian houses only came to accept the teinds of 37 churches between them. The most prolific appropriators were monasteries belonging to other orders. Kelso Abbey enjoyed the revenues from 37 parishes, Arbroath Abbey 34, Paisley Abbey 28 and Holyrood Abbey 25. Some dioceses were equally well endowed. Glasgow Cathedral was drawing on the incomes of about 35 churches by 1200. By 1300 over 60 per cent of parishes had their teinds siphoned off in this way and by the Reformation the figure had risen to 86 per cent compared to about a third for England. The resources which were creamed off from local communities in this way helped to finance the impressive phase of cathedral and abbey construction of the later twelfth and thirteenth centuries. The debit side was that instead of beneficed priests more and more parishes came to be served by perpetual vicars and later by chaplains and curates, poorly educated, poorly paid and poorly motivated. There would also have been a negative effect on the construction and maintenance of parish churches.

The period of real poverty for the parish clergy did not begin until the later fourteenth and fifteenth centuries when their fixed incomes were eroded by inflation. Thirteenth-century vicars and chaplains were paid fixed pensions rather than a share of the teind. After the Fourth Lateran Council in 1215 Scottish vicars were granted a stipend of ten merks. Such an income, provided that it was paid in full, appears to have been adequate in the thirteenth century, placing them on a par with wealthier peasant farmers or small freeholders, a social status comparing not unfavourably with that of many seventeenth-century ministers.

It is easy for the condition of the church in the fifteenth and early sixteenth centuries, with its poor provision at parish level, to colour our view of the medieval church causing us to underestimate its tremendous vitality and energy. It had evident shortcomings in terms of pluralism and nepotism. One can find examples of lay patrons using parishes in their charge as a means of providing livings for younger sons, absentees who often did not even bother to take holy orders and who left the running of the parish to poorly paid chaplains. Even so, there is less indication that insufficient resources were applied at a parish level to ensure the proper provision of spiritual care and welfare in the twelfth and thirteenth centuries than in later times. There is plenty of evidence of genuine religious devotion among the clergy and a real desire to bring the word of God to the population. The piety of landowners is also evident in their building and endowment of churches and their grants of land to religious houses.

Popular devotion and the quality of religious provision at parish level is hard to assess. If the new cathedrals seemed distant to most people and the activities of monks in the abbeys to have little relevance to their own lives the new parish kirks, simple and plain though they may appear to us, must have been impressive in settlements where they were the only stone buildings. Genuine faith is suggested by the popularity of pilgrimages; to St Andrews which had been a focus for pilgrims from the tenth century, to the shrine of St Kentigern in Glasgow and to many other places. Nevertheless, the rituals of the mass, no matter how well performed, may have meant little to the average peasant.

THE INTRODUCTION OF THE MONASTIC ORDERS

The establishment of dioceses and parishes involved the extension of a system which already existed in embryo. More innovatory was the introduction of continental monastic orders. In the time of Malcolm III and Margaret there were, as Barrow[7] has pointed out, no religious communities at all in Scotland south of the Forth. Further north there were groups of Culdees at some sites and a number of isolated hermitages but these lacked organisation and their observances were out of line with the Roman church. The new monasticism began under Queen Margaret with the establishment of a group of Benedictine monks at Dunfermline as an offshoot of Christ Church, Canterbury. The church that the monks built was extended during

7. Barrow, *Kingship and Unity*, pp. 77.

the reign of David I who raised it to the status of an abbey around 1128. The encouragement of a range of religious orders has been seen as a family enterprise on the part of Margaret and her sons, a policy pursued with purpose and dedication. If this was the case, however, the process accelerated markedly only in the reign of David I. The introduction of continental monasticism by Margaret was in a sense a false start. The monks of Dunfermline may even have been driven out of Scotland during the anti-foreign reaction under Donald Ban following the deaths of Malcolm and his wife.

During the reign of Edgar a Benedictine priory was founded at Coldingham. Under Alexander I, between 1115 and 1120, Augustinian canons were brought from Nostell in Yorkshire to found a house at the ancient religious site of Scone. Alexander also appears to have initiated the process which established Augustinian canons at Scotland's chief ecclesiastical centre, St Andrews. Under David I, however, the number of new foundations and the variety of religious orders increased dramatically. David's patronage of monastic orders was wide-ranging but not indiscriminate. He was the first person to bring to Britain monks from the new austere order of Tiron only a few years after its foundation. He established them near Selkirk in 1113 but in 1128 the monks moved to Kelso, a better site close to the growing royal burgh of Roxburgh. Kelso became one of the richest and most influential monasteries in Scotland, establishing daughter houses at Arbroath, Kilwinning and Lindores. The orders which came to Scotland were French in origin but their first monasteries were established as offshoots of English houses, staffed initially with English monks, strengthening contacts south of the Border as well as with the Continent. Once settled in southern Scotland these new religious communities began to found daughter houses of their own further north.

The Cistercians were introduced by David I at Melrose (1136) and Fergus, Lord of Galloway at Dundrennan (1142). The Cistercians eventually owned about a dozen houses in Scotland. The Burgundian Valliscaulian order, not represented in England, was established in relatively isolated locations within and near the Highlands, at Ardchattan, Beauly and Pluscarden. Augustinians canons were brought in to take over and update several old Culdee communities and other churches with a strong Celtic element. Under David I they were also established at Cambuskenneth and Holyrood. As the Augustinians were not a closed order they went out from their houses and served the community. A number of nunneries were also founded, the earliest being one at Berwick by 1153. In 1300 there were 11 nunneries in Scotland, some with revenues from appropriated churches, most with lands. David I's patronage also extended to the Knights Templars and Hospitallers. In the 1230s, during the reign of Alexander II, Dominican and Franciscan friaries were set up in many of the larger burghs. By the end of the thirteenth century there were over 20 in Scotland.

The endowments which religious houses received varied. For some of the nunneries they were relatively modest. In the case of the Cistercians, whose rule forbade them to live off rents and teinds, grants often included large areas of upland grazing which, under monastic management, were converted into huge sheep ranges. Most of the lands given to monasteries established by the crown came from royal demesne and represented a significant depletion of royal resources, something which later Scottish kings were to regret. Most early monastic foundations had royal patrons but some of the great Anglo-Norman lords also endowed religious houses. Hugh de Morville, Constable of Scotland under David I, was the first to bring the Premonstratensians to Scotland, establishing them at Dryburgh in 1150. Roland and Alan, lords of Galloway, founded other Premonstratensian houses at Soulseat and Tongland and brought the Cistercians to Glenluce while Uchtred, son of Fergus of Galloway, is credited with founding the Benedictine nunnery at Lincluden. Reginald, son of Somerled, founded Saddell Abbey in Kintyre, the Benedictine abbey of Iona and an Augustinian nunnery on the same island. The Cluniacs were established at Paisley by Walter the Steward. Also of significance was the continuing flow of smaller endowments to already established houses whose need for resources increased as their building programmes expanded. The generosity of large feudal landholders was sometimes carefully calculated though. As with David, Earl of Huntingdon, who founded a monastery at Lindores in Fife, endowments often took the form of revenues from parish churches rather than land. This limited the diversion of valuable capital assets into what has sometimes been seen as a non-productive sector.

By the late thirteenth century all the main monastic orders apart from the Carthusians were established in Scotland and the monastic settlement was almost complete. The Cistercians, Tironensians and Augustinian canons were the most important orders and although there was a concentration of religious houses in central and southern Scotland the new monasticism had spread far into the north and west. This was the peak of monasticism in medieval Scotland. The fourteenth century brought decline due to war damage. Even after large-scale hostilities ceased in 1328 many religious houses close to the Border remained vulnerable to attack.

The new religious orders had an important impact as landowners (Chapter 3) but also exerted a considerable influence on society. They introduced new standards for the performance of Divine Office and with this came new fashions in architecture and better organised hospitality and charity. The example of their disciplined communal life must also have been profound. While royal patronage of the monastic orders slowed down after the 1170s landowners continued to endow new foundations into the mid-thirteenth century. By this time the scale of building by the wealthier abbeys and priories was becoming increasingly impressive. To finance construction work on this scale even the Cistercians relaxed their rules about accepting incomes which did not come from the direct working of their own lands. With the provision of the more comfortable living quarters there must, almost inevitably, have been a trend towards greater worldliness among the cloisters though the Cistercians at least seem to have kept to a simple diet. The relative comfort of the monastic life began to attract many people who did not have a true vocation, something which may have come to count for less than the value of the endowments that prospective novices or their families could bring to a community. This did not bode well for the future.

CHAPTER 3

MEDIEVAL ECONOMY AND SOCIETY

POPULATION

Any figures for the population of medieval Scotland are pure guesswork. There is no equivalent of Domesday Book or the fourteenth-century English lay subsidies to provide even a rough basis from which calculations can be made, nothing before the hearth tax returns of the 1690s. Population estimates have been made by assuming a ratio between the carrying capacity of Scotland and England of around 1:6. The pitfalls of such an approach hardly require emphasis. Nevertheless, using this and other estimates it is possible to suggest that Scotland may have had a population of around one million by the early fourteenth century. Indirect evidence such as the creation of new settlements and the expansion of cultivation limits shows that, as over most of Western Europe, Scotland's population increased substantially in the twelfth and thirteenth centuries, possibly reaching a peak in the late thirteenth or early fourteenth century. At this time overall densities may have been around 35 persons per square mile. While this may seem low, average population densities were only slightly greater in the seventeenth and early eighteenth centuries, when a greater proportion of the population was concentrated in the towns. Medieval Scotland then was hardly an empty country. Many areas must have been as well populated in the early fourteenth century as they are today. Indeed some districts, especially in the north, may have supported more people than in later times.

Although estimates suggest a doubling of Scotland's population between the eleventh and fourteenth centuries, it is not certain to what degree this put pressure on resources in the way which occurred for parts of England. On present evidence population pressure in Scotland by the early fourteenth century appears to have been less acute than in England. Surveys of the lands of the Priory of Coldingham and Kelso Abbey at the end of the thirteenth century indicate that townships in the Merse had large areas under crop and, seemingly, little pasture. The implication is that cultivation had reached or even exceeded its long-term viable limits. The evidence for an advance of cultivation to high levels in the Lammermuirs, with the opening up of royal hunting forests and private chases for grazing, cultivation and settlement increased pressure on the land. Evidence for a substantial expansion of cultivation in the twelfth and thirteenth centuries is strongest for eastern Scotland from the Merse to Strathmore and the Mearns. By no means coincidentally these were the areas with the densest concentration of burghs through which agricultural surpluses could be channelled for export.

There is little information for medieval Scotland on short-term demographic episodes such as subsistence crises to compare with the details which are provided by the Irish annals though there are stray references to famines in the thirteenth century. The first two decades of the fourteenth century brought harvest failure and livestock mortality, as in northern England, though whether more or less severely is unclear. It is not known how badly the great European-wide famine of 1315–18 affected Scotland. but Scottish raids into northern England in the 1320s may be seen in this context as, in part, an attempt to make up natural losses by means of plunder. The beginnings of a population decline before the Black Death have been identified in England and, more recently, in Ireland due to a combination of a worsening climate, harvest failures, famines and outbreaks of livestock disease during the first quarter of the fourteenth century. In Scotland population losses may also have occurred as a result of war with England but so far there is no clear evidence of population decline before the mid-fourteenth century.

The Black Death, which reached Scotland in 1349, caused the most savage cut in population of any demographic crisis on record. Nevertheless, the scale of the disaster is uncertain. Later chroniclers claimed that around a third of the population perished in the initial epidemic while other outbreaks of plague later in the fourteenth century also took a heavy toll. It has been suggested that, as a result of lower population densities. Scotland may have suffered less severely than England from fourteenth-century plague attacks. In Scotland there was no legislation comparable to the English statute of labourers. In England shortages of labour made landowners reluctant to abandon serfdom while in Scotland it died out during the fourteenth century. Such evidence can be interpreted as indicating that Scotland did not experience so drastic a fall in population during the fourteenth century as England. Even if this was so, there must have been a significant alteration in the balance between population and resources with major social and economic repercussions. The paucity of subsistence crises during the later fourteenth and fifteenth centuries, evidence for increases in holding sizes, falls in rents, the leasing of demesnes and indications that the diet of ordinary people included a substantial component of meat and animal products confirms this.[1] Cultivation limits also retreated. This may have been due in part to background influences like climatic deterioration but it was

1. A. Grant, *Independence and Nationhood 1306–1469* (London 1984), pp. 77–9.

undoubtedly encouraged by the availability of good quality land in less marginal locations as a result of a drop in population. After the initial disaster of 1349 there were further outbreaks of plague in 1361–62, 1379–81, 1392, 1401–3, 1430–32, 1439–42, 1455–56, 1468–72, 1475–80 and 1496–1500. The mortality caused by these must have prevented any significant growth of population throughout the later fourteenth and much of the fifteenth century. It is unlikely that there was any significant upturn until well after 1500. Overall, the food supply situation appears to have been adequate throughout the fifteenth and early sixteenth centuries. In European terms Scotland may have been a poor country but its population was not a starving one.

SETTLEMENT

Early charters, our main source of evidence regarding the medieval Scottish countryside, tell us something about territorial units but little about the settlements within them. Consequently, ideas concerning medieval settlement tend to be based on backward projections from the better documented fifteenth and sixteenth centuries. Charters and place-name evidence show that even before the rise of population discussed above Scotland was far from being empty. In most areas, however, settlement was probably thinly spread at the end of the eleventh century. There was plenty of scope for the growth of existing places, for the infilling of the settlement pattern and for the spread of population into new areas. The actual form of settlement is less clear. Over most of Scotland, as in later times, the pattern is likely to have been a dispersed one of small hamlet clusters and isolated dwellings. Such a pattern has similarities with other areas of North-Western Europe including Ireland, Wales, south-west England and Brittany. It was well adapted to conditions where extensive areas of free-draining soils, capable of supporting large communities, were restricted, and to an economy orientated towards livestock rearing. Nevertheless, the fact that such settlement patterns also occurred in more fertile lowland areas like Strathmore with larger extents of high-quality land should make us wary of explaining settlement patterns purely in terms of environmental influences.

Just as the territorial framework of medieval Scotland reflected influences extending back into early-historic and even prehistoric times, so elements of the settlement pattern are likely to have reflected long-term continuity. This has been demonstrated by the excavation of some sites in the Northern and Western Isles. At the Udal in North Uist, occupation spans a period of some 5,000 years. The multi-phase site at Jarlshof in Shetland extends from the Bronze Age to the seventeenth century. Similar continuity is likely in southern Scotland but has yet to be demonstrated as clearly. Settlement excavations have focused on the northern and western fringes of Scotland and there has been a lack of investigation of medieval settlement sites in southern Scotland. The caputs or centres of many multiple estates were clearly places of importance with at least centuries of existence behind them when they first enter the documentary record in the twelfth and thirteenth centuries. In the Lowlands continuity of settlement locations from pre-medieval to post-medieval times may help to explain why there is so little trace of the medieval settlement pattern in the landscape. A recent study of crop mark sites on the gravels of the Lunan Valley south of Montrose identified plenty of prehistoric settlements.[2] Medieval, or at least pre-improvement, landscape features like cultivation ridges, field boundaries and trackways were also abundant but no trace of a medieval building was found. If the considerable changes of the eighteenth and nineteenth centuries have failed to alter settlement patterns in areas like this the more gradual changes of the first millennium AD are likely to have had even less impact.

Between the eleventh and the early fourteenth centuries the settlement pattern is likely to have evolved under the influence of population growth but the chronology of the colonisation of waste and the foundation of new settlements, extensively studied in other parts of Europe, is not clear. The process is only identifiable occasionally, and generally indirectly, from medieval charters. Sometimes the wording of a grant of an area of arable land makes it clear that the land has been newly cleared from the waste and is likely to have been associated with the creation of a new settlement. In other instances reference to the expansion of arable land occurs in a context that merely suggests that an existing settlement was growing. The splitting of existing settlements and their fields to create smaller units, which will be discussed more fully in Chapter 8, can also be identified.

Duncan has detected in medieval charters a contrast between eastern Scotland north and south of the Forth with a greater emphasis on arable farming in the Lothians and the Merse compared with areas further north.[3] It is in this context that evidence for a different settlement pattern in the south east may be considered. When documentation becomes more abundant in late-medieval times we find nucleated villages in this region similar to those of north-east England. Some villages have regular layouts with parallel rows, sometimes focusing on a central green, comparable with examples from the Eden Valley in Cumberland and County Durham. It seems unlikely, as was once thought, that such settlements were established as regular villages with extensive open fields during the Anglian occupation of the area. On the other hand, surveys of the lands of Kelso Abbey and Coldingham Priory indicate that some of these places were village-sized agglomerations by the end of the thirteenth century, parish centres with a church and often a lord's hall and demesne. It is possible that the scale and layout of some of these settlements may reflect re-planning by Anglo-Norman landholders during the twelfth and thirteenth centuries, contemporary with the creation of many regular village plans in northern England. It is possible that the regular layout of green villages like Ancrum, Bowden and Maxton may have been the result of

2. D. Pollock, The Lunan Valley project: medieval rural settlement in Angus, *PSAS*, 115, 1985, 357–401.
3. A.A. Duncan, *Scotland: The Making of the Kingdom* (Edinburgh 1975), pp.309–25.

re-planning when they were granted market charters in the sixteenth and seventeenth centuries. In the case of the East Lothian village of Dirleton, however, documentary evidence shows that the present layout of the settlement existed in the sixteenth century and was not the result of a comparatively late re-planning exercise.[4]

The most dramatic evidence for the expansion of medieval settlement and cultivation comes from the Lammermuirs. Parry has identified traces of settlements associated with ridge and furrow cultivation at altitudes where, under present climatic conditions, a crop of oats would hardly ever ripen.[5] His calculations show, however, that during the warm climatic phase that spanned the twelfth and thirteenth centuries it would have been possible to gain subsistence yields of oats on a reasonably regular basis at altitudes up to 1,200 feet. Settlement and cultivation would thus have been viable over all but the highest areas of this rolling hill country. Documentary evidence shows that most of these high settlements sites were abandoned between 1300 and 1600 while others at lower levels went out of use in the seventeenth and early eighteenth centuries. The immediate cause of abandonment might reflect a range of social and economic influences, but Parry has argued persuasively that climatic deterioration from the fourteenth century is likely to have been a background influence. Similar chronologies of settlement expansion and retreat probably occurred in other upland areas but have yet to be identified. Nevertheless, the advance of cultivation to such high altitudes in the Lammermuirs should not be taken as indicating that all available land at lower levels had been brought under the plough or that population pressure on resources was considerable. Some high-level ridge-and-furrow may have represented temporary, opportunistic, cultivation of land around summer shielings, a process which can be seen operating in the Highlands in post-medieval times. Even where settlements were more permanent they are likely to have leapfrogged a lot of land at lower altitudes which was more gently sloping and harder to drain.

The Scottish medieval farming economy appears to have involved the widespread use of systems of transhumance in which livestock, especially cattle, were sent to hill grazings or shieling grounds during the summer. In the Southern Uplands the tying up of large areas as royal and private hunting forests, the spread of commercial sheep farming and the expansion of settlement and cultivation, are likely to have brought the use of shielings to an end in most areas during the twelfth and thirteenth centuries. A dispute over pasture rights between the monks of Melrose Abbey and the inhabitants of the valley of the Gala Water in the late twelfth century may have been caused by an attempt on the part of the monks to encroach on shieling grounds. The existence of settlements whose names include the element

4. I.D. Whyte, The evolution of rural settlement in Lowland Scotland in medieval and early-modern times: an exploration, *SGM*, 97, 1981, 4–15.
5. M.L. Parry, Secular climatic change and marginal agriculture, *Transactions of the Institute of British Geographers*, 64, 1975, 1–14.

'shiel' testifies to the former existence of shielings. At Penshiel in the Lammermuirs the remains of a monastic grange show how the status of the site changed from temporary to permanent occupation.

At a time when the medieval economy was beginning to expand extensive areas of Scotland became tied up, for a time, as hunting forests.[6] The idea of maintaining forests as private hunting reserves was another Anglo-Norman innovation introduced by David I. Before his reign, neither monarchs nor magnates appear to have set specific areas aside for this activity. David began to designate royal forests from the 1130s and to issue grants of forests to barons and ecclesiastical corporations. The latter may have sought such grants as a means of excluding baronial hunting parties from their grazing areas. Along with royal forests came special forest laws enforced by the justiciars. The main royal forest in southern Scotland was Ettrick. North of the Tay were the forests of Alyth and Cluny. Further north still there were extensive royal forests on Deeside and in Moray. Large areas of the Southern Uplands were granted as baronial forests to families including the Bruces in Annandale, the Avenals in Eskdale and the Crawfords in Clydesdale. At one time royal and baronial forests formed a near-continuous block of territory from the Pentland Hills to the Solway. By the later thirteenth century, however, many forests were being reduced in size and thrown open for grazing and settlement. The royal forest of Gala and Leader was disafforested by Alexander II due to economic pressure. In the fourteenth century the crown disposed of many of its forests, along with other lands. New royal forests were established in the fifteenth century but they were located in more remote areas of the Highlands such as Glenfinglas and Mamlorn.

AGRICULTURE, ESTATE MANAGEMENT AND RURAL SOCIETY

The information relating to agriculture and estate management which can be gleaned from early charters and other documents is limited but badly needs a comprehensive reassessment. Early writers on the history of Scottish farming believed that there had been a pre-fourteenth century golden age of agriculture, particularly under the supposedly enlightened management of the monastic houses. This was followed by a decline in standards of husbandry from the fourteenth to the seventeenth century. However, the evidence for either the golden age or the subsequent decline is questionable. It seems likely that the quality of monastic estate management before the fourteenth century and its deficiencies in late-medieval times have been exaggerated. It should not necessarily be assumed that because so much of the surviving documentation relating to thirteenth-century estate administration comes from

6. J.M. Gilbert, *Hunting and Hunting Reserves in Medieval Scotland* (Edinburgh 1979).

monastic lands that their management was necessarily more efficient than estates in lay hands. Equally, fifteenth-century records relating to the lands of the abbey of Coupar Angus appear to indicate the use of systems of convertible husbandry like those which made such an important contribution to change in sixteenth- and sevententh-century English farming. But whether such techniques were a new development or the continuation of long-established practices and to what extent farming on this estate was typical of agriculture elsewhere in fifteenth-century Scotland is uncertain.

The evidence indicates the existence of open field systems and the fragmentation within them of lands belonging to individual cultivators in a similar pattern to large areas of medieval Western Europe. A charter of c1250 by Cicely of Mow in Roxburghshire, granting 26 acres (10.5 hectares) of her demesne to Kelso Abbey, shows that the land lay in eight different places, at some of which it was scattered in several plots, indicating a complex pattern of subdivision and intermixture. Sometimes the allocation of land within open fields was done on a regular basis by means of shares drawn by lot or in sequence, as in a grant of 1205 of 'every fifth rig' of land in a township in Fife. The use of a heavy plough drawn by a substantial oxen team can be inferred from surviving ridge and furrow cultivation which appears to date from the fourteenth century and earlier. Whether such ploughs were wheeled and how much variation there was in plough design and team size between different regions and different soils is unclear. The way in which the open field systems were organised, the crop rotations used and the overall extent of arable cultivation can only be guessed at, along with the ways in which cultivation systems were adapted to cope with the increased intake of land that must have occurred in most areas during the twelfth and thirteenth centuries. Nor can we offer any more than guesses about how standards and techniques of husbandry differed between demesnes and peasant holdings.

Inferring rotations from the sparse and indirect information on crop production is fraught with danger. Two- and three-course rotations on a Midland English model have been suggested as has the continuous, intensive, infield-only cropping of small plots. There is no evidence for the cultivation of legumes in the twelfth and thirteenth centuries. Wheat was certainly grown in some of the best-favoured districts but probably covered a limited area compared with oats and bere (a primitive four-row barley) especially north of the Tay. Some rye was grown and it has been suggested that its cultivation declined in favour of wheat during the twelfth century. Wheaten bread was eaten in the monastic houses and doubtless in the households of the better-off lay landowners, suggesting that wheat may have been more important as a demesne than a peasant crop although peasants were sometimes required to pay it in rent and may have grown it specially for this purpose.

The limited survival of documentation for lay estates in medieval Scotland means that information relating to estate organisation and management comes largely from the lands of the religious orders. As landlords, monastic communities appear by the later thirteenth century to have preferred to commute rents in kind into money. This inevitably involved a reduction of demesne cultivation and the leasing out of demesne land. The great wealth of monastic houses like Kelso and Melrose lay not in arable demesnes but in their sheep flocks. The size of the flocks owned by Melrose Abbey has been estimated at upwards of 12,000. The abbeys of Coupar Angus, Kelso and Newbattle may have had 7–8,000; sheep farming and wool production was clearly a major source of income. It has sometimes been implied that the monasteries, especially Cistercian houses, were the only exporters of wool in twelfth- and thirteenth-century Scotland. This was not true; they were indeed the largest producers but their total contribution to wool exports has been estimated at about a fifth. Moreover, the idea that the monastic houses were super-efficient estate managers also requires re-examination. The Cistercians tended to enter into long-term advance contracts with merchants for the purchase of their wool. Although this was designed to give them a guaranteed income it inevitably brought them lower prices per sack. Even worse, over-optimistic estimates of expected wool yields sometimes forced them to buy wool from other sources in order to make up the quota they had undertaken to deliver. Duncan has suggested that even the Cistercians' attitude to estate management was rough and ready with little sign of the long-term perspective of the improving landlord.[7] The lack of estate documents from before the end of the thirteenth century is, he argues, not entirely due to destruction but to the fact that such records hardly existed before this time, further evidence of a lack of long-term strategy in estate management.

Lands belonging to Cistercian houses were, as elsewhere, organised with a system of granges housing groups of lay brothers. The rules of the order required them to seek out remote areas away from worldly distractions but Melrose, in the heart of the fertile Tweed Valley or Newbattle, close to Edinburgh, hardly fit this description. There is likely to have been some displacement of existing population in order to establish the lowland granges on such estates. Although the Cistercians undoubtedly improved and developed the upland areas that they acquired even here they are unlikely to have taken over lands which were complete wilderness. There are indications that in the Lammermuirs, for instance, their sheep flocks may have replaced earlier systems of transhumance based on cattle rearing. While some monastic houses managed their lowland demesnes in large compact granges others, like Coldingham Priory, had areas of demesne scattered through many of their townships, presumably to make it easier for tenants to discharge labour services.

Compared with the wealth of detail which is available for English medieval society the documentation for twelfth- and thirteenth-century Scotland is so sparse that we have only a few glimpses of social structures and relationships. Unravelling the structure of the peasantry is further complicated by the terms

7. Duncan, Scotland, pp. 431–2.

that were used to denote various social strata. These differ from one region to another as well as over time. The significance of such variations is hard to evaluate. In broad terms, rural society in most areas between the end of the eleventh century and the fourteenth century appears to have included an upper stratum of free tenants, a substantial class of dependent peasants cultivating the land and pasturing livestock, and an ill-defined group at the bottom of rural society including smallholders and the totally landless. These last must have depended on selling their labour for work either on demesnes or on the holdings of the wealthier peasants. In central Scotland in the mid-twelfth century we find peasants, termed bonders, paying food rents but only fairly light labour and carriage services. In the early thirteenth century north of the Tay a class of free tenants is recorded. They owed cain rents in produce to the king's thanes but were otherwise free. Below them was a class of unfree tenants, scolocs, probably comparable with the earlier bonders further south. Under them was a group of less well off cottagers with mainly grazing rights and some small plots of arable but only burdened with fairly light labour services. There is no overall contemporary term which embraces the mass of the peasantry. Nativi or 'neyfs', roughly equivalent to the English villein, was the term most often used. The lowest levels of neyfs were known as fugitivi in the twelfth century and servi (serfs) in the thirteenth. In the twelfth century there may still have been some people who were genuine slaves. The term neyf covered a wide social range including relatively wealthy families but whether servi or not they were all considered to be bound to their lord by their places of birth and the residence of their families. Generalising, the bonders of the twelfth century became the neyfs of the early thirteenth and the husbandmen of the late thirteenth century while over the same period the scolocs became fugitivi and then cottars.

South of the Forth, where the extent of arable may have been greater, landowners were able to impose more labour services than further north but even here they were light compared with the classic areas of English manorialisation. This reflects the importance of pastoral farming in the Scottish economy and the more restricted extent of demesnes. Indications are that demesne cultivation was not very important in the early twelfth century but that demesnes increased during the later twelfth and early thirteenth centuries. This may in turn have led to an increase in labour services. The evidence suggests that demesne expansion was largely confined to southern Scotland and had little impact north of the Forth. Given that the quotas of knights' service demanded from the great feudal lordships were modest compared with Angevin England there may have been less pressure to move towards intensive demesne production for commercial sale.

By the end of the thirteenth century demesne farming on estates like Coldingham Priory and Kelso Abbey was declining. By 1300 Kelso had leased out nearly half its 3,000 acres (1,214 hectares) of arable, granting the farms to tenants complete with stock and equipment as well as commuting some labour services to money and produce. It can only be assumed that demesne cultivation on lay estates followed a similar trend. Even at the peak of demesne cultivation a good deal of hired labour must have been needed. In settlements like Swinton in the Merse, where the extent of the demesne has been estimated at around 500 acres (202 hectares) at the end of the thirteenth century, the labour services of the villagers could only have made a limited contribution to its cultivation. This in turn implies the existence of a substantial landless group among the rural population employed as labourers on the demesnes and perhaps also on larger peasant holdings.

Duncan has suggested that labour services may have been retained mainly as a token of bondage.[8] The late thirteenth-century survey of Kelso Abbey's lands shows that as well as paying a money rent husbandmen gave labour at harvest time and did some ploughing and harrowing on the abbeys demesne lands as well as carriage services and helping to wash and shear the sheep. Cottagers paid a money rent and provided labour at harvest time. Tenants were thirled to the local mill and brewhouse, and paid heriot and merchet (payment for permission to give a daughter in marriage). Husbandmen had their holdings intermingled in the common fields of their settlement. Cottars appear to have had separate small plots of land, usually under two acres and often much smaller. As well as holdings which were scattered through the common fields of a township there were also compact holdings, sometimes held free of labour services. The largest of these, up to one ploughgate in extent, may have been survivals of early ministerial holdings belonging to thanes but the smaller ones are likely to have been recent intakes from the waste. Within peasant society there were marked contrasts in wealth and status. At Swinton at the end of the thirteenth century the 24 husbandmen each held half a ploughgate of land but there was a wide gap between them and the cottars holding two acres or less. Elsewhere husbandmen had a greater range of holding sizes and divisions within the peasantry may have been less sharp.

We have little information about the economy of peasant farming during the twelfth and thirteenth centuries. By analogy with other parts of medieval Western Europe it can be assumed that conditions did not remain static and that as well as short-term variations caused by differences in harvest quality and outbreaks of livestock disease there must have been longer-term shifts caused by changes in the relationships with the landowning classes, the ebb and flow of demesne cultivation, and population trends. Unfortunately such changes can barely be identified far less assembled into a meaningful chronology.

ECONOMIC DEVELOPMENT AND TRADE

The limitations of our knowledge of peasant agriculture in medieval Scotland highlight the lack of information concerning the economy in general. Nevertheless, some broad trends can be identified. A notable feature of the

8. Ibid., pp. 343–8.

twelfth and thirteenth centuries was the shift to a money economy and, closely associated with it, the development of overseas trade and the rise of the burghs. Indications are that during the reign of Malcolm III the use of money and the volume of trade was restricted. Once more David I appears to have laid solid foundations on which later developments were based. Although coinage may have been used increasingly by the late eleventh century in the embryo towns it was under David I, around 1136, that the first Scottish coinage was minted. The old idea that David actually introduced the use of coins to Scotland must, however, be rejected as there was clearly already a developed money economy in existence by this time linked to the burghs and established patterns of trade.

David opened mints in Perth and Aberdeen as well as Berwick, Carlisle, Edinburgh and Roxburgh suggesting that money was already in regular circulation north of the Tay. During the long reign of William I there was an increasing production of Scottish coins which, along with the growing circulation of foreign coins, encouraged a transition to a money economy. In 1250 the Scottish coinage was changed to conform with that of England and earlier Scottish coins were withdrawn for reminting. Another re-coinage occurred towards the end of the reign of Alexander III but only in the later thirteenth century did Scottish coins become fairly plentiful. The spread of the use of money throughout the country during the thirteenth century is indicated by the fact that the re-coinage in the 1250s involved production from mints situated not only in the burghs used by David I but also in Ayr, Dumfries, Forfar, Glasgow, Inverness, Kinghorn, Lanark, Montrose, Stirling, St Andrews, and Renfrew though Berwick continued to be the main centre of coin production. The evidence of coin hoards suggests that English coins formed up to 95 per cent of the money circulating in Scotland during the later thirteenth century, emphasising the importance of trade links with England before the Wars of Independence. The pattern of hoards dating from the period 1100–1360 shows a concentration in the Lowlands and an absence from the far north and west. Their distribution is, however, widespread in rural areas as well as in and around the burghs.

The burghs have been seen, naturally enough, as the principal sources of cash and of money income for the crown at this period. For much of the twelfth century this was probably the case. However, by the end of the twelfth century the ability of Scotland to raise large sums of money, as in 1190 for cancelling the Treaty of Falaise and in 1209 to meet the terms of the Treaty of Norham, shows that more cash was circulating. Evidence suggests that by the end of the twelfth century rents in money were becoming more common in rural areas, especially on estates belonging to religious houses. Mills, fisheries and salt-pans were potential sources of cash rents but as the wool trade developed and became more profitable the rent of pasture came increasingly to be reckoned in money. The development of the burghs as market centres (Chapter 4) provided a means for turning surplus agricultural produce from demesnes and rents into cash. The role of towns in stimulating arable farming is shown by an assessment of monastic incomes for Lothian and the Merse in 1293. Religious houses like Newbattle and Holyrood, close to Edinburgh, had larger demesnes whose arable land was more highly valued than abbeys in the Merse like Melrose, more distant from urban centres.

By the early thirteenth century the Scottish economy appears to have been firmly based on the use of money and continued to develop steadily thereafter. It has been estimated that the amount of money in circulation in Scotland may have increased around ten times between the mid-twelfth and late thirteenth centuries, with particularly fast growth occurring in the third quarter of the thirteenth century. This expansion of the money supply occurred 50 years or so after a comparable one in England and ought to have caused a rise in prices. Duncan has detected a tendency for rents to rise, more steeply before 1250, more slowly thereafter.[9]

All this points to a steadily expanding economy. Calculations relating the growth of money supply to levels of population suggest that in later thirteenth-century Scotland there may have been as much money in circulation per head of population as in England. It is even possible that at certain periods Scotland may have been richer, in relative terms, than England. If this sounds improbable it should be remembered that by the later thirteenth century the English economy had peaked and was starting to decline, that pressure of population seems to have been less of a problem in Scotland, and that Scotland was well suited environmentally to the production of wool, that great medieval money-spinner. Our picture of a sharp contrast between a prosperous England and a poverty-stricken Scotland has perhaps been unduly influenced by conditions during the better-documented sixteenth and seventeenth centuries when differences between the economic performance of the two countries were probably at their greatest. Certainly the relationship between money supply and population suggests a healthy balance of trade which contrasts with the deficit of later centuries. It also implies that merchants, lightly taxed, must have been making considerable profits. Given this, the lack of development of credit facilities in Scotland is perhaps surprising but it may be that trends in this direction were curtailed by the outbreak of war with England.

These healthy economic indicators might seem to confirm that the reign of Alexander III in the later thirteenth century was indeed a 'golden age'. Undoubtedly it was a period to which later chroniclers looked back as a time of prosperity and plenty when favourable climatic conditions would have improved crop yields and allowed an extension of cultivation in hill areas. Recent re-interpretations favour faster economic growth in Scotland during the early thirteenth century, emphasising the extent to which later growth was based on foundations going back to the time of David I. It has also been suggested that Scotland in the later fourteenth century,[10] after the Wars of Independence and the Black Death, may have been a better candidate for the

9. Ibid., pp. 339–42.
10. Grant, Independence and Nationhood, pp. 76–9.

label 'golden age' than the reign of Alexander III – for the peasantry at least. Nevertheless, the later thirteenth century was a period of peace, population growth, the flourishing of towns and particularly of growing money supply which has prompted the suggestion that if not exactly a golden age then 'silver age' might be an appropriate description.[11]

The social impact of this economic growth has yet to be evaluated adequately. The urban merchants ought to have risen socially as well as profited financially from favourable conditions for trade and light taxation. Yet the merchants do not seem to have been able to capitalise on their success in social or political terms. We know of no thirteenth-century merchants who rose to positions of importance comparable to fourteenth-century ones like John Mercer. Moreover, it was in the later fourteenth century, not the thirteenth, that burgesses were summoned to attend Parliament on a regular basis. For the nobility living standards were clearly rising in the thirteenth century as evidenced by the building of stone castles and the growing consumption of luxury imports like wine, but even the most prosperous Scottish magnates were strictly middle-rank by English standards of wealth.

How much wealth filtered down to the peasantry is uncertain. The later fourteenth century with lower population levels, falling rents and favourable conditions for the leasing of land may have been a better time for the upper levels of the peasantry than the later thirteenth century when there are one or two stray indications that, under pressure of population growth, average holding sizes may have been falling. Nevertheless, many of the coin hoards from the later thirteenth century are of a size which suggests that money was changing hands among the peasantry as well as higher levels of society.

The growth of the economy of medieval Scotland was closely linked with the development of trade, particularly the export of wool to Flanders. Evidence for trade in mid-eleventh century Scotland is very limited. The biographer of St Margaret claims that she encouraged foreign traders to come to Scotland and certainly during Malcolm's reign trade was profitable enough for fixed customs duties to be applied. But even in the early twelfth century the number of communities recorded as engaging in foreign trade was small, Berwick, Perth and Aberdeen being the chief centres. The volume of trade expanded dramatically during the twelfth and thirteenth centuries, part of the general expansion of trade throughout Europe, encouraged in Scotland by low customs duties on exports and none at all on imports.

Although we have only limited data concerning Scottish trade in the twelfth and thirteenth centuries the basic patterns are clear.[12] Many of its features including the commodities exported and imported and the main trading partners remained little changed down to the seventeenth century. Exports focused heavily on a limited range of raw materials, the natural products of a

11. N.H. Reid, *Scotland in the Reign of Alexander III* (Edinburgh 1990), pp. 53–66.
12. M. Lynch, in M. Lynch, M. Spearman and G. Stell (eds), *The Scottish Medieval Town* (Edinburgh 1988).

pastorally orientated economy. By far the most valuable export was wool, sent principally to Flanders but also to France and England. The development of the wool trade with Flanders transformed the Scottish economy leading to a concentration on sheep rearing and strongly influencing the nature of urban development. Scottish wool exports in the later thirteenth century were perhaps a fifth of those of England. It is not clear when the wool trade first began to grow substantially but it was well established before the thirteenth century. By the end of the reign of William I large areas were already given over to sheep pasture. In the longer term Scotland's dependence on the export of wool to Flanders had its drawbacks, especially in the fourteenth and fifteenth centuries when Bruges came to engross much of Scotland's trade. This monopoly, together with the ease with which Scotland could import manufactures from Flanders, stifled local industries. The import of dye-stuffs indicates that in the twelfth century some burghs, notably Perth, had a significant clothing industry but this appears to have declined due to Flemish competition. As a result the dyeing and finishing of cloth, activities which brought prosperity to many English towns, were not prominent in Scottish burghs. The limited industrial base of Scottish towns is another theme which emerges in later centuries. Extreme dependence on the export of a narrow range of raw materials and semi-finished products made the Scots vulnerable to external influences beyond their control.

Although much less valuable than wool, leather skins and fish (especially salmon, herring and cod) were also significant exports. In the thirteenth century fishing was an important element in the economy of towns like Aberdeen and Berwick and was the main reason for the prosperity of smaller east-coast burghs like Crail. Imports included raw materials such as timber, manufactured goods like fine cloth from Flanders and Italy, iron, woad and other dye-stuffs for the native woollen cloth industry and luxury items like wine and spices. Wine came from Normandy, Maine and, increasingly important through the thirteenth century, from Bordeaux, providing a major source of revenue for the burghs as standards of living rose and wine consumption increased.

Although it is impossible to quantify the volume of trade with England or even to estimate its importance relative to other sectors of the economy there is no doubt that England was one of Scotland's main trading partners by the outbreak of the Wars of Independence. Growth of trade with England during the twelfth century is likely although there is very little direct evidence for it but there is no doubt of its importance during the thirteenth century. A substantial coastal trade in grain from England to Scotland had developed by the later thirteenth century. Much of this was in English hands and English surnames became common in Scottish burghs. The emphasis on sheep farming in Scotland coupled with population growth may have encouraged the import of English grain, particularly wheat, a risky crop in Scotland under medieval farming practices. Shipping technology also favoured close contacts with England. Until the introduction of cogs in the late thirteenth century vessels trading to Flanders and France were small and generally hugged the east coast of England calling en route at ports like Dunwich and Yarmouth. During the thirteenth century there were Scottish merchants, perhaps even communities, in Dunwich, Lynne and Yarmouth. There was probably also a considerable overland trade in wool to England. Trade with Ireland is also recorded with Scottish merchants operating in Dublin and Drogheda and grain being exported from Ireland to Ayr. But compared with the volume of east-coast traffic west-coast Scottish trade was still small scale. Trade with Flanders was so important that a substantial Scottish community was established in Bruges by the end of the thirteenth century while trade with Norway and the Baltic is also recorded.

Little information is available concerning the activities of individual Scottish merchants. However, some details of one of them, Thomas of Coldingham, a Berwick merchant who died in 1316, have been pieced together.[13] As Berwick was the largest wool-exporting burgh in Scotland it is not surprising to find that wool comprised the bulk of Thomas' business and that he was a large-scale operator buying wool from the priory of Durham as well as within Scotland. He operated with partners on some occasions and it is clear from other evidence that partnerships or 'companies' were becoming common in the larger Scottish towns by the later thirteenth century. One of his partners, John of Chilton, mayor of Berwick in 1136 and 1337, appears to have taken over much of Thomas' business after his death. Thomas of Coldingham's interests were not confined to wool though. He was also involved in exporting leather, with fisheries on the Tweed and in land speculation.

It is not clear how much Scottish trade was handled by native merchants and how much by foreigners. Flemish, Italian and English merchants were certainly active in the wool trade. Flemish traders had their own headquarters or 'factory' at Berwick which was destroyed when English forces sacked the town in 1296. By the early fourteenth century merchants from Cologne, Hamburg and Lubeck were also active in the trade in wool and hides. It has been suggested that they too may have had a permanent base at Berwick. Dundee is the only other burgh which is known to have had a similar privileged group of foreign merchants.

The monasteries also traded on their own account, importing grain and exporting wool. Some even owned their own ships. Duncan has suggested that in the twelfth and early thirteenth centuries the Cistercians had a system for collecting wool for export from all their houses under the control of the abbeys of Melrose and Coupar Angus, operating via storehouses in Berwick and possibly also in Perth.[14] The abbeys of Melrose, Newbattle and Arbroath are also known to have chartered vessels for direct trade with England and the Continent.

If information on foreign trade is scanty details of internal commodity flows are even more meagre. Within estates like those of the great abbeys we can

13. J. Donnelly, Thomas of Coldingham, merchant and burgess of Berwick upon Tweed (died 1316), *SHR*, 59, 1980, 105–250.
14. Duncan, *Scotland: The Making of the Kingdom*, p. 45.

visualise movements of produce in rents and from demesnes to estate centres for consumption and processing. The size of many monastic communities was probably large compared with the households of lay proprietors and must have required correspondingly complex victualling arrangements. Many monasteries were indeed unable to supply all their basic requirements from their own estates. They maintained establishments in the larger towns to handle grain brought in from England and to deal with exports of wool and other commodities from their estates. Berwick had more religious town houses than any other centre although Roxburgh, Edinburgh and Stirling were also important. This serves as a reminder that the development trade cannot be considered separately from the rise of towns and it is to this theme that we now turn.

CHAPTER 4

MEDIEVAL TOWNS

Compared with many parts of Europe urban development came late to Scotland. Nevertheless, the foundation and growth of towns in medieval Scotland shared the same basic features of the urban revival that occurred throughout Europe. Burghs, often associated with royal castles and possessing administrative as well as trading functions, were yet another instrument by which Scottish kings from David I onwards consolidated and extended their control. Because it developed later the Scottish urban hierarchy was still evolving in the sixteenth and seventeenth centuries, long after the English urban system had achieved a measure of stability. Nevertheless, by the fifteenth century Scotland's towns had developed distinctive features, particularly regarding their monopolies, patterns of trade, organisation and socioeconomic structure.

To understand how this occurred we need to consider the origins of urban development in Scotland before examining the economies and societies of Scottish medieval towns. This is not easy due to the paucity of documentary evidence. The earliest series of burgh records, for Aberdeen, only begins in 1395 and sources remain thin until almost the end of the fifteenth century. The lack of information is particularly bad for the earliest phases of burgh development in the twelfth century. Despite these handicaps there has been important new work in recent years on Scottish medieval towns, especially their social and economic life. Re-examination of familiar manuscript sources, exploration of previously unused ones, plus important contributions from the new field of urban archaeology, have provided fresh insights into the lives and activities of medieval town dwellers.

URBAN ORIGINS

The topic of urban origins in Scotland has provoked controversy partly due to the difficulty of deciding when a settlement developed sufficient functions to be considered truly urban.[1] Such problems can be as hard to resolve for the

1. B. Dicks, The Scottish medieval town, a search for origins, in G. Gordon and B. Dicks (eds), *Scottish Urban History* (Aberdeen 1983), pp. 23–51.

seventeenth century as the twelfth. If towns in medieval Scotland are defined in a narrow sense as places which had special trading privileges conferred on them by king or another overlord then the origins of Scottish towns lie firmly in the twelfth century. On the other hand, if towns are considered in broader terms as settlements with concentrations of trading and manufacturing activities then earlier origins may be postulated. In recent years historians of medieval English towns have stressed the importance of the pre-Norman contribution to urban development. For Scotland it is equally unrealistic to suppose that towns were created simply by David I and his successors conferring the title of 'burgh' on a series of virgin sites. Burghs either required time to develop commercial, industrial and administrative functions or were grafted on to existing nucleations which already possessed such attributes, even if only in embryo form.

The Anglo-Norman burgh was more of an innovation in Scotland than Norman chartered boroughs were in England. There were no Roman towns in Scotland to provide continuity of urban life or fabric, nothing comparable to the Anglo-Saxon and Danish fortified burghs. While the Scandinavian settlement in Ireland gave rise to a number of trading centres, the Norse occupation of northern and western Scotland seems to have been purely agrarian in character. The only exception was Kirkwall, already a market centre in 1117 according to Oryneyinga Saga, which is likely to have grown further following the start of construction of St Magnus' cathedral in 1137. Yet before the case for pre-burgh urban origins in Scotland is dismissed it is worth reflecting on Duncan's contention that because there is no evidence for towns before the later eleventh century this does not necessarily mean that they did not exist.[2]

Various sites which pre-dated the burghs had concentrations of political power, economic activity and population which were almost urban in character. Late Iron Age tribal centres like Eildon Hill North and Traprain Law appear to have been occupied permanently by substantial populations. Traprain Law has provided evidence of almost continuous occupation for around 1,000 years from the middle of the first millennium BC to the fifth century AD, a longer history than any medieval burgh can boast. Excavations there have revealed traces of a dense concentration of settlement with houses built around small courtyards arranged on either side of streets.

Civilian settlements grew up outside a number of Roman forts including Bearsden, Carriden, Cramond, Croy Hill and Inveresk but these can only have been occupied briefly. Conditions in post-Roman Scotland do not seem to have favoured the continuation or re-establishment of large hillforts like Traprain Law. The trend was towards smaller more easily defended citadels. Sites like Dunadd, Dumbarton Rock and Dundurn, despite their limited area, had some of the functions which characterised later towns. Nevertheless, it is significant that these examples did not develop into medieval burghs

---

2. A.A. Duncan, *Scotland: The Making of the Kingdom* (Edinburgh 1975), p. 465.

although at other early-historic fortress sites like Edinburgh and Stirling there was probably continuity of settlement through to the first phases of burgh development. Religious centres like Glasgow and St Andrews also acted as foci for settlement development. A study of the layout of St Andrews has suggested that the pre-burghal settlement was located immediately outside the precincts of the Pictish monastery.[3] The new burgh, established by Bishop Robert around 1150, extended along the line of two tracks leading to the cathedral precincts. It superceded, and may have partly overlain, the earlier settlement.

Elsewhere there are other indications that settlements with proto-urban functions pre-dated the establishment of burghs. At Peebles the main street of the burgh founded in 1152–53 ran from the royal castle down a wedge of land between the confluence of the River Tweed and the Eddleston Water. On the far side of the Eddleston Water, with the parish church and an early-Christian site, a settlement known as 'Old Town' maintained a distinctive, separate identity for centuries and appears to have pre-dated the foundation of the burgh. At Aberdeen it has been suggested that the pre-burgh nucleus covered an area between the medieval parish church of St Nicholas and the Dee estuary.[4] This site offered limited scope for expansion, hemmed in as it was by the estuary on the south, the Den Burn on the west and the steep slope of St Katherine's Hill to the east. By the later twelfth century a move had been made to a more spacious site a little way to the east, closer to the castle. Sites like Perth and Stirling, at the head of navigation of their respective estuaries and the lowest crossing points of major rivers, were obvious locations for early trading communities as were Aberdeen and Berwick at the mouths of estuaries with long-established ferries. The early existence of timber bridges at places like Ayr, Berwick, Perth and Stirling were important elements in the growth of trade as were the fording points on the Tweed and Teviot close to the site of Roxburgh.

The example of Glasgow illustrates the problems of determining the influence of pre-burghal settlement on the growth of a medieval burgh. There were two potential early nuclei for development. One lay around the cathedral and shrine of St Kentigern, situated on the edge of the gorge of the Molendinar Burn some distance from the Clyde. Glasgow's first recorded cathedral was dedicated in 1136, some 40 years before the date of the burgh charter, and the grant of a weekly market between 1175 and 1178 may merely have formalised an existing assembly. The other site was close to the river at a convenient fording point. Various patterns of development have been suggested, one possibility is that the area around the cathedral formed the core of the medieval burgh which gradually expanded southwards towards the river. Another theory is that there was no significant early

3. N.P. Brooks and G. Whittington, Planning and growth in the medieval Scottish burgh: the example of St Andrews, *Transactions of the Institute of British Geographers*, NS 2, 1977, 278–95.
4. J.C. Murray (ed.), *Excavations in the Medieval Burgh of Aberdeen 1973–81* (Edinburgh 1982).

settlement around the cathedral and that the pre-burghal nucleus lay close to the river. A further idea is that the awkward site of the community around the cathedral was considered too cramped for development and that it was replaced by a new planned burgh nearer the Clyde. Detailed study of the layout of early-modern Glasgow, combined with hints from the documentary record and archaeological evidence, suggests that the last theory is the most plausible, though there is no reason why there should not have been a pre-burghal settlement beside the river crossing as well as by the cathedral.

THE FIRST BURGHS

Early in the twelfth century certain places began to be granted the status of burghs with trading monopolies over the areas around them so that no one could buy or sell except in the market-place of the burgh where a toll was payable by all who were not privileged inhabitants or 'burgesses'. David I led the way by establishing Berwick and Roxburgh as burghs before he became king in 1124. His motive may have been to try to modernise the Scottish economy using a well-established model. He would have been aware of the success of such foundations elsewhere and of the contributions which tolls and rents from urban property could make to royal revenue. The earliest burghs were royal demesne centres to which rents were brought and at which surpluses were disposed of, locations where traders and craftsmen were probably already gathering. By the time of David's death in 1153 18 burghs had been established. By the end of the reign of William the Lion in 1214 there were some 37 burghs in Scotland and around 50 existed by the early fourteenth century (Map 4.1).

There has been considerable debate about the reasons behind the foundation of the earliest burghs, the importance of defensive, trading, and administrative functions being stressed by different historians. The lack of contemporary documentation has produced much theorising on a limited base of evidence. It is unrealistic to look for a single all-embracing theory to account for the appearance of burghs or for a coherent master plan behind their creation. The rationale behind burgh foundation probably reflected a number of motives whose relative importance varied between different sites and through time.

The military aspect of burgh foundation with the need for strategic control of territory can be seen in the plantation of the burghs of Elgin, Forres and Inverness. In 1130 the earldom of Moray was suppressed and the crown took over direct control of the province. Castles and associated burghs were established to increase royal control in the region as well as royal revenues. In western Scotland burghs like Ayr, Lanark and Dumfries, associated with royal castles controlling the exits from Galloway, also had an important strategic role.

In some cases a garrison function was clearly pre-eminent where a new burgh was closely associated with the castle and caput of a feudal lordship. A

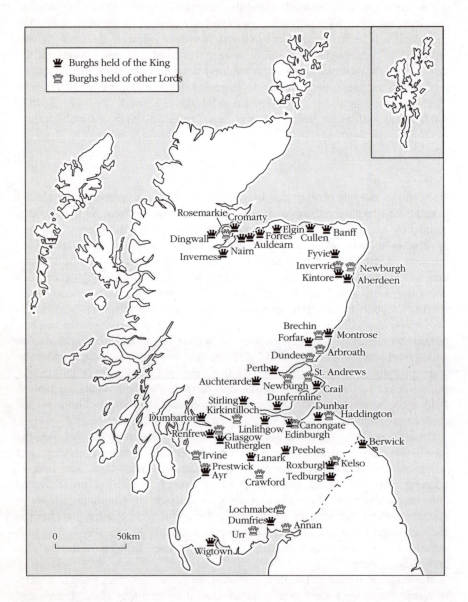

Map 4.1 Medieval Burghs

good example is Inverurie, established at the end of the twelfth century in association with the castle of David, Earl of Huntingdon in his new lordship of Garioch.[5] It is unlikely that Inverurie was designed for more than local trade and the aim behind its foundation seems rather to have been to

5. K.J. Stringer, *Earl David of Huntingdon 1152–1219* (Edinburgh 1985) pp. 69–72.

establish a range of specialist services on a restricted scale in association with the castle, supplying provisions and, if necessary, manpower. Early burghs in Galloway, long vanished, which were associated with large mottes as at Urr and stone castles like Buittle were probably similar in character. Several early inland burghs like these failed to develop more than a purely local economic role and either remained small or disappeared.

Royal administration was also a significant aspect of burgh creation. There was a close relationship between burghs (many of them former demesne centres), royal castles and sheriffdoms. Of 31 royal burghs founded before 1286 only seven were not associated with royal castles (Aberdeen, Banff, Cupar, Haddington, Montrose, Selkirk and Wigtown), and all but four (Dundee, Inverkeithing, Kinghorn, and Montrose) were the head burghs of sheriffdoms. Theories stressing the importance of the trading role of these centres have tended to ignore the fact that their trading privileges developed slowly and were not formalised into a fully integrated system before the later fourteenth century.

Most, but not all, of the earliest burghs were founded directly by the crown. Similar trading rights were also granted to ecclesiastical centres like Glasgow. The earliest non-royal burghs, St Andrews and Canongate had received their charters by the 1170s, towards the end of David I's reign, about 25 years after the first king's burghs, Berwick and Roxburgh. Ten of the 13 Scottish cathedral sites developed burghs plus Elgin where the cathedral was built after the burgh had been established. Another 25 centres associated with ecclesiastical and lay landowners were founded during the next three centuries including burghs associated with bishoprics as at Glasgow, religious houses like Arbroath, Kelso and Newburgh, and baronial centres like Dunbar and Prestwick. These early church and baronial centres were mostly assimilated into the ranks of the king's burghs and by the sixteenth century there was no real distinction between the two groups, both having full rights to engage in foreign trade. Seigneurial foundations with more restricted privileges appeared later, and much more slowly, than in England. Large numbers were created only during the sixteenth and seventeenth centuries. In the later fifteenth century, however, charters erecting burghs of barony established the basic rights of this group; to buy and sell goods within the burgh, to hold markets and fairs, to have craftsmen and burgesses and to have the right to elect baillies and other officers. Foreign trade was not a privilege granted to baronial burghs (Chapter 10).

Most burghs established during David I's reign were, however, pre-eminently trading colonies with a high proportion of foreign residents. Incomers were drawn from England, Normandy and especially from Flanders, the most densely populated and highly industrialised region of Northern Europe. There was a large influx of Flemings after 1155 when they were expelled from England. These immigrant merchants and craftsmen added a cosmopolitan element to the first burghs; their family and business contacts were important in the development of trading links. In Glasgow the surnames of inhabitants during the first century of the burgh's existence suggest a wide origin for settlers within Scotland and England. Although many of the original settlers were outsiders there is also evidence of migration to the new burghs from the surrounding countryside. By the fourteenth century Scottish surnames were becoming common suggesting increasingly local origins for the burgesses.

The creation of the first burghs may seem to have been a piecemeal, *ad hoc* process but there are hints even in David I's reign of a significant degree of organisation and control. A charter of c1180 confirms an earlier grant by David of a free trade area among the burghs north of the Mounth. This and one or two other stray pieces of evidence have been interpreted as indicating the existence of three regional groupings of burghs; south of the Forth, from Forth to Mounth, and further north, within which the liberties or trading areas of individual burghs were defined, a system which would have helped the crown to oversee mercantile activity.

When new burghs were established settlers were offered a piece of land rent free for a certain period known as 'kirset', usually a year but in the case of more isolated burghs such as Dingwall, 10 years, within which time they were to build houses on their plots. Burgess privileges depended on occupying, not just owning, a burgage plot which could be inherited or purchased. Traders required substantial inducements to come to the new settlements with their capital and expertise. As a result the burghs were granted wide trading privileges. Merchant burgesses were given a monopoly over exports of wool, hides and animal skins. Foreign merchants could trade only with burgesses within the burghs and not direct with rural producers. At an early date burgh trading monopolies were extended to defined hinterlands or liberties within which no one could buy or sell staple commodities except in the market-place of the burgh. These hinterlands often extended over entire sheriffdoms. Where more than one burgh was established within a sheriffdom, such as Dundee and Montrose, or Ayr and Irvine, disputes over the extents of their respective monopolies were inevitable and sometimes protracted. Burgesses also enjoyed freedom from tolls throughout Scotland. In return for these benefits burgesses, as tenants of the king, were required to make a substantial contribution towards occasional royal taxation; in the thirteenth century this amounted to a third of national levies.

BURGH LAYOUT AND DEVELOPMENT

The study of the development of the plans and built environment of medieval towns is well established in other European countries but little detailed work has been done for Scotland. Studies of the topography of urban sites combined with detailed scrutiny of documentary sources have provided information on the evolution of a number of towns including Ayr, Glasgow, Perth and St Andrews. In addition, we now have a growing body of archaeological evidence relating to medieval Scottish towns. Urban archaeology in Scotland only developed in the 1970s and much of the available information comes from a handful of towns, notably Aberdeen, Elgin, Inverness and Perth. It was rapidly discovered that the medieval layers of towns on rocky sites, like Edinburgh, had been largely destroyed by later building. Moreover, the deep foundations required for nineteenth- and twentieth-century construction have destroyed much of the medieval evidence for towns such as Dundee and Glasgow. Perth, with medieval deposits averaging two to three metres thick, has provided the richest assemblage of structures and finds[6].

The commonest burgh plan, found throughout Western Europe, was a single main street widening into a market-place with the burgage plots running back at right angles in a herring-bone pattern, often terminating in back lanes parallel to the main street. A dozen early burghs have more complex street patterns with two or more parallel thoroughfares intersected by minor lanes to form a grid pattern. Retrospective studies of urban morphology may oversimplify the processes of burgh planning and growth by suggesting that towns were laid out fully-fledged as the result of a single master plan rather than growing in a series of stages. Complex plans need not have been established in their entirety during early phases of development. There is evidence that in the early stages of growth the layouts of burghs like Ayr, Lanark and Perth were sometimes changed markedly as the main axis of development was completely re-aligned.

A detailed study of St Andrews, whose plan involves three main streets which converge on the precincts of the cathedral, has demonstrated that the central thoroughfare, Market Street, was a later insertion between North and South Streets.[7] The reconstructed pattern of the medieval burgage plots provides clear evidence for the sequence of development. The first phase, dating from around 1150, was close to the cathedral precincts. It was followed by new blocks of burgages extending further west until the town's late-medieval limits, marked by the position of the surviving West Port, were reached. The first stage of the burgh involved a simple layout of two wide streets leading towards the cathedral, each one flanked by long burgage plots with a standard width of 12 paces. Although the area of the first burgh was small its plan influenced the subsequent development of the town for centuries.

The nucleus of medieval Edinburgh was probably the present Lawnmarket stretching from the precincts of the castle to the site of St Giles church, the continuation down the ridge to the Nether Bow being a later development. In towns like Edinburgh and St Andrews the line of pre-existing trackways appears to have influenced the layout of streets and burgage plots in the early phases of growth. As population increased burghs expanded by the creation of new blocks of burgages, usually at the ends of existing streets. The limits of medieval towns like St Andrews are often marked by the locations of

6. P. Holdsworth (ed.), *Excavation in the Medieval Burgh of Perth 1979–81* (Edinburgh 1988).
7. Brooks and Whittington, Planning and growth.

friaries which were generally established at the fringes of the built up area from the mid-thirteenth century onwards.

For Perth detailed analysis of the widths and layout of the burgages indicates a complex evolution. By the sixteenth century, Perth had developed a grid layout with two main streets running east-west intersected by narrower cross-streets. Superficially this plan might seem to have been laid out as a single exercise yet study of the documentary and topographic evidence shows that the town reached this form gradually. The first phase, dating from the early twelfth century or before, consisted of a single row of burgages running from Watergate down to the River Tay. By the middle of the twelfth century expansion on either side of what was to become the High Street had begun, at right angles to Watergate running away from the river. The building of a castle to the north of the town at a slightly later date led to a new access way, Skinnergate, being driven through the burgages north of the High Street. By the late twelfth century expansion was continuing further away from the river on either side of the High Street. In the early thirteenth century the area of the burgh was expanded substantially by the creation of a new street, South Street, parallel to the High Street. Through the thirteenth century expansion continued away from the river along High Street and South Street to limits defined by the town's fourteenth-century defences. By the fifteenth century, two suburbs had grown up beyond the walls.

The market-place of a burgh might be relocated as the town grew, something which happened with St Andrews in the 1190s and at Crail where the market was transferred from Nethergate to the High Street running parallel but further inland and later still to a third widened street, Marketgate. Specialised markets within burghs existed from the fifteenth century if not earlier. Few Scottish medieval towns had defences apart from the protection afforded by proximity to a royal castle or by natural features. At Aberdeen a loch, marshy ground to the east of the town and the Den Burn to the west gave considerable natural protection. Some early burghs had earth and timber defences though; William the Lion ordered a ditch and palisade to be constructed to protect Inverness. Perth and Roxburgh had earthwork defences which were later rebuilt in stone. Berwick, when attacked by Edward I's army in 1296, had a rampart and ditch which, in the event, provided little impediment to the attackers. Fourteenth-century Dumfries had a wall of stone in addition to earthworks. By the fifteenth century Edinburgh and Stirling both had substantial stone defences. Many burghs were located near river mouths at the lowest convenient crossing point before tidal water. In such locations bridges provided access for trade and also allowed the easier collection of tolls and the control of traffic. Fine fifteenth-century stone bridges survive at Ayr, Dumfries, Haddington and Stirling replacing earlier timber structures.

In early burghs large grants of property were made to religious houses. Monastic property in Scottish medieval towns was much more extensive than land belonging to the nobility. The church had a greater landholding presence in Scottish towns than in English ones. Elsewhere in Western

Europe religious houses were often prevented from owning urban property but the monastic stake in Scottish burghs grew during the twelfth and thirteenth centuries as a result of gifts and outright purchase. By the end of the thirteenth century 24 religious houses had property in all of the 50 or so burghs. In some towns only one or two properties were in the hands of the monasteries but in Berwick, the leading burgh in Scotland, the religious presence was stronger.[8] Fifteen religious houses held property in Berwick. Monastic property in towns served a number of functions. It provided accommodation for the abbot if the king required his presence in the town. Urban land could also be rented out as a source of income. Particularly in the hands of the Cistercians, urban holdings acted as commercial bases for supplying the mother house with imports and handling the monastery's exports of wool and other commodities.

The term 'burgage tenure' suggests a degree of uniformity in urban property holding which had ceased to exist by the fourteenth century as sub-letting and grants to the church complicated the pattern of landholding. Burgh lands could also revert to the crown for failure to pay rent, lack of heirs, or forfeiture. The crown could grant burgages to the church and some burgages were acquired by local landowners through purchase or marriage. Despite this major lay landowners were not greatly interested in acquiring urban property, or indeed in the burghs at all before the fifteenth century. There was, however, an increasingly active market in urban property among the burgesses themselves. By the fourteenth century some burgesses were acquiring additional burgages as investments; they provided a steady income in rents and could be sold to raise capital when necessary. The rents of burgages could be granted to the church or burgages sub-let to tenants. Burgage tenure gave townspeople greater freedom to alienate lands but elements of feudalism still survived as with the service of watch and ward.

Early grants of burgh lands to the church mainly involved abbeys and bishoprics. By the fourteenth century urban property was increasingly being granted to the orders of friars. The friars said prayers for the townspeople, provided aid for the poor, accommodation for travellers and education. Hospitals for the care of the sick and elderly also existed within the burghs while leper hospitals were located at a little distance from the towns. Not all medieval burghs had their own parish church. Altars in the naves of the churches of adjacent religious houses served the urban community at Canongate, Jedburgh, Kelso and Melrose while parish altars were erected in cathedrals at Glasgow and Old Aberdeen. At St Andrews, however, the burgh community had its own church, separate from the cathedral, by the mid-thirteenth century.

Apart from churches and castles virtually no surviving buildings in Scottish towns pre-date the sixteenth century. However, houses dating from the late sixteenth and early seventeenth centuries contain structural features which

8. W.B. Stevenson, The monastic presence in Scottish burghs in the twelfth and thirteenth centuries, *SHR*, 60, 1981, 97–118.

echo earlier building techniques. Documentary sources, and in recent years a good deal of archaeological evidence, provide additional information on building construction. Nearly 40 buildings have been excavated from the medieval layers of Scottish towns, especially Aberdeen, Inverness and Perth. Due to the availability of open space for excavation within the modern towns most of the excavated structures have been located at the rear of burgage plots and not on the street frontages. Structures in such locations would, in many cases, have been lower-status houses and workshops. This may explain why many of them were of simple post and wattle construction though similar structures have been found on some frontages too. Wattle plastered with clay, dung or possibly turf was either set directly in the earth or into a sill beam, sometimes itself on stone foundations which slowed rotting. Frequent rebuilding with a lifespan of 25 years or less is probable. Walls of timber planks have also been discovered but these are likely to have been more expensive than wattle and were probably less common.

Many of the excavated medieval buildings in Scottish towns appear to have been single-storey structures with only one room but two-storey houses also existed although even at this date it is possible that some of them may have been divided into flats. Some long buildings on the Perth backlands may have been terraces of cottages similar to those of medieval Winchester. The smallest houses consisted of only one room. Byre-dwellings with animals accommodated under the same roof as their owners have also been found. The houses in Scottish medieval towns were almost entirely built with wood, wattle and thatch; stone construction was rare before the sixteenth century. Nevertheless, stone houses existed in Aberdeen and Ayr by the early fourteenth century and may have been more common in larger burghs like Berwick and Perth. Domestic refuse was often disposed of in the backlands. The richness of the finds from rubbish pits in such locations suggests that much of the waste material must have come from wealthier buildings on the forelands. The backlands were also used for keeping horses, cattle, pigs, geese and poultry while several excavated buildings in such locations provide evidence of industrial activity as well as domestic occupation, possibly craftsmen living above their workshops. Apart from burgh churches the main public buildings were town houses or tolbooths. The earliest surviving tolbooths date from the late sixteenth century and reflect increased pressure on royal burghs to provide prisons, but tolbooths are known to have been built from at least the fourteenth century, providing a purpose-built assembly place for burgh courts which had previously been held in the open or in the houses of individual burgesses.

URBAN ECONOMIES

The burghs had a role in the economy of medieval Scotland out of all proportion to their size. In the thirteenth century, as we have seen, prosperity in the burghs was linked to the demand for Scottish wool from the cloth towns of Flanders. There is much more evidence for overseas trade than for internal commodity flows though information even for the former is scanty enough. Local trade must have been important to all the burghs though, with foreign trade merely being the icing on the cake for many of them. In England it was common to have markets outside towns but in Scotland markets were restricted to the burghs.

Nevertheless, as concentrations of population Scotland's medieval towns were small. Fourteenth-century Perth had about 370 burgages. Edinburgh in 1400 had around 400 houses. Aberdeen in 1408 had only 344 burgage holders. These figures suggest that the largest burghs may have had populations of upwards of 2,000 in the late thirteenth and fourteenth centuries and that in most other burghs the population was probably numbered in hundreds rather than thousands. But size was not necessarily a good indicator of economic importance as is shown by the rise of late-medieval Edinburgh to engross more and more of Scotland's export trade with only a modest growth of population.

By the end of the thirteenth century there were 38 royal burghs and 18 non-royal ones. There is little doubt that Berwick and Perth were the leading centres. Excavations at Perth have provided evidence of an urban community which was both prosperous and densely packed.[9] A wide range of exotic imports and the heavily built up nature of the burgages demonstrates that Perth was a centre of major importance. Berwick, however, was the fastest growing town in the thirteenth century. These two burghs were followed by a number of second-rank centres including Aberdeen, Roxburgh, Edinburgh and Stirling. Excavations in Aberdeen show that despite its key position as the major trading centre north of the Mounth, standards of living and the density of building were lower than in Perth marking the town as more of a provincial centre. The old-established shire centre of Dundee was already an active trading centre at the end of the twelfth century when it was granted to David, Earl of Huntingdon, who acquired burgh status for the community.[10] By the early thirteenth century Dundee's merchants were trading with London and East Anglia. Soon Dundee was challenging Perth whose merchants were, by 1209, trying to stifle its competition. In this they were unsuccessful for after the fall of Berwick Dundee rose to become one of the most important towns in medieval Scotland. Below the level of these centres were the lesser burghs. Some coastal towns like Crail, if smaller than the main burghs, were still prosperous trading centres. Inland burghs like Inverurie and Kintore, without direct access to the sea, must have depended almost entirely on local trade.

Because Scotland's export trade concentrated heavily on raw materials, and because Bruges craftsmen were able to flood the domestic market with a wide range of manufactures, urban industry remained restricted, even as late as the sixteenth century. There were far fewer craft guilds in Scotland than in England and many of these were composite organisations. Nevertheless, a

9. Stringer, *Earl David*, pp. 74–9.
10. Holdsworth, *Excavation*.

range of manufacturing and processing activities did exist in Scottish towns. Surnames in thirteenth-century Perth indicate the existence of craftsmen in basic trades such as tailors, tanners and smiths as well as specialists like armourers and goldsmiths. Something of the diversity of industrial activity in medieval burghs has been discovered from recent excavations. From Perth, where site conditions were especially favourable for the preservation of organic material, several hundred pieces of medieval textiles have been recovered, most of them relatively poor-quality woollen cloth, suggesting that the best wool was exported though it is not clear how much cloth was woven in the surrounding countryside rather than in the town itself. Needles of bone and metal testify to the activities of tailors. After wool, hides were the most valuable raw material and their preparation and processing was an important urban occupation. A wide range of objects carved in bone emphasise the importance of this often forgotten raw material. Metal- and wood-working, baking and brewing are also attested by archaeological evidence. Excavations at Inverness have provided evidence of iron-working showing that not all ironware was imported. Many burghs were also substantial producers of pottery. A Scottish pottery industry existed from the thirteenth century at least although English and continental wares were imported in quantity. In the late thirteenth and early fourteenth centuries local pottery became much more common; it is possible that the Wars of Independence, by cutting Scotland off from continental suppliers, stimulated domestic crafts including pottery manufacture.

Towns were not divorced from the countryside; urban and rural areas were interdependent, the towns providing mechanisms by which the resources of the landward areas were marketed and distributed. Their rural hinterlands were sources of basic foodstuffs, building materials and fuel as well as commodities for trade. In Aberdeen many rural landowners had town houses overlooking the market-place while from the fourteenth century Aberdeen burgesses were investing in rural estates and marrying into local landed families. By the late thirteenth century and increasingly in the fourteenth century burgesses were acquiring land beyond the limits of their burghs. Such land provided burgesses with status, collateral for business ventures, income from rent, and produce if farmed directly. Burgesses seem to have been able to marry into landed families quite easily. Burgesses could also further their careers by royal service; as auditors of the Exchequer accounts for instance, supplying provisions for the royal household, and as masters of mints. Adam Forrester, a noted Edinburgh merchant, was clerk of the customs rolls south of the Forth in 1363 and 1366, auditor of the Exchequer accounts 1388–1410, sheriff of Lothian in 1382 (by which time he was also a prominent rural land-holder), and deputy chamberlain in 1391. John Mercer of Perth (d1380), another of these early 'merchant princes', described by a contemporary as having 'inestimable wealth', had a similar career and married into a baronial family.[11]

11. E. Ewan, *Townlife in Fourteenth Century Scotland* (Edinburgh 1990), pp. 121–34.

BURGH SOCIETY AND ADMINISTRATION

Burghs grew into small tight-knit communities united by their trading privileges, their distinctive tenure and their trading and craft activities. By the early fourteenth century even the burgesses of ecclesiastical burghs were acquiring rights of self-government from their superiors. Royal burghs already had greater independence which probably increased during the fourteenth century when royal administration was weakened under the impact of war with England. This was reflected by the crown granting burghs feu ferme charters in which they enjoyed the benefits of all revenues except customs on exports in return for fixed annual payments. A charter to Aberdeen in 1319 was the first, probably formalising a process which already existed on a more *ad hoc* basis in many burghs.

'Burgh' and 'burgage' are essentially legal concepts; the status and privileges of the burghs were protected by laws from David I's time. A charter of William I refers to laws passed by David giving burghs the monopoly of buying and selling, of making woollen cloth, and also restricting the keeping of taverns outside the burghs, a partial monopoly possibly connected with the lucrative import trade in wine. By William's reign a body of law evidently existed regarding the burghs, both legislative and customary, much of it probably similar to the rest of Western Europe, especially England. Rather than being superimposed on an existing background of feudal laws, burgh privileges developed gradually as an integral element of feudalism which arrived in Scotland at much the same time, incorporating many rights which were seen as normal by incoming foreign burgesses. Scottish burghs were not separate from the feudal society and economy; rather they were a distinctive element within it.

The best-known compilation of burgh laws is the Leges Burgorum, large parts of which are modelled on the mid-twelfth century customs of Newcastle upon Tyne at a period when Northumberland was under Scottish control. Other parts of the Burgh Laws seem to have been added later. It is not clear whether the original core of material was formulated under David I and was added to in the thirteenth century or whether the whole body of legislation was collected together in the thirteenth century incorporating some earlier laws. Other evidence points to the reign of William (1165–1214) as a period when a good deal of burgh law was first written down.

Scottish burghs were more uniform in terms of their laws and customs than English boroughs and as early as the fourteenth century they were a more unified force in national politics. It is probable that from the beginning each burgh had its own court to settle disputes between inhabitants and with outsiders. Such courts were originally presided over by the sheriff but by the late twelfth century this had given way to an officer chosen by the burgh community. Burgesses owed suit to the burgh court as landward tenants in chief did to the sheriff court. Burgh courts were not separate from feudal law but formed a parallel system similar to other courts in medieval Scotland.

Three head courts were normally held each year allowing burgesses to be tried by their peers but under a system which did not differ materially from the rest of the country. Burgh courts had limited criminal jurisdiction at first. Only in the fourteenth and fifteenth centuries did they begin to acquire similar powers to the sheriff courts; crime was too profitable in the form of fines, escheats and pardons to be left entirely in the hands of the burgesses. In 1394 Robert III granted to the provost and burgesses of Perth the sheriffship of the burgh, expanding its legal jurisdiction to that enjoyed by the sheriff and allowing burgh courts to try major criminal cases. Similar grants to other burghs followed in the fifteenth century.

By the early thirteenth century a higher authority, the Court of the Four Burghs, had developed to deal with the collective interests of towns, especially regarding taxation. The Court of the Four Burghs originally comprised four burgesses, one each from Berwick, Edinburgh, Roxburgh and Stirling. It served as a court of appeal from individual burgh courts, dealt with questions of interpretation of burgh law, and provided a forum for burgesses from different towns. From it developed the Convention of Royal Burghs which was formally constituted in 1487 (Chapter 10).

Burghs had little independence at first. In the twelfth century they were under the control of an officer appointed by the king or other overlord, often the sheriff. By the late thirteenth century, as trade expanded and population grew, burgh administration had become more complex. The sheriff was originally assisted by officials; prepositi or ballivi (baillies) who helped to collect burgh revenues. By the twelfth century, perhaps earlier, these were being chosen from among the burgesses in some burghs and then by the burgesses themselves. By the mid-fourteenth century the prepositus (provost) had become the head of the burgh community while the baillies were still concerned with collecting revenue. The Berwick Statutes of the Guild, a set of bye-laws from the second half of the thirteenth century, show a well-developed structure of burgh administration. The provost was usually a prominent merchant, occupying an office with a good deal of prestige but often rather limited real power. The baillies also organised justice, presiding over the head courts, administering burgh lands, collecting tolls and fixing prices. The larger burghs came to be run by councils acting on behalf of the community but in smaller burghs affairs continued to be conducted by open assemblies of burgesses.

In the early days of the burghs much trading was probably done by the craftsmen who actually made the goods. The expansion of overseas trade in the thirteenth century led to the development of increasingly influential groups of merchants, encouraged by the crown which confirmed their privileges in 1364. By this time the growing national importance of these merchant elites was reflected in their contribution to royal revenues, their participation in parliament and, at a local level, by their increasing dominance of burgh society.

The government and community of the medieval burgh was focused on the head court and the guild merchant. The crown granted the burgesses of some towns, including Perth and Stirling, the right to have a guild in the thirteenth century. Aberdeen's charter of 1222 confirmed that a merchant guild already existed with a range of monopolies including that of making cloth within the burgh. At least 19 burghs had a guild merchant by the fourteenth century. Berwick had a guild in the twelfth century, as did Perth and Roxburgh. In the early thirteenth century Aberdeen, Ayr, Dumbarton, Dundee, Inverkeithing and Stirling had them but in many small burghs merchant guilds were not established until the sixteenth or seventeenth century. Until c1400 the guild merchant was the main burgh institution concerned with trade. Because burghs existed primarily for trade there was some overlap between the activities of the guilds and burgh government but the guilds did not take over burgh administration. Before the mid-fifteenth century the merchant guilds were mainly concerned with the cloth trade though actual manufacturers were excluded from membership. When this source of wealth declined guilds were increasingly involved in regulating trade in staple commodities such as wool, woolfells, and hides.

The function and composition of early guilds have been debated; they have been seen by some historians purely as associations of merchants, defending their members against encroachments on their privileges by craftsmen. In practice many guilds were probably less exclusive. Guild members formed a community within a community. The emergence of craft guilds in Scottish towns occurred a century later than in England and much later than on the Continent. The distinction between merchant and craftsman was not very precise in fourteenth-century burghs. The conventional story of conflict between merchants and craftsmen has been overdrawn and presented too simplistically. By the fifteenth century, when records first become available, the composition of the merchant guild varied from one town to another. In Dunfermline the guild numbered around 50, about a third of the male inhabitants. In Perth, with a much larger population, the guild merchant was not much bigger but included craftsmen as well as merchants. In Aberdeen the guild was much larger and no distinction was made between inland and overseas traders though no craftsmen were included. In Edinburgh on the other hand around 15 per cent of the merchant guildry were craftsmen by the mid-sixteenth century.[12]

The Laws of the Four Burghs and the Statutes of the Guild of Berwick evolved during the twelfth century becoming a model for most Scottish guilds. They show that the guild merchant had social and religious as well as mercantile functions. The records of the merchant guild of Dunfermline from 1433 are the earliest surviving ones. Sons of guild members or husbands of daughters of guild members were admitted free; otherwise the entrance fee was 40 shillings (against 6s 8d for admission as a burgess). Given that about a third of Dunfermline's burgesses were guild members the guild cannot have been too exclusive. It contained many craftsmen and indeed references to merchants are comparatively few. The term used by contemporaries was 'the

12. Ibid., pp. 58–63.

guild' not 'guild merchant' and the fraternity was open to both groups. Only in the sixteenth century did such guilds evolve into elitist trade organisations dominated by merchants to the detriment of craftsmen. Craft incorporations did not appear until the second half of the sixteenth century in Dunfermline; before that craft activities were regulated by the merchant guild. The guild financed improvements in the town such as paving the streets and repairing the tolbooth. A significant proportion of guild funds went to support the church. The guild also helped impoverished members and, to judge by the expenditure on food and drink, conviviality was a principal function of its meetings.

THE LATER MIDDLE AGES: DECLINE AND DECAY

From the early or mid-fourteenth century until the later sixteenth century it is likely that Scottish towns shared the general pattern of commercial decline which affected the whole of Western Europe. The flowering of urban life in the twelfth and thirteenth centuries gave way to crisis and decay centred around a long-term deterioration in overseas trade. Given the lack of evidence compared with towns in late-medieval England the nature of urban decline in Scotland is not always easy to identify but the overall decline in exports is clear enough, a trend exacerbated for many towns by the growing proportion of the diminishing volume of exports which was engrossed by Edinburgh's merchants. Edinburgh handled 21 per cent of the export trade in wool in the 1320s but 32 per cent by the 1370s and 57 per cent by the 1440s.

With several major outbreaks of plague between 1349 and 1455, an increasingly adverse balance of trade, falling exchange rates, a shortage of coin and the collapse of overseas markets it is hard to believe that there was not a decline in the economy of most burghs. There were periods of revival leading to church building and some urban growth (as with the expanding suburbs of Perth in the fifteenth century) but these relatively brief interludes were superimposed on a long-term decline in trade. Although there was some improvement in the late fifteenth and early sixteenth centuries there was no general revival of urban fortunes until the 1560s and especially the 1590s. Nevertheless, decline has been assumed rather than proven due to the lack of clear evidence and it is not certain whether it took the forms that have been postulated for late-medieval English towns. The occupational structure of the main towns changed as their inhabitants adjusted to the less encouraging economic climate. Poor-quality Scottish cloth, most of it woven in rural areas, was still allowed into Flanders but not better quality cloth. As a result the clothing and textile trades were not as prominent as in English towns. Decline in wool exports also led to towns diversifying their economies, some into leather processing.

The crown maintained a tight grip on the burghs in the thirteenth century but this became looser from the fourteenth century. The crown intervened in trade and tried to encourage exports, especially cloth, and also attempted to restrict the export trade to a smaller group of established merchants. The sense of community among the inhabitants of different burghs was beginning to find political expression by the mid-fourteenth century with the recognition of burgesses as the third estate of the realm. This was helped by the lack of sharp differentiation between royal and non-royal burghs regarding taxation. The Court of the Four Burghs became recognised as a forum for seeking advice on burgh law and custom. Burgesses were probably present in the early parliaments of Robert I and were officially summoned to Parliament in 1326. They were regular attenders from 1357, their political representation being due in particular to the crown's need for money to pay the installments on David II's ransom between 1357 and 1373. This growing financial burden began to cause a split between those burghs which were represented in Parliament and those which were not. This gulf was to widen in later centuries as the burghs represented in Parliament pressed for greater privileges to offset the burden of taxation that they bore, emphasising the stresses which existed in the late-medieval economy.

CHAPTER 5

LATE-MEDIEVAL SCOTLAND: ECONOMY AND SOCIETY IN TRANSITION

The wars with England which began in 1296 continued until 1323. War broke out again in 1332 and dragged on into the 1350s, only ending with the Treaty of Berwick in 1357. The scale of long-term dislocation as well as short-term devastation was considerable. The campaigns associated with William Wallace and Robert Bruce are well known but war damage in the years immediately following 1296 was probably less severe than during the second quarter of the fourteenth century. Though the Treaty of Berwick was followed by a generation of peace close contact with England, such as had existed in the later thirteenth century, was not resumed. The legacy of mistrust between the two countries was to last for another 300 years and more, a state of latent hostility punctuated by intermittent war which had profound effects on Scotland's social and economic development.

THE LATE-MEDIEVAL ECONOMY

The economic impact of war during the first half of the fourteenth century is difficult to assess. Many parts of the country were laid waste by English attacks and the scorched-earth policies of the Scots. The most developed regions of southern Scotland bore the brunt of the fighting although districts north of the Forth were not immune. Rural areas were swift to recover from military activity though, as were the towns. Aberdeen was burnt in 1336 but within five years the inhabitants were delivering their fermes to the crown as usual. In Berwick, despite the slaughter of the townspeople in 1296, merchants continued to trade under English occupation until 1318 and then under Scottish control. By 1327 Berwick had recovered its position as the main exporter of Scottish wool though its lead was less prominent than before and it was increasingly being challenged by Edinburgh.

Despite the resilience of the Scots severe damage to the economy undoubtedly occurred, not least due to the fact that contact with England, one of Scotland's main trading partners in the later thirteenth century, was broken. In addition, Scottish trading routes, particularly to France and the Low Countries, were vulnerable to English attack. Before the Wars of

Independence Scotland's overseas trade had been more broadly based but contacts with Germany and western France as well as with England declined making trade with Flanders, especially Bruges, proportionally more important. By the mid-fourteenth century, conditions were more stable. Most of our evidence is for links with France and the Low Countries. Information on contacts with the Baltic and Scandinavia is scanty and indirect, mostly relating to voyages which went wrong through shipwreck, piracy or some dispute rather than to successful trading ventures. There is little evidence of Scottish merchants in Norway at this time. The economies of Scotland and Norway were competing rather than complementary. Norway was not a major producer of cloth so there was little demand for Scottish wool. Norway and Scotland both exported leather and fish, both imported cloth, salt and grain, commodities which Scotland could only supply to Norway in limited amounts.

During the fourteenth and fifteenth centuries Norway came increasingly under the influence of the Hanseatic League which limited contacts with Scotland. Trade only revived with the growing need for Norwegian timber in the early sixteenth century. Trade with Denmark suffered from fewer restrictions but was limited before the later fifteenth century. The marriage in 1468 of James III to Margaret, daughter of Christian I, opened up Denmark to Scottish merchants who began to settle in increasing numbers. By the end of the fifteenth century Scots were active in Aalborg, Bergen, Copenhagen and Elsinore. Trade with the Baltic was more important to late-medieval Scotland though its volume is hard to estimate before the end of the fifteenth century when the Sound Toll Registers become available. These indicate that vessels from Leith and Dundee dominated the Scottish Baltic trade. But the Scots were small fry in the Baltic and wool, their major export, was less and less in demand there though skins, cloth and salt could be sold. As Scottish merchants experienced increasing problems in selling their goods, imports from the Baltic probably rose, including grain which could no longer be obtained regularly from England, arms, iron and, surprisingly, herring. Despite the richness of Scotland's fisheries Scottish merchants are recorded buying Baltic herring in Scania from the late fourteenth century. Overall, Scottish trade with the Baltic is likely to have been heavily in deficit by the fifteenth century.

Trade with the Low Countries, especially the export of wool, continued to be Scotland's most vital overseas link. In the fourteenth century Scotland supplied a significant proportion of the wool consumed in Flanders and Artois. The volume of the export trade is reasonably clear as Scottish customs records exist for some years in the early fourteenth century and on a regular basis from the 1360s. As there was no general tariff on imports until the end of the sixteenth century there is much less information on commodities entering Scotland. The imposition of the 'great customs' on the export of wool, woolfells and hides seems to have begun before the end of the thirteenth century in imitation of the system instituted by Edward I for England. The monitoring of such exports by the crown to ensure full payment was easier if the bulk of taxable exports was channelled through a single centre like Bruges. In the fourteenth century Bruges came to dominate Scottish overseas trade and manufactures from there flooded into Scotland. The importance of Scottish trade with Bruges is shown by a treaty made in 1407 which confirmed privileges established by earlier grants in 1359 and 1394 and added new ones including the appointment of a conservator to regulate and safeguard Scottish trade. Some kind of trading staple at Bruges probably existed by the 1340s. The concessions were not as full as those enjoyed under the later staple but they showed that Scottish trade was far from negligible in importance. The staple remained at Bruges until 1477. From then till 1500 it was probably at Middelburg. In 1507 or 1508 it was moved to Veere. The advantages of Veere lay less in the size of its market than its readily accessible deepwater harbour.

A triangular trade from the Baltic to Scotland then with staple goods from Scotland to Flanders and so back to the Baltic appears to have been a regular pattern. It was on one such voyage in 1406 that the ship carrying the 12-year-old son of Robert III, the future James I, was captured by an English vessel. Despite the danger of the sea routes France continued to be a major trading partner and wine a costly import. Almost all Scotland's overseas trade in the fourteenth and fifteenth centuries was channelled through east-coast ports, notably Aberdeen, Dundee (which had captured much of Perth's export trade) and to an increasing degree Edinburgh. One of the most notable features of late-medieval Scottish trade was the increasing degree to which it was monopolised by Edinburgh's merchants. Given that the volume of trade was declining this presented problems for merchants in other burghs. There was little trade from west-coast ports apart from some contact with Ireland. Staple goods for export from the western Lowlands were brought overland to Leith or to Blackness, the outport for Linlithgow, a flourishing entrepot whose trade around 1400 was almost as great as Aberdeen's.

In European terms late-medieval Scotland was a major exporter of wool and leather. The Scots were also important producers of fish and, increasingly, coarse woollen cloth. Exports of wool had, by the 1360s, returned to the fairly buoyant level of the late 1320s, peaking in 1372, when around 9,252 sacks of wool were exported. At this time Scotish wool exports may have been over a quarter of English ones. By 1376, however, they were down sharply. Exports of hides peaked a decade later; in 1381 over 72,000 were exported. The boom of the 1370s was short-lived as the whole of Europe began to slide into recession. The return of David II from captivity in England in 1357 and the need to meet his ransom payments led to higher taxation. By 1368 export duties on wool, fleeces and hides had been quadrupled. Higher duties did not affect exports immediately; there was an export boom in the early 1370s, but the increased tariffs had an adverse effect in the longer term. Scotland's balance of payments fluctuated during the fourteenth century but was probably reasonably favourable overall until the 1390s when it fell sharply into deficit with a major slump in exports and problems with the exchange rate. Wool exports declined during the 1380s and 1390s, dropping to a low point in the early fifteenth century. English wool exports showed a similar downward trend but were balanced by the expansion of the cloth industry. Although production of Scottish cloth increased its low quality and price did not allow it to make more than a modest conbtribution to export revenues.

Although war in Flanders during the 1380s affected cloth manufacture there the slump in Scottish wool exports at the end of the fourteenth century was only partly due to a drop in demand. Other detrimental influences included an English naval blockade of Scotland from 1400. The decline in trade is highlighted by the drop in the numbers of vessels leaving Scottish ports for foreign destinations. In 1328–31 around 30 vessels left Leith each year. By the 1410s this had fallen to 16. The drop for Aberdeen over the same period was even more dramatic; from 36 vessels a year to around five. Due to the threat of English piracy many of these ships were relatively large and often sailed in convoy for protection. The need to use such big vessels increased the investment involved in trading ventures and meant that losses due to piracy and shipwreck were correspondingly serious. The threat of piracy has perhaps been overestimated but most of the maritime nations surrounding the North Sea preyed on their neighbours' shipping and piracy, whether in local waters like the Firth of Forth or in more distant locations, caused serious difficulties at times.

The Scots, however, were not merely passive victims; they earned a measure of notoriety as pirates. With the decline of trade from the end of the fourteenth century frustrated Scottish skippers, with their big, well-armed vessels, turned increasingly to piracy. Aberdeen skippers in the early years of the fifteenth century did so on a large scale, supported by powerful backers including the Earl of Mar and the burgh's provost. The obvious conclusion is that a decline in the town's trade drove skippers to piracy but there is more than a suspicion that the relationship may have operated the other way with trade falling off due to a focus on piracy as a more lucrative source of income. The capture of neutral as well as English vessels worsened relations with some of the Scots' trading partners. The activities of Aberdeen's pirates were directly responsible for the Hanseatic League imposing an embargo on Scottish trade. The reluctance of the Scottish authorities to compensate victims of piracy by their countrymen also soured relations with Flanders in the 1420s.

The slump which set in at the opening of the fifteenth century was the start of a long period of decline and economic instability. War between France and England, the hostility of the Hanseatic League, and deteriorating political conditions in Flanders combined to make trading tougher for the Scots. The years after the return of James I in 1424 were better than the first quarter of the fifteenth century and contact with England resumed on a scale not seen since the reign of David II. In 1426 James cut the duty on wool exports in an attempt to boost trade, a measure which brought some temporary success. But to compensate new duties were introduced on a range of commodities including cloth, salmon and salt. James I also passed measures to restrict overseas trade to merchants with goods amounting to at least three sacks of wool or the equivalent value. This had the effect of further entrenching the position of the wealthier merchant burgesses whose financial support James urgently needed. Overseas trade could still allow individual entrepreneurs to make their fortunes and such men were a good source for loans. This was the first of several measures to restrict foreign trade to a small elite. At a time when economic conditions were deteriorating there was some sense in this but it also restricted the activities of men who were ambitious but not well-connected.

The recovery of the 1420s was short-lived. Customs receipts on exports, over £9,000 a year in the early 1370s, reached only £5,695 a year in the late 1420s, fell to just over £2,000 by the late 1450s and remained under £3,000 for the rest of the century. Receipts from wool dropped by two-thirds from the late 1420s to the late 1450s. Overseas trade was badly hit by the renewal of war with England in 1436. There was a brief upturn again in the mid-1440s, then prolonged depression in the 1450s. Although exports of wool declined, the production of coarse woollen cloth seems to have expanded. We have little indication of the quantities produced before the introduction of duties on exported cloth in 1426 but it has been argued that the industry was already taking a significant proportion of the Scottish wool clip by the 1370s. Although the duty on cloth was much lower than that on wool by 1434/5 customs receipts for cloth amounted to some 10 per cent of that from wool and exports may have been as high as 75,000 yards in some years. Coarse woollen cloth found a ready market among the urban poor of Flanders due to its rock-bottom price. Exports, though fluctuating considerably from year to year, seem to have peaked in the 1420s. They had fallen by about two-thirds in the mid-fifteenth century but then began to rise reaching a peak in the early 1540s. Exports of hides showed a similar trend. Revenue from salmon exports rose rapidly in the 1470s, fell dramatically in the mid-1480s, then rose more slowly into the sixteenth century. Unlike most sectors of the export trade Edinburgh handled only a limited amount of salmon, Aberdeen being the main centre. By the early sixteenth century exports of wool accounted for about 56 per cent of the receipts of the Scottish customs, hides 12 per cent, woolfells 9 per cent, cloth 9 per cent and salmon 6 per cent.

In the late fifteenth century foreign trade was less important to the towns than at any time before. The extent of the decline is seen in the fall in the proportion of taxation contributed by the burghs from a third to a fifth and eventually a sixth. Set against this, however, Scottish domestic crafts may have benefited from a shortage of money for imports. The boom in the construction of tower houses as well as royal projects must have benefited the building trades while in other areas of skilled craftsmanship, such as the manufacture of artillery and shipbuilding, Scotland was making significant advances. It was against this background of increasing difficulty for merchants and the rise of domestic industry that, during the reign of James III, urban craftsmen began to be incorporated (Chapter 11).

Landowners were also facing difficulties. The overall national assessment for land fell by half between the late thirteenth century and 1366. In part this may have been the result of a fall in productivity and deflation but it is also likely to have reflected the drop in population after the Black Death. A shortage of labour is probably the underlying explanation for trends like the leasing of demesnes and increases in the sizes of peasant holdings which can be discerned from the few surviving estate documents of the late fourteenth century. The boom in exports of wool and leather in the 1370s and 1380s suggests that a switch to livestock farming occurred which, with a shortage of labour and high wages, is likely to have been more profitable to proprietors than arable farming. With the disappearance of serfdom landowners could probably only retain their tenants by offering lower rents. For a generation or more in the later fourteenth century, before the slump in exports set in, conditions may have been especially favourable for prosperous peasant farmers who may have been able to lease large holdings at comparatively low rents. The economic difficulties of the fifteenth century, with the decline of exports of pastoral products, is likely to have favoured a renewed expansion of arable farming. It is probably no accident that it is at the end of the fifteenth century that the term 'outfield' first appears in charters suggesting an intake of new land for cultivation (Chapter 8).

Economic difficulties were exacerbated by problems with the coinage.[1] These were part of the general shortage of silver throughout Europe. Scotland would have been affected (though perhaps less severely) even if there had not been an export slump and interference with the currency. Unfortunately, one effect of the shortage of money was the realisation that more could be created by reducing the weight of the coins in circulation. When this was done to excess the result was a shift from deflation to inflation, a trend which is evident in Scotland by the early fifteenth century. Until the late fourteenth century Scotland's coinage was tied to England's with similar weights, standards, denominations and even designs. The value of both currencies fell in the first half of the fourteenth century but more or less in step. However, After Edward III prohibited the use of coins of David II in England this system of parity came to an end. In 1367 devaluation in Scotland reduced the groat (six Scottish pence) to five-sixths of the value of its English equivalent, the start of a trend which was to continue through the fifteenth century. In the thirteenth century the Scottish pound had contained 5,400 grains of silver. By 1390 this had fallen to 2,764, by 1451 to 1,178 and from 1470 it stood at 780 grains. There was a rapid and severe reduction in the value of Scottish coins against English ones. By the mid-fifteenth century the Scottish pound was worth only a third of its English equivalent, by 1603 a twelfth. Wages for labourers and artisans in Scotland rose between the early fourteenth and early sixteenth centuries at levels which seem to have at least compensated for the drop in the value of the coinage over the same period (about two thirds), while rents rose at a comparable, if not a greater, level.

1. D.M. Metcalf (ed.), Coinage in medieval Scotland 1100–1600, *BAR*, 45 (Oxford 1977).

A fall in exports with a healthier demographic regime than in England, and a correspondingly steady demand for imports may explain the net loss of bullion from Scotland which was a problem from the later fourteenth century. Legislation by James I in 1424 tried to tackle the problem by placing a tax on all silver and gold that left the country and by requiring fixed amounts of bullion to be brought into Scotland for each sack of wool or its equivalent that was exported. The periodic enactment of these measures is ample evidence of their ineffectiveness. The realisation that the profits from exports were being spent on luxury imports rather than returning to Scotland as bullion led in the 1460s and 1470s to limitations on the wearing of silk, bans on the import of English cloth, and other restrictions. Bullion continued to flow out of Scotland, sometimes to pay ransoms like those of David II and James I. Substantial amounts also went to Rome as sweeteners to encourage the confirmation of benefices. This led to the invention of the offence of 'barratry', the unauthorised purchase of benefices in Rome, in an effort to check the loss. Inflows of money in the form of royal dowries provided useful injections of cash into the economy but failed to balance the outflows.

THE NOBILITY

The nobility of late-medieval Scotland amounted to perhaps 2,000 heads of families or 10,000 members in all, perhaps a little over 1 per cent of the population, a figure comparable with contemporary France. Within this group there were at any time perhaps 50 or so magnates who played a significant role in national affairs. Below this there were a few hundred substantial landholders. At their lower end they merged into the peasantry being distinguished by their tenures rather than their wealth. Unlike England, where the peerage was sharply defined and distinguished from the gentry, a Scottish peerage did not emerge until the mid-fifteenth century. This blurring of distinctions helps to explain why in Scotland a gentry class with a clear sense of identity was so late in developing. Landed society, indeed society in general in late-medieval Scotland, was more fluid with greater social mobility than many societies elsewhere in Europe.

The structure of the higher nobility changed markedly between the mid-fourteenth and the mid-fifteenth centuries. Before the Wars of Independence the nobility was still a territorial one in which status and power were directly related to land. The dozen earldoms were huge, compact blocks of country within which the earls' influence was paramount. The rest of the nobility comprised the barons who had been granted special jurisdictional powers and below them the freeholders without special privileges. Within the barons Grant distinguishes three groups.[2] First, there were those who held great feudal lordships, some, like Annandale, as extensive as earldoms. At a lower level were men with groups of baronies.

2. A. Grant, *Independence and Nationahood, 1306–1469* (London 1984), pp. 124–7.

Their importance was distinctly greater than the rest of the barons who held only one or two baronies each.

Many ancient earldoms and provincial lordships survived into the period after the Wars of Independence due to Robert I's essentially conservative policies. By the end of the fourteenth century this pattern was beginning to change. One important feature was the increasing concentration of earldoms and lordships in fewer hands. By the 1390s the Stewarts had acquired a dozen of them and the Douglases several more. With the forfeiture of various Stewart nobles by James I and the Douglases by James II much of this land came into the hands of the crown during the fifteenth century. By the mid-fifteenth century the nobility was starting to become more personal in nature and more distinctly divided between the lords who were parliamentary peers and the lairds, a group which included all other nobles. New earldoms and lordships, instead of having a firm territorial base, were coming to be personal honorific titles which did not necessarily have close links with specific localities. The earldom of Douglas, created in 1355, was the first of the new type a personal honour covering territories scattered in nine sheriffdoms including four lordships, 16 baronies and many other fragments. At the same time many of the traditional territorial earldoms were disappearing by forfeiture or division among heiresses. As this occurred the traditional role of the earls in mustering and leading the common army declined. To the new earldoms were added dukedoms, the first being those of Albany and Rothesay created in 1398, again honorific ranks not tied to particular localities. By 1438 only five of the old provincial earldoms survived. The rest had come into the hands of the crown by forfeiture or escheat.

The great provincial lordships followed a similar pattern. By the mid-fifteenth century many had reverted to the crown, been absorbed by the Douglas earldoms, or been fragmented. It was in this context that the barons who did not hold provincial lordships, but whose lands were nevertheless extensive, assumed greater political importance. The new earls and lords of parliament were drawn mainly from this group. The removal of the Stewart and Douglas earldoms by James I and II allowed members of this group to rise to the top of the nobility becoming some of the most important families in Scotland. A distinct Scottish peerage developed in the mid-fifteenth century with the practice, from the reign of James I, of summoning certain lords to attend parliament. These 'lords of parliament' came to form the lower rank of the peerage and were distinguished from the 'small barons' who were summoned to Parliament as a group. Most of the new lords of parliament were the heads of long-established families. The disappearance of many of the earls by forfeiture and failure of their male lines allowed the lords of parliament to rise in status. The result was a refashioning of the upper levels of the nobility so that it was more homogeneous with fewer really wealthy magnates, the new honorific earls not necessarily having estates any greater than those of the other nobles.

Grant has provided interesting insights into the structure of the late-medieval Scottish nobility by calculating the rates of extinction of families and comparing the results with other countries.[3] In England and France the survival rates of noble families were roughly similar. Turnover was rapid with most families becoming extinct in the male line. In each 25–year period around a quarter of noble families died out in this way. In Scotland, however, the extinction rate for dukes and earls fell from 27 per cent in the first half of the fourteenth century to between 16 per cent and 17 per cent in the second half of the fifteenth century. The extinction rate for barons and lords of parliament dropped from 24 per cent in 1325–49 to between 5 per cent and 7 per cent for the last three-quarters of the fifteenth century. When the two data sets are combined the aggregate rate of extinction for Scottish noble families falls steadily from 28 per cent in 1325–49 to 10 per cent in 1475–1500, contrasting markedly with England where the rate held steady at around 25 per cent throughout the fifteenth century. There was a major difference in the survival rate of families in late-medieval Scotland compared with England and France.

The high levels of extinction of Scottish dukes and earls in the first quarter of the fourteenth century can be attributed to war with England. There is no indication that plague was important in extinguishing families in either Scotland or England after the mid-fourteenth century. It is possible that the lack of internal unrest in late-medieval Scotland compared with England may have aided family survival but differences in fertility between Scottish and English noble families may also have been important. Grant has suggested that marriage with older female heiresses for political and economic advantages was less common in Scotland because such heiresses were fewer and that Scottish magnates were more likely than their English counterparts to marry women of childbearing age with a greater probability of producing enough sons to carry on the male line. If the origins of this noble marriage pattern are uncertain some of its implications are clear. In England the failure of male lines led to a high turnover of landownership. In Scotland the estates of the nobility were more stable and the scope for making very large additions to one's territory by marriage less considerable. In England the acquisition of estates by marriage tended to produce a fragmented pattern of land ownership working against the strong and continued influence of magnate families in particular localities. The prolonged disputes over inheritance that resulted from the marriage pattern of the late-medieval English nobility, a major cause of local instability, was less of a problem in Scotland. The degree of continuity in the occupation of land in Scotland contributed to stability within landed society. The fertility of noble families led to a surplus of younger sons who often managed to establish cadet branches. Younger sons were more likely to be granted lands from those already in their fathers' possession than from ones belonging to an heiress mother, a feature which helped to entrench families within particular localities.

The establishment of cadet branches within the territories dominated by existing landed families helps to explain the importance of kinship in late-medieval Scotland. Younger sons of noble families frequently married

3. Ibid., pp. 127–30.

into the families of local lairds which further cemented kinship links within particular localities. Feudal lordship, now based less on traditional knight service than on broader concepts of personal service, reinforced kinship. The clearly defined regional spheres of influence of Scottish magnates which resulted from the geographical concentration of their estates and the importance of their jurisdictions in baronies and regalities was powerfully supported by family ties. It is in this context that a switch from a recognition of kinship on a cognatic to an agnatic basis seems to have occurred. Cognatic systems, acknowledging relationships through the female as well as the male line, produce large, loose kinship groups with weak links. Agnatic systems, recognising relationships only through the male line and defined by the possession of a common surname, appear to have become typical in Scotland by the end of the fifteenth century. Their persistence explains why kinship remained so important among Scottish landowning society long after its role had been reduced elsewhere.

Although agnatic kinship systems were a feature of early Celtic society this does not explain why they should have re-emerged in late-medieval Scotland. Grant argues that the spread of the practice of entailing estates so that they passed only to sons, brothers and others in the male line and not to heiresses, which became common at this time, provides an explanation.[4] Once entails had been in place for a generation or two they effectively created a system of agnatic kinship within a landholding class which was producing so many sons and cadet branches.

Agnatic ties were strengthened by geographical proximity. Particular surnames came to be identified with specific localities as, with a lack of heiresses, a family's landholdings often remained stable for generations. Another way in which landed families could strengthen their regional influence was through bonds of manrent, written contracts of allegiance and mutual support between two men, usually a lord and a laird.[5] Such bonds extended the influence of the magnate and backed up the lairds in their localities by giving them powerful allies. The bonds did not indicate a new development in terms of loyalty, merely a desire to confirm existing relationship in writing in an increasingly literacy-conscious age. The relationships were the same as those which were expected within a framework of kinship and involved an extension of values based on kinship to people who were not related. This emphasises the importance of kinship in late-medieval Scottish society and stresses how kinship and lordship supported each other. The possession of clearly defined regional spheres of influence buttressed by landownership, kinship and kinship-type ties with non-related families by means of bonds of manrent was one of the most distinctive features of late-medieval Scotland, a system of regionalised power structures which only began to break down in the later sixteenth century.

4. Ibid., pp. 136–40.
5. J. Wormald, *Court, Kirk and Community in Scotland 1470–1625* (London 1981), pp. 30–5.

MONARCHS AND MAGNATES

The nobility of late-medieval Scotland has received a bad press from historians as has the period itself, often dismissed as a wasteland of warring factions with, at the top, a continuing struggle for power between a weak crown and over-powerful magnates. In the last two decades there has been a major revision of ideas regarding the nature of late-medieval Scottish society, particularly the relationship between the crown and the nobility. The most vigorous exponent of this new interpretation has been Wormald.[6] The revised viewpoint suggests that the relationship between the Stewarts and their magnates was in general based on co-operation rather than conflict, on a consensus view that a balance between royal and noble power had to be maintained for the good of all. The crown and the nobility worked to maintain a responsible partnership and a generally peaceful and positive relationship.

The traditional picture of over-mighty magnates and struggling kings has been based largely on sixteenth-century chroniclers whose works have been shown to be riddled with bias and invention. The position of the fifteenth-century Stewart kings has been substantially reassessed. The relationship between the crown and the nobility operated best with a king who had a strong personality, yet who did not try to overturn the system. James I and II in particular now appear as tough, powerful, sometimes unscrupulous men who ruthlessly hounded the two greatest magnate families of their day, the Stewarts and the Douglases. Despite the fact that James I and III were both murdered, there was no serious challenge to the Stewart dynasty as a whole – a very different situation from England where for most of the fifteenth century the crown passed back and forth between the houses of Lancaster and York. Crown/magnate problems only occurred in Scotland during 16 of the 128 years between 1341 and 1469. It was not until the second half of the sixteenth century that faction fighting and violence became a major feature of Scottish society. Even then stability was soon re-established under James VI.

There were indeed 66 years of royal minorities between 1341 and 1469. That the Stewarts survived such misfortune itself indicates the strength of their position. A further pointer to the stability of the relationship between nobility and crown is that the Stewarts, having got rid of noble families which they considered troublesome, felt secure enough to promote others in their place. James I reduced the number of earldoms from 15 in 1424 to 8 in 1437, largely by seizing those which were in the hands of branches of the Stewart family. His actions have more the appearance of a family feud than of a confrontation with the magnates as a group. The removal of so many Stewart earldoms allowed other families to rise, notably the Douglases who by 1449 held three of the remaining earldoms.

6. Ibid., pp. 3–26.

Equally, after the forfeiture of the Douglases James II's relations with his remaining magnates were generally good. He created three new earldoms and a number of new lords of parliament, the first of two sets of promotions which altered the character of the Scottish peerage, elevating families which were to become prominent in the sixteenth century including the Campbells and the Gordons (Chapter 14). The old view of James III as a renaissance monarch who spent his time with low-born talented favourites and was overthrown in favour of his son by an indignant, barbarous nobility has been exposed as a sixteenth-century invention. The fact that such an abitrary, incompetent king survived for so long is an indication of the respect with which the monarchy was viewed by the magnates. The rebellion which led to the king's death at Sauchieburn in 1488 may have been designed merely as a protest with the king's murder an unexpected accident. The interests of the nobility lay then in co-operation with the crown rather than opposition. Royal service and favour was the path to reward, particularly in view of the shortage of heiresses, while opposition might provoke a ruthless royal reaction.

In the fifteenth century the Scottish administration, although paralleling the institutions that existed in England, was much simpler in structure. It was only during the fifteenth century that a central court of justice and a professional group of lawyers developed and there was no Scottish equivalent of the English House of Commons. By English standards the Scottish crown was impoverished, its reserves at best barely a tenth of those of England. Lack of money prevented the development of a sophisticated central administration, but at the same time the lack of complex institutions reduced the need of Scottish monarchs for money to run them. The judicial system financed itself and Scottish kings did not employ paid armies. Compared with England, Scotland's population was taxed infrequently and lightly so that a complex and expensive money-gathering apparatus was not required. Direct taxes were only imposed in 22 years between 1306 and 1469.

It can, of course, be queried whether Scottish kings failed to tax their subjects because they saw no need to do so or because they had no realistic hopes of making taxation effective. Nevertheless, the fact that even in times of national emergency, when armies had to be raised or when national prestige was at stake, they did not try to impose taxes suggests that decentralised *laissez-faire* rule was as much deliberate royal policy as *faute de mieux*. Developments in administration and law during the fifteenth century did not necessarily involve greater centralisation. The eventual creation of a central court of justice was less an acknowledgement that the decentralised system of feudal courts was ineffective than an indication that as Scotland's economy and society continued to develop there were new aspects of the law which such courts were ill-equipped to deal with.

It has been customary to write off late-medieval Scotland's system of heritable sheriffdoms, regalities and baronies as ineffective and weak compared with the sophisticated, centralised system of justice in England. Under the Scottish system local disputes and problems were dealt with by local people under a system of amateur judges. This contrasted sharply with the professionalism of English judges. But while the English legal system became increasingly cumbersome and even unworkable the Scottish one retained a more flexible commonsense approach which may have worked at least as well in its way. The king still relied on his magnates for raising armies and running the localities. The lack of centralisation is emphasised by the fact that it was only in the reign of James III that Edinburgh finally became the permanent capital and administrative centre of Scotland. Because the Scottish Parliament, unlike the English House of Commons, did not have the responsibility for raising taxes there was less need for the lairds to attend it. This did not mean that the Scottish Parliament was weak or ineffective compared with the English one – only that its role was different. The way in which it stood up to James III and pointed out his shortcomings demonstrates this clearly.

THE LATE-MEDIEVAL CHURCH

In late-medieval Scotland at any time there were possibly fewer than 4,000 men in holy orders. Nevertheless, this group was immensely influential providing a pool from which government administrators were still mostly drawn and dominating the practice of law. The clergy who staffed the cathedrals were an educated elite often connected by family ties to the nobility and enjoying a comfortable lifestyle in contrast to the growing poverty of the ordinary parish clergy. It was from their ranks that literary figures like Gavin Douglas, William Dunbar and Robert Henryson were drawn, men whose achievements were significant in European, not merely Scottish, terms. The traditional picture of the late-medieval Scottish church as a system in decline, ridden with secular values and gross abuses, has been coloured retrospectively by the seeming inevitability of the Reformation. The picture is far from simple though. Certain aspects of the church were falling out of favour. Monasticism was undoubtedly less popular than in earlier centuries. The lifestyle of many monks was comfortable and secularised. Yet there is also evidence of real devotion and a sense of vocation. At some abbeys, notably Cambuskenneth, Jedburgh and Melrose, ambitious building programmes were undertaken. Outside the cloisters concern for spiritual matters and belief in the efficacy of prayer was still evident. This is seen in the continuing popularity of pilgrimages to Scottish shrines as well as to foreign centres like Compostella, the Holy Land and especially Rome. James IV regularly visited shrines as distant as Tain and Whithorn. In the towns many burgh kirks were renovated or rebuilt, some of the grandest like St Mary's at Haddington being almost cathedrals in scale. Within these kirks large numbers of altars were founded by guilds and individuals. There was also a development of religious ceremony and processions in many towns which reinforced links between the church and guild membership. Candlemass and Corpus Christi processions became regular features of the calendar of several towns as did religious plays put on by particular guilds.

New religious orders continued to be introduced to Scotland. James I established the Carthusians at Perth in 1429. In the reign of James II, c1462–63 Observantine friars settled in Edinburgh. During the next half century they opened seven more houses in other burghs. New Franciscan nunneries were set up at Aberdour (1480), Dundee (1501/52) and Sciennes near Edinburgh (1517). At least 20 new hospitals were founded during the fifteenth century.

Continued faith is also evident in the establishment, mainly by private landowners, of collegiate churches in which colleges of clerks held votive masses for the dead. Votive masses were increasingly seen as more efficacious than monastic prayers and instead of granting lands to abbeys it became fashionable to pay for the services of one or more chaplains to say regular masses for the souls of the patron and his family, an option which was available to those of moderate wealth as well as to larger landowners. Collegiate churches were merely an extension of this with several chaplains organised into a corporate structure. They could be founded at a far lower cost than endowing a new religious house and provided a more tangible return for their patrons than granting lands to existing monasteries. Collegiate churches were the most visible aspect of the late-medieval trend towards the belief that repeated prayers, pilgrimages and penances could shorten the time spent by the soul in purgatory. Some were established in existing parish churches, some as private chapels but rebuilding on an impressive scale was usually considered necessary. Enthusiasm for endowing collegiate churches, which were major status symbols, usually ran ahead of resources and many, including the richly decorated Roslin Chapel, were never completed.

Balanced against this evidence of continuing vigour were signs of decay. This was evident in the closure of some religious houses, like Saddell Abbey in Kintyre which was suppressed in the early sixteenth century. The Trinitarian friary at Peebles had, by the mid-sixteenth century, absorbed the ones at Berwick, Dunbar and Houston. Scottish nunneries had become notorious for their breakdown of discipline and widespread unchastity. Even so the larger priories and abbeys continued to operate without indications of serious decline. There are signs that individual abbots tried to improve standards or religious observance, behaviour and education within their monasteries. Men and women with genuine vocations were still entering the cloisters, but the ideal of corporate property had given way to private possessions, jealously guarded. James I encouraged reform in Scottish monasteries, writing to the heads of Augustinian and Benedictine houses in 1425 and urging them to combat moral decay. His introduction to Scotland of the Carthusians with their strict ascetic rule seems to have been designed, unsuccessfully, to shame existing monastic orders into better behaviour. Ironically, the Charterhouse at Perth, the last medieval monastery to be established in Scotland, was the first to be destroyed at the Reformation.

Despite James I's interest in reforming the monasteries the beginnings of the system which was to secularise them can be seen in his reign with the practice of granting abbeys and priories 'in commendam' to churchmen who already held benefices. Originally designed as a temporary measure this developed into a system of granting the revenues of religious houses out in perpetuity. Monasteries became mere sources of income for their commendators, leading to exploitation and demoralisation. Under James IV and V commendatorships were manipulated ever more cynically as a way of providing for royal favourites and bastards. In 1498 James IV granted the abbey of Holyrood to his brother the Duke of Ross, aged 18. Grants of Dunfermline Abbey followed in 1500 and Arbroath Abbey in 1503. James also assigned Cambuskenneth Abbey to his Secretary, who was not even in priest's orders, and Glenluce Abbey to his Treasurer. James V extended this policy despite professions of concern for the state of the monasteries. Between 1534 and 1547 the abbeys of Coldingham, Holyrood, Kelso, Melrose and St Andrews were granted to three of the king's illegitimate sons.

As elsewhere in late-medieval Europe formal instruction in religion and preaching were in short supply. Nevertheless, the church instituted important developments in education during the fifteenth century. The main diocesan centres provided some instruction, perhaps to a relatively advanced level at St Andrews and Glasgow, the two richest and most important ones. Schools were also set up in the major burghs from the twelfth century and by the fifteenth century were found even in some quite small baronial burghs like Tranent. Song schools at cathedrals and religious houses taught potential churchmen how to read Latin and sing plain song. Cathedrals also had grammar schools for teaching Latin as did the major towns. Scholars pursuing higher levels of education had, however, to travel abroad to Bologna, Paris, Oxford or Cambridge.

The outbreak of war with England at the end of the thirteenth century closed Oxford and Cambridge to Scottish students and encouraged them to go to France, especially Paris for theology and Orleans for law. The theological schools at friaries like those in Ayr and Perth were the nearest thing to institutions of higher education that existed in Scotland before the fifteenth century. Scholars like Duns Scotus, who achieved an international reputation, had to pursue their careers outside Scotland. Ambitious churchmen seeking advancement would normally go to a foreign university to study arts and especially law in preparation for a career as an administrator either in the church or in government. Of the 400 or so Scottish graduates in the later fourteenth and early fifteenth century whose careers are known around half had obtained degrees in law. Literacy was spreading slowly among the nobility, the lairds and the urban elites but probably more slowly than in England because of the lack of demand from a complex administrative bureaucracy. The limited extent of literacy in Scotland is suggested by the fact that there was little demand for printing until the sixteenth century.

Scotland's first university, at St Andrews, was established in 1412. Another college was founded there in 1450 for the study of theology and philosophy. Colleges created at Glasgow in 1451, Aberdeen in 1495 and further ones at St Andrews in 1513 and 1538 show that Scotland participated in the rapid growth in higher education which was occurring throughout Europe. It was an ambitious programme which is likely to have been matched by an expansion of schools in the burghs. Nevertheless, university curricula remained narrowly focused on the arts with little attention to medicine and law and only modest provision for the study of theology. The number of graduates from Scottish colleges was small; under a dozen each year from St Andrews in the mid-fifteenth century, perhaps 30 a year by the end of that century and no more than 100 a year from all Scotland's colleges in the 1540s. The training provided was still fairly basic. Students usually arrived at the age of 15 or even younger and normally had to spend some time improving their Latin before they could understand the lectures. The curriculum involved an introductory study of grammar, rhetoric and logic followed by more advanced subjects like music, arithmetic, geometry and astronomy. After perhaps 18 months of basic grounding in Latin students were allowed to matriculate and after a further two years they might obtain their master's licence, something which was achieved by only about a third of the entrants. Those graduates who wanted to rise within the church still had to go abroad for further study, generally of civil and canon law.

Economic decline within the church matched moral decay. The finances of many monasteries were already in difficulties during the fifteenth century. In the 1530s James V imposed crippling demands on the church, taking advantage of the Pope's concern that Henry VIII's reformation might spread to Scotland to extract extra concessions. Ostensibly the taxes were levied for defence and to set up a College of Justice but in practice they went to fill the royal treasury. James' exploitation of the church was not a new phenomenon; its origins can be traced to concessions granted to the crown during the reign of James III. James IV also extracted a good deal of money from the church but the scale of appropriation under his son was far greater than anything seen previously. The church raised much of the money by large-scale disposal of its property.

The sphere in which the late-medieval church was undoubtedly weakest was in the provision of worship for the parish community. Although the overall state of disrepair of parish kirks may have been exaggerated by some writers many kirks were far from being wind and watertight and some were ruinous. Parish priests, recruited mainly from the tenantry and smaller freeholders, were poorly educated and increasingly poorly paid. Most had little hope of advancement. With their quarter share of the teinds or, more usually, a fixed pension, vicars and curates were forced to squeeze whatever extra income they could from their parishioners. Not surprisingly they acquired a reputation for rapacity. In the fourteenth century their position was probably not too bad and their income probably put them on a par with wealthier peasants and small freeholders. During the fifteenth and especially the sixteenth century, however, inflation eroded the value of their fixed incomes.

How much religion meant to ordinary people is unclear. Attendance at church for normal Sunday masses seems to have been far from regular although most people seem to have gone to mass at Easter, the only time of year when most of them took communion. The overlap of parish and barony, of ecclesiastical and secular administration, may have helped to bind the church to the community at a local level. This may explain the seemingly limited support in Scotland for the Lollards and the lack of evidence for outright dissatisfaction with, or opposition to, the church. References to activities such as football, wrestling and archery practice taking place in churchyards can be interpreted as indicating a lack of popular concern for religion but, seen in another light, they may merely emphasise the close links that existed between church and community. The worst abuses of the late-medieval church, such as the sale of indulgencies, false relics and pardons, were not as widespread in Scotland as in England. Demands for reform of the church were less widespread, being confined to a minority among the landowners and urban middle classes who viewed religion in less blind and mechanical terms than the bulk of the population. As the sixteenth century progressed, however, signs of discontent began to grow.

RURAL SOCIETY AND THE FEUING MOVEMENT

The structure of the lower levels of Scottish rural society in the fourteenth century is almost impossible to determine due to lack of data. In the late fifteenth and early sixteenth centuries, however, the volume of evidence increases and sheds more light on rural communities. The picture which emerges is complex and varied. Most families who farmed the land were tenants but there was considerable variation in their status. One group, perhaps the majority in many areas, were tenants-at-will, holding from year to year by verbal agreements. In a stronger position legally were tenants with written leases or tacks for a specific number of years or for life. More secure still were rentallers, so called because they held a copy of the entry in the proprietor's rental book which confirmed their possession. Rentallers, equivalent in many respects to English copyholders of inheritance, could normally expect to pass on their holdings to their heirs. While population growth was sluggish and labour in short supply it was in a landowner's interest to keep the land occupied in this way. Even where tenants held tacks for only a few years the normal expectation was probably that they would be renewed. Even tenants at will were often members of families which had been established in particular holdings for generations. The customary right for heirs of tenants to succeed in this way was known as 'kindness', tenure based on kinship with the previous occupier. Kindly tenants might hold their lands as rentallers, leaseholders or at will but their right to succeed, widely recognised by local and royal courts, could be assigned, compensated for, renounced or even bought and sold.

The holdings occupied by tenants varied considerably in size. On estates where detailed records are available, principally ecclesiastical ones, tenants can be traced moving from one holding to another, leasing extra land, and negotiating with neighbours to consolidate land into larger, less fragmented parcels. Below the tenants were a large, poorly recorded group of cottars and sub-tenants about which we know little. Overall the picture of tenant society is one with elements of both stability and mobility, similar to the better-recorded farming communities of the seventeenth century (Chapter 9). This was a society where rents were still paid largely in kind and labour but where money nevertheless circulated widely, a society where tenants could appear assertive rather than downtrodden, where failure to pay one's rent due to adverse circumstances did not lead automatically to summary eviction.

Rural society was not static though. A trend towards the enlargement of holdings on some estates in the early sixteenth century is likely to have had implications for social structures. A much more profound transformation occurred in the middle of the century as a result of the widespread granting of church lands in feu ferme. Feu ferme was a hereditary tenure conferring much greater security of possession than leasehold. A superior who granted land in feu usually required a substantial initial cash payment and an annual feu duty. This was designed as an economic rent for the land and might be as great or greater than the rent of the same land under leasehold. In order to make up for the loss of payments or 'grassums' which were often charged on renewal of leases additional periodic charges might be imposed on the feuar with a double feu duty on the succession of an heir.

Feu holders thus paid heavily for their security. In the longer term, however, inflation eroded the real value of feu duties and other payments. Because of this, and because feuing permanently alienated land from the superior's control, feuing was mainly an emergency expedient for raising money. Its chronology is clear from over 3,000 surviving feu charters. While some feu ferme grants were made in the late fifteenth and early sixteenth centuries the bulk of them occurred between the 1530s and 1580s. The main impetus for feuing in the 1530s was James V's massive taxation of the church, but high taxation continued under the regency of James' widow, Mary of Guise. The 1540s brought widespread destruction of churches and religious houses in southern and eastern Scotland by English armies and a need for money to rebuild them. Such reasons are sometimes specified in feu charters but one suspects that the money so raised was often used for other purposes. Canon law forbade the alienation of church property without good reason; rebuilding a devastated abbey or meeting royal taxation provided acceptable excuses.

The feuing movement has been seen as a disaster for small men, especially tenants whose customary rights to the continued occupation of their lands were set aside when their land was feued over their heads to rack-renting lairds and nobles. Sanderson's study of feuing has shown that this is an oversimplification.[7] Overall more than half the feus granted went to sitting tenants, only about 3 per cent to the nobility and 29 per cent to lairds, many

7. M.H.B. Sanderson, *Scottish Rural Society in the Sixteenth Century* (Edinburgh 1982).

of whom were very small landholders. Only 8 per cent of grants went to burgesses and 3 per cent to clergy and professional men. There was considerable variation in the pattern of grants between estates. Most of the grants on the lands of Paisley and Scone Abbeys went to existing occupiers against only 13 per cent on the estates of Crossraguel Abbey.

Feuing did bring considerable social changes though. Large areas of land were transferred out of the hands of the feudal classes to a new social group which lay outside the traditional circle of power. The gradual increase in the status and influence of smaller landholders is a theme which will recur in later chapters. Many existing laird families increased their landholdings and status, many noble families established cadet branches in their own estates. Although sitting tenants may have obtained more than half the grants they obtained a much smaller proportion of the total area involved for many grants to lairds and nobles comprised large blocks of territory. In areas like Strathisla, where two-thirds of the grants and about half the land went to former tenants, there was a major change in the structure of rural society as many new small proprietors and feuars were created. Becoming a proprietor, however modest, induced new attitudes towards local society and the world at large. The broadening of the base of the pyramid of landownership shifted some power from the nobility towards the middle ranks of rural society, as occurred in England during the same period. The policies of abbeys like Kilwinning and Paisley in feuing most of their lands to sitting tenants helped create the pattern of small, independent proprietors in parts of the western Lowlands which gave this area such a distinct identity in terms of religious attitudes in the seventeenth century. The enhanced status of many feuars was expressed by the construction of new tower houses, clusters of which sprung up in several areas. Many of these families continued as small proprietors into the seventeenth and even the eighteenth century. The new pattern of landholding created by feuing did not remain static for long though. Inevitably some were more successful than others; some sold out while others absorbed the lands of their neighbours. The role of feuing in opening up the land market and facilitating the purchase of estates by merchants and professional men has yet to be explored in detail.

For many newly established feuars the burden of raising the initial lump sum and meeting the annual feu duties was considerable. That so many tenants were able to purchase their feus may seem surprising until it is realised that, as leasehold tenants, many had already faced the problems of meeting large periodic grassums. This cautions us against the assumption that all social groups below the level of the lairds were impoverished. Not all tenants could afford to buy their feus, not all were given the opportunity, but even close to large towns like Edinburgh and Glasgow, where one might have expected competition from merchants and professional men to have been keenest, many small tenants were able to find the necessary resources.

On the other hand for every tenant who obtained a feu charter there was another whose lands were granted over his head to an outsider. What Sanderson has called the dark side of feuing; rack-renting of former tenants by speculators from outside the community who had bought up the feus, or eviction to make way for the feuar's chosen tenants, undoubtedly occurred.[8] Such stresses only surface occasionally in official records but tenants who were being oppressed or squeezed out by new landlords may not often have been able to seek redress through the courts. The threat as well as the reality of change may have had an unsettling effect on rural society. Such tensions, at a time of increasing political uncertainty, did not bode well for a church which, panicked into disposing of its lands, had set in motion changes and created a groundswell of discontent which helped to undermine its authority even further.

8. Ibid., pp. 153–65.

CHAPTER 6

THE REFORMATION AND ITS IMPACT

The Reformation has been seen as the most significant watershed in early-modern Scottish history. The political dimensions were complex but a significant element was rejection of the long-established association with France. French assistance had been vital in countering English attacks in the 1540s but the price was French domination. In 1558 the marriage between the young Queen Mary and the Dauphin seemed likely to many Scots to lead to Scotland becoming a mere appendage of France. The Reformers, by firmly rejecting the religion of Rome, reorientated Scotland's political links away from France and the 'auld alliance', drawing Scotland much closer to England. The Scottish Reformation was only accomplished with English assistance and the Treaty of Edinburgh in 1560 marked the start of a long period of increasing convergence of interests between the two countries. Economic and social trends were slower to follow political changes. Trade and cultural contacts with France continued to be significant to Scotland. Nevertheless, contacts with England grew steadily more important in the century and a half after the Reformation, underpinned by economic and social changes which slowly brought the two countries closer together.

The Reformation has attracted much partisan writing. The problem of assessing its nature and impact is made harder because the Reformers were such vigorous self-publicists. Traditional interpretations have viewed it as a great popular revolution backed by large numbers of people drawn from a wide range of society, the result of a massive groundswell of dissatisfaction with the church of Rome. Seen in these terms the Reformation becomes an inevitable process, fuelled by the protracted decline of a church which has been described as remarkable, even by the low standards of its time, for the depth of its corruption.

Recent interpretations have painted a more complex picture. Like most revolutions the Reformation was confused, the issues and allegiances involved being far from clear-cut. As with revolutions elsewhere, some aspects of the Scottish Reformation marked a break with the past while others emphasised continuity. In particular, stress has been laid on the limited spread and belated growth of support for Protestantism, on the attempts of the old church to reform internally, the slowness with which the new church was established and consolidated in many areas, and on the uniqueness of the political circumstances which brought about the Reformation. It is sometimes implied that the reformed church was established in all its essentials in 1560 as a monolithic entity which remained unchanged into modern times. In fact the Reformation was only the start of 130 years of evolution, of trial, error and compromise. It was not until after the settlement of 1690 that the kirk emerged in its familiar modern Presbyterian form.

THE CHURCH ON THE EVE OF THE REFORMATION

Due to the limited survival of pre-Reformation parish and diocesan records, impressions of the church during the first half of the sixteenth century are dominated by the writings of those who criticised it. The picture of a decaying institution which was a sink-hole of corruption is almost certainly overdrawn. The condition of the Scottish church was probably no worse in the sixteenth century than it had been in the fifteenth, no worse than in other parts of Europe. Most people appear to have been indifferent to it rather than hostile. It was not so much that the church deteriorated during the sixteenth century as that the expectations which the laity had of it rose. The church proved incapable of responding sufficiently to the changing needs and demands of society, certain sectors of which were more literate and better educated than before, more able to question and criticise.

Evidence for continuing vitality and new initiatives within the church is as striking as signs of decline. Cathedrals and abbeys were still being rebuilt and embellished. Some monasteries, notably Kinloss under the influence of two outstanding abbots, Thomas Chrystall and Robert Reid, were still functioning as major intellectual centres. Religious processions, pageants and plays were a prominent feature of urban life. Pious burgh councils continued to endow song and grammar schools. There was a rich tradition of church music. New almshouses continued to be established. The last collegiate church was founded as late as 1546.

Even so, a negative aspect of the church was its lack of able leaders. This is hardly surprising considering that appointments to higher offices were made largely on the basis of political influence and family connections. The system has been likened to an employment agency for the illegitimate sons of the crown and nobility. The highest offices in the church were often held by men who played key roles in government; between 1511 and 1546 the post of chancellor was held almost continuously by the archbishops of St Andrews and Glasgow. Equally, royal servants were often rewarded with ecclesiastical appointments. Nevertheless, while the system was not well-designed to appoint the best people for the job it did produce some able men including William Elphinstone, Bishop of Aberdeen, Robert Reid, Bishop of Orkney, John Hamilton, Archbishop of St Andrews and even his much maligned predecessor, Cardinal David Beaton. Many of the initiatives which such men tried to set in motion might, given more time and different political circumstances, have succeeded in reforming the church from within. It is ironic that one of the new church's achievements in the sphere of education, the foundation of a new university in Edinburgh, was made possible by a grant of 8,000 merks bequeathed by Robert Reid two years before the Reformation.

The monasteries, perhaps less secularised or crippled by the system of commendators than has sometimes been suggested, continued to function and to attract new recruits. Donaldson has described them as aged and devitalised institutions, a view reinforced by the failure of the monks to make any significant contribution to either side of the Reformation debate.[1] On the other hand, their training did not fit them for preaching or theological discussion. The charges levelled against them by contemporary satirists suggest that their lifestyles had become worldly and comfortable rather than immoral. The lack of hostility towards monks and monasteries after 1560 indicates that people bore them little animosity and may have had some regard for them even if they saw them as increasingly irrelevant to the needs of contemporary society.

If the monasteries were detached from society by their function of prayer the friaries were closely involved in everyday life; in preaching, charity, education and in providing the lay population with legal expertise. The fact that they continued to receive endowments from lay patrons suggests that they were still respected, useful institutions. The friaries produced some outspoken critics of the church. Before the Reformation several friars were exiled for their views and after 1560 many of them served the new church. The fact that friaries were targeted for attack in the early stages of the Reformation may partly reflect their location which made them convenient targets for urban mobs. There is more than a suspicion, however, that their destruction was deliberately orchestrated by the reformers because the friars were more formidable intellectual opponents than the monks.

As we have seen, the defects of the church were especially noticeable at a local level. Spiritual duties were delegated to those at the bottom of the church hierarchy while most of the revenues were enjoyed by those at the top. The appropriation of revenues continued as new foundations such as university colleges and collegiate churches drew off even more resources from the parishes. The parish clergy were inevitably ill-educated for nobody with the ability to rise higher would have contemplated entering their poorly paid ranks. They were frequently forced to acquire more than one living or engage in secular activities like trading to make ends meet, as well as pressing their parishioners hard for offerings. Problems like lack of celibacy and poor education were hardly a new feature of the parish clergy though. They may not have been doing too bad a job, given their limitations, for there is no indication of a substantial groundswell of anti-clerical feeling in mid-sixteenth-century Scotland. This suggests that while parish priests may not always have been respected they were not widely hated. Part of the

1. G. Donaldson, *The Scottish Reformation* (Cambridge 1960).

problem was that lay participation in the church was limited. The laity had some say in the appointment of new priests, rather more in electing parish clerks and kirkmaisters, comparable in many respects with English churchwardens. Nevertheless, there were no official channels by which the laity could convey their views regarding the structure and operation of the church. The result was widespread popular indifference to the church, manifested in poor attendance or by irreverent behaviour from those who did turn up to hear mass.

Many clerics as well as laymen were aware of the church's failings and appreciated the need for change. During the 1540s and 1550s the church made several attempts to institute reforms. It is often suggested that these measures were 'too little, too late' a purely cosmetic exercise designed to deflect criticism rather than a serious effort to encourage change. It must be admitted that the central issue, the need to improve the provision of resources and standards of pastoral care at parish level, was not seriously addressed. It is also clear that these attempts to transform the church foundered due to reluctance by the majority of its leaders to disrupt their comfortable lifestyles in order to set an example to the lower clergy. As a result they failed to give a clear message to the laity that changes were under way. Nevertheless, these attempts should not be dismissed as totally ineffectual. Several of their aims closely matched those of the reformers.

As early as 1541 the Scottish Parliament had passed an act 'for reforming of kirks and kirkmen'. General councils of the Scottish church met in 1549, 1552 and 1559 to draw up a programme of reform which is usually associated with Archbishop Hamilton but which may have been set in motion by his predecessor Cardinal Beaton. Efforts to check problems like concubinage, pluralism, non-residence, church repairs and the endowment of the illegitimate offspring of priests from church revenues are hardly surprising but the recommendations also contained some quite radical proposals which were distinctly anti-papal in tone. There was to be more emphasis on preaching and teaching the laity through the use of the vernacular. Hamilton produced a vernacular catechism in 1552 designed to be read regularly by parish priests to their congregations. The council of 1559 introduced vernacular prayers. There was to be more strict and regular inspection of parishes and religious houses by bishops and more emphasis on raising educational standards among the lower clergy as well as changes within the universities.

As an attempt at a counter-reformation before the Reformation itself the plans were well-intended but too limited. There was no effort to improve the quality of training for the priesthood, little progress in raising the stipends of parish clergy and not enough effort to get the higher clergy to preach, given that parish priests had not been trained for such work. It is possible that the limited amount of heresy which appears to have existed in Scotland before the mid-1550s made church leaders complacent and overconfident. The implementation of the new measures was delayed by squabbles within the higher levels of the church and there seems to have been a good deal of variation between dioceses in the extent to which they were introduced. The changes were merely tinkering with the existing, inadequate system rather than a major attempt to transform it. By the time that the Council met in 1559 it was already being overtaken by events.

THE GROWTH OF PROTESTANTISM

One of the key debates concerning the Scottish Reformation is the extent to which there was a long-established, broadly-based tradition of Protestantism during the first half of the sixteenth century. There is little documentary evidence for the existence of heresy but many sources which might have had a bearing on this issue have not survived. The authorities were evidently wary of the influence of heretical ideas and concerned to restrict their spread. One reason for the establishment of St Salvators College at St Andrews and King's College, Aberdeen was to counter the supposed spread of heresy. There is a stray reference to an outbreak of Lollardy in 1494 among the laity in the Kyle district of Ayrshire, an area which a focus for Protestantism in the early phases of the Reformation, but its significance is hard to evaluate. It has been seen as the start of a continuing tradition of radical Protestantism in the region but it might equally have been an isolated occurrence. By the 1520s trading contacts with the Baltic were acting as channels for the flow of Lutheran literature into Scotland, leading in 1525 to a ban by Parliament on their import. Nevertheless in the early 1530s the use of Tyndale's English bible became common. Despite the growing spread of Protestant ideas there were not many Scottish martyrs. Patrick Hamilton, burnt in 1528 for preaching Lutheran doctrines, and the charismatic orator George Wishart, executed in 1546, were among the most notable. A number of men with Protestant views were, however, driven out of Scotland, depriving the movement of valuable leadership.

So far as can be judged, the Protestant movement was still limited in size by the mid-1550s, scattered in small cells with a simple programme for action focusing on the preaching of the Gospel, prayers in the vernacular and a strong commitment to personal faith. Groups of Protestants forming secret congregations were served by preachers most of whom, like John Knox, were priests who had broken from the established church. The suggestion that by 1559 there was an organised alternative church in many parts of the Lowlands waiting for the right circumstances to stage a takeover seems to be pushing the evidence too far. Protestantism was strongest in certain regions, notably Angus and the Mearns, Fife, the Lothians and Ayrshire. Within the larger towns a sizable body of Protestant support can only be identified in Dundee and Perth.

Yet small though their numbers may have been the influence of the Protestants may have been considerable. Protestantism appears to have appealed to a wide cross-section of society but there was an important concentration of support from the middling groups, especially the lairds and the urban middle classes. Even so the success of the movement depended on its gaining sufficient support from the magnates. A recent study by Frank Bardgett has shown that in Angus and the Mearns all the influential nobles had some Protestant leanings in the 1540s.[2] Below them came about 30 lairds who favoured the new ideas. They formed a minority among the local gentry but were a coherent and organised group. Under their influence Protestantism seems to have been spreading downwards through society and gaining ground at a popular level. There was only a small group of Protestants in Edinburgh but they included several influential burgesses and professional men who were in touch with Protestant sympathisers at court.[3] By the later 1550s Protestant ideas seem to have been spreading down through Edinburgh society, attracting men of lower status such as small merchants and craftsmen, a group who were to give the Reformation in the city a distinctive, if short-lived, character.

Although in the 1550s the Protestant movement was still small and disorganised it had the advantage of not being under serious pressure from the authorities. The political situation under the leadership of the Queen Regent, Mary of Guise, did nothing to discourage it. Between 1550 and 1558 there were no executions for heresy and Mary failed to give reformers within the established church a clear lead. She needed the political support of various nobles with Protestant leanings and, whether from inclination or expediency, she tolerated their beliefs. Even so, it needed something more to turn Protestantism into a truly national movement. In the later 1550s two key factors emerged; a group of nobles to provide leadership and a patriotic dimension to broaden support.

During the later 1550s various sources of resentment against the church and other preconditions for change began to converge. Certain key magnates who were sympathetic to the Protestant cause, including the Earl of Argyll, the Earl of Morton and the Earl of Arran, felt that they were being denied power by Mary of Guise. In 1557 they and other Protestant lords signed an agreement which committed them to trying to establish the reformed faith in Scotland. The political situation favoured decisive action by the Protestant magnates. The marriage of Queen Mary to the Dauphin in April 1558 increased the fear of French domination. An upsurge of anti-French feeling gave the movement a new respectability based on patriotism while the accession of Elizabeth I in November 1558 held out the possibility of English aid for the reformers.

Harder to pinpoint and operating on a longer time-scale were other sources of dissatisfaction. The increase in royal control over the church at the expense of the papacy, especially from 1535 when the Pope accepted the right of James V to nominate rather than merely recommend candidates for vacant appointments, had led to flagrant abuses. The property of abbeys and bishoprics was increasingly being treated as crown resources to be used at

2. F.D. Bardgett, *Scotland Reformed: the Reformation in Angus and the Mearns* (Edinburgh 1989).
3. M. Lynch, *Edinburgh and the Reformation* (Edinburgh 1981), pp. 68–86.

will. When appointments were made to vacant sees large portions of their revenues were often reserved as royal pensions to laymen. At a more local level there was resentment by smaller lairds against the payment of teinds and social stresses caused by the feuing of church lands. Both those who had lost out by not being able to obtain a feu and those who had been successful but were struggling to meet high feu duties may have objected to the exactions of the church. Moveover, many feuars were becoming conscious of their new status, more assertive and keen to play an active role in local society. Protestant beliefs offered them a way to achieve these ambitions.

THE REFORMATION AND ITS AIMS

In 1559–60 there was a sudden change of pace from the slow growth of Protestant support to the widespread adoption of the new faith. The Reformation was sparked off in May 1559 by a riot following a sermon preached by John Knox in Perth, a town characterised by sharp economic and social tensions with a tradition of anti-clericalism. The riot snowballed into rebellion and by October Mary of Guise had been deposed. The towns played a key role as centres of Protestant support in the early days of the revolution. Several burghs north of the Forth rapidly declared for the Protestant cause; Brechin, Dundee, Montrose, Perth and St Andrews, as well as Ayr in the west. The Reformation could never have succeeded if it had been a purely urban phenomenon though. The support of rural landowners was crucial. In several cases it was the influence of local lairds which was vital in persuading burgh councils to change their allegiance. Edinburgh was more hostile to the Protestant cause and elsewhere the changeover was often carried through by a powerful minority who seized the initiative.

The rebellion, which had limited popular support in a country where political thought was intensely conservative, was a tremendous gamble which only succeeded with outside help. English aid was decisive once the military efforts of the reformers became bogged down. In February 1560 the Treaty of Edinburgh laid the foundation for a new alliance with England and in June of that year the Scottish Parliament accepted the Protestant religion in the name of Queen Mary, abolishing the authority of the Pope, forbidding the Latin mass and accepting the reformed Confession of Faith.

The reformers had two initial problems; to secure legal recognition and to transform their ideas for the structure of the new church into reality. In its first years the new church was in a shaky position legally. Queen Mary accepted the church tacitly but did not ratify the legislation passed in her name by the Reformation Parliament or abandon her Catholic faith. It was not until she was deposed in 1567 that the church was fully accepted by the state and then not quite on the terms which many of the reformers had wanted.

Difficulties regarding its legal position were one explanation for the slow progress made by the church in its earliest years. Another was a crippling lack of finances. Many of the aims of the reformers relating to education or the need for discipline and supervision within the church did not differ materially from the ideas of those who had tried to change the church from within during the 1550s. It was in the proposed massive shift of resources to parish level that the reformers' ideas were most radical and it was here that they experienced greatest difficulty. Not surprisingly, but not altogether realistically, they laid claim to most of the revenues of the old church. They failed to get them. The new church could appoint ministers to serve parishes but for several years it was unable to gain control of the benefices to finance them. The initial financial settlement made for the new church by the Privy Council was that two-thirds of the revenues of benefices in the old church should stay with their Catholic holders while the remaining third should be divided between the new church and the state. This led to a struggle between the kirk and the crown over the division of their third; inevitably the crown won.

Only after 1567 could the work of the new church really get under way with what amounted to a second reformation, more radical and Calvinist than the one of 1559–60. Much of the new dynamism was due to the co-operation of the government with the reformers and particularly the influence of the Regent Moray who was as responsible as anyone for the new more Calvinist tone of the church. This rapport between church and state was short-lived. After Moray's assassination his successors as regent, Mar and Morton, were not trusted as much by the reformers. A widening gap between church and government began to appear which was to lead to conflict when James VI began his personal rule.

The aims of the reformers were set out in a programme known as the First Book of Discipline. Their vision did not stop with the creation of a Protestant church but embraced a 'godly Commonwealth', a society which, by submission to divine will would come to be a mirror of the Kingdom of God, a partnership in which the state governed in accordance with the church and where the church had the backing of the secular authorities in imposing moral discipline. It is, however, the practical side of the First Book of Discipline which impresses most. Although uneven and bearing the signs of hurried composition, it was a clear straightforward statement of faith, with its concern for the preaching of the word, the proper administration of the Sacraments, prayers in the vernacular and education in religion for everyone. Ministers were not to be allowed to hold secular offices, ending (for a time) the clergy playing a leading role in politics. There was an emphasis on the need for the new system to operate effectively by inspection and monitoring of ministers. The focus of the new church on the parish required a major redistribution of resources away from the cathedrals, collegiate churches and religious houses to finance an effective ministry. Education formed an important part of the programme with the aim of having a schoolmaster in every parish and education, free if necessary, for even the poorest. At a higher level reform of the universities was clearly necessary, too, if they were to produce the trained graduate ministry which was seen as essential for the success of the new church. Provision for the poor was also an important element.

This ambitious programme was crippled by insufficient funds. The reformers' aim was to divide the income of the old church in roughly equal proportions to finance the new ministry, build schools and help the poor, with the lands of the former bishoprics going to support the universities. Unfortunately there were too many vested interests in control of the finances of the old church to allow this. The Book of Discipline wanted ministers' stipends to be within the range of 100–300 merks a year, something which proved impracticable at first. John Knox, installed as Edinburgh's first Protestant minister, was promised a stipend of £400 per annum but he actually received less than half of this. The larger towns competed with each other to attract notable preachers offering handsome stipends which they then had difficulty in paying. In Edinburgh, as further ministers were appointed and the costs of financing the new church rose alarmingly, the desperate expedient of levying a regular tax on all households was tried. The scheme proved so unpopular that it had to be abandoned.[4]

Despite severe financial difficulties the new ministers were usually better off than their pre-Reformation counterparts. By the end of the sixteenth century their testaments suggest that they were emerging as a new fairly well-to-do group within the middle ranks of society, possessing sufficient resources to act as moneylenders in many cases. By the 1620s the increases in their stipends may have been running behind the rise in prices but under Charles I and the Covenanting regime they did well with rises that were ahead of inflation so that many ministers had incomes comparable to or exceeding those of small estate owners. Put in another way they were perhaps 12 or 15 times as wealthy as the cottars and farm servants who made up the bulk of rural congregations or labourers in the towns. The pre-Reformation clergy had been poor and struggling. The Reformation created a new wealthy social elite.[5]

Despite early setbacks the ideals of the new church endured and what is particularly striking is the consistency with which the church worked to implement them. As regards its beliefs the Reformation represented a sharp break with the past; out went the mass, the use of Latin, altars, confession, the cult of Mary and the saints, holy days and feast days, prayers for the dead, belief in purgatory, crucifixes, images, elaborate vestments, organs, choirs and plainsong. In came simple services in the vernacular with an emphasis on preaching, prayer, the psalms and the reading of the bible. Out went elaborate ritual performed before a congregation who were mere spectators. In came active participation in worship by the people. Strong emphasis was placed on the Sunday service. It was originally envisaged that Communion would be held four times a year in urban parishes, twice a year in rural ones, but this was not always possible due to the shortage of ministers and because the established practice of holding Communion only occasionally was hard to break. The basis of the normal Sunday service was,

4. Ibid., pp. 174–5.
5. W. Makey, *The Church of the Covenant 1637–51* (Edinburgh 1979), pp. 106–22.

100

in fact, those elements of the Communion which did not directly involve the celebration; a confession of sins, psalms, lessons, prayers and a long sermon. Ministers were expected to work their way through the bible systematically so that their congregations should come to know it well. The masters of households were required to ensure that their families and servants had sufficient religious knowledge to survive an annual examination by the minister.

Yet there was continuity too. The structures of pre-Reformation rural and urban society were too strong to be readily changed overnight. After the first burst of enthusiasm in 1559–60 the story of the Reformation is, in many ways, one of how the original radical aims of the reformers were modified to accommodate the new church to the enduring patterns of Scottish society. After 1560 the privy kirks in the burghs grew less by expanding their original radical core of committed Protestants than by spreading their nets to include a more passive majority, making the new church less dynamic and more diluted in the process. As Lynch has observed for Edinburgh the Scottish Reformation succeeded best where it changed least. In a society so conservative and so conscious of rank, privilege and tradition the Reformation only made progress where it did not disturb the fabric of society unduly.[6] Inevitably this constrained the way in which the new church developed as early radical ideas were dropped in favour of compromise and conciliation.

There was also considerable continuity between the old church and the new in terms of personnel. Three of the pre-Reformation bishops came over to the new church and it has been estimated that overall at least a quarter of the rank and file Catholic clergy – and in some areas more than half – did as well. Many of the new ministers and readers were recruited from the ranks of former parish priests, friars, canons regular and even monks. Continuity was also evident in the new church's handling of problems such as education and social welfare. Here they built on foundations established by the old church.

The structure which the early reformers planned for their new church was simple compared with the complex hierarchy of the old church. At its core was the parish served by ministers whose key duties were preaching and the administration of the Sacraments using a liturgy closely modelled on the English one. In its early years, however, the church was desperately short of trained ministers. It made widespread use of exhorters who could preach and conduct normal Sunday services as well as lay readers who were appointed to say prayers and read scripture. From 1572 readers were also authorised to conduct baptism and marriage services and to catechise children, becoming similar in many respects to Anglican deacons. Even in the mid-1570s as many as three-quarters of Scotland's parishes were still served by readers rather than ministers. Lay participation in the church was centred on the kirk sessions, committees comprising the minister of a parish and a dozen or more lay elders, initially elected annually from among the most worthy local men. Kirk sessions were designed to ensure the obedience of congregations to the

6. Lynch, *Edinburgh and the Reformation*, pp. 214–22.

new church. Some developed even before the Reformation to regulate some of the secret Protestant congregations or 'privy kirks'.

The need for a system of supervising ministers as well as their congregations was also appreciated. The initial plan was for regional superintendents who have been viewed as bishops in all but name, presiding over powerful courts and receiving salaries comparable with the incomes of some pre-Reformation bishops though subject to greater control. In the event only five superintendents were ever appointed and oversight of the church in many areas was organised on an *ad hoc* basis by granting special commissions to ministers to take on supervisory work, an untidy but far cheaper system. In 1572 a convention at Leith agreed to retain the pre-Reformation dioceses and to appoint to them bishops nominated by the crown but approved by committees of ministers. Once elected, however, the bishops were also subject to supervision. At the highest level a General Assembly was created largely because it was impossible for Queen Mary, a Catholic, to be head of the new church. The General Assembly was initially modelled on Parliament, being made up of representatives of the three estates. Gradually though, as it became clear that the nobility and the burgesses were not always good attenders, the Assembly became a forum mainly for ministers and elders.

Once Mary had been deposed and replaced by her infant son the government actively supported the church and financing it became easier. Ministers became entitled to succeed to benefices in the old church and as these gradually became vacant they released more funds. From 1573 a reorganisation led to more regular payments of stipends at higher rates. It was only from the 1590s, however, that the church began to receive sufficient money to expand its ministry throughout Lowland Scotland on a scale which started to realise many of the ideals of Knox and other early reformers.

The success of the Reformation in its early years was due in no small measure to the fact that the reformers concentrated on practical matters rather than doctrine, with setting up an effective parish system providing spiritual care for the population rather than arguing over the polity of the kirk. The church had developed from the bottom upwards, coalescing around the congregations of the early privy kirks. The First Book of Discipline was more concerned with the election of elders and deacons than with the appointment of superintendents and the role of the General Assembly. In 1572 the church became overtly episcopalian. The early reformers, even Knox, saw a need for ministers to be supervised, and were not opposed to episcopacy. Indeed, by appointing active men who were not distracted from their ecclesiastical work by affairs of state the Reformation revived the episcopate. The reformed church in its early years was certainly not Presbyterian. Donaldson has described the system as one of congregationalism tempered by episcopacy.[7]

A major change of approach was soon to follow though, disturbing the

7. G. Donaldson, *Scotland: Church and Nation Through Sixteen Centuries* (Edinburgh 1972), p. 63.

evolving structure of the church and directing it on a new course. In 1574 Andrew Melville returned to Scotland after several years in Geneva where he had been influenced by the teachings of Calvin's successor, Theodore Beza. Melville was a scholar, an impressive teacher, a coldly rational theoretician without the practical pastoral experience of Knox. His uncompromising view was that the new church had failed in its mission due to its reliance on the laity. What was needed was a church of dedicated professionals which would transform a society rather than merely reflect it. He also believed that this church should have no bishops. Bishops were considered to be unscriptural because they raised some ministers above their colleagues and because the early Christian church was thought to have had a non-hierarchical organisation. On the other hand, the work of ordinary ministers had to be supervised. Melville considered that this should be done through a structure of church courts with presbyteries and synods above the kirk sessions. Presbyteries, meetings of groups of ministers from designated areas, could admit new ministers and supervise the work of existing ones. A Presbyterian structure had advantages over a diocesan system. As some 60 presbyteries were planned they would be able to exercise closer supervision over the church at a local level. The work of committees of ministers was also less likely to be disrupted by changes of personnel than in a diocese where death or promotion of a bishop might put the organisation into limbo until a replacement was appointed.

Melville considered that the laity should be excluded from a significant say in church affairs. This did not involve abolishing kirk session elders but making them part of the church establishment by electing them for life rather than annually. His aim was to make the elders paid professionals but finances were never sufficient to allow this. Many of the original reformers opposed Melville but he drew together a determined pressure group of younger supporters who managed, in 1578, to get their proposals approved by the General Assembly. The government was less inclined to accept Melville's ideas; bishops appointed by the crown were a useful means of strengthening royal control over the church. Parliament rejected the proposals and in 1584 James VI reaffirmed his authority over the church and his support for an episcopal structure. It was not until 1592 that Parliament approved a Presbyterian system. Within a year or two some 50 presbyteries came into existence but not as part of the full structure which Melville wanted. A compromise was achieved, the first of several over the next century or so, in which bishops were retained along with a system of presbyteries. The power of the bishops was reduced but James became skilful in manipulating the General Assembly so that moderate rather than extremist opinions prevailed. In 1610 he succeeded in having bishops reinstated with greater power while retaining presbyteries. This compromise was widely accepted and worked quite well. Melville himself had been exiled five years earlier for going too far in his opposition to James but a small group of his supporters continued to press for a totally Presbyterian system.

THE CONSOLIDATION OF THE NEW CHURCH

An important feature of the Scottish Reformation was its relative peacefulness and lack of violence. The number of Protestant martyrs executed before 1560 and Catholic ones after this date were small compared with the 300 or so Protestants who died under Mary Tudor and the 200 Catholics under Elizabeth I. In Scotland 28 executions for heresy are known to have been carried out between 1528 and 1558. From 1567 saying mass became a capital crime but at the most only two executions are thought to have taken place. Even the murderers of Cardinal Beaton were dealt with remarkably leniently, being imprisoned or, like Knox, sent to the French galleys rather than executed. The activities of the armies of the Protestant Lords and Mary of Guise in 1559–60 involved more manoeuvring than conflict. Equally, once the Protestant cause had triumphed there was little vindictiveness against the Catholic clergy. Political circumstances did not allow the reformers either to compel existing clergy to accept the Reformation or to remove them. The pre-Reformation clergy were left with two-thirds of their former incomes even if they did not support the reformed church. For the first few years after 1560 the structure of the old church continued to survive, its bishops still sitting in Parliament and serving on the Privy Council, the lower clergy granting charters and leases of revenues to which they were still legally entitled.

Nor, contrary to popular belief, was there wholesale destruction of ecclesiastical buildings by the reformers. Urban mobs did sack the friaries and there was widespread removal of 'images' but outside the towns most religious houses were left alone under their lay commendators. The monks remained in residence, gradually dying out as the fabric of their abbeys and priories crumbled around them. Where cathedrals and abbey churches were too large to meet the needs of the reformers the nave or chancel was often retained as a parish kirk and the rest of the fabric was left to decay. It was mainly where they were isolated, as on Lismore, or where there was already a suitable parish church, as at St Andrews, that cathedrals were completely neglected.

Given the legal and financial problems faced by the reformed church it is not surprising that its impact in the early years was mixed, its consolidation and spread slow. The first success stories were in the burghs in some of which a regular ministry was operating even before the Reformation Parliament gave official approval to the new church. In several towns kirk sessions, often extensions of the secular burgh courts, were soon in place compelling something close to universal church attendance and enforcing strong moral discipline. Even in the towns success was not instantaneous though. Even as late as 1565 it is doubtful if Protestantism was accepted by the bulk of Edinburgh's inhabitants. In the countryside the church had spread from its original bastions of strength in areas like Angus, Fife and Ayrshire to cover most of the Lowlands south of the Tay by the end of the sixteenth century. Progress north of the Mounth was more mixed and the impact of the church on the Highlands, outside Argyllshire and parts of Perthshire was limited.

Of Scotland's 1,080 parishes about 240 were being served by the new church in some way by the end of 1561, perhaps 850 by 1567 and over 1,000 by 1574. This sounds more impressive than it really was for three-quarters of the parishes still had only readers. It took time for the universities to turn out the body of trained graduates required for the new ministry. In Angus and the Mearns 88 parishes had been incorporated into the new church in 1563 but only 28 had proper ministers. Even by 1590 this had only risen to 59 ministers. A list of ministers drawn up in 1573 shows that many Border areas were still poorly served and that over the country as a whole there was only one minister for every three or four parishes. Nevertheless, data from relatively remote areas like Galloway, Orkney and Perthshire show that in the first years after the Reformation provision by the new church, if patchy, was not inconsiderable. Of course a Reformed minister did not guarantee a reformed congregation. Realistically, it cannot be claimed that the church achieved a firm grip over the minds of its congregations throughout the Lowlands until perhaps the 1620s.

In the Highlands the structure of the old church was dismantled but was slow to be replaced. The superstitions of Catholicism survived long after the actual faith had decayed. The vacuum continued in some areas until 1690 and beyond due in part to an acute shortage of Gaelic-speaking ministers. It was only in the nineteenth century under the influence of the Free Church that many parts of the Highlands received proper religious provision. Highland chiefs saw the new religion as a threat to their way of life and did little to help it outside Argyll which was converted at an early stage of the Reformation under the influence of its Protestant earl and John Carswell the energetic first superintendent of Argyll. This vacuum gave the Catholic church an opportunity to mount a counter-attack and from the late 1570s Jesuit missionaries from the Scotch College at Douai succeeded in reviving the Catholic faith in parts of the Highlands. Their numbers were too few, however, and their impact too small to constitute a serious problem for the reformed church.

Adherence to Catholicism continued in many parts of the Lowlands well into the 1570s and even 1580s with masses still being celebrated in rural churches. If the towns had provided good environments for the survival of Protestant privy kirks before the Reformation they were equally suitable for the continuation of Catholic cells after 1560 with support for the old church remaining entrenched among particular crafts and families. Much of this represented a traditional, conservative reaction against innovation rather than a positive preference for the old religion. In the Lowlands Catholicism had died out in most areas by 1600 but lingered on in some districts under the influence of powerful families like Huntly in the north east and Maxwell in the south west. Overall the success of the new church was remarkably complete. This was aided by its unity. Throughout the period from the Reformation to the settlement of 1690 tensions, especially between episcopalians and Presbyterians, were successfully contained within the church which was able, by a series of compromises, to accommodate a wide range of opinions without breakaway groups developing. Conflicts between episcopalian and Presbyterian viewpoints concerned organisation rather than basic doctrine. So the hard-line Presbyterians who supported Melville's view after 1610 continued to agitate from within the established church rather than leaving it. The more extreme views of the Covenanters after 1637 threatened to split the church for a while but failed to break its unity.[8] The period of enforced religious toleration under Cromwell was too short for Anabaptists, Congregationalists and Quakers to gain significant followings. After 1660 the Covenanters formed the strongest dissenting group which the church had seen.[9] But even they wanted to take over control of the established church, not split from it. The Church of Scotland was more monolithic and cohesive than in England or other Protestant countries due in part to the control over society exerted by kirk sessions and presbyteries.

THE IMPACT OF THE REFORMATION ON SOCIETY

The Reformation was a radical movement trying to make headway in a conservative society which put powerful brakes on its development. The vision of Knox was of a godly society with far more equality than existed in contemporary Scotland. That vision rapidly faded as the original moral certainty of the reformers was compromised by practical considerations. Nevertheless, in the longer term the impact of the Reformation on Scottish society was so profound and all-pervading that it is hard to isolate specific aspects of its influence. Many of these will be pursued in subsequent chapters. Here, three themes are considered; the impact of the church on social attitudes, poor relief, and entrepreneurship.

While the Reformation touched the whole of Scottish society not all groups were affected equally. Although it had been the actions of a group of magnates which had helped start the Reformation support from the nobility was relatively limited and lukewarm with a sizable proportion of them still adhering to the old faith after 1560. Moreover, the magnates appreciated that some of the ideas of the reformers challenged their control of society. Even after the new church began to strengthen its grip on society large landowners could continue to do much as they pleased and escape censure – though not always. Smaller landowners were more often successfully disciplined by kirk sessions. At the bottom of society the shifting vagrant population was not much affected by the new church either. The new church appealed particularly to middling groups; burgesses, lairds, feuers and large tenants from whose ranks many of the new ministers were drawn. These groups accepted most willingly the discipline of the new church and imposed it on

8. Makey, *The Church of the Covenant.*
9. I.B. Cowran, *The Scottish Covenanters 1660–88* (London 1976).

those below them. The Reformation Parliament in 1560 was attended by over 100 lairds, the first time they had appeared in such numbers, emphasising their growing self-awareness and sense of identity. The smaller lairds were often enthusiastic elders; the church's demand for an educated laity fitted in with their own social aspirations. In the towns the new faith added a religious dimension to existing civic pride. The church offered the middle groups in urban and rural society the role of the Calvinist godly magistrate to enhance and justify their secular power, providing religious support for their existing social role.

The later sixteenth and early seventeenth centuries saw an important shift in power in society away from feudal magnates and nobles towards these middling groups. In a sense the kirk session elders came to represent the society of seventeenth-century Scotland more realistically than the magnates. The parish and its kirk session began to replace the barony and its court as the unit of local administration. Each parish was served by upwards of a dozen elders who, collectively, often represented a formidable amount of local power. In many parishes where large landowners were absentees the kirk session was dominated by small proprietors, estate officials and larger tenants, men of similar background to many of the ministers. At times the kirk session might be augmented by the heritors of the parish, but only by invitation. Kirk sessions were dominated by men who had a degree of local influence but were outside the traditional power structure of feudal society. The ministers formed a new elite which identified closely with this group. Walter Makey's analysis of the backgrounds of mid-seventeenth-century ministers shows that where their origins are known over half were the sons of ministers but that most of the rest came from the ranks of smaller landowners, feuars, tenants and burgesses.[10]

After the relative indifference of the pre-Reformation church to secular society the new church brought a far closer interest in the lives of ordinary people. This attention was focused on the parish community. In the late sixteenth and seventeenth centuries in most parts of the Lowlands parishes had populations of under 700, many of them under 500. To the existing ties of community; neighbourhood, kinship and lordship the church added a new and powerful element. As ties of kinship and lordship weakened the church took over many of their former functions, notably poor relief. As the influence of local baron courts declined the parish church and its associated organisations became the main institution providing cohesion at a local level. In the earliest days of the Reformation the involvement of the local community in the affairs of its church was at a maximum; at Communion they gathered around the table with the minister as a group. Congregations could elect their own elders and censure, even depose, their minister. Gradually this egalitarian system changed as elders were appointed for life and not annually. The maintenance of the church, manse and school, the payment of the minister's stipend and the schoolmaster's salary became the responsibility of

10. Makey, *The Church of the Covenant*, pp. 97–105.

the heritors in a parish rather than the whole congregation. Despite this, local people were still far more involved with their church – and the church much more involved with them – than had been the case before 1560.

The early reformed church was not especially puritan in character. It was only with the spread of Melville's ideas after 1574 that a more sustained attack on the celebration of religious festivals and stricter Sabbatarianism developed. It is in this area, as well as in their moral control of parish society, that the approach of the reformers seems harshest as middle-class respectability was forced on the lower orders of society in a way which often seems smug, rigid and narrow-minded. The new kirk sessions developed what has sometimes been seen as a moral and spiritual tyranny over everyday life. By about 1620 most parishes, except in the more remote parts of the Highlands, had active kirk sessions enforcing strict moral discipline. The church could not force people to believe but it successfully imposed outward conformity, the work of the kirk sessions being backed up by the church's control of education and poor relief. The high moral standards set by the kirk sessions were rigidly and persistently imposed. Their concentration on sexual offences rather than on the other deadly sins has often been commented on as unhealthy and distasteful but in practice such offences were often easiest to define and detect.

The success of the discipline imposed by the church was partly due to the support it received from the civil authorities. This was evident at the very start of the Reformation when baillies in the burghs used their secular powers to establish the new church. The state continued to support the church by making a number of moral offences crimes; adultery in 1563, fornication in 1567, Sabbath breaking in 1579 and drunkenness in 1617. Anyone excommunicated by the church was also outlawed by the state. From 1572 excommunicated people were not allowed to hold any office or act as witnesses. From 1609 they were banned from receiving the income of lands and rents. Civil penalties for excommunication were retained under Charles II and were only abolished in 1690. In 1712 the Toleration Act prevented civil authorities from forcing people to submit to kirk discipline and the disciplinary link between church and state was dissolved.

With regard to poor relief the reformed church took over the approaches and some of the infrastructure of its predecessor. The years immediately around the Reformation were a bad time to be poor in Scotland for existing mechanisms of charity provision were disrupted and discontinued before new ones could be put in their place. The distinction between able-bodied, undeserving poor and the infirm and helpless poor which became the mainstay of the kirk's approach to poor relief was inherited from the pre-Reformation church. The First Book of Discipline contained ambitious plans for social welfare but this element soon disappeared, probably due to the control over the new church exerted by lairds and burgesses. In 1597 supervision of poor relief was handed over to the kirk sessions, a tacit recognition that they were the only effective organisation at a local level capable of doing this. Voluntary contributions and fines become the main source of money for poor relief along with occasional legacies. As will be seen in Chapter 9 provision for the poor remained limited throughout the seventeenth century compared with England where compulsory assessment became normal.

Another aspect of the Reformation which has generated debate is the extent to which Calvinism encouraged entrepreneurship and economic development. Smout has argued against a direct link between Calvinism and the rise of capitalism in Scotland, on the basis of the time-lag between the Reformation and the rise of a capitalist economy in the later eighteenth century.[11] Medieval restrictions on free competition, such as burgh guilds, the Convention of Royal Burghs and the staple at Veere survived long after the Reformation. The kirk's attitude to poverty was similar to that of the pre-Reformation church and its condemnation of avarice hardly encouraged capital accumulation. Smout has viewed the contribution of Calvinism to economic expansion as indirect through the gradual provision of better education and the establishment of a serious-minded strain of sobriety and industriousness in the Scottish character. This could only influence economic development once the seventeenth-century obsession with narrow doctrinal aspects of religion had diminished and intense piety had started to become unfashionable. Only then could the sense of purpose and single-mindedness generated by Calvinism be channelled into business, trade and agricultural improvement, releasing Calvinism as a psychological force for economic change just when it was losing its power as a religion. According to this theory Calvinism did not cause the Industrial Revolution, but it ensured that when opportunities for growth came the Scots were psychologically equipped to make the most of them.

More recently Marshall has produced a new interpretation of this debate.[12] In a re-examination of Weber's ideas on the relationship between religion and the rise of capitalism he emphasises Weber's distinction between the origins of modern capitalism itself and the spirit of modern capitalism. Weber postulated that the Protestant ethic fostered the development of the spirit of capitalism which was only one factor responsible for the rise of modern capitalism. It was perfectly possible for the spirit of capitalism to exist but due to unfavourable economic and social conditions for the development of capitalism itself to be delayed.

Marshall reduces the time-lag between the Reformation and the rise of capitalism by arguing that the early reformed church was more Lutheran than Calvinist in doctrine and that true Calvinism developed only slowly through the later sixteenth and early seventeenth centuries. As has been pointed out the early reformers were more concerned to establish the church at a parish level than with developing a sophisticated body of theological doctrine. On the basis of contemporary theological commentaries Marshall suggests that the classic Calvinist ideas of predestination and the duty of diligence in one's

11. T.C. Smout, *History of the Scottish People 1560–1830* (London 1969), pp. 88–93.
12. G. Marshall, *Presbyteries and Profits* (Edinburgh 1980).

everyday work, which Weber considered fostered the spirit of capitalism, were still poorly developed in late sixteenth-century Scotland. During the seventeenth century the idea of predestination took a firmer hold. This incorporated the beliefs that the elect chosen by God should be seen to lead godly lives, and that to attain assurance that one was of the elect systematic worldly activities, including diligence in one's calling, were required as a duty and as proof of election. Weber considered that these influences on everyday conduct were significant for the development of the spirit of capitalism.

Marshall, examining the manufactory movement in later seventeenth-century Scotland and in particular the detailed records of the Newmills Cloth Manufactory, claims that the spirit of capitalism is evident in the attitudes of the management regarding the running of the company. This is mostly seen indirectly through the working practices which were operated. Only rarely did individuals record the ethos which lay behind their actions, or their attitudes towards profit and its accumulation. Similar attitudes, clearly related to his religious beliefs, are evident in Sir John Clerk's attempts to run his collieries at Lasswade efficiently. For Clerk, trying to get his colliers to accept new work disciplines which would turn them into a capitalist labour force went hand in hand with the imposition of his own Calvinist morality. On this argument then the Reformation encouraged a spirit of entrepreneurship in Scotland but background social and economic constraints prevented its full expression until well into the eighteenth century.

The institutions which were established at parish level by the reformers in the decades after 1560; the new ministry, the systems of education and poor relief and especially the kirk sessions, proved to be enduring and resilient in the face of the religious and political upheavals of the seventeenth century. Superficially the kirk underwent a series of major changes during this period; the confirmation of episcopacy in 1584, the acceptance of Presbyterianism in 1592, a return to episcopacy in 1610, the reintroduction of a Presbyterian system under the Covenanters in 1638, the restoration of episcopacy in 1661 and finally William of Orange's reluctant acceptance of a Presbyterian structure in 1690. It is important, however, to appreciate that the church did not oscillate between completely episcopalian and Presbyterian systems. The disagreements were about means rather than ends. Mostly what was tried were compromises with various shades of emphasis which attempted to reconcile different elements within the Kirk. There were periods when divisions went sufficiently deep to cause disruption at parish level, when there was no minister or the work of the kirk session was interrupted. In 1661 for instance nearly 300 ministers, unwilling to support Charles II's episcopalian regime, left the church. In 1690 around 500, more than half the ministry, did likewise rather than submit to the new Presbyterian system. Nevertheless, in terms of theology, forms of worship and pastoral care the differences in the organisation of the church under the various regimes were slight and the structures created by the reformers remained in place developing an all-pervasive influence on Scottish society which will be evident in later chapters.

CHAPTER 7

POPULATION c1500–c1750

The study of pre-industrial population is beset by problems, particularly in the case of Scotland. Earlier Scottish historians side-stepped these difficulties by ignoring them. More recent writers have begun to explore population trends and their influence on Scotland's economy and society. The limited quantity and poor quality of the sources relating to Scotland's population have severely restricted the range of questions which can be meaningfully posed. Many of the sophisticated analytical techniques developed for the study of English population in the pre-census period cannot be used for Scotland. It is worthwhile, therefore, considering some of the difficulties caused by the nature of the available sources.

Compared with most other parts of Western Europe, especially England, the materials for Scottish historical demography are limited in coverage, late in date and imperfect in content. A requirement that every Scottish parish should keep some kind of register was first introduced in 1552 but it was not until 1616 that ministers were enjoined to keep full registers of baptisms, marriages and burials. Like much legislation from this period, enforcement proved impossible even in the later seventeenth and early eighteenth centuries. The number of parish registers which have survived is low compared with England and most other parts of Western Europe. Few exist for the sixteenth and early seventeenth centuries. Even for the later seventeenth century survival is patchy; a high proportion of existing registers come from the eastern Lowlands. The West, the North and particularly the Highlands are very badly served. For the early eighteenth century parish registers become more detailed and abundant though, as in other parts of Europe, baptism and marriage records begin earlier and are more complete than registers of burials. The monolithic structure of the Church of Scotland probably reached its maximum effectiveness in terms of control over society at this period. Nevertheless dissent, limited during the seventeenth century, was growing with the gradual development of episcopalian congregations in some areas and an increasing number of secession movements. It is also unclear to what extent the large size of many Scottish parishes may have hindered the accurate recording of vital events.

Baptism registers survive most frequently and appear to be fairly well kept.

Indications are that the baptism generally followed within two or three days of birth. In Haddington between 1653–80, 93 per cent of children born and in Kilmarnock 1740–51 94 per cent, were baptised within a week. Relatively few parishes kept burial registers and many surviving ones are incomplete with substantial under-registration of child deaths. Marriage registers often record the proclamation of banns, the intention to marry rather than the actual ceremony. In Scotland various legal forms of marriage were possible as well as marriage in church by the parish minister.[1] Irregular marriages were uncommon before the 1660s but after the Restoration there were always some Protestants who did not want to be married by the established church. Irregular marriages had the curious status of being illegal yet valid. They were punished in the seventeenth century but a blind eye was increasingly turned on them in the eighteenth century and they became more common.

Hearth and poll taxes were instituted during the 1690s to meet the wartime costs of the army and navy. They provide invaluable information on demography and social structure at a local level, though the quantity and completeness of the surviving lists is variable. The poll tax returns are more detailed than the hearth tax lists but, unfortunately, their survival is very irregular. Some areas such as Aberdeenshire, Renfrewshire and the Lothians are well covered, but in many other regions returns survive only for isolated parishes. For both sources information on the Highlands is extremely limited. Pre-census listings of the type that have served English historical demographers so well are extremely rare for Scotland before the second half of the eighteenth century and are seldom complete enumerations of all the inhabitants of a parish or estate.

POPULATION TRENDS AND DISTRIBUTION

At some point in the later fifteenth or sixteenth century population began to grow once more. The evidence for demographic expansion is indirect, including a new wave of settlement creation with the splitting of existing townships and the creation of new ones, along with the expansion of cultivation around existing settlements. Problems relating to increasing population pressure become apparent by the later sixteenth century. Between 1550 and 1600, Lythe has calculated that there were 24 years of dearth on a local or national scale. Poverty and vagrancy became a problem, provoking legislation.[2] Economic difficulties such as rising taxation, high inflation and falling real wages exacerbated the problems of bad harvests. Further outbreaks of plague may have had some effect in slowing population growth but the disease was increasingly confined to the towns.

1. T.C. Smout, Scottish marriage regular and irregular, 1500–1940, in R.B. Outhwaite (ed.), *Marriage and Society* (London 1981), pp. 204–36.
2. S.G.E. Lythe, *The Economy of Scotland in its European Setting 1575–1625* (Edinburgh 1963), pp. 15–23.

In broad terms there is a good deal of comparability between population trends in England and Scotland from the sixteenth to the later eighteenth centuries. Population in both countries rose during the later sixteenth and early seventeenth centuries, then levelled off or even fell before starting to rise very gradually once more in the early decades of the eighteenth century. We are, however, less certain about the scale of secular changes in Scotland. Although population grew during the sixteenth century the amount of increase is unclear. Population growth appears to have continued through the first two decades of the seventeenth century but it is uncertain whether the overall trend of population during the seventeenth century was upwards or downwards. Even for the later seventeenth and early eighteenth centuries the broad outlines of Scotland's demography are still uncertain. Although it is impossible to calculate rates of population growth for Scotland it seems unlikely that they matched the buoyant rates of increase which occurred in sixteenth-century England.

Estimates of population totals around 1500 have been in the 500,000–700,000 range. For 1700 suggestions have varied from 800,000 to 1,270,000 although a figure of 1,100,000 has been most favoured by historians. We are fairly sure of the total population of Scotland at the end of our period. Alexander Webster's private census of 1755 seems to have been reasonably accurate and his figure of about 1,265,000 can be accepted with some confidence. Between c1500 and c1750 England's population grew by around 2.8 times. If Scotland's population in 1500 is taken as half a million this gives a rate of increase of 2.5 times, only slightly less than England. But the slow growth of Scotland's population in the later seventeenth and eighteenth century suggests that a figure of half a million inhabitants in 1500 is too low. A population at this date of 700,000 gives a more realistic overall growth rate for the next 250 years of 1.8 times. At any rate population growth in the sixteenth and early seventeenth century was substantial. The social and economic impacts of this increase have yet to be properly investigated but population expansion is likely to have been an important factor behind a major change in diet. During the sixteenth century there was a shift in the diet of ordinary people in the Lowlands away from meat and animal products and towards oatmeal. A similar trend occurred in the Highlands during the seventeenth and early eighteenth centuries.[3] Lack of certainty regarding population totals at the end of the seventeenth century has led to speculation regarding whether Scotland's population increased or stagnated during the first half of the eighteenth century, and how quickly the losses caused by the famines of the later 1690s were made up. Recent calculations by Robert Tyson based on the 1691 hearth tax returns give a population for Scotland at this date of 1,234,575, only 31,000 fewer than in 1755, with growth between the two periods being a mere 2.5 per cent.

3. A. Gibson and T.C. Smout, Scottish food and Scottish history 1500–1800, in R.A. Houston and I.D. Whyte (eds), *Scottish Society 1500–1800* (Cambridge 1989), pp. 5–81.

In some regions growth was faster: the western Lowlands appear to have increased their population by some 12 per cent between 1691 and 1755. In regions which were hard hit by the famines of the later 1690s recovery may have been much slower. Tyson's detailed study of population change in Aberdeenshire between 1695 and 1755, based on a comparison of calculations from the 1695 poll tax with Webster's census, estimates that the population of the county in 1755 was still 7 per cent lower than in 1695. The growth of the city of Aberdeen by over 50 per cent during this period only partly offset a drop of rural population of nearly 11 per cent in the lowland part of the county and 12 per cent in the uplands.[4] Even at the end of our period population growth over Scotland as a whole was very slow. The estimated annual growth rate during the 1750s is only 0.4 per cent, per annum similar to France but far lower than the 1 per cent of England.

Webster's 1755 census provides the first reasonably accurate picture of the distribution of Scotland's population. Although falling at the very end of our period it occurred at a time when population growth was still slow. Scotland's population had probably only just recovered to its c1690 level and may still have been lower than in the early 1640s. Over the country as a whole there were around 43 persons per square mile, less than half the figure for England at this date. Most of the Highlands had population densities below the national average, generally under 20 persons per square mile (Map 7.1). The relative fertility of Caithness and particularly Orkney is emphasised by population densities more comparable with the Lowlands. The carrying capacity of most of the Highlands was fairly low but not much less than some Border counties. Over most of the Lowlands, outside the environs of the larger towns, a population density of 50–60 persons per square mile, some 2.5–3 times that of the Highlands, appears to have been normal (Map 7.2). In Lowland counties where the density was greater than this factors such as the existence of large towns, a disproportionate number of smaller burghs, and a concentration of economic activity on trade and industry were important influences.

The purely Highland counties of the north and west (including Perthshire but not the interior of the north east) held about 30 per cent of Scotland's population and the counties north of the Tay 53 per cent. This emphasises the demographic importance of the Highlands despite lower population densities than areas further south. Within the Lowlands the contrast between east and west is striking. East-coast counties south of the Mounth held 30 per cent of the population with another 18 per cent in the north east against only 20 per cent for all the counties of the western and south-western Lowlands. The pattern of population distribution in 1755 is probably a reasonably accurate reflection of that of earlier times. The growth of many burghs in the late sixteenth and early seventeenth centuries, and the expansion of Edinburgh and Glasgow in the later seventeenth and early eighteenth

4. R.E. Tyson, The population of Aberdeenshire 1695–1755: a new approach, *North Scotland*, 6, 1984–5, 113–31.

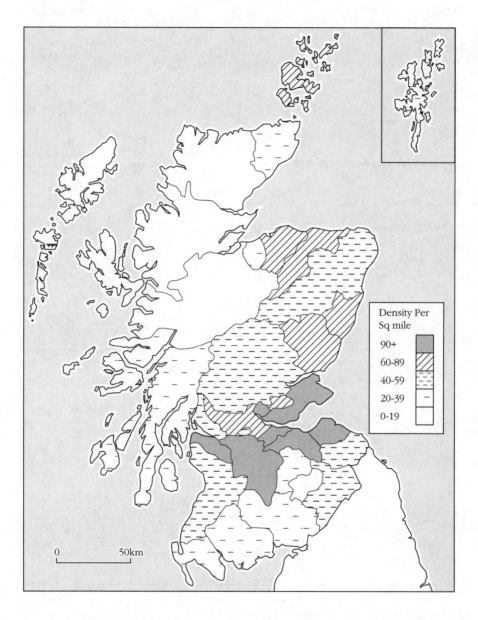

Map7.1 Population Density 1755

centuries, would have increased the contrast between population densities in central Scotland and other areas but otherwise the pattern of population densities was probably not much different at least as far back as the later sixteenth century.

Map 7.2 Percentage distribution of population 1755

THE SCOTTISH DEMOGRAPHIC REGIME

From what has already been said it will be evident that there are problems in identifying significant trends in Scottish mortality and fertility. Nevertheless, while the general features of Scotland's demography are comparable with those of other pre-industrial societies in North West Europe there are interesting differences in detail which hint at some distinctive aspects of Scotland's demographic regime. Although mean household size and the age structure of the population was broadly comparable with England, Scotland appears to have experienced a more high-pressure demographic regime than England with a higher birth rate and a substantially higher death rate. Calculations by Hollingsworth for the mid-eighteenth century based on Webster's census suggested that in Scotland the crude birth rate was over 41 per 1,000 compared with 33–34 for England. This figure is now considered to be too high. Mitchison has recalculated it at c35 per 1,000, levels more in line with England.[5]

The crude death rate around 1755 has been calculated at c31 per 1,000 for Scotland against c26 south of the Border. Calculations of life expectancy at birth in 1755 give figures of 31 or 32 against 36–37 for England. Much of the difference was due to higher infant and child mortality in Scotland. An infant mortality rate during the first half of the eighteenth century of over 220 per 1,000 compared with c195 per 1,000 in England seems likely. Conditions appear to have been improving for some sectors of the population at least. Houston's study of Edinburgh advocates has indicated that life expectancy at age 30 was 27.4 years between 1650 and 1699 but that this rose to 33.4 between 1700 and 1749.[6] This was at least a third better for this privileged group than the estimate of 25.8 for the population as a whole in 1755. Demographically, eighteenth-century Scotland had more in common with Denmark, Norway and Sweden, countries where the birth rate was fairly stable and there was a substantial improvement in mortality, than with England. In several respects Scotland's demographic experience was closer to France than England. Recent work has suggested that the homeostatic regime which adjusted population to resources in England through changes in the ages of women at first marriage responding to the standard of living was a less prominent feature of Scottish demography. Instead, population growth was checked by more swingeing mortality caused by epidemics and famines.

Within Scotland there seem to have been regional variations in population characteristics. The most marked contrast was between the Highlands and the Lowlands although within these broader divisions there were smaller regions like the north east and Fife which may have had distinctive demographic features. The scarcity of data for the Highlands makes it hard to assess the individuality of this region but there are hints that, like Ireland, the Highlands may have had a demographic regime characterised by almost continuous population growth throughout the period. It is possible that the region may have had an even higher-pressure regime than the Lowlands, along with a lower average age of first marriage, in the western Highlands and Islands at

5. R. Mitchison, Webster revisited, a re-examination of the 1755 'census' of Scotland, in T.M. Devine (ed.), *Improvement and Enlightenment* (Edinburgh 1988), pp. 62–77.
6. R.A. Houston, Mortality in early-modern Scotland: the life expectancy of advocates, *Continuity and Change*, 7, 1992, 47–69.

least. There are indications that the rapid build up of population that occurred in the Highlands during the second half of the eighteenth century began earlier and that land hunger existed from the sixteenth century. The Highlands suffered more severely than the Lowlands from the famines of the later 1690s. It is not clear how severe pressure on resources was by c1690 but the population cuts caused by these famines may have removed pressure for many decades so that renewed build-up of population only became a serious problem from the mid-eighteenth century.

In Scotland it was technically easy to get married but the evidence, virtually all from the eighteenth century, suggests that average age of marriage was relatively high and that a significant proportion of the population never married. Although only limited data are available there are indications that the Scottish marriage pattern was similar to England, with most women not marrying until their mid-twenties and men a year or two later. A study of 1,000 court deponents between 1660 and 1770 has given a mean age at first marriage for Lowland women of 26–27.[7] There are some indications that women may have married earlier in the towns than in the countryside. In mid-eighteenth-century Kilmarnock women in the town married at around 23–24, those in the rural part of the parish at 26–27.[8] This factor, along with in-migration, may have helped sustain the rapid growth in urban population which occurred during the later sixteenth and early seventeenth centuries (Chapter 10). A substantial proportion of women did not marry; calculations from various samples range from around 11 per cent to over 20 per cent. Together with the relatively high age of first marriage this level of female celibacy must have had a marked effect in reducing overall fertility.

The power of the kirk sessions may have limited pre-marital conceptions compared with England but there is plenty of scope for further research into the existence of regional variations in bridal pregnancy. Illegitimacy rates in Lowland Scotland were slightly higher than for England. A recent study of regional variations in illegitimacy in Scotland during the later seventeenth and eighteenth centuries has shown that illegitimacy rates were always under 4 per cent in the Lowlands and were below 2 per cent in Fife and the Lothians between the 1740s and 1760s.[9] Comparable figures were 3 per cent for mid-eighteenth-century England, 1.5 per cent for France and 2 per cent for Sweden. Illegitimate children were sometimes the result of sexual activity before an intended marriage which had to be postponed or abandoned. In other cases kirk session records show that servant girls might be taken advantage of by their masters.

In the Highlands illegitimacy was more common with rates of between 6

7. R.A. Houston, Age at marriage of Scottish women c1660–1770, *Local Population Studies*, 43, 1984, 63–6.

8. R.A. Houston, Marriage formation and domestic industry: occupational endogamy in Kilmarnock Ayrshire 1697–1764, *Journal of Family History*, 8, 1983, 215–29.

9. R. Mitchison and L. Leneman, *Sexuality and Social Control in Scotland 1660–1780* (Oxford 1989).

per cent and 9 per cent in the later seventeenth century. The north east and Caithness had a pattern which was closer to the Highlands than the central Lowlands. The trend of illegitimacy was steadily downwards from the 1660s to the mid-eighteenth century in Caithness, the north east and the Highlands demonstrating the spread of church discipline. By the early eighteenth century in most areas the church was succeeding in keeping sexual activity firmly within marriage. Only in Ayrshire and the south west was there a tendency for rates to rise in the 1750s and after. This may be considered as the start of an upturn towards the high levels of the mid-nineteenth century when the level for Scotland as a whole exceeded 9 per cent. The reason for the distinctiveness of the west and south west is not clear. The inhabitants of the south west showed more resistance to church discipline than other Lowland regions. This is seen in the proportions of women who refused to give the names of the fathers of their illegitimate children, the numbers of women who ran away rather than face kirk discipline, and the percentage of men who would not admit responsibility, all of which were higher than in other areas. Overall levels of illegitimacy and pre-nuptial pregnancy were less than in England, suggesting that nuptuality and fertility varied less in Scotland during the later seventeenth and early eighteenth centuries.

Another important influence on Scottish population trends was the high level of emigration. From medieval times Scots were prominent in many parts of Europe as scholars, soldiers and traders. Scotland had a long tradition of supplying mercenaries to foreign armies. Many Scots were involved in wars in Ireland in the late Middle Ages. During the Hundred Years' War significant numbers of Scots fought in France against England. They were later organised into the Scots Guard. The Scots Brigade in Holland performed a similar function in the later seventeenth century. Scandinavia was another important destination for Scottish soldiers. Some mercenaries returned home but wastage was high. It might be argued that many such men were probably younger sons who, had they stayed at home, might not have been able to marry but even if this was so in a proportion of cases the demographic drain must still have been considerable. The number of Scots fighting in the Thirty Years' War has been estimated at around 30,000 but there were significant numbers of Scots in foreign service before its outbreak in 1618. Licences granted by the Privy Council allowing the recruitment of soldiers in Scotland for foreign service – probably the tip of the iceberg – are common from the 1570s onwards. Between 1625 and 1627 alone 14,000 men left the country. From 1625 to 1642 licenses were granted for over 47,000 men to leave Scotland. The actual number who left was probably smaller but estimates of emigration to Scandinavia during the first half of the seventeenth century run at about 25–30,000. Although levels of recruitment were influenced by political conditions within Europe it is probably no coincidence that this wave of emigration for mercenary service occurred during a period of rising population. Military service abroad may have provided a convenient way of siphoning off surplus population, particularly problem elements like beggars, vagrants and criminals.

Emigration for less warlike reasons also occurred on a significant scale. Numbers of Scots traders abroad are difficult to estimate but may have been considerable judging by the size of the Scots merchant communities in individual cities. Around 1700 the Scots community in Rotterdam numbered around 1,000 and many other Dutch and Baltic ports had substantial Scottish groups. Scots were active as pedlars, merchants and craftsmen in Scandinavia and the Baltic from the end of the fifteenth century. Numbers in Poland expanded rapidly from about 1570. In the early seventeenth century the number of Scots in Poland, many of them small merchants, has been estimated at 30–40,000. Few appear to have returned to their homeland. In the first four decades of the seventeenth century wave after wave of emigrants left Scotland pushed out by population pressure and attracted by opportunities abroad. The Ulster plantations in the early seventeenth century attracted a substantial flow of colonists. By 1647 some 20–30,000 Scots may have settled there, mainly small tenants and cottars from western and south-western Scotland.

For the first half of the seventeenth century a net outflow of 85–115,000 has been suggested, a loss of perhaps 2,000 a year, most of them males between the ages of 15 and 30. Perhaps a fifth of all young men left Scotland at this time. Emigration on this scale must have had a major effect in checking population growth. We know less about emigration during the second half of the seventeenth century. Movement to Scandinavia and Poland diminished, the main destinations being Ulster, England and the Netherlands. Emigration to America was of minor importance before the second half of the eighteenth century though the transportation of Scottish prisoners after the battles of Preston (1648), Dunbar (1650) and Worcester (1651), as well as a number of Covenanters during the later seventeenth century must not be forgotten. Movement to the New World, principally the Caribbean, has been estimated at c7,000 for the later seventeenth century. Movement to Ireland is hard to calculate because of the two-way nature of the flow but a net loss of 60–100,000, much of it in the middle of the century and during the 1690s seems plausible. Contemporary estimates claim that 50,000 or more emigrated to Ireland between 1689 and 1700 – a figure approximating to around 5 per cent of the population. Emigration on this scale must have wiped out the effects of natural increase for several years at a time. Overall estimates of emigration during the second half of the seventeenth century run at 78–127,000, similar to the first half. The main difference was that more women and families were involved so that the proportion of young men leaving Scotland was probably nearer 10 per cent than 20 per cent.

In the first half of the eighteenth century emigration was at a lower level though movement to England and the New World probably increased. A figure of 30,000 migrants to America between 1700 and 1760 has been suggested. Migration to England in the seventeenth and early eighteenth centuries is difficult to estimate and has yet to be studied in detail. Many itinerant Scottish traders operated south of the Border by the end of the seventeenth century. Over half the Newcastle keelmen were of Scottish origin by 1740. Movement to the Tyne had started on a seasonal basis but was becoming permanent by this period. Most of the Scots keelmen came from the eastern Lowlands especially the mining, salt-making and shipping communities around the Forth.

Emigration from Scotland must have been an important safety-valve reducing demographic pressure at home. Emigration from England was sufficient to reduce population growth rates in the 1630s and 1640s and to turn the rate for the later seventeenth century into a firmly negative one. The proportional impact of emigration in Scotland is likely to have been greater and does not appear to have been balanced by significant immigration. The size of foreign communities in Scottish burghs seems to have been small, due partly to the vigour with which merchant and trades incorporations maintained their privileges. There is no evidence of a big influx of Protestants from the Low Countries and France during the late sixteenth century as happened to English towns like Norwich. Overall, emigration was an important reason behind the failure of Scotland's population to grow significantly during the seventeenth century.

Scotland's demographic regime differed from that of Ireland as well as England. Even when conditions in Scotland favoured population growth it was slower and subject to greater regional variation than in Ireland. As well as emigration Scottish population growth during the early eighteenth century was restricted by the rate of celibacy and the relatively high average age of first marriage. In combination these influences must have constituted a powerful check on fertility. In Ireland, which experienced rapid population growth in the first quarter of the eighteenth century, the average age of first marriage appears to have been lower than in Scotland. These influences combined to restrict the growth of Scotland's population even when conditions were most suitable. The widespread availability of land in Ireland through subdivision of holdings may have encouraged earlier marriage while in Scotland the strict controls which most proprietors imposed on the creation of sub-tenancies had the reverse effect.

MORTALITY CRISES

Despite their deficiencies for calculating long-term trends, Scottish parish registers are a valuable source of information on short-term population fluctuations particularly mortality crises. In common with much of Europe these were frequent in Scotland during the sixteenth, seventeenth and early eighteenth centuries. Crises caused by famine, disease and war were followed by periods of recovery and slow population growth. The net result was that the secular trend for population was at best only gradually upwards. For most of the fifteenth and sixteenth centuries it is necessary to rely on stray references in chronicles and other literary sources to identify demographic crises. The fifteenth and early sixteenth centuries seem to have been relatively free from famine despite climatic deterioration. Thereafter the situation worsened. There are signs of famine in the early 1550s, 1562–63, 1571–73, 1585–87, 1594–98 and, in the Highlands, in 1604.[10] There is no indication of the scale of mortality associated with these crises or their geographical extent. It is unclear whether any of them produced a reduction in Scotland's population as severe as the cut of up to 20 per cent that has been postulated for England in the late 1550s. Serious outbreaks of bubonic plague are also known to have occurred in 1455, 1475, 1493, 1529–31, 1568–69, 1574, 1584–88, 1597–99 and 1600–9. The revival of trade during the sixteenth century may have increased the frequency with which plague was introduced to Scotland. From the later fifteenth century records suggest that most outbreaks of plague were concentrated in the towns, although that of 1601 reached the West Highlands. It is possible that a combination of influences, including the more scattered distribution of the rural population, slightly cooler climatic conditions, poorer communications and even the flimsy nature of most rural dwellings, helped to limit the spread of bubonic plague through the Scottish countryside compared with England.

In the second half of the sixteenth century population pressure and a growing dependence upon cereals as the dietary basis of the bulk of the population may have increased vulnerability to harvest failure. Scotland continued to suffer from recurrent famines and epidemics into the early seventeenth century. Thereafter major crises occurred less often. Plague vanished after the 1640s and the famine of the 1690s was the only nationwide demographic crisis during the last century of our period.[11]

We know far more about demographic crises in the seventeenth century than in the sixteenth. The range of sources improves and above all there is information on fluctuations in grain prices. There has been considerable debate regarding how closely variations in grain prices reflect the availability of food. In England the price series which have been reconstructed have a distinct southern bias and are often derived from the records of institutions whose activities may not accurately reflect the operation of normal market forces. Scotland is better served by runs of county lists of grain prices, which were struck at Candlemass each year to regulate rents and payments of wages in kind. From the early seventeenth century they provide continuous and standardised series of price data for most regions and types of grain. Even so, given the dispersed nature of Scotland's population, poor transport, the vagaries of the weather and differences in the social and economic structure of communities, it is possible that fiars prices may mask local variations in the cost and availability of food. The limited degree of commercialisation in Scottish rural society, for the earlier part of the period at least, might have restricted the purchasing power of the population so much that a shortage of food would not necessarily have driven prices as high as might have been expected.

After the subsistence crises of the mid-1590s food supply seems to have

---

10. Lythe, *The Economy of Scotland*, pp. 15–23.
11. M. Flinn (ed.), *Scottish Population History* (Cambridge 1977).

been more favourable during the first 20 years of the seventeenth century, a period of economic growth and increasing prosperity. During the seventeenth century three exceptionally severe mortality crises affected most of the country in 1623, the 1640s and the late 1690s as well as others, often equally savage, which were limited to particular regions. These included a severe famine in the Northern Isles in 1634, one in parts of western Scotland in 1634–35 and another in the Highlands around 1690. The scarcity of parish registers for these areas means that reliance has to be placed on diaries and other sources; many local famines may not yet have been identified. Bubonic plague, which inspired as much fear in Scotland as elsewhere in Western Europe, is relatively well recorded while smallpox is also mentioned specifically but other diseases like typhus are harder to identify, particularly due to the poor quality of burial registers.

The first major crisis of the seventeenth century was a severe famine in 1623 caused by harvest failure in the two preceding years.[12] In some parishes the numbers of burials rose to eight times the levels of previous years. In Dumfries up to 15 per cent of the population perished. In Dunfermline and Kelso the figure was 20 per cent and for Burntisland a third although refugees from surrounding rural areas may also have been included. Baptism registers show a substantial drop in births in many parishes. The impact of the harvest failures was increased by the failure of either church or state to provide effective aid. Panic measures by the Privy Council, designed to mobilise county authorities into levying an assessment on landowners to provide funds for poor relief, met a negative, even hostile response. It is not clear how great was the cut in population but on a national scale mortality was substantial.

Population levels can barely have recovered when the last major outbreak of bubonic plague hit many towns and some rural areas between 1644 and 1649. The movement of armies during the Great Rebellion helped spread the disease into remoter districts like Kintyre and Islay but the most severe effects were in the burghs. In 1645 9,000 or even 12,000 people died in Edinburgh and its environs, somewhere between a quarter and a third of the population. Other towns, including Crail, Dunfermline, Paisley, Perth and Stirling, were severely affected in the same year with scattered outbreaks in rural parishes. The 3,000 deaths which are believed to have occurred in Perth represent a higher proportion of the population than died in Edinburgh. Further outbreaks followed in 1646 and 1647. One source suggests that up to two-thirds of the population of the small burgh of Brechin perished in 1647 and 1,600 people in Aberdeen. Outbreaks in 1648 and 1649 hit Dundee and Montrose. Over Scotland as a whole mortality is unlikely to have been more than about 2–3 per cent of the population but the impact locally, especially in urban areas, was far more severe. Perhaps one town dweller in five succumbed to plague during this period. It is uncertain how long it took for the worst affected towns to recover but the apprenticeship registers for Edinburgh show that the plague years were followed by a wave of

12. Ibid., pp. 116–26.

immigration from the countryside as young people moved in to take up the available opportunities that the savage cut in population had created.

The third great mortality crisis of the seventeenth century occurred in the later 1690s, again due to harvest failure. Its impact was all the more severe as it came after some 40 years during which food supply had been generally good and there had been no major epidemics. There may have been some growth of population between the mid-seventeenth century and the 1690s. Certainly there are indications of rising levels of vagrancy in the years immediately preceding the crisis caused perhaps by overpopulation and a slump in industrial production due to economic dislocation caused by war with France.

The famine of the later 1690s is recorded in more detail than earlier crises.[13] It was the last time when large numbers of people in the Lowlands died of starvation and, as a result, it had a striking impact on folk memory. Although this period went down as the 'Seven Ill Years' most areas had three or four poor harvests between 1695 and 1699. Bad conditions may have set in earlier in northern Scotland where there are reports of the harvests of 1693–95 being deficient. The severity of this famine was increased by unsettled political and economic conditions. The aftermath of the Revolution of 1688 had brought high taxation, and war with France a disruption of trade. Poor relief had broken down in many parishes because ministers had been ousted following the return to Presbyterianism in 1690. Grain prices in 1696 reached levels which had not been seen for decades. Waves of starving people poured into the towns. In Edinburgh the burgh council set up a refugee camp in the Greyfriars churchyard. A better harvest in 1697 brought some relief but 1698 was a bad year over most of Scotland. The harvest year of 1698–99 was the worst for poverty, vagrancy and begging until the better harvest of 1699 eased conditions. The provision of effective poor relief at a parish level was patchy even in areas like the Lothians. It is likely that Scotland's population was cut by around 13 per cent. About half of this was due directly to increased mortality, most of it probably from disease rather than outright starvation, the remainder to a drop in the birth rate and to emigration.

In some regions, such as the interior of Aberdeenshire, mortality was substantially higher. A recent study suggests that Aberdeenshire experienced a more serious mortality crisis than anywhere else in Scotland outside the Highlands; perhaps 20 per cent of the population died.[14] Conditions were worsened in this area by the collapse of the export trade in woollens. Poor relief was dislocated because a third of the parishes in the county had no minister due to the re-establishment of Presbyterianism. In Lowland parishes like Old Machar the weekly donations to local and vagrant poor increased fivefold but the sums received by individuals fell as the numbers of people in need rose. The influx of starving poor into Aberdeen prompted the burgh council to try and expel non-resident beggars as well as raising more relief

13. Ibid., pp. 164–50.
14. Tyson, The population of Aberdeenshire.

from voluntary contributions. Imported grain was sold at comparatively low prices to those in need. The crisis was most severe for those groups which were always at risk; spinsters and widows, the elderly and infirm, children, dismissed servants and wage-earning tradesmen whose products no longer commanded a market due to high food prices. Conditions were so bad that many people of higher social status; substantial tenants, schoolmasters, merchants and urban craftsmen, were forced to seek relief or were even found dead of starvation. Mortality was so heavy in many parishes that residents and strangers alike were buried in mass graves with a minimum of ceremony. The drop in Aberdeenshire's population had not been made up by the time of Webster's census in 1755. Elsewhere the scale, timing and even the nature of the crisis varied considerably from one district to another. While most parishes seem to have experienced a fall in baptisms some, like Fenwick in Ayrshire and Kettins in Angus, showed barely any increase in mortality.

Nevertheless, famine and epidemic disease seem to have had no impact on long-term rates of population growth. Demographic crises were accidental rather than an integral part of the structure of the demographic regime. Recent work on England has shown that 'national' mortality crises were really aggregations of a large number of local ones, with a majority of parishes not being affected at all in 'crisis' years. In Scotland the impact of severe weather conditions on the grain harvest was mediated through a range of variables: topography, drainage, altitude, soils – and when to this is added variations in social structure and farming systems it is not surprising that the incidence of crises was patchy in Scotland too. On the other hand, the poor quality of parish register data makes it hard to examine the distribution of such crises even at a regional level.

Many of the factors which Appleby has identified as making North West England particularly vulnerable to famine also applied to Scotland.[15] Environmental influences included a more marginal climate for cereal cultivation, coupled with more severe climatic conditions than England at the nadir of the Little Ice Age. Among economic factors were inefficient cultivation techniques and livestock management, the persistence of small-holdings, the inability of farmers to accumulate capital reserves, the limited development of commercialisation, and the poor quality of internal transport. The dependence of Scottish farmers on spring-sown cereals limited their flexibility compared with husbandmen in many parts of England who sowed a mixture of winter and spring-sown cereals and thus spread the risk of crop failure. The dependence upon oats and bere meant that there was no possibility of 'trading down' and eating inferior grains at a time of crisis as happened in England. These conditions applied even more forcefully in the Highlands helping to explain the continuation of periodic famines there throughout the eighteenth century. The rise of the cattle trade in the Highlands from the later seventeenth century, and the growing reliance of many Highland districts upon imported grain, set against a background of

15. A.B. Appleby, *Famine in Tudor and Stuart England* (Liverpool 1978).

rising population rendered the region especially vulnerable. Temporary migration to Lowland districts increasingly provided an alternative mechanism for coping with such crises.

There were fewer mortality crises in Scotland during the century after the 1650s than in the previous hundred years. The incidence and scale of famines and epidemics declined substantially. The reduction in the occurrence of bubonic plague may have been linked to more effective quarantine procedures within Scotland as well as in France and Italy where vigorous measures helped to keep the disease away from the British Isles. Successful quarantine saved Scotland from the outbreak which attacked England in 1665–66. The Scottish Lowlands escaped from the grip of major subsistence crises later than England but ahead of other European countries like France and Ireland. It is easier to identify the factors which made Scottish society more vulnerable than England than to determine the changes which removed the threat of famine. Within communities mechanisms for reciprocity existed between proprietor and tenant, tenant and servant or cottar, with the provision of informal assistance within the rural population. Such mechanisms were especially important as formal poor relief was only designed to supplement aid from family and neighbours. The readiness of ordinary people to assist the vagrant poor despite the strictures of kirk sessions and landlords suggests that there a good deal of help was probably available within communities. The widespread availability of credit within Scottish society, including the delayed payment of rents, must also have helped. The activities of heritors in providing assistance to the people on their estates during the crisis of 1740–41 is well established but it is possible that many proprietors were providing help by means of the subsidised sale of grain at an earlier date. There may also have been a slight improvement in the productivity of arable farming, in parts of the Lowlands in the late seventeenth and early eighteenth century. Better transport and marketing eased the flow of grain from one region to another, as is demonstrated by the increasing convergence of county prices for grain. Most important of all was a considerable improvement in the provision of poor relief in the first half of the eighteenth century with landowners accepting more responsibility for maintaining the poorer inhabitants of their estates during times of crisis.

From the early eighteenth century there was no longer a close relationship between high food prices and high mortality. The harvest failures between 1739 and 1741, a period of difficulty throughout North West Europe, highlights the progress that society in Lowland Scotland had made towards the elimination of famine since the 1690s. In Ireland the crisis of 1741 killed around 10 per cent of the population but outside the Highlands there was no crisis in Scotland. In the Lowlands the worst hardships appear to have been felt by the urban and industrial population. As well as more effective relief a modest rise in living standards for much of the rural population due to profits generated by the commercial spinning of linen yarn may have helped ease the situation. Mortality in 1739–41 was substantially higher than in previous years but did not reach seventeenth-century crisis levels. Sharp fluctuations in death rates from year to year and from one region to another were linked with outbreaks of disease but the impact of these tended to be local rather than regional or national. Conditions were worse in the Highlands where the provision of poor relief by kirk sessions and aid from proprietors was still patchy.

During the eighteenth century smallpox emerged as a major scourge though it killed a smaller proportion of those infected than bubonic plague, flaring up more frequently against a background of endemic occurrence. Smallpox was probably endemic throughout the Lowlands from the later seventeenth century unlike England where it was endemic principally in London. It is probable that, as in eighteenth-century England, such infections were often peripatetic, hitting individual communities hard then moving on and not returning for some years, always present somewhere but not on a scale which would have had a marked impact on national levels of mortality in any year. The later 1740s were characterised by a number of localised epidemics. The diseases involved are difficult to determine. Parish registers often show patterns of mortality which lead one to suspect smallpox but other epidemics such as chickenpox, dysentry, influenza, malaria, measles, and scarlet fever are known to have occurred. Smallpox is best recorded because it was easier to identify. Over half the deaths from smallpox were of children under two years of age and where bills of mortality are available the disease accounted for around a sixth of all deaths. Detailed studies of Alva and Tranent have shown that the trend at this time was for population to grow for three years or so.[16] Then a smallpox outbreak in the fourth year would wipe out any increase in this and an additional year so that overall the disease offset about half the natural growth.

MOBILITY AND MIGRATION

Recent research has demonstrated that Scottish society was highly mobile geographically. Sources such as testificates, statements of good moral conduct issued by kirk sessions which were needed for settlement in another parish, show that movement was normal, particularly among younger people, though usually over limited distances. The most significant divide in early-modern Scotland which limited mobility was the Highland–Lowland boundary. Its permeability gradually increased from the later seventeenth century. Contact across this frontier included a two-way traffic in agricultural produce, with grain being imported into the Highlands, and cattle exported. Greater contact between the Highlands and Lowlands is demonstrated by a study of Highland migration into Greenock. In 1700 around 6 per cent of the town's population had originated in the Highlands but by 1755 this had nearly doubled to 11 per cent while the actual numbers involved had increased fivefold.[17] Highland society, however, was still largely closed to Lowlanders while, before the end of the seventeenth century at least, Highlanders who ventured

16. Flinn, *Scottish Population History*, pp. 223–4.
17. Ibid., pp. 472–9.

into the Lowlands were regarded with suspicion and mistrust.

There were attempts to 'colonise' parts of the Highlands and Islands with Lowlanders to help bring the areas concerned under the rule of law. An early example was the influx of Lowlanders into Orkney from the end of the fourteenth century and Shetland in the late sixteenth. This helped consolidate Scottish rule over these formerly Norwegian possessions. Less successful were the efforts of the Fife Adventurers to colonise Lewis at the end of the sixteenth century. A group of Lowland lairds acquired a lease of Lewis and in 1599 they mounted an expedition there with over 400 hired soldiers plus gentlemen volunteers and ordinary settlers. The incomers built a settlement at what is now Stornoway but they had underestimated the hostility of the local population. In 1602 they were attacked by Macleod clansmen. Many of the colonists were killed or captured and a second attempt to re-occupy Lewis made in 1605 lasted for only two years. Larger in scale and much more permanent in impact was the plantation of Kintyre in the seventeenth century, a private initiative by the House of Argyll to strengthen their hold on this former MacDonald territory. The Earl of Argyll had established the burgh of Lochead, later Campbeltown, in 1609. The settlement still had only around 30 families by 1636, barely half of them Lowlanders. In the 1650s the Marquis of Argyll initiated a more ambitious scheme for settling Lowlanders in the peninsula to strengthen political and military support for him there. He granted leases of large blocks of land to a dozen west-country lairds who brought in many followers. The ravages of war and especially the plague of 1647 had left many holdings vacant so that the settlement scheme was achieved without large-scale displacement of the existing population. A further phase of colonisation occurred after 1669 when many persecuted Covenanters from the western Lowlands found a refuge there.

Scotland had few extensive empty areas into which frontiers of colonisation could expand. The build up of population in areas like Deeside led to an expansion of settlement on a small scale during the seventeenth and early eighteenth centuries. On the other hand, people were also moved out of certain areas. The most significant clearance probably occurred in the eastern Borders in the late seventeenth and early eighteenth centuries linked to farm enlargement and the rise of commercial sheep farming. Other early clearances to make way for commercial livestock farming occurred in parts of the eastern Highlands, such as the depopulation of Glen Lui in the late 1720s.

Scotland had no counterpart to the contrast which existed in England between upland and wood-pasture regions as areas of in-migration and squatter settlement and champion arable areas in which settlement was difficult and from which people tended to move out. Nevertheless, subsistence crises produced waves of migration from upland to lowland districts. The continuation of such crises to the end of the seventeenth century in the Lowlands and throughout the eighteenth century in the Highlands meant that the kind of movement which has been termed 'subsistence migration' persisted longer than in England. By the eighteenth century, however, most of this movement within the Lowlands involved

Highlanders and it was not always possible to distinguish between migrant harvest labour and wandering beggars.

In Scotland there was no legislation comparable to the English Settlement Act of 1662 which helped to reduce long-distance mobility. Legislation designed to control vagrancy was almost inoperable at a local level before the eighteenth century while the provision of some relief to non-resident poor by kirk sessions, and more generally by communities, encouraged vagrancy. Scotland had a fluid group of vagrant beggars, always substantial but liable to increase dramatically during crisis years. Kirk sessions had an influence over population movement by their issue of testificates. Landlords also had considerable control over population movement within their estates through the granting of tenancies and restrictions on sub-tenancy.

Rural–urban migration was an important element in population mobility throughout Western Europe in early-modern times. Two broad categories of migrant to pre-industrial towns have been identified: betterment migrants who were generally young, single and upwardly mobile including apprentices, servants, scholars and trainee professionals, and subsistence migrants motivated by influences driving them out of the country as much as by the positive attractions of the towns. Both groups can be identified moving into Scottish burghs. Together they produced a pattern in which, against a background of steady in-migration, the larger towns experienced periodic surges of incomers in the wake of crises such as the outbreaks of plague which hit most of the major burghs in the 1640s.

The proportion of Scotland's population living in the larger towns nearly doubled between 1500 and 1600, and doubled again by 1700 (Chapter 10). Much of this growth must have been generated by in-migration, producing a shift in the balance of urban against rural population. It is likely that urban mortality rates were higher than in the countryside. Edinburgh in particular, with its awkward site, poor water supply and refuse disposal problems and unusually dense concentration of population, must have been particularly unhealthy. In a city like this endemic diseases, though poorly recorded, were probably far greater killers than occasional but well-publicised epidemics. Migration to the larger towns and higher levels of mortality from epidemic and endemic diseases must have been another factor which helped check population growth in the seventeenth and early eighteenth centuries.

Patterns of migration into the towns can be studied from apprenticeship registers. Apprenticeship migration was not a surrogate for all urban in-migration but was probably fairly representative of the movement of young, single people who formed the most dynamic component of the migration stream. The pattern of apprenticeship migration to Edinburgh in the seventeenth and eighteenth centuries shows that the capital had a national migration field, drawing recruits from every part of the country.[18] Not

18. A.A. Lovett, I.D. Whyte and K.A. Whyte, Poisson regression analysis and migration fields: the example of the apprenticeship records of Edinburgh in the seventeenth and eighteenth centuries, *Transactions of the Institute of British Geographers*, NS 10, 1985, 317–32.

surprisingly there was a marked distance-decay effect with a higher proportion of migrant apprentices being drawn from areas close to the capital than from more distant regions. Some areas, however, sent disproportionately more or fewer apprentices in relation to their populations and distances from the capital. In the late seventeenth century the city recruited larger numbers of apprentices than expected from the lightly urbanised south east and from Aberdeenshire, fewer from areas like Fife and Tayside which had many smaller towns. In this period the pull of Glasgow was not sufficient to check the flow of migrants from west-central Scotland to Edinburgh.

During the eighteenth century Edinburgh's apprenticeship migration field contracted as the system declined while other towns grew and offered opportunities more locally. The rise of Glasgow and its satellites cut the flow of apprentices from west-central Scotland but Edinburgh began to attract more migrant apprentices from the Highlands. A reduction in the flow of apprentices from the border counties may reflect the growing attraction of Tyneside for Scottish workers. The changing pattern of recruitment to Glasgow complements that of Edinburgh. Glasgow's apprenticeship migration field expanded steadily in the early eighteenth century. As well as attracting apprentices from the nearby counties of Lanark, Renfrew and Dumbarton, an increasing proportion of apprentices was drawn from the Highlands. By the mid-eighteenth century Argyllshire was supplying 22 per cent of Glasgow's migrant apprentice tailors compared with under 3 per cent at the start of the century.[19] By contrast patterns of migration to Aberdeen and Inverness remained remarkably stable. These towns dominated lightly urbanised regions with no real competing centres. Seventy-five per cent of migrants to each town were drawn from within a 40-kilometre radius. Aberdeen's migration field, however, became increasingly curtailed southwards, probably as a result of the growth of Dundee.

While migration to the towns became increasingly important during the seventeenth and early eighteenth centuries movements within the countryside were far more significant in total. Levels of mobility were high but mostly over distances of only a few kilometres. Much of the turnover was due to the frequent movement of farm servants, producing peaks around the hiring times of Whitsunday and Martinmas. Cottars were more mobile than tenants, women more migratory overall than men. It is not yet clear whether levels of population turnover were as high as in England, but Lowland Scotland was similar in that a high proportion of young single men and women in rural areas left home in their teens to work as farm and domestic servants in other households. The origins of this system in England go back to late-medieval times at least. In Scotland farm servants are too numerous in the sixteenth century for this group not to have existed at an earlier date. Farm servants are not well documented; they seem to have been more frequent in lowland arable areas than in the pastoral uplands of southern Scotland.

19. I.D. Whyte, Population mobility in early-modern Scotland, in R.A. Houston and I.D. Whyte, *Scottish Society* (Cambridge 1989), pp. 37–58.

We know less about population movements within the Highlands. The structure of clan society with its emphasis on kinship and inter-clan hostility does not appear conducive to high levels of geographical mobility. This has yet to be demonstrated convincingly though and there are pointers which suggest that population turnover in the Highlands was greater than has sometimes been assumed. Regular contacts with Ulster and trade with the Lowlands are important features of the Highlands in the seventeenth century. The level of inter-clan violence diminished markedly in the later seventeenth and early eighteenth centuries, and there was less homogeneity of surnames among the lower levels of clan society than has often been supposed suggesting that Highland society was not as tightly compartmentalised as has sometimes been portrayed. A study of marriage patterns in the parish of Laggan from late-medieval times has indicated that persistant directional patterns of marriage contact existed.[20] There was relatively little contact southwards with Perthshire or with the south-west and eastern Highlands and none into the Lowlands. Instead, contacts were channelled down the Spey valley, possibly reflecting economic linkages with the Moray Firth lowlands including the purchase of grain and the taking in of lowland cattle to summer shielings.

Migration is harder to measure for the eighteenth century than for the seventeenth as the source material becomes less informative. There are indications of some broad internal movements, such as the rise of temporary migration from the Highlands to help with the Lowland harvest, already a feature of labour mobility in the late seventeenth century. Sometimes it is hard to differentiate between this kind of movement and subsistence migration. During the crisis of the 1690s many Highland shearers refused to leave the Lowlands and return home because they knew that there was no food for them there while in 1741 food shortages in the Highlands prompted larger than usual numbers of Highland harvest workers to leave early for the Lothians, some of them dying in Edinburgh soon after their arrival. To understand migration and demographic patterns in general we need to look at agriculture and rural society in more detail.

20. A.G. Macpherson, Migration fields in a traditional Highland community 1350–1950, *JHG*, 10, 1984, 1–14.

CHAPTER 8

THE COUNTRYSIDE c1500–c1750

The traditional picture of the pre-improvement Scottish countryside is of a landscape that was unchanging and a rural economy that was backward. The sweeping away of this system during the later eighteenth and early nineteenth centuries under the impact of the 'Agricultural Revolution' has been one of the most enduring images of Scottish economic history. Within the last few years new research has substantially altered our perception of early-modern Scottish agriculture. It is clear that there was much more regional and local variation in farming systems and, in particular, more change at an early period than has been realised. In the process of dispelling old myths, however, many new questions and problems have been thrown up.

RURAL SETTLEMENT

By the sixteenth century the pattern of rural settlement, barely recoverable for medieval times becomes clearer. Over most of the countryside settlement was dispersed, often in hamlets or ferm touns. These have usually been portrayed as clusters of between six and a dozen households, mainly tenants working a farm jointly. Other types of organisation, such as a single tenant farm worked by cottar labour or a group of smallholdings might produce settlements of a similar size but different social structure. Estate plans and surviving deserted settlements show that most ferm touns were loosely scattered or strung out without any signs of planning. The flimsy construction of pre-improvement housing meant that the sites of individual farms might change over time making settlement layout fluid. Some settlements were anchored by the presence of a more permanent structure such as a church or a tower house but in other cases considerable locational drift might occur over the centuries.

Most hamlets were purely agricultural in function but some larger clusters developed under the influence of various nucleating forces. In the Lowlands the parish church generally provided the focus for a larger hamlet, the kirk toun. In the Highlands such nucleations were less common and it was more usual to find churches and chapels in isolated locations. Other nucleating elements are emphasised by place names such as 'bridgton', 'castleton', 'chapelton' and 'milton' which are frequent on modern maps. The mains or home farm of an estate often formed another settlement cluster, frequently with a group of tradesmen/smallholders. Along the coast fisher touns reflected a distinctive way of life that was often quite separate from neighbouring agricultural communities. They were particularly characteristic of the north east from Angus to the Moray Firth. Some of them date from the fifteenth and sixteenth centuries, developed by landowners to increase revenue as well as supplies of fish. These fisher touns were often laid out in rows close to the shore, their houses built with their gables to the sea for protection from wind and weather.

As with any settlement pattern elements of both continuity and change can be identified. For Lowland Scotland a comparison of any sixteenth- or seventeenth-century estate rental with a modern large-scale map shows that a high proportion of the old settlement names survive despite the changes caused by agricultural improvements in the eighteenth and nineteenth centuries. Elements of change are also evident. From the sixteenth century or even the later fifteenth there is evidence that settlement margins were expanding once more. New ferm touns can be identified by comparing successive estate rentals. They often differed from established settlements by paying money rents rather than ancient customary rents in kind. Their names sometimes incorporated elements such as 'bog', 'hill', 'moss' and 'muir' showing the kind of environment from which they had been created.

Another process of settlement change which can be identified from documents and place names was township splitting where an existing ferm toun was divided into two or more settlements.[1] Sometimes this occurred because of patterns of land ownership. Where land in a settlement came to be held by more than one proprietor a division into separate units might be advantageous. Most townships appear to have been split due to population growth. When a ferm toun reached a size where the complexity of its field systems started to become unmanageable it seems to have been normal to split the toun into smaller settlements rather than permit unrestricted growth. The modern map is dotted with groups of farms possessing a common name but distinguished by prefixes like Easter, Mid and Wester, Over and Nether. It was once thought that these split settlements had originated in the eighteenth and nineteenth centuries by the division of pre-improvement ferm touns into consolidated farms. Documents often show, however, that division occurred much earlier. Sometimes subsidiary settlements were hived off from a parent one which retained its original site. In other cases new townships were established on fresh sites and the original one was abandoned. The process became more complex when it happened more than once, the townships created by an initial division themselves being split at a later date.

As well as the creation of new touns in the interstices between existing settlements and the splitting of townships there were some frontiers where

1. R.A. Dodgshon, *Land and Society in Early Scotland* (Oxford 1981), pp. 195–204.

colonisation on a larger scale was possible. These included royal and baronial hunting preserves which were disafforested. One of the largest of these was Ettrick Forest which returned to crown hands with the forfeiture of the Douglases in 1455.[2] At this date it was sparsely settled, inhabited mainly by rangers occupying forest stedes or holdings with attached grazing rights. In the late fifteenth century the forest stedes were converted into large sheep farms, some held directly by the crown others leased to tenants. In Glen Strathfarrer the process of disafforestation and colonisation occurred even later. The area was retained as a hunting preserve well into the seventeenth century. From the late sixteenth century permanent colonisation pushed up the valley and by the end of the seventeenth century the glen had a considerable population.

In the Highlands settlement expansion, which may have been linked to the growth of both population and demand, often involved the permanent colonisation of shielings. Documentary sources sometimes provide evidence of the transition from shieling to farm. A report prepared in 1712 by one of the Earl of Mar's estate factors stated that the earl's Deeside feuars, in contravention of their charters were leasing shielings to tenants who were converting them to permanent steadings and were cultivating the ground around them. New shielings were being pushed higher into the deer forests between the head of the Dee, Glen Shee and Glen Tilt.[3] Albert Bil's recent study of shielings in Perthshire shows that this process was occurring in Atholl and around the Tay valley between c1720 and c1740 but also happened in the seventeenth century and earlier.[4]

In England, it has been said, you are rarely more than a few miles from the site of a deserted medieval village. In Lowland Scotland, by contrast, the landscape was so thoroughly transformed during the eighteenth and nineteenth centuries that remains of deserted settlements are less frequent. The smaller size of settlements and the flimsier construction of their buildings means that they have often left little trace in the landscape compared with the larger settlements of more solid peasant houses found in late-medieval England. Nevertheless, a number of deserted hamlets and villages are known although reasons for abandonment are often hard to establish. Some settlements were removed to allow the extension of the policies around a country house. When the Marquis of Tweeddale was laying out the policies around Yester House in East Lothian at the end of the seventeenth century he had the old village of Bothans demolished and replaced by the settlement of Gifford further away from the house. Sometimes the amalgamation of two parishes or the relocation of a parish church caused a kirk toun to decline

2. J.M. Gilbert, *Hunting and Hunting Reserves in Medieval Scotland* (Edinburgh 1979), pp. 41–2.

3. I.D. Whyte, Infield-outfield farming on a seventeenth-century Scottish estate, *JHG*, 5, 1979, 391–402.

4. A. Bil, *The Shieling 1600–1840* (Edinburgh 1990), pp. 255–77.

and even disappear. Other settlements were replaced by planned estate villages on new sites during the eighteenth century.

Other deserted ferm touns occur on the fringes of the improved land in marginal locations. Sites like Lour, Old Thornilee, Glentress and Langhaugh in the Tweed valley are associated with the foundations of small tower houses and field systems. They are likely to have been inhabited into the seventeenth or even the eighteenth century. Their abandonment may relate to farm amalgamation associated with the development of a more commercialised livestock economy in the late seventeenth and early eighteenth centuries, a trend which seems to have led to a considerable amount of unchronicled depopulation. Recent survey work in areas like Eskdale suggests that sites of this type may be widespread throughout the Southern Uplands.

Despite a retreat from the levels reached before the fourteenth century the maps drawn by Timothy Pont at the end of the sixteenth century suggest that cultivation limits in south-east Scotland were still high by modern standards. This did not necessarily mean that more ground was cultivated than in later times, though lower yields due to climatic deterioration in the sixteenth and seventeenth centuries may have meant that more land had to be worked to produce a given amount of grain. Before the improvement of transport in the eighteenth century every rural community tried to be self-sufficient in grain while it was often easier to cultivate higher well-drained slopes than lower marshy ground. Despite local variations there are indications of an expansion of the arable area in many parts of Scotland during the sixteenth and seventeenth centuries. Often this process is indicated by evidence of township splitting and the appearance of new touns in estate rentals. In the Lothians and other parts of central Scotland an advance of cultivation occurred in the early seventeenth century with the spread of liming, allowing the intake of previously acid marginal soils. In areas like the rolling plateau below the escarpment of the Moorfoot Hills south of Edinburgh or the moors between the Lothians and North Lanarkshire liming allowed a considerable intake of new land at altitudes of around 180–200 metres.

PRE-IMPROVEMENT AGRICULTURE

Pre-improvement Scottish agriculture has received a bad press until recently. The model of agricultural development for the Lowlands accepted by earlier writers involved a medieval golden age of farming aided by a warm climatic phase and spearheaded by efficient commercial management on the monastic estates. This was succeeded by centuries of stagnation and decline. Internal strife, wars with England and climatic deterioration combined to reduce the efficiency of agriculture. The nadir was reached during the harvest failures of the later 1690s. In the early eighteenth century one or two forward-looking landowners began to try agricultural improvements in the face of indifference and opposition from their neighbours and tenants. It was not until the 1760s, however, that economic and social conditions favoured widespread agricultural change. When the transformation of the rural economy and society began in earnest the process was extremely rapid, a true agricultural revolution which altered Lowland agriculture and rural society within a couple of generations.

Much of the evidence on which this interpretation was based came from the flood of descriptive writings on agriculture which appeared in the later eighteenth century. Insufficient attention was paid to the fact that the improving writers were biased and often ill-informed in their descriptions of traditional agriculture. The whole ethos of the improving movement favoured the condemnation of everything that had gone before. This chronology has been modified as exploration of contemporary rather than retrospective sources has provided a clearer picture of pre-improvement agriculture. There is no doubt that there was indeed a sharp acceleration in the rate of change from the 1760s. It is clear, however, that pre-improvement Scottish farming systems were by no means static and that much of the groundwork which allowed the rapid burst of improvement in the later eighteenth century had been undertaken, slowly and unobtrusively, during the previous century.

Throughout Scotland agriculture was organised using a form of open-field farming known as infield-outfield. This has, in the past, been dismissed as primitive and inefficient, ill-suited to large-scale cereal production, merely an adjunct to a basically pastoral economy and incapable of significant improvement. It seemed to combine two of the most primitive elements of agriculture; shifting cultivation and continuous cropping. Its origins were postulated as being pre-medieval, possibly prehistoric. Dodgshon has demonstrated, however, that far from originating in remote antiquity and remaining unchanged into the eighteenth century, fully-fledged infield-outfield systems only evolved in late-medieval times.[5] Moreover, where detailed documentation from the seventeenth and eighteenth centuries is available, it is clear that field systems were more varied regionally than had been allowed for, more flexible, and capable of evolving into more sophisticated forms.

Dodgshon has suggested that initially the distinction between infield and outfield was a tenurial one. Infield was the original area of assessed land, laid out in fixed numbers of land units. These units originally denoted a fixed amount of land which might vary from one area to another or through time but which were consistent within individual touns. From the thirteenth century the assessments of most touns remained fixed. New land taken into cultivation was not absorbed into existing land units but was treated separately so that most touns came to have cores of old assessed land units surrounded by fringes of more recently reclaimed land measured in acres. How did this tenurial distinction produce the differences in farming techniques which led to the creation of infield and outfield? Dodgshon suggests that by the time the intake of new land was contemplated the original assessed area would already have been under intensive cultivation,

5. Dodgshon, *Land and Society*, pp. 184–95.

using all the manure produced by the township's livestock during the winter half of the year when the animals were grazed on the stubble and housed. As this manure was already committed to maintaining returns from the existing arable area any attempt to expand cultivation needed to utilise the otherwise wasted manure produced during the summer when animals were grazed on the common pasture. The solution was to fence the animals on areas of the pasture allowing them to dung it in preparation for outfield cultivation.

As long as it is remembered that models of infield-outfield farming are only generalisations they provide a basis from which to explore local and regional variations. Infields and outfields were not large, continuous areas of cultivation except in the best drained and most fertile areas of eastern Scotland. On most farms they comprised a series of scattered blocks separated by access ways, areas of permanent pasture and marshy hollows. The infield, normally on the best soils and closest to the settlement, was cultivated intensively by the application of most of the farmyard dung and the manure from animals grazed on the stubble after harvest. Additional fertilizers included turf pared from outfield and rough pasture, seaweed, urban refuse and, increasingly in certain districts, marl and lime.

In most areas the infield formed a small proportion of the total cultivated area, ranging from about a third to a seventh or less. In the most intensively cultivated areas the infield could account for most of the arable area while in upland valleys like Eskdale and Liddesdale some farms may have had no infields at all. Studies of testaments suggest that in Angus infield accounted for around half the cultivated land on the fertile coastal plain and in Strathmore but as little as 10 per cent in the glens penetrating the Grampians. Infields were cultivated with continuous rotations of cereals. In many areas oats and bere, a hardy variety of barley, were the only crops sown. Oats were tolerant of exposure and soil acidity. Bere ripened more quickly than two-row barley and did particularly well on lighter, sandy soils but some barley was grown in the most fertile areas of the south east. In Galloway many infields were cropped solely with bere, a practice also recorded from the fringes of the Highlands. In the best-favoured areas from the Black Isle to the Merse as well as in lower Clydesdale and central Ayrshire, wheat was grown. Peas and beans, whose nitrogen-fixing properties were known if not understood, were more widespread being raised throughout the eastern Lowlands, in Galloway and west-central Scotland. Small amounts of rye were grown in some areas and single infield rigs were also sown with flax and hemp. Bare fallowing on the infield was sometimes practised but this does not seem to have been common.

Outfields were sown only with oats, sometimes a hardier variety than on the infield. In years when returns of outfield oats were especially low the straw may have been valued more highly than the grain. Blocks of outfield were often manured by folding livestock at night in summer within temporary turf dykes. The land was cropped for two or three years, sometimes longer, and then left to revert to pasture for a few years before being ploughed up again. In the north east there were two categories of outfield; folds which were manured and faughs which were simply ploughed up after being rested. In late-medieval times outfield cultivation may have begun on an *ad hoc* basis as temporary intakes from the waste. In areas where waste was extensive outfield cultivation probably retained this character until the eighteenth century. By the seventeenth century, however, outfields had become carefully controlled in most Lowland townships, with regular rotations operating over clearly defined plots. In townships with little permanent pasture, like many in the Merse by the end of the seventeenth century, outfields in fallow were a vital source of grazing. Outfields also provided turf for compost, roofing, walling and building dykes. The intensity of outfield cultivation varied greatly. As much as two-thirds might be under crop in any year in parts of south east Scotland. Elsewhere a half was more normal and the proportion might fall to a quarter or a fifth.

In the more arable-orientated areas of the Lowlands, especially the Lothians and the Merse, infield-outfield systems had evolved considerably by the later seventeenth and early eighteenth centuries. Infield rotations had become more complex with four-course systems of wheat, bere, oats and legumes. Five-course rotations including these crops and a year of bare fallow have been recorded, especially in Berwickshire and Roxburghshire where fallow may have taken the place of lime which was not available locally. Efforts were often made to maximise yields of wheat, the highest-priced cereal, by the sowing legumes the previous year, sometimes in conjunction with liming.

The intensification of cultivation in the Lothians was aided by the adoption of liming in the early seventeenth century. As field systems in this region became more intensive and the area of pasture on each farm diminished, the amount of animal manure must also have been reduced. At some point further increases in crop production would have become impossible without an alternative method of maintaining the fertility of the land. Seaweed and urban refuse helped but the adoption of liming was of more widespread significance. For Berwickshire and Roxburghshire, Dodgshon has suggested that outfield cultivation became more intensive in the later seventeenth and early eighteenth centuries with two-thirds under crop in any year in some areas.[6] A switch to cattle rearing in the early eighteenth century, with a consequent need for more pasture, may have reversed this process in some cases. Another trend in the south east was for infields to be expanded at the expense of outfields. At Dundas near South Queensferry in the mid-seventeenth century the infield had been enlarged to cover 70 per cent of the cultivated area.[7] This was aided by the adoption of liming which appears to have been first tried at Dundas in 1624. Liming allowed outfield to be upgraded to infield, encouraged the use of more sophisticated infield rotations and the spread of wheat. Outfield cultivation at Dundas was equally intensive: over half the outfield was under crop in any year. The use of

6. Ibid., pp. 231–3.
7. Whyte, Infield-outfield farming.

legumes combined with liming seems to have allowed a significant change in the balance of infield to outfield producing an intensive arable-orientated system in which livestock had become relatively unimportant.

It must be emphasised, however, that such intensive cropping systems were relatively late developments and were confined to fertile areas adjacent to large towns. The demands of the rapidly growing Edinburgh market (Chapter 10) were probably an important influence. Nevertheless, it highlights the flexibility and adaptability of infield-outfield farming. By the later seventeenth century there was a considerable contrast between such field systems and those in areas where cultivation was merely an adjunct to a basically pastoral economy. The traditional infield rotation of bere/oats/oats was certainly widespread, though local variations with fallow courses and legumes are recorded in some places. In areas with sandy soils or near towns where there was considerable demand for malt, rotations concentrating on bere were sometimes used with two or even three crops of bere followed by oats. For outfields it was common to stipulate that no more than three or four crops of oats should be taken before a comparable period of fallow. The use of lime allowed the intensification of outfield cultivation with as many as seven or eight consecutive crops followed by only a brief period of fallow.

In the Highlands, despite the unsuitable environment, arable farming was still important. In medieval times plough cultivation using mainly horses may have been the normal mode of tillage. From the sixteenth century growing population pressure led to changes. The more intensive cultivation of existing arable land was leading to a reduction in fertility in some parts of the Highlands, such as Tiree, by the seventeenth and early eighteenth centuries. Population growth also forced an expansion of cultivation on to more marginal land. The intake of land around shielings and sometimes their conversion to permanent settlements was one symptom of this pressure. Another was the expansion of outfields. A further sign of pressure was the spread of hand cultivation. The creation of lazy beds has been viewed as an archaic and primitive survival from ancient times. In fact it may have been a relatively late development, a response to the problem of feeding a growing population in a difficult environment. Hand cultivation was extremely labour intensive. One contemporary estimate was that it required three times as much effort as plough cultivation for a return only a third as great again. But the Highlands had plenty of labour and in some areas more land was under hand than plough cultivation by the early eighteenth century. The way in which Highland communities responded to land pressure by developing new techniques demonstrates a flexibility and adaptability that has not previously been looked for in what has been seen as a backward, culturally conservative area.

The yields obtained from infield-outfield cultivation have usually been considered as uniformly low with a break-even yield of three times the quantity of seed sown as a normal return. Traditionally this left a third of the harvest for seed, a third for rent and a third for direct consumption by the farmer's household. There are indeed plenty of indications that this return was seen as a basic minimum. In Commissary Court testaments it was usual, when making valuations of growing crops, to estimate their likely product at three times the quantity of grain sown. Doubtless such estimates erred on the side of caution but there is other evidence that a three to one return was accepted as a reasonable minimum from infields while yields from outfields might fall even lower.

Records of cultivation on Lowland mains farms managed directly by proprietors provide specific information on crop yields and are likely to represent the best of contemporary husbandry. A comparison of crop yields on the Cassillis estate near Stranraer for the late 1650s and early 1660s, and the better-favoured Dundas estates near Edinburgh between 1637 and 1662 is instructive.[8] At Cassillis yields of bere on some infield plots ranged from 8:1 down to 2:1 but were normally between 3:1 and 6:1. The return of oats ranged from under 2:1 to around 3.5:1. At Dundas the average return of wheat was only 3:1. Although returns of up to 6:1 have been recorded from some Roxburghshire farms this suggests that wheat was a marginal crop even under the best conditions. Bere at Dundas gave an average return of 5.3:1 with yields from individual plots in some years exceeding 8:1. Infield oats produced 3.7:1 and outfield oats 3.5:1. The first crop of oats from outfield land which had been rested for a number of years was probably often better than average returns from nearby infields. Returns at Dundas were, overall, better than a break-even yield of 3:1. That such yields were not exceptional is confirmed by the more general observations of contemporary commentators. In Buchan the normal yield of oats on infield land was considered to vary from 4 to 6:1 depending on whether turf had been added to animal manure. Outfields gave a lower return overall but the first crop of rested plots might produce 7:1.

Some types of cultivation could produce far higher returns from limited areas with careful tillage and heavy application of manures. The paring and burning of land on the edges of peat bogs might give 10, 15 even 20:1 and comparable returns are recorded from the Outer Hebrides with the use of spade cultivation and large quantities of seaweed. Average yields over most of Scotland were below those of contemporary England but perhaps not any worse than returns from northern England. Scottish yields were certainly no poorer and perhaps somewhat better, than those from much of central, eastern and northern Europe. It is also likely that there was an improvement of yields in some areas during the seventeenth and early eighteenth centuries due to the adoption of liming and better rotations. This is suggested by data from the Mains of Yester in East Lothian, from 1697 to 1753.[9] The series begins at the end of the disastrous harvests of the late 1690s as it does not show how low yields were in the worst years of the crisis. Conditions were certainly bad enough for the cultivation of wheat to be abandoned and not resumed until 1712. Over the period as a whole the mean return of bere was

8. I.D. Whyte, *Agriculture and Society in Seventeenth Century Scotland* (Edinburgh 1979) pp. 74–6.
9. I.D. Whyte, Crop yields on the Mains of Yester 1698–1753. *Transactions of the East Lothian Antiquarian Society*, 22, 1993, 23–30.

5.0, oats 4.2, peas 2.8 and wheat 9.1. The high yields of wheat are impressive but the area sown was smaller than for other cereals suggesting that wheat did not form a complete course on all the infields and that it may have received special inputs of manures and fertilisers. Yields of wheat and bere at Yester rose during the first half of the eighteenth century and returns of oats showed a similar, though less marked, trend.

As with open field systems elsewhere the holdings of individual cultivators were fragmented into strips and parcels scattered throughout the arable area. The term 'runrig' was often used to describe the way in which land was allocated within such a system. Runrig has been misunderstood in the past, having been seen as synonymous with infield-outfield. Dodgshon has shown that runrig was a system for allocating land between different cultivators. At an early stage in the evolution of runrig periodic re-allocation of shares may have been common but instances of this are rare by the time documentation becomes more detailed in the sixteenth and seventeenth centuries.[10] Consolidation out of runrig by the exchange of strips can be identified as early as the sixteenth century and may have been on the increase.

Other elements in the farming system included meadowland, usually ill-drained areas beside streams or in marshy hollows where natural hay was cut for winter fodder. By the early eighteenth century the deliberate flooding of water meadows in winter to encourage the earlier growth of spring grass was being tried in some areas. Beyond the arable land lay the uncultivated waste. The head dyke delimiting the arable area was the most important division on the farm. It protected crops from damage by livestock and baron courts frequently passed acts requiring tenants to maintain head dykes in good condition. Waste might belong to individual proprietors but much upland pasture was commonty, land whose ownership was shared between a number of proprietors. Commonties could be divided by universal agreement between the heritors having rights to them but in many cases the numbers of people involved were too great to allow this. Such areas could only be maintained in joint ownership if they were kept as pasture; ploughing and sowing part of a commonty was a declaration of property. Such encroachments were usually strenuously resisted and were checked by periodic perambulations. To prevent overgrazing commonties were often stinted or 'soumed', one soume being equal to half a horse, a cow 10 sheep, 30 lambs and so on. As with common pastures elsewhere such regulations were frequently ignored, tenants overstocking them with their own animals or livestock brought in from other areas for a fee.

Almost all farms, Highland and Lowland, were mixed. Even the intensive arable farms of the south east kept a few sheep, as much for their manure as for wool and meat, and a few dairy cattle in addition to draught oxen and horses. In the eastern Borders specialised sheep farms had developed by the late seventeenth century with large areas of hill grazings and limited arable and meadow in the valleys. In Galloway and western Scotland the accent was

10. Dodgshon, *Land and Society*, pp. 141–57.

on cattle, the animals being raised for meat in the south west, with dairying starting to become a speciality around Glasgow. In the Highlands both cattle and sheep were kept as well as goats which could forage over rougher terrain. Goat-keeping was more limited in the Lowlands, being confined to areas like the uplands of Galloway and the Upper Tweed. Pigs were kept in small numbers throughout Lowland Scotland but less so in the Highlands were there was a prejudice against eating pork. Horses were reared in large numbers in parts of the southern and eastern Highlands and were sold in Lowland markets. The principal bottleneck in pre-improvement farming was the lack of winter fodder. Livestock could graze the stubble on infields and outfields after harvest, as well as ranging over uncultivated areas of outfield. Some of the straw from the crop and natural hay provided additional feeding but even this might be barely adequate. It was normal to kill off a substantial proportion of animals at Martinmas.

In summer, to protect growing crops, the bulk of the livestock of many townships was sent beyond the head dyke to pasture under the control of a common herd. The animals were brought back at night to be folded on outfields that were being prepared for cultivation. In areas with extensive reserves of waste transhumance was practised. In summer the dairy cattle were sent to upland pastures or shielings along with part of the community, particularly women and children, who stayed with the animals making butter and cheese and living in temporary huts. Although shielings went out of use in parts of the Southern Uplands during the twelfth and thirteenth centuries they may have continued in some areas into the sixteenth century; on the moorlands between Clydesdale and West Lothian or in Ettrick Forest for instance. In the Highlands shielings remained in general use until the introduction of commercial sheep farming at the end of the eighteenth century.[11] The development of the droving trade with its emphasis on raising lean animals for beef may, however, have reduced the emphasis on shielings in many areas. Shielings were linked with dairy cattle which needed regular milking and close supervision while animals reared for meat could be more loosely tended by smaller numbers of herdsmen.

Dodgshon has identified a sectoral shift towards livestock farming in Scotland between the mid-seventeenth and mid-eighteenth centuries.[12] Sheep farming in the eastern borders and cattle rearing in Galloway were becoming more specialist and commercialised from the 1660s as a result of the growing demand from England for beef, mutton, lamb and wool. There is also evidence that some Lowland farmers, especially around Edinburgh and Glasgow, were changing entirely to grass. Probably more widespread in the early eighteenth century was a trend to expand livestock production on Lowland arable farms by reducing the extent of outfield cropping and so increasing the amount of pasture. This may have developed as a means of

11. Bil, *The Shieling*, pp. 297–360.
12. Dodgshon, *Land and Society*, pp. 255–65.

cashing in on the booming cattle trade with England with estates starting to buy in lean Highland cattle for fattening.

AGRICULTURAL CHANGE AND IMPROVEMENT

The extent and significance of agricultural change in seventeenth- and early eighteenth-century Scotland are badly in need of more detailed research. The wealth of source material relating to agriculture which becomes available in the later eighteenth century has tended to focus attention on this period with the classic 'agricultural revolution' beginning in the 1760s. It has been assumed that per capita production in Scottish agriculture stagnated or even declined between the early sixteenth and later seventeenth centuries. There may, however, have been some improvement in productivity between c1650 and c1750. With the exception of the freak years of dearth in the later 1690s food supply in Lowland Scotland improved markedly after 1660. In this period estates as far north as Sutherland, Caithness and Orkney were producing substantial quantities of grain for export and landowners such as Viscount Tarbat were investing in the provision of warehouse and harbours to facilitate the trade. Grain prices were low and grain was exported, often in large quantities, in most years. The causes of this are unclear but may have included more favourable weather conditions, the reduction of feudal households resulting in larger surpluses being available for the market, an expansion of the cultivated area and improved returns from existing arable land in some areas due to innovations like liming and improved rotations. The development of more effective marketing systems had begun to reduce regional contrasts in grain prices within the Lowlands by the 1680s and had eliminated them by the 1730s. This favourable food supply situation was not necessarily encouraging for landowners, or even their tenants. Many farmers were still paying rents in kind and the efforts of east-coast proprietors to dispose of the large quantities of grain that they received often have an air of desperation as much as entrepreneurship. Low grain prices did not allow either landlords or tenants to make substantial profits and accumulate significant capital. This in turn discouraged investment in agricultural improvements.

In recent years there has been a revision of ideas regarding the course of agrarian change in eighteenth-century England with the emphasis on the first four decades of the century as a period of strong growth in agricultural output followed by 50 years of slower growth, even stagnation. While such ideas cannot be transferred north of the Border without modification they nevertheless suggest a need to examine more carefully assumptions regarding the nature and timing of agricultural change in Scotland. There are grounds for suggesting that many gradual, unobtrusive changes occurred in the century or so preceding the rapid acceleration of improvement. These were important preconditions for improvement which removed or at least reduced structural constraints on development within the rural economy and society.

Changes in Scottish agriculture during the later seventeenth and early eighteenth centuries were underpinned by a series of acts passed by the Scottish Parliament between 1661 and 1695.[13] The statutes represent a sustained effort at encouraging improvement on a scale and at a pace which was realistic in the contemporary economic climate. The earliest act in 1661 was designed to promote enclosure for planting, crops and livestock by means of tax concessions, allowing the diversion of roads and sharing the costs of enclosure on estate marches. In 1669 this act was supplemented by provisions for the exchange of parcels of land to straighten property boundaries and facilitate enclosure. In 1685 the tax concessions on enclosed land were renewed.

That this legislation was actually used is shown by a number of applications to the Privy Council to divert roads to allow enclosure. Agreements for straightening estate boundaries to aid enclosure are also known. References in the records of some baron courts also indicates that the statutes were were widely known and actively used by proprietors. The programme of improving legislation culminated in 1695 in two acts relating to the division of commonties and lands lying runrig. The legislation utilised straightforward legal processes, through the Court of Session and Sheriff Courts. Too much may be made of this legislation; the 1695 statute relating to runrig was not the general enclosure act some writers have claimed while both the runrig and commonty acts were not widely used until well into the eighteenth century. Nevertheless, while divisions of commonty under the 1695 act only became frequent after the 1750s a number are known from the first half of the eighteenth century, some involving several thousand acres. Likewise, while consolidation of proprietary runrig touns mainly occurred after the 1760s a number of feuar touns in the Merse had their holdings consolidated before 1750. Although instances of its use in the early eighteenth century are relatively few, the legislation nevertheless represented a progressive, forward-looking approach to agriculture.

The most marked change in the rural landscape in the later seventeenth and early eighteenth centuries was the creation of blocks of enclosures on the policies surrounding the homes of landowners. This trend may have started earlier in the seventeenth century but did not become widespread until after the Restoration. This fashion often went hand in hand with the extension and improvement of existing tower houses and castles, or their replacement by neo-classical mansions. There was a strong aesthetic element in this enclosing activity. Most schemes involved the planting of trees. Blocks of woodland in an otherwise treeless landscape made estate policies stand out, emphasising the dominance of their owners over rural society. Few could have ignored the commercial possibilities though. The Earl of Strathmore reckoned the value of his newly planted trees at Castle Lyon and Glamis, when mature, to be more than equal in value to a full year's rental of his estates. By the end of the seventeenth century the scale of afforestation around some country

13. Whyte, Agriculture and Society, pp. 94–110.

houses was impressive. At Yester the enlarged policies had a perimeter of several miles within which were thousands of acres of new planting. On most estates, however, the scale of activity was smaller. The 128 acres of planting around Panmure House, with about 45,000 trees, was considered the most extensive in Angus.

Enclosure encouraged the first experiments in selecting livestock breeding, especially cattle, using imported English and Irish animals. Where all or part of the mains was enclosed along with the policies it was possible for proprietors to experiment not only with new rotations but also with new crops such as sown grasses and turnips. Large-scale enclosure of land beyond the policies first developed in Galloway under the stimulus of the cattle trade with England. By 1684 Sir David Dunbar of Baldoon had constructed a huge cattle park capable of wintering up to 1,000 animals, some purchased from neighbouring landowners and tenants, others bred from Dunbar's own imported Irish cattle. Dunbar's annual turnover was some 400 animals which were driven to England for sale. At four or five years of age these crossbred animals sold for up to £72 Scots compared with the £20 or less for ordinary Galloway cattle. Dunbar was not the only Galloway landowner to begin large-scale enclosure for commercial cattle rearing. The expropriation of land from tenants to create cattle parks continued through the first quarter of the eighteenth century, encouraged by rising cattle prices. Fear of further enclosure and dispossession precipitated the Leveller's Revolt of 1723–25, a rare Scottish example of large-scale rural protest. Gangs of small tenants and cottars went around parts of Galloway throwing down the enclosure walls which they considered as a threat to their tenancies and slaughtering some of the cattle within them. The government sent in dragoons to patrol the area but few prisoners were taken. There were no executions and only one or two people were sentenced to transportation. The sensitive handling of the Leveller's Revolt suggests that there was considerable sympathy for the protesters and recognition that dispossession on this scale was something new and, at the time, undesirable in terms of landlord–tenant relations.

The use of parks for commercial livestock rearing was not confined to Galloway though elsewhere the scale of operations was smaller. The introduction of English and Irish cattle for breeding is recorded from estates in Ayrshire, Perthshire, the Carse of Gowrie, and the Lothians. Other estates including some in the Merse adjacent to the main drove routes to the Border began to buy in lean Highland cattle for fattening, the animals being sold to local burghs or to English buyers. The scale of enclosure for arable farming was still small. The 100 acres of enclosed land at Panmure and the 350–400 acres at Castle Kennedy near Stranraer were exceptional. Even so these areas acted as test beds for new crops and techniques, including convertible husbandry which is known to have been tried on a number of estates in different parts of the Lowlands. In the early years of the eighteenth century sown grasses, clover, lucerne and turnips were all integrated into rotations on an experimental basis on enclosed estate mains.

The Scottish rural landscape on the eve of the first main phase of enclosure is strikingly depicted portrayed on the Military Survey of 1747–55. In the most highly commercialised and forward-looking districts, like the Lothians, the Merse and the country around Glasgow, enclosure had progressed so far that extensive areas of country were already parcelled out into a landscape of regular fields. The pace of change varied greatly from one estate to another though. In other areas, such as lowland Aberdeenshire and the Laigh of Moray, the landscape hardly seems to have changed from medieval times with only isolated islands of enclosure amid the sea of waste and open-field cultivation.

The harvest failures and famines of the later 1690s seem to have concentrated the minds of many landowners on the weaknesses of Scottish agriculture and the need for improvement, resulting in a brief flurry of pamphlets emphasising the need for change. Sir Robert Sibbald, in an unpublished manuscript, and Lord Belhaven, Andrew Fletcher of Saltoun and James Donaldson in published works, were remarkably consistent in the faults that they identified.[14] Rack renting and the lack of long leases, insufficient interest in agriculture by landowners, the continuation of rents in kind and feudal services, lack of enclosures, limited provision of winter fodder, overstocking of pasture, and the need to divide commonties were among the failings they emphasised. It is doubtful if this literature had much direct influence. Its importance lies in its reflection of a mood of increasing dissatisfaction by many landowners in the performance of Scottish agriculture and the realisation that things could be improved.

A few men operating during the first half of the eighteenth century have become celebrated as early improvers, notably John Cockburn of Ormiston, the Earl of Haddington, and Sir Archibald Grant of Monymusk. They have often been presented as isolated figures of heroic stature battling against the prejudice and ignorance of the majority of their contemporaries. There has been a tendency in recent years to topple the legendary innovators of eighteenth-century England such as Coke, Townshend and Tull from their pedestals. It is possible that the roles of men like Cockburn have been similarly exaggerated. There are indications that a broader spectrum of landed society was aware of the need for change. A detailed study of change in Scottish agriculture during the first half of the eighteenth century is badly needed. It is likely that such research would show that many proprietors were transforming their estates, though often on a small scale, and that innovations such as root crops and sown grasses probably occurred earlier and were more widespread than has been believed.

It has often been suggested that the efforts of the earliest improvers, during the first half of the eighteenth century, were stimulated by increased contact with England following the Union of 1707, particularly as some of the men who sat in the new Westminster Parliament became well-known agricultural innovators. The way in which landowners like Cockburn and Grant brought English experts and equipment north to their estates indicates that there was

14. See Whyte, ibid., for a full discussion.

indeed an element of this. It is important to note, however, that nearly all the changes which occurred in the first half of the eighteenth century: enclosure, the planting of trees, long leases, selective livestock breeding, had already been tried during the late seventeenth century. The efforts of these 'early' improvers were a continuation of existing trends rather than a new approach. The only real innovation in the early eighteenth century was the first experiments with new crops like turnips, potatoes, clover and sown grasses and even here the dates of the first trials of some of these might well be pushed back before 1707 with further research.

A study of one early eighteenth-century landowner, George Dundas of Dundas, illustrates the constraints within which many Scottish proprietors at this period had to work.[15] Dundas succeeded to a small estate near South Queensferry in 1706 at the age of 16. From 1708 he began to improve the policies around Dundas Castle. He created a nursery and began planting trees and enclosing land with hedges and stone walls. The labour force and resources that he committed to this work in any year were modest. Never more than 5 per cent, and usually around 3–4 per cent, of the estate's income was spent upon improvement and in some years a good deal of this outlay was offset by the profits that he made from selling seeds and plants from his nursery. By the mid-1730s most of the planting had been finished. During the 1740s he turned his attention to enclosure for livestock and crops, experimenting with sown grasses and clover. The notes that he made from books on agricultural improvement by English authors showed that he was as familiar with the new husbandry of sown grasses and root crops as John Cockburn but more cautious in the pace at which he tried to innovate. The Dundas papers contain a series of letters from Cockburn written during the period 1737–39 when, following the death of his father, he was undertaking large-scale development of his estates. An interesting feature is that, despite the obvious interest of both men in agriculture, their letters were mainly concerned with coalmining ventures. This emphasises the danger of attaching labels to men like Cockburn who were clearly not concerned solely with agriculture but were interested in economic development on a broad front.

A major brake on improvement was the widespread occurrence of entails. Under an Act of 1685, entailed estates could not be alienated from specific heirs and, more critically for agricultural change, estate owners could not contract debts against the estate making the raising of long-term loans for agricultural improvement virtually impossible. By the mid-eighteenth century as much as a third of Scotland was held under entail and the strict provisions which limited development were not relaxed until 1770.

Innovations such as new crops and rotations, the developments of new breeds of livestock and enclosure are conventionally seen as the hallmark of agricultural improvement. Another type of change, relatively neglected, was

15. I.D. Whyte, George Dundas of Dundas; the context of an early eighteenth century Scottish improving landowner, *SHR*, 60, 1981, 1–13.

equally important in creating improved farming systems. This included structural adjustments which led to the creation of a more commercialised farming system. Changes of this type are less easy to identify as they often occur gradually but they affected many parts of the Lowlands during the seventeenth and early eighteenth centuries. Although they were only modifications of the existing farming system they were nevertheless important prerequisites for improvement. During the later seventeenth century written leases or 'tacks' for specific lengths of time became more common, gradually replacing verbal agreements between proprietor and tenant, and tenancies at will which ran from year to year. While many written tacks were for short periods, longer leases for 19 years became more frequent. It also became more common, in arable-orientated lowland areas, to insert clauses into such leases specifying particular rotations and other practices to be adopted by the tenant. By the early eighteenth century true improving leases had developed with clauses requiring tenants to enclose land, plant trees, and carry out other work. While insecurity of tenure under the old system may have been more notional than actual, tenants were unlikely to have undertaken improvements at their own expense without the security from rent increases or eviction provided by a long written lease.

The structure of farms changed too. On many Lowland estates a gradual process of holding amalgamation occurred in the later seventeenth and early eighteenth centuries. The number of tenancies on multiple tenant farms was reduced and in many areas larger single-tenant units worked by farm servants and cottars rather than the families of several small tenants, were becoming common. In Aberdeenshire the poll tax lists highlight a sharp contrast between farms in remote areas like the upper Dee and Don valleys, with a great many small tenants, and touns in many lowland parishes which were held by a single, more prosperous farmer. The process of amalgamation was by no means irreversible and must often have depended on the availability of suitable tenants but by the early eighteenth century single-tenant farms, often quite large, had come to dominate some areas, notably the Lothians but also parts of the Southern Uplands and the western Lowlands.

In the Southern Uplands the shift towards more commercial farm structures occurred earlier than in the adjacent lowlands.[16] A tradition of commercial sheep farming in the eastern borders went back to monastic times. By the late seventeenth and early eighteenth centuries farms with flocks of over 1,000 sheep were by no means uncommon. The animals were raised for their meat as much as their wool with the colliers of Tyneside providing a growing market. A gradual reduction of the number of tenancies on such farms appears to have been under way by the later seventeenth century. Such farms did not become fully commercialised immediately though. The uncertainty of grain supply from nearby lowlands kept much of the best valley bottom land

---

16. R.A. Dodgshon, Agricultural change and its social consequences in the Southern Uplands of Scotland 1660–1780, in T.M. Devine and D. Dickson (eds), *Ireland and Scotland 1600–1850*, pp. 46–59.

under crop, reducing the amount of winter fodder available and hence the size of the flocks that could be kept. During the first half of the eighteenth century as grain supply improved there was a systematic reduction in the amount of cultivation and further rationalisation of tenancies.

The process of consolidating holdings marked a gradual move towards a more polarised rural society in which, as the number of tenancies was reduced, more working capital was needed to take on a holding and tenants became more sharply differentiated in wealth and status from their cottars. This process, continued over two or three generations, led to the gradual accumulation of capital and management skills that was required to create the first generation of tenants who wholeheartedly embraced the new improved agricultural systems. This was the thin end of a wedge which was ultimately driven between tenants and cottars, once overlapping social groups, leading to the creation of a capitalist farming class and a landless proletariat.

Another important step on many estates was the gradual commutation of rents in kind, particularly in arable-orientated areas where rents were paid mainly in grain. This isolated tenants from the market and hindered the development of more commercial attitudes. Farmers only needed to market small amounts of produce to offset any shortcomings in the subsistence-orientated production of their holdings. Commutation occurred in the first half of the seventeenth century in some districts but became more frequent after the Restoration. As the size of old-style feudal households was reduced proprietors could no longer consume all the produce they received as rent. Those in the vicinity of major burghs began to convert grain rents to money and let the tenants do the marketing. This was done on the Clerk of Penicuik estates near Edinburgh as early as 1646. Other estates in the Lothians, around Glasgow, and in the north east followed during the later seventeenth century. The combination of gradual holding enlargement and the switch to money rents must have helped to give farmers more flexibility in their farming systems and to create more commercially orientated attitudes. It is clear, however, that the nature and pace of change in agriculture was strongly influenced by the structure of Scottish rural society, and to this we now turn.

CHAPTER 9

LOWLAND RURAL SOCIETY c1500–c1750

Many questions regarding early-modern Scottish society remain unanswered, such as the role of kinship, patterns of debt, credit and inheritance, social mobility, and the ways in which communities were affected by the impact of agricultural change. We are still unclear even about basic frameworks like patterns of landownership and the distribution of wealth. Nor have there been many detailed studies of individual communities of the kind which has added so much to our understanding of rural life in early-modern England. Nevertheless, it is clear that Scottish society exhibited important differences from, but also some significant parallels with, contemporary England.

SOCIAL STRUCTURES AND RELATIONS

An initial problem in trying to describe social structure is the lack of contemporary assessments by Scots or outsiders. John Major, writing in 1521, divided the Scots into Highlanders and Lowlanders. He did not attempt a full analysis of social structure but he recognised that social mobility was significant. He also appreciated the importance of vertical ties with his comment that when two nobles were at feud the quarrel descended the social scale so that 'their very retainers cannot meet without strife'. Bishop Leslie, writing in 1578, distinguished the inhabitants of the Borders as a distinct group because of their propensity for reiving. Within the rest of Lowland society he identified two clear groups, the nobility and the church. He graded the nobility into dukes, lords, barons, lairds and ordinary gentlemen, the last of these including younger sons of the nobility and members of families of good birth but without titles. Nobility was conferred by birth but he appreciated the dramatic changes that had occurred in the fortunes of some landed families with the redistribution of church estates during the sixteenth century. His remaining category, the common people, was subdivided into three; soldiers, merchants and, lowest in status, a group which included the craftsmen and also, by implication only, the cultivators of the land. Leslie's imprecise and confused ordering of Scottish society matches the one produced for England in 1577 by William Harrison. Both writers had a similar focus, dividing the nobility into several strata but failing to differentiate the bulk of the population. Leslie also recognised that primogeniture caused downward mobility from the nobility with younger sons becoming soldiers of fortune, scholars and merchants. Less precisely he also appreciated that wealth allowed upward mobility, especially in the towns.

When we attempt a more detailed analysis of Scottish society we run into problems of terminology, particularly in the ill-defined zone at the base of the gentry and the upper levels of the peasantry. In England designations like 'yeoman', 'husbandman' or 'labourer' were based on an amalgam of tenure, wealth and status which provided a reasonable guide to their position in society. In Scotland designations like 'feuar', 'tacksman', or 'wadsetter' were based on tenure giving little indication of wealth or status. A high proportion of the people who worked the land were tenants and by the later sixteenth century most of them held by ordinary leasehold. Scottish tenants have been treated as a single homogeneous mass but marked differences existed in the sizes of their holdings, and thus presumably in their wealth and status.

Although wealthy tenants existed there was less of a steady gradation upwards into the ranks of the small landowners than south of the Border. An English commentator in the 1580s identified the lack of a middling class in Scottish rural society as a distinctive trait. According to him, Scotland lacked a 'middle rank of subjects' to 'tie together the two extremes of society'. A major gap separated those who worked the land from those who owned it. In sixteenth- or seventeenth-century England a family could, with good luck and good fortune, rise in two or three generations from the ranks of the husbandmen, move through the yeomanry, and achieve gentry status. In Scotland this was made more difficult by the nature of the land market. It was relatively uncommon for land to become available in small parcels, in contrast to the vigorous peasant land market which characterised England from medieval times. Landowners might give their tenants the status of temporary proprietors by borrowing money on wadset. Wadsets were loans in return for which access was granted to land rent free or at a reduced rent in lieu of interest payments. The land reverted to the proprietor upon repayment of the capital sum and wadset land was not often permanently alienated to the lender. The larger proprietors' hold on the land market was sufficiently strong to ensure that when land was disposed it was sold in large blocks to other established proprietors or occasionally to wealthy merchants rather than being broken up piecemeal and made available to men of lesser means.

In early-modern English society one of the most significant divides was between those who had access to some land, however little, and those who depended on selling their labour to others. In Scotland this distinction was less marked because access to land was more widespread. Scotland lacked a large landless class and in this respect was similar to Ireland; many people, as cottars and sub-tenants, had access to some arable land and grazing although their plots were often very small. There has, however, been little attempt to study regional and local variations in the structure of Scottish rural society.

Scottish society has sometimes been portrayed as relatively open and not markedly stratified. This assumes that upward social mobility was easy, expressed by the popular figure of the 'lad o' pairts', the talented boy from humble origins who was able to use the superior Scottish educational system to achieve social advancement. This image has been based on a few striking but probably atypical examples. The extent of social mobility in early-modern Scotland is yet another topic awaiting systematic study. This picture of a fluid society with easy upward movement is almost certainly overdrawn. Education might elevate a man of humble origins to a position as a minister or schoolmaster but these occupations possessed limited influence compared to that wielded by the landowners, entry to whose ranks was difficult. Compared with England, where social mobility has been seen as widespread, Scottish society may have been less flexible though by no means as rigid as continental peasant societies. Upward mobility did occur but it may have been less easy than has sometimes been suggested. It is also likely that social stratification became more sharply defined during the later sixteenth and early seventeenth centuries. Population growth seems to have expanded the base of the social pyramid by creating a larger class of poor while at the same time providing opportunities for some higher groups to increase their wealth.

Vertical ties based on reciprocal links of paternalism and deference bound society together at all levels. The practice of the Crown making major landowners responsible for their vassals and tenants, and of local courts making tenants answerable for the actions of their cottars and servants illustrates the importance of such linkages. The old feudal tenure of wardholding gave proprietors the right to call upon vassals and tenants to provide military service. As long as proprietors needed armed followings, and as long as their supporters needed protection from armed aggression, this emphasised the reciprocal nature of the relationship. Despite feudal survivals such as labour services and thirlage, feudal relationships were weaker in Scotland than in many parts of Europe. Some historians have suggested that personal ties and mutual interdependence went sufficiently far to create a social consensus producing a relatively egalitarian society within which social divisions were relatively unimportant, a society with a level of social harmony unusual in Europe. This is almost certainly an over-idealised view but the absence of certain types of popular protest like peasant uprisings may indicate a degree of social harmony. Deference and obedience might vanish, however, when the lord–vassal or landlord–tenant relationship became too exploitative and the traditional responsibilities of the landowners towards the inhabitants of their estates were abandoned. As feudal ties declined during the seventeenth and early eighteenth centuries group solidarity characterised by horizontal linkages became more important. The rise of the use of the term 'heritor' from the late seventeenth century, an all-embracing word denoting those who owned land, stressing property rather than feudal superiority, highlights the increasing group solidarity of proprietors.

During the sixteenth century linkages in society operated through personal lordship and kinship rather than through land. Kinship was the basic form of obligation in local society. The extent to which kinship links were valued, beyond the bounds of the nuclear family, declined from the sixteenth century even for the upper levels of society. Over much of the Lowlands by the later seventeenth century kinship was probably as unimportant as a framework for economic, social and cultural relationships as it was in England at the same period. Scottish kinship was agnatic unlike the cognatic system of England. Descent and kin bonds were recognised between males, identification being helped by the use of a distinguishing surname. Women were added to or subtracted from the male kin group at marriage. This is shown by the way they retained their own surnames after marriage.

The central importance of the nuclear family is confirmed by the poll tax lists of the 1690s. A range of relations were sometimes found in gentry households but at lower levels the two-generation family without any other resident kin was normal. There is little information on the role of kinship among the lower levels of rural society. It was probably less important than among the landowners. To what extent people had relatives living locally, and what degrees of kinship were recognised, is hard to determine. The limited range of both Christian names and surnames within many communities complicates studies of kinship densities. Bearing in mind levels of population mobility, however, kinship densities were probably low placing considerable emphasis on help from friends and neighbours.

Relationships between proprietors and tenants could involve oppression and exploitation. This was encouraged by the tremendous power wielded by landowners. Examples of rack-renting and summary eviction are known. On the other hand, landlord and tenant were both ultimately dependent on the same basic resource, the land. This produced a degree of mutual interdependence between them. Paternalism is shown by the readiness of landowners to grant remission of rent to hard-pressed tenants in difficult years. The importance of 'good neighbourhood', reciprocal obligations between people of more or less equal status which imposed constraints on individual action for the good of the community, must also be emphasised. It is most clearly seen through acts in baron court books relating to farming practises such as the regulation of activities within the open fields and on the common moor. It is evident too in the existence of a range of mechanisms for debt and credit which spread the resources within a community to maximum effect. The need to maintain good neighbourhood is also seen in the action taken to stop anti-social behavour such as scolding, slander, habitual drunkenness and physical violence.

Little work has so far been done on the family in Scotland. It has been assumed that there was strong patriarchal control by husbands over wives, fathers over children and masters over servants but there is no evidence of especial brutality, or of a major change in attitudes towards marriage and childhood. Evidence regarding the considerations which lay behind the choice of marriage partners is neither abundant nor direct, particularly for the lower levels of society. After the Reformation there were fewer restrictions on marriage particularly when they occurred against the wishes of kin. Under Scottish law marriage depended entirely on the mutual consent of the two partners. Paternal consent to marriage was seen as very desirable but not absolutely essential. In a high proportion of cases it is likely that people would have chosen partners from their own social level. Within this kind of constraint free choice of partners subject to parental approval is likely to have been normal as in England rather than marriages arranged by parents. Among the gentry and nobility the importance of property, perpetuating the family and the need for dynastic alliances may have weighed more heavily in the choice of marriage partner leading to greater parental or even official control over the choice of partner. Dowries, still paid in cattle as well as cash, continued to be paid in the Highlands in the early eighteenth century. How affectionate marriages were in practice is hard to determine as the few surviving diaries provide little direct evidence. The role of women in marriage was seen by society as a whole as essentially subordinate, submissive, even servile, but at an individual level there was scope for a variety of arrangements.

The status of women in Scotland remains unclear. Most sources were male-orientated and tend to marginalise, trivialise or ignore womens' concerns. Did Scottish society offer women as much freedom as in England or were they subject to greater constraint like women in southern and eastern Europe? Women were excluded from politics and from church government, even at the level of the kirk session, though the church recognised them as independent moral individuals. In law, however, they were not accepted as independent criminals or reliable witnesses. They were also disadvantaged educationally resulting in higher levels of illiteracy than among men. Women formed a major element in the labour force. As farm servants they undertook a range of tasks including all but the heaviest labouring. As bearers in coal-mines, where they outnumbered men by two to one in many east-coast pits, their work was even harder and more degrading. When married they had to undertake a wide range of household tasks as well as employment which brought in additional cash such as spinning linen yarn. Up to 80 per cent of all Scottish women were estimated to be engaged in spinning in the mid-eighteenth century. The wages that women received were inferior often only around half the male rate although the differential was less marked for harvest work. Such wages were clearly designed to be adequate only when combined with a man's income. Low wages made spinsterhood or widow-hood a precarious proposition for anyone below the laird class.

If the freedom of women to sell their labour was restricted so were their rights regarding property. A wife's moveable property came under the control of her husband; he could dispose of it without her consent but she could not do so without his permission. Property acquired during marriage remained firmly in the control of the husband but a wife could bequeath her own property by means of a will. Widows were entitled by law to at least a third of their husbands' moveable estate. Women's rights were stronger with regard to land. A married woman could not dispose of land without her husband's agreement, but he had no right to do so. Unmarried women were in an even stronger position and the status of widows with regard to property was almost equivalent to that of men. Women, especially widows, can be found with independent roles in society; taking over the tenancies of farms or the running of businesses in towns. At most social levels the opportunities for adult women to lead a separate existence were limited though. Independent spinsterhood was a more feasible proposition for daughters of the lairds and nobility who could live off the income of rents or investments. Nearly a third of the daughters of lairds in the mid-eighteenth century chose to remain single.

LANDOWNERS AND THEIR ESTATES

Throughout the period landowners dominated Scotland's political life, society and economy. Scottish proprietors had the reputation of being the most absolute and powerful in Britain because of the survival of many feudal structures which had long disappeared in England. Among these were legal powers through the local jurisdictions of barony and regality (Chapter 12). The stability of the greater landowning families and their estates over long periods was another notable feature of Scottish society, evident as early as the fifteenth century. There were certain periods, notably during the reigns of James II and James IV, when new peerages were created but the families that benefited were generally ones of middling rank which had already displayed stability and continuity for generations.

Scottish landowners formed a relatively small, closely connected group. During the seventeenth and eighteenth centuries there were probably around 5,000 of them but a high proportion were small lairds and owner occupiers. At the apex of the pyramid were perhaps 1,000 substantial families, and a hundred or so great ones. At the end of the sixteenth century in a county like Aberdeenshire there were some 500 landowners but 50 of them held two-thirds of the county. The largest magnates had estates which were almost mini-kingdoms in terms of their size and independence. Any division of the landowning group must be arbitrary but the most important distinctions were between the great landowners, generally the nobility, most of whom held their lands direct from the crown, the smaller estate owners or lairds who were often vassals of the nobility though sometimes holding direct from the crown, and 'bonnet lairds', owner-occupiers who worked their land in person. There was a wide social gulf between bonnet laird and magnate but in between there was a lot of interaction between the lairds and the nobility who were united by ties of kinship as well as social and economic interests.

There was a substantial increase in the number of proprietors during the later fifteenth and sixteenth centuries. This was partly the result of the break up of some great landholding units like the earldom of Mar but it was also due to the feuing movement. The sixteenth century saw the virtual demise of the crown as a significant landowner and the rapid decline of the church as a proprietor. As a result, from the later sixteenth century little land was held by institutions. Most land in this category was within or adjacent to the major burghs and comprised property belonging to hospitals, colleges and other charitable organisations. An exception during the early eighteenth century was the York Buildings Company, a dubious group of speculators who bought up many of the estates of prominent Jacobites which were forfeited after the rebellion of 1715.

During the seventeenth century, particularly after 1660, and continuing into the eighteenth century a reverse trend set in with numbers of landowners in most regions falling. Many owner-occupiers and small lairds were forced to sell out as a result of the mid-seventeenth century crisis, the lean years of the 1690s, misguided investment in the Darien Scheme or the South Sea Bubble and other misfortunes and misjudgements. There was also a trend away from the granting of portions to younger sons and towards keeping estates intact. In Aberdeenshire the average number of heritors per parish fell from 9.7 in 1667 to 6.5 in 1741, the total number of landowners from 621 in 1667 to 250 in 1771. Low grain prices in the later seventeenth century made it harder for smaller landowners to make ends meet unless they lived frugally, at a time when levels of consumption among lairds as well as the nobles were tending to rise. The lands of those who sold out were absorbed by lairds and magnates. The balance of landholding between the greater proprietors and the lairds does not seem to have changed very much: it was the smallest men who went to the wall.

Patterns of landownership varied from one region to another. During the eighteenth century the dominance of the great landlords was especially strong in the south east and the Borders, as well as in much of the north east, the Highlands and the Northern Isles. By contrast Fife, the central and western Lowlands and parts of Galloway had a greater proportion of lairds and owner-occupiers. In some western counties bonnet lairds held 15 per cent or more of the valued rent, the great landlords under a quarter. This reflected the pattern of feuing in the sixteenth century. Where a good deal of land was feued in small parcels the process left a distinctive stamp on the structure of rural society. This distinctive pattern of landholding helped to give society in the western Lowlands its independent religious views which were especially evident during the Covenanting times of the mid- and later seventeenth century.

Despite a standardised record of land transactions, the Register of Sasines, from 1617 relatively little work has been done on the land market in Scotland. Indications are that there was a gradual increase in land transactions through the sixteenth and seventeenth centuries, particularly after the Restoration. Many proprietors were ruined by the wars of the 1640s and the high taxation of the Commonwealth. Debts and bankruptcies increased the turnover of land as did the system of apprisal under which a person could buy up all a landowner's debts, owed to a number of individuals, and then force him into bankruptcy. This was a legally acceptable way of acquiring land as well as an underhand means of getting back at an enemy. About a third of the land that changed hands during the seventeenth century did so in this fashion. It was to check the growth of this practice that the law of entail was introduced in 1685 to prevent the forced sale of estates as a result of the concentration of debts in the hands of single creditors.

The Scottish nobility expanded during the seventeenth century. James VI used the lands of the monasteries as rewards for those who had served him well in government, especially after 1603, creating a new aristocracy of service. There were 44 peerages when James began his personal reign. By 1603 he had created 14 more and a further 29 had followed by his death in 1625. This altered the character of the nobility but not as drastically as the numbers might suggest for the amount of land, wealth and influence enjoyed by these new members of the nobility, was modest compared with established magnates. The lands granted to these career administrators were often fragmented and scattered rather than in large compact blocks which would have helped strengthen their power in the localities. By doing this James ensured the loyalty of those whom he had rewarded by making it difficult for them to succeed without his continued favour. Many of the new peers were the sons of lairds and barons and it took a long time for them to become accepted on equal terms by the established nobility.

Other incomers entered the landowning elite from trade and the legal profession via marriage and purchase. From the late sixteenth century there was a trend for land around the major burghs to be acquired as estates by more prosperous merchants and lawyers, and in smaller parcels by craftsmen burgesses. There was no social gulf between old-established landowning families and trade or the legal profession. Younger sons of landowners had long been channelled into such careers and intermarriage between rural and urban wealth was common. Demand for estates increased through the eighteenth century, especially around the larger towns, with a broader range of people buying land. As well as merchants and lawyers men from military backgrounds or with colonial wealth began to purchase estates. Despite these examples of successful incomers much of the land remained in the hands of ancient families who could trace their posessions back for centuries. The disruptions of the mid-seventeenth century, the Revolution of 1688 and the Jacobite rebellions often had significant effects on landownership at local levels but most of the land lost by leading families was acquired by established laird families who were moving upwards.

The rise of the lairds was a gradual one punctuated by one or two periods when their influence increased relatively quickly. The beginnings of their rise can be seen in the penetration of literate laymen into royal administration and the law at the expense of clerics, first evident during the reign of James III. Even in the fifteenth century lairds were far from being totally subservient to the magnates. An indication of their new wider horizons is the way in which large numbers of them went to Reformation Parliament when few had previously attended Parliament at all. Their place in Parliament had not been clear in the fifteenth and early sixteenth centuries and this sudden influx highlighted the potential threat which their uncontrolled attendance might pose to the influence of the magnates. In 1587 their position was regularised by making provision for the election of two representatives from each shire, with the exception of the two small counties of Clackmannan and Kinross which were allocated only one each. The Reformation abruptly curtailed the role of churchmen in government and the law offering greater scope for ambitious laymen. Although James VI was happier to rely on his magnates in a traditional manner, royal administration nevertheless expanded rapidly during his reign, most of the offices being held by men who had made dual careers in the law and administration. Some laird families were able to establish legal dynasties whose success eventually elevated them to the peerage like the Earls of Haddington who began as a cadet branch of the Hamiltons.

The traditional power of the aristocracy, exercised through kinship, feudal lordship and military leadership, was gradually replaced by political patronage. Following the Union of 1707 the attention of the magnates focused increasingly upon London and they became less directly involved in local affairs leaving a vacuum which was filled by active and ambitious lairds. The aristocracy forfeited their local dominance in their pursuit of wider goals.[1] This in turn strengthened the role of county government and the Justices, Sheriffs and Commissioners of Supply. Even so the county never developed into the strongly identified social and political unit that existed in England and the Justices did not acquire the authority of their English counterparts. As a result there was less prestige in the holding of offices of this sort than south of the Border.

In any consideration of Scottish rural society we must remember the power which proprietors had over the inhabitants of their estates. Controlling the number and size of tenancies was one mechanism. By allowing subdivision of existing holdings, the splitting of townships and the intake of new land they could increase the number of people on their lands. In areas where society remained disturbed until relatively late, close to the Border or on the margins of the Highlands for instance, the desire to preserve a large following of tenants which could be mobilised in time of need might result in the maintenance of relatively small holdings. Conversely, by amalgamating holdings and resisting subdivision landowners could create a more markedly polarised society. They could also control the numbers of cottars employed on each farm through their baron courts, or by conditions attached to leases. In addition, they had considerable influence over kirk sessions and their distribution of poor relief.

In a country where rural settlement was dispersed it is difficult to define those structures which bound the rural population into communities. The parish with its church, minister, kirk session and school provided a growing community focus from the later sixteenth century. Most Scottish parishes, even in the Lowlands, were large compared with their English counterparts though. Estates, particularly their judicial subdivisions or baronies, were also

1. R. Mitchison, *Lordship to Patronage, Scotland 1603–1746* (London 1983), pp. 161–76.

important in the day-to-day life of the population. Each barony had a defined caput or centre where courts were held, rents were paid and services discharged. A group of baronies, not necessarily contiguous, might be raised to the higher level of jurisdiction known as a regality. Regalities were in effect petty kingdoms in which royal authority was restricted to a very few major offences.

Baron courts have been viewed as instruments of feudal oppression by which proprietors could extort fines and extra services from their tenants or pursue private grudges rather than administer impartial justice. Doubtless this did happen but there was also a more positive side to their activities. Like English manorial courts they provided a forum where the tenants could meet and interpret custom. While many courts were dominated by the proprietor in his role of baron others maintained the older system of having cases judged by juries drawn from the tenantry. Court and estate officers were usually tenants too, faced with the same problems and pressures as their fellows and thus likely to be sympathetic to their difficulties. Proprietors could use their baron courts positively by passing acts encouraging tenants to make improvements such as sowing legumes and planting trees or to protect improvements. The court helped to bind the inhabitants of the barony together, providing an institution which, properly used, was fairly impartial. It was convenient to have a source of justice near at hand where cases could be dealt with quickly and judged by people who know the circumstances.

THE TENANT FARMERS

Below the landowners the tenant farmers formed the most important social group in terms of wealth and status. The condition of the tenantry is central to an understanding of early-modern Scottish rural society but they have received surprisingly little attention. Even so, we know more about them than any other group below the proprietors because they are mentioned in estate documents. Such records, however, inevitably reflect the preoccupations of landowners and their estate officers. Eighteenth-century writers on agricultural improvement saw them as reactionary, ignorant and conservative. Historians have tended to portray them as impoverished, fairly homogeneous and hardly differentiated from their cottars. There was more variation in Scottish rural society than has often been realised.

The proportion of the rural population made up of tenants and their families varied. They accounted for only around 20–25 per cent of heads of household in many parishes in lowland Aberdeenshire in the 1690s. In the Lothians and the Merse, where holdings were larger, the figure fell as low as 15 per cent; in Renfrewshire, with smaller farms, the figure was around 30–40 per cent. In parts of upland Aberdeenshire the figure rose as high as 80 per cent. There was considerable variation in the sizes of tenants' holdings between regions and on particular estates. At the lower end of the scale were crofters and pendiclers (smallholders) who must often have had by-employments and who were only distinguished from cottars by virtue of leasing their land direct from the proprietor rather than sub-letting from a tenant. At the other extreme were the occupiers of lowland arable farms assessed at two ploughgates or more, or the tenants of the 1,000-acre sheep runs of the eastern Borders.

The structure of the tenantry on any estate depended on landlord policy. Until well into the eighteenth century a substantial proportion of farms in many areas were worked by groups of tenants. Sometimes they held by a single joint lease, being communally responsible for the rent. More commonly tenants leased specific fractions of a farm and paid separate rents. Holdings on multiple-tenant farms tended to be small and there must have been a good deal of co-operation between the tenants in pooling equipment and labour for the main tasks in the agrarian year. In some areas sizable farms worked by a single-tenant family aided by cottars and servants were more common. Such holdings were not necessarily a new feature; substantial peasants leasing more than one holding are recorded from the fifteenth century. In the long term there appears to have been a gradual trend towards a reduction in the number of small tenancies on many estates and the creation of larger units. Such changes, though slow, had implications for the social structure. In communities where multiple-tenant farms divided into relatively small holdings were common, society was probably not markedly differentiated, distinctions between tenants and cottars being blurred. In areas where larger single-tenant farms were dominant society must have been more sharply polarised into tenants and cottars.

Several sixteenth- and seventeenth-century commentators stressed the adverse effects of insecurity of tenure. The prevalence of tenancies at will and short leases was blamed for poor farming standards and the lack of any desire to institute improvements. Such tenancies, allowing rents to be readily adjusted to match price fluctuations, were also considered to encourage rack-renting. Modern writers have assumed that insecurity of tenure was normal. Nevertheless, although sixteenth-century terms like 'kindly tenant' and 'rentaller' (Chapter 5) disappear after the early seventeenth century enduring paternalism and the strength of custom probably ensured that continuity was normal from lease to lease, generation to generation at rents long fixed by tradition. Studies of the tenantry are needed for a range of estates before firm conclusions can be drawn regarding stability and levels of turnover. In one example, the Panmure estates in Angus, there were elements of both stability and mobility among the tenantry.[2] Sixty-five per cent of the short written leases which were normal in the later seventeenth century were renewals to sitting tenants. Eighteen per cent recorded moves within the same barony of the estate, 3.5 per cent from other estate baronies and only 13.5 per cent were leases granted to tenants coming from outside. Forty-five per cent of the tenants stayed on holdings within the estate for under five years

2. I.D. Whyte and K.A. Whyte, Continuity and change in a seventeenth-century Scottish farming community, *Agricultural History Review*, 31, 1981, 151–69.

but 30 per cent stayed for over eleven years. Where moves were made within the estate, or on to the estate from outside, the distances involved were short; mobility was very localised.

Paternalism was still important in the later seventeenth century. On the Buccleuch estates in the central Borders the accounts of the annual land settings at Hawick show that it was normal, when a tenancy fell vacant, to offer it automatically to the tenant's heir, seemingly regardless of his abilities. If no son or close relative was willing to take on the holding it was offered to anyone else on the estate. Only as a last resort would lands be set to an outsider. This occurred under a system of annual leases and suggests that on many estates tenants could keep their farms for as long as they could work them and then pass them on to a son, provided that the family kept out of trouble and paid their rents fairly regularly. There must have been a good many holdings which had been occupied by the same family 'beyond memory of man'. Under such circumstances the tenant's identification with 'his' land must have been strong even if his legal rights to the continued occupation of it were not.

Holding size was crucial to the ability of tenants to survive a crisis and accumulate capital. This is often difficult to determine as most holdings continued to be measured in customary units such as ploughgates, husbandlands, oxgangs and merklands which had lost their original close relationship to the amount of land worked. In the seventeenth and eighteenth centuries it was possible for a more prosperous tenant to occupy a farm of perhaps 300 acres in the south-eastern Lowlands or a pastoral one of 1,000 acres in the Southern Uplands. Most tenants worked much smaller areas. The occupiers of many multiple tenant touns may have held only 30–40 acres or less in many parts of the Lowlands. In the north east, where holdings seem to have been smaller, 20–30 acres may have been more normal. When it is remembered that some of this land would have been uncultivated outfield in any year and that portions of infield were sublet to cottars it is easy to see why so many tenants lived close to the margins of subsistence.

On the Panmure estates there was a certain amount of mobility up and down the farming ladder with some tenants starting with small holdings and working their way up to larger ones.[3] This was not particularly common, however, and most farmers ended their careers on a similar-sized holding to the one that they started with. The amount of capital required to stock one of the largest farms on the estate was some 15 times that of a smaller holding. Capital accumulation on this scale within a single generation can rarely have been achieved. On the other hand, extreme downward mobility does not seem to have been great either. In the barony of Downie between 1660 and 1714 out of 118 tenants only 12 ended up on the poor roll and nine of these were smallholders. Indications are that social mobility from the cottar class into the tenantry was limited. This suggests that the various strata within the tenantry may have been entrenched and that it was not easy to work one's

3. Ibid.

way up from modest beginnings to occupy one of the largest farms. This in turn emphasises the importance of inherited wealth, whether as cash or farming stock. Various socioeconomic cycles may have existed within the rural community. A narrow one in which the children of cottars became farm servants and then, once married, became cottars can be postulated as well as more complex ones where a married cottar was able to use the labour of his children and take on the tenancy of a larger unit, subsequently reverting to cottar status when the children left home or alternatively using the labour or other cottars and servants to continue working the holding.

The evidence of testaments suggests that most farmers operated with slim reserves. Seventy-eight per cent of Panmure tenants in the later seventeenth century had debts at their death which, if they had all been called in at once, could only have been met by selling off some of the farming stock and equipment. Only a handful had a substantial credit surplus. On the other hand, a high proportion of most farmers' debts were rent arrears which may be considered as a special category. On Lowland farms where rents were paid in grain, the system of reckoning arrears during bad years worked against the tenant. Arrears were chalked up as cash values based on the market prices obtaining in the years of default. When rent arrears accumulated due to a bad harvest grain prices rose. These inflated cash arrears then had to be paid off from the meagre profits of succeeding years of glut and low prices. Arrears accumulated in a single bad season might hang over a tenant for years afterwards. At Panmure, following the crisis of the later 1690s, rent arrears from this period continued to be entered separately through the 1720s into the 1730s, falling only gradually as tenants died off rather than because sums were being repaid.

The picture of an impoverished tenantry must not be overdrawn, since wealthier tenants did exist. There were opportunities for accumulating capital through moneylending, trading and taking on posts in estate administration. A study of the Panmure tenantry suggests that during the seventeenth century the position of smaller tenants, in terms of their ability to accumulate capital, hardly improved but that larger tenants were distinctly better placed by the end of the century, probably widening divisions within rural society.[4] Even in the sixteenth century the sums of money owing in testaments indicates that there must have been flourishing, if usually small-scale, trade within the rural community, and an active money economy. Some tenants, even cottars, are recorded as having died in possession of sizable sums of ready cash or money out on loan. Cottars lent money to tenants, tenants lent to lairds and even to nobles. As in England widows, spinsters and the elderly were important providers of credit. Debt and credit was related to different life-cycle phases, many families probably being net recipients of credit at some stages of their lives and net providers at others. Smaller tenants and

4. I.D. Whyte and K.A. Whyte, Debt and credit, poverty and prosperity in a seventeenth-century Scottish rural community, in R. Mirchison and P. Roebuck (eds), *Economy and Society in Scotland and Ireland 1500–1939* (Edinburgh 1988), pp. 70–80.

cottars received and provided most of their credit within the farming community. Larger tenants drew on urban capital to a greater degree. Landowners were not significant suppliers of credit to the rural population, apart from allowing rent arrears, but were happy to borrow from the inhabitants of their estates.

No research has yet been done on the inheritance strategies of the farming population of early-modern Scotland. For tenant families the most important element must have been the ability to pass on their holdings along with the stock and equipment with which to work it. Given that proprietors did not usually subdivide holdings between the sons of deceased tenants, there must have been a continual pool of younger sons who may have tried to obtain other tenancies, sunk downwards into the ranks of the cottars, or moved out of farming.

Levels of rents were crucial in determining the prosperity of the tenants and of rural society as a whole. A traditional Scots saying, 'ane to saw [sow], and to gnaw, and ane to pay the laird witha', reflected a basic division of the product of a farm into a third for direct consumption, a third for seed corn, and a third for rent. That this level of calculation was indeed seen as normal is suggested by the custom of charging 'third and teind' (a third of the crop for rent plus a tenth for tithes) on land which had been recently brought into cultivation until its average product could be assessed or when land was granted in steelbow tenure where the proprietor provided the tenant with the necessary seed stock and implements as part of the lease. In eastern Lowland areas rents on assessed lands which had been fixed by custom in medieval times, were usually paid in victual. Where new land was taken into cultivation its rent was generally paid in money. Pastoral holdings in the Borders, many parts of the western Lowlands and along the margins of the Highlands generally paid rents in money either because they had been set for cash from early times or because commutation had occurred, the products of pastoral farming being more easily transported and marketed than grain surpluses.

The grain rents of farms in the eastern Lowlands were inflation proof and had long been fixed by custom. Assuming that they had originally been well adjusted to productivity there was little reason to alter them unless there was an expansion of the arable area or a new technique like liming increased yields. Makey has argued that in the western Lowlands customary rents in money also remained fixed and were steadily devalued by the effects of inflation in the later sixteenth century. Only in the mid-seventeenth century did proprietors in these areas begin to raise rents to compensate for devaluation.[5] Tenants in such areas should have enjoyed a boom period during the later sixteenth and early seventeenth centuries as the real value of their rents fell, followed by a period of adjustment in the middle and later seventeenth century when capital accumulation was harder. Rents did not always remain static and instances of rack-renting are known from the seventeenth century. A particularly short-sighted practice was to offer vacant holdings to the highest bidder, a process which tended to put off careful

5. W. Makey, *The Church of the Covenant* (Edinburgh 1979), pp. 164–78.

farmers and led to ridiculously high rents being offered by more optimistic men who rapidly went bankrupt.

Tenants were also liable for a range of small payments in kind; most often hens and eggs but also dairy produce, live animals, wool and coarse linen cloth. Such payments went a long way towards providing the basic food requirements of landlords' households though with the reduction in the size of feudal followings from the sixteenth century there was an increasing tendency to commute these rents to money payments. Other relics of feudalism which survived into the eighteenth century were labour services, notably on Lowland arable estates. These included work on the mains or home farm; ploughing, manuring, harrowing, harvesting and mowing hay. In addition, cutting peat and transporting it to the landowner's residence was often required while tenants who paid rents in grain were frequently bound to transport it to the nearest market centre or port. Such work was probably often performed by cottars rather than the tenants themselves. Many proprietors seem to have retained their mains under their own management merely to keep labour services in being. The system of thirlage, by which tenants were bound to have their grain ground at a particular estate mill, was widely resented. Mills were leased by the proprietor and the miller charged multures, a fixed proportion of their grain often around a twentieth but sometimes higher. Helping to maintain the fabric of the estate mill was a further imposition. The profitability of thirlage is demonstrated by the way that proprietors clung to it on some estates until the end of the eighteenth century.

THE PEOPLE BELOW

A high proportion of the rural population throughout Lowland Scotland was below the tenant class but little is known about them. They are rarely mentioned in estate records and although their names occur in parish registers, kirk session records, court books, poll tax listings and occasionally in testaments, they remain shadow people. The terminology used to categorise them is variable and complex. It is not always clear to what extent this reflects differences in usage between sources or variations in nomenclature through time and between regions. The most numerous social group were cottars who sublet small portions of arable land from the tenants with some grazing rights and a kaleyard for growing vegetables in return for providing labour. The term 'cottar' was a broad one which included people referred to in various sources as grassmen, hinds, half hinds, herds, shepherds and taskers. In areas like the Lothians hinds were really married servants, paid mainly in wages but the distinction between them and cottars paid in land is not always clear. In addition there was a landless group dependent upon wages such as dyke-builders, masons, slaters or common labourers whose numbers were probably fairly small.

Some cottars were full-time agricultural workers but many were part-time tradesmen. From this group were drawn the shoemakers, tailors, weavers and wrights who supplied the basic services required by rural communities. Single women, widows and spinsters, are also referred to as cottars. Testaments show that cottars rarely had much agricultural equipment; their plots were usually ploughed by the tenant for whom they worked. Clauses in leases suggest that cottar families were often attached to particular tenants and would move with them from one holding to another. The subdivision of what were often already small, marginal holdings to accommodate cottars, and the maintenance of such a significant smallholding element on the land was one of the most distinctive features of Lowland rural society and a barrier to improving agricultural productivity.

Living-in farm servants were another important element in Scottish rural society. They represented a life-cycle phase rather than a separate social group being young and unmarried. It must have been the normal experience of most cottar children and many from tenant families to leave home in their early teens and go into service in another household, often only a short distance away. In areas where holdings were small and could often be worked by family labour farm servants formed a small percentage of the rural workforce. Male farm servants accounted for only 8–9 per cent of recorded adult males in parts of upland Aberdeenshire in the poll tax lists of the 1690s. In the Lothians and Berwickshire, where larger holdings needing more hired labour predominated, the figure was as high as 40 per cent in some parishes.

Male and female servants were given bed and board as well as wages in kind and money. Wages rose with increasing age and experience. The fees of female servants in the Lothians in the 1690s ranged from £5–6 Scots a year to as much as £18 though relatively few earned more than £12. There was some difference in average wage levels between regions; they were higher in the Lothians, possibly due to the proximity of Edinburgh, than in the north east or western Scotland. Servants' contracts were normally for a year and as in England, they frequently left at the end of a contract and sought a new master. Movement of farm servants in this way was an important component of population mobility within the countryside. Because servants were young, unattached and mobile they were often seen as troublesome and disruptive. A high proportion of the cases of fornication coming before kirk sessions involved servants while Parliament tried to safeguard tenants by restraining the mobility of servants.

Rural communities contained craftsmen such as millers, smiths, weavers, tailors and wrights who were often part-time industrial workers with smallholdings. In some places, however, specialised industrial communities with full-time workforces occurred, most notably in coalmining and salt-making districts. In these communities labour relations and social conditions were highly distinctive. The rapid expansion of coal and salt production from the later sixteenth century, combined with the unpleasant and dangerous nature of the work, made it difficult for coal masters to recruit and retain a labour force. It was against this background that an Act of 1606 made colliers and salt-workers into serfs, a situation which was not fully ended until the later eighteenth century. There are indications that a form of bondage existed in mining areas in Fife in the later sixteenth century. Poor law legislation in 1579 and 1597 which allowed vagrants to be bound for life to employers may have provided the mechanism for this. The Act of 1606 seems to have been designed to prevent the poaching of labour by unscrupulous coal masters. Like many Scottish statutes of the period it probably set an official seal of approval on practices which were already widespread. The Act provided that colliers, coal bearers and salters could not be employed without a certificate from their previous master, or at least an explanation as to why they had left. Anyone who gave work to a collier without a proper certificate could be required to return them or face a fine. Serfdom arose as a by-product of this legislation. To retain their labour force, coal masters merely had to withhold certificates to prevent their workers from leaving. An Act of 1641 extended these measures to other specialist colliery workers such as gatesmen and windsmen. In 1661 a further Act ratified these statutes while one in 1672 allowed owners of coalmines, salt-works and manufactories to seize vagrants and put them to work.

Although in law a collier became bound simply by starting work in a mine, as a certificate was then needed before he could leave, custom required either a formal agreement or a longer period of service. It was accepted that colliers could become bound to their masters either by entering into a formal pact or by working for a year and a day. A runaway collier who remained at liberty for the same period was considered to have won his freedom. It became acknowledged that colliers could be sold or leased with their mines or moved from one pit to another at the will of their master. Formal contracts involved the payment of 'arles', a bounty on recruitment, and the entering of the collier's name in a record book. The children of colliers were often bound at baptism.

There were, however, some counterbalancing benefits for colliers.[6] Their wages were higher than those in agriculture and better than in English mines. Their housing was provided free or at a nominal rent and they also received a coal allowance. Cases of colliers receiving brutal treatment from mine foremen are recorded but under paternalistic proprietors like the Clerks of Penicuik their bondage may not have been seen as a serious handicap. Work disciplines were often relaxed but conditions were far from easy. In the Forth coalfields male colliers were expected to supply female bearers; wives, daughters or sisters, to haul the coal to the surface. Horse gins were not commonly used for raising coal before the eighteenth century and the women had to climb sets of ladders bearing burdens of a hundredweight or more. Even when winding equipment was installed the coal still had to be dragged to the shaft by women hauling sleds or primitive wheeled hutches, work which seems hard and degrading beyond belief.

In the past, salt-workers have been lumped together with colliers as one of

6. R.A. Houston, Coal, class and culture: labour relations in a Scottish mining community 1650–1750, *Social History*, 8, 1983, 1–18.

the most disadvantaged groups in early-modern Scottish society because they were included in the 1606 Act in similar terms. Whatley's recent studies of the Scottish salt industry has shown, however, that they were by no means as downtrodden as has sometimes been claimed.[7] Like coalmining salt boiling was hard, unpleasant and dangerous work but the master salters in charge of each pan received relatively high wages. The skills involved were considerable and seem to have been passed on from father to son making it unlikely that casual vagrant labour can have been used on a large scale. The possession of these skills gave the master salters considerable bargaining power with their employers. This, along with evidence that colliers were by no means as separate and isolated as has sometimes been portrayed, indicates that the status of colliers and salters may not have been so different in practice from other social groups.

Most visitors to Scotland in the sixteenth and seventeenth centuries who recorded their impressions commented on the country's poverty. For a high proportion of the rural population it would only have taken some random misfortune such as accident, illness, or the death of a spouse, to push them into real difficulty. The elderly, unable through age and infirmity to earn sufficient to maintain themselves, were particularly vulnerable as were orphaned children. So were widows and spinsters bearing in mind that rates of pay for women were much lower than for men. There was also a class of people who were fit to work but who were unemployed. Given the widespread access to land provided by the cottar system this group should, in theory, have been relatively small. Nevertheless, there were always those who, temporarily or more permanently, were cut off from a normal role in society; discharged soldiers and seamen, broken and bankrupt tenants, industrial workers during trade slumps. The authorities tried to make a clear distinction between those who were genuinely in need of assistance and 'sturdy beggars' who were not. In practice, however, there must have been a sliding scale within any community ranging from families who only needed occasional temporary assistance and those who were maintained permanently by official and unofficial charity.

Following the Reformation there was no co-ordinated effort to deal with the problem of poverty until an Act of Parliament in 1574 which was confirmed with only minor changes in 1579. The provisions of the Act were closely copied from the English statute of 1572 which set up the Elizabethan poor law. The different circumstances of Scotland, particularly the difficulty of enforcing such legislation in the localities, resulted in the Scottish act being virtually ignored until well into the seventeenth century. The legislation was not amended sufficiently to fit the structure of authority in Scotland. Responsibility for enforcing the legislation was placed on officials who did not exist using mechanisms which were patently unworkable. The reformed

7. C.A. Whatley, *The Scottish Salt Industry 1570–1850* (Aberdeen 1987) and A cast apart? Scottish colliers, work, community and culture in the era of 'serfdom' c1606–1799, *Scottish Labour History Society Journal*, 26, 1991, 3–20.

church and its kirk sessions took over poor relief, officially from 1592. Kirk sessions' poor funds came from voluntary contributions from parishioners and fines levied on those who offended against the kirk's discipline but the payment of sums from the poor box to both resident and vagrant poor was more an expression of simple Christian charity rather than an indication that kirk sessions were implementing a standardised poor law system.

Subsistence crises apart, there was a general problem of vagrancy during the sixteenth and seventeenth centuries. As with Tudor England, the Scottish authorities seemed obsessed with the problem of vagrancy. Scottish legislation echoed that of England in considering the able-bodied poor who were idle yet capable of work as a threat to social order, while reserving charity for the old and infirm. It is likely that, as in England, a rise in population lay behind the problem of vagrancy. There was a considerable difference between the official view of vagrants as a threat to the state, and reality. In a country where population was dispersed in small clusters and single dwellings there may, however, have been some reason for ordinary people as well as the legislature to be concerned about vagrancy. 'Sorning' or begging with menaces could threaten small outlying communities. With so much unsettled upland and moorland it was easy for beggars to move around and congregate. It was rare in England for vagrants to travel in large groups. In Scotland gangs of beggars may have been more common. The carrying of weapons seems to have persisted longer north of the Border and it was easy for gangs of armed vagrants to terrorise the countryside as did the band led by the celebrated gipsy James MacPherson who was hanged in Banff in 1700.

Kirk session records provide a more realistic view of vagrancy than official legislation. In many parishes where details have survived a substantial percentage of relief payments went to non-resident poor. In Monikie parish in Angus between 1660 and 1710 20 per cent of payments went to groups of 'strangers'.[8] Presumably these must often have been individual vagrants crowding together at the kirk door after a service. Insufficient research has been undertaken to determine whether patterns of vagrancy were similar to those in England, with net flows from upland areas to lowlands, from country to town. Some movements seem to have been more localised, often within specific circuits. At Monikie there are instances of particular named vagrants turning up and receiving relief for several years at the same time of year. Such movements may have been tied into seasonal rhythms in the market for casual labour. The proportion of men and women receiving relief, often around 75 per cent and 25 per cent respectively, compares with those in studies of English vagrants. Kirk session registers often hint at the reasons behind vagrancy. Blindness, infirmity and illness were the most important causes. The loss of homes and possessions by fire was a smaller but significant category. Some people such as shipwrecked seamen, discharged soldiers and the victims of highway robbery were clearly only receiving

8. I.D. Whyte and K.A. Whyte, Geographical mobility in a seventeenth-century Scottish rural community, *Local Population Studies*, 32, 1984, 45–53.

assistance temporarily. There were surprisingly few bankrupt tenants but a considerable number of payments to people who had once had some social status; people designated as former gentlemen and gentlewomen, ministers, schoolmasters, burgesses or their widows.

Many circumstances might reduce people to poverty. Widowhood, spinsterhood, old age, physical or mental infirmity or unexpected pregnancy are only a few. It is harder to determine the factors which forced people to take to the roads. Women tend to figure more frequently than men in lists of resident parish poor and so probably formed a majority of the poor in most communities. There were probably more old women in most rural communities than old men. Accidents and early death due to occupational hazards may have resulted in male life expectancy being significantly lower than that for women. The dominance of women in parish poor lists may also indicate that it was easier for men to obtain casual employment which kept them off the poor list. The fact that women accounted for a small proportion of vagrants suggests that they must often have been cared for within their respective communities. Relief from the parish poor fund would not have been sufficient to maintain them at home without charity from relatives or neighbours. Perhaps it was when such sources failed that women took to vagrancy. Women were sometimes recorded as travelling with their husbands and sometimes only with their children. The harsh side of vagrancy is also seen in kirk session registers with expenditure for graves and winding sheets to beggars found dead and for the burial of children of vagrant women. Many payments went to people with testaments who may have been travelling in search of work, requiring only temporary assistance. Some vagrants who received relief in East Lothian parishes had come from England; it is possible that casual relief may have been more generous north of the Border.

CHAPTER 10

URBAN DEVELOPMENT
c1500–c1750

Studies of early-modern Scottish urban development have tended to focus on the legal and institutional development of the burgh rather than the economies and societies of towns. Recent research has produced some important re-interpretations, integrating early-modern Scottish towns more closely with mainstream European urban history. Between the early sixteenth and mid-eighteenth centuries the economy and society of Scotland's towns changed considerably. The revival of trade in the later sixteenth century was linked with substantial population growth in Scotland's larger towns. One result of this was a marked increase in the proportion of Scotland's population which was urbanised. These and other influences altered the social and economic structure of the medieval burgh, transforming its tight-knit, relatively unstratified community. Change continued in the later seventeenth century, symbolised by the act of 1672 which dismantled most of the trading monopolies enjoyed by the royal burghs. Even so there were strong elements of continuity, particularly in institutional structures. These, often only slightly modified, continued to serve the pre-industrial town as well as the medieval burgh providing an important element of stability in urban life.

INSTITUTIONAL FRAMEWORKS

By the fifteenth century two groups of burghs had emerged, royal burghs and burghs of barony and regality. In the fifteenth and sixteenth centuries the royal burghs consolidated their system of trading monopolies which was strong by European standards. They became a more homogeneous group and their ability to define and pursue common interests gave them great unity and solidarity. This in turn gave them considerable political influence which allowed them to maintain their monopolies into the later seventeenth century. These privileges were granted and upheld by the crown in return for a major contribution to national taxation.

The solidarity of the royal burghs was reinforced by the development of the Convention of Royal Burghs, an independent assembly free from direct crown control which met up to four times a year, more often than any other national gathering, and to which each burgh sent representatives. The Convention apportioned the burghs' tax contribution among its members, regulated their affairs, promoted their interests and defended their rights. By the late fifteenth century burgh representatives, accustomed to meet in Parliament, were beginning to hold separate assemblies to air grievances, settle disputes and decide on common policies. These meetings grew into the Convention which was formally constituted in 1487 but became more prominent from the mid-sixteenth century. The Convention was thus created by the burghs themselves rather than the crown. It reflected the *laissez-faire* attitude of the Scottish monarchy and the decentralised nature of authority in late-medieval Scotland. The Convention was unique within Europe: it was not an independent political entity like the Hanseatic League but within a national framework it was extremely powerful. It regulated foreign trade through the staple at Veere and after 1707 it was the principal body in Scotland representing trading and industrial interests.

The privileges of royal burghs included the sole right to engage in foreign trade within specified hinterlands or 'liberties' which might embrace an entire sheriffdom. There is no parallel in Western Europe for the size of the liberties of Scottish royal burghs or for the completeness with which they carved up the country. During the sixteenth and seventeenth centuries the creation of new royal burghs, usually by the promotion of baronial burghs, was vigorously opposed by existing royal burghs because the liberties of new centres had to be carved out of those of the old ones to the detriment of their trade. The pace of creation of new royal burghs was thus slow.

By the sixteenth century early ecclesiastical burghs like Glasgow and St Andrews were being treated in a similar way to those founded by the crown. From the fifteenth century, however, another category of trading centre began to emerge, burghs of barony and regality held from lay and ecclesiastical landowners. Their merchants were not allowed to engage in foreign trade and could only buy and sell within the confines of the burgh, not in the surrounding countryside which fell within the liberty of some royal burgh. The development of baronial burghs was opposed by neighbouring royal burghs and more generally by the Convention. The full privileges of the royal burghs were confirmed in 1633 but the very fact that such a confirmation was felt necessary suggests that their position was under attack. Some baronial burghs in the early seventeenth century were openly flaunting the restrictions placed on their trading activities. After the Restoration the tide of opinion began to turn against the royal burghs and their monopolies which were increasingly seen as restrictive and outdated. An Act of 1672 gave baronial burghs most of the rights to overseas trade enjoyed by royal burghs. The latter won back some concessions in 1690 but the old monopolistic system was effectively dismantled leaving baronial burghs free to compete with their royal neighbours.

PATTERNS OF URBANISATION

According to figures calculated by de Vries in 1500 under 2 per cent of the population of Scotland lived in towns with more than 10,000 inhabitants.[1] Most burghs were small, mere villages in scale whatever their pretensions. If levels of urbanisation are used as a measure of economic development then Scotland at this time had more in common with other peripheral areas of Europe like Scandinavia and Ireland than with more highly urbanised countries like England, the Low Countries and Italy. As Table 10.1 shows, this position began to change in the later sixteenth century. Between the sixteenth and the late eighteenth centuries Scotland had one of the highest growth rates of urban population in Europe. Scotland appears to have been the only European country to share the English pattern of a steady expansion of urban population throughout the period irrespective of whether national population totals were growing or stagnating. By 1750 Scotland was already more highly urbanised, on this measure, than France, Germany or Iberia, and was rapidly catching up with England.

Towns with over 10,000 inhabitants were the tip of the iceberg. If larger centres grew at a different rate from smaller towns, particularly if they increased their populations at the expense of smaller burghs, the picture in Table 10.1 may be misleading. This point is especially important as de Vries has characterised the period from the first half of the seventeenth century to c1750 as one in which, throughout Europe, urbanisation tended to stagnate with cities growing at the expense of smaller towns. Moreover, urban population growth and prosperity were not always directly linked.

Scottish overseas trade had been depressed for much of the sixteenth century leading to increasing competition between towns for larger shares of a diminishing income. Edinburgh, and to a lesser extent Aberdeen, Dundee, Glasgow and Perth, consolidated their positions relative to other towns. An inevitable result was the decay of many middle-rank towns. Equally, Scotland's distinctive pattern of trade, dominated by the export of unprocessed or partly processed primary products and imports of manufactures, hindered the development of urban industry and encouraged a proliferation of small centres whose role in overseas trade was disporportionate to their size. Many of the most important middle-order towns, such as Ayr, Dumfries and Inverness, were relatively remote from the large regional centres and this may have helped give them a more independent role.

During the later sixteenth and early seventeenth centuries many towns grew rapidly. Edinburgh may have had a population of about 2,500 in the fourteenth century. By 1560 this had risen to around 12,000, or perhaps 15–18,000 if the suburbs and Leith are included. By the 1640s Edinburgh's

1. J. de Vries, *European Urbanization 1500–1800* (London 1985), p. 39.

Table 10.1   Urbanisation in Scotland, England and Wales[2]

Percentage of total population in towns with over 10,000 inhabitants

	1500	1550	1600	1650	1700	1750	1800
Scotland	1.6	1.4	3.0	3.5	5.3	9.2	17.3
England and Wales	3.1	3.5	5.8	8.8	13.3	16.7	20.3

Population in towns with over 10,000 inhabitants (thousands)

	1500	1550	1600	1650	1700	1750	1800
Scotland	13	13	30	35	53	119	276
England and Wales	80	112	255	495	718	1021	1870

Percentage increase in urban population from previous date

	1500	1550	1600	1650	1700	1750	1800
Scotland	–	0	130	17	51	124	132
England and Wales	–	40	128	94	45	42	83

population had doubled as had those of other large burghs such as Aberdeen. In the early 1640s plague abruptly checked urban growth in Edinburgh and other large towns with around a fifth of the population perishing. It is possible to use various sources including an assessment of the rents of property in the royal burghs in 1639, the hearth tax data for 1691 and Webster's census of 1755 to calculate the approximate proportions of the Scottish population living in towns of various sizes (Table 10.2). Scotland was clearly a country of many small towns. Centres with populations of under 5,000 had almost as large a share of the urban population as those with over 10,000. Like many other European countries there was a lack of medium-sized towns in the 5,000–10,000 range. The percentage of the population living in smaller urban centres was larger than in England until the later eighteenth century. Relatively little is known about the activities that went on in these smaller burghs, how they varied in their economic and social structures, and how they were linked with the larger towns. Nor is it easy to distinguish between small towns and settlements which were essentially rural. Many royal burghs, tiny in terms of population, had corporate structures and engaged in foreign trade. The poll tax records for the

2. Ibid.

Table 10.2 Percentage of total population in Scottish towns

	1560	1639	1691	1755	1790s
Capital	1.1	2.7	4.5	4.5	5.6
Other towns over 10,000	0.0	3.5	2.7	4.4	10.8
5,000–9,999	0.6	3.3	1.6	3.2	3.2
2,000–4,999	0.8	2.2	3.1	4.2	6.4
1,000–1,999	?	?	3.5	?	6.3
500–999	?	?	?	?	3.4
Total in towns over 2,000	2.5	11.7	11.9	16.3	26.0

1690s suggest that there was a divide between urban and rural at a population of around 450–500. Small burghs of this size such as Fraserburgh and Peterhead had a range of professional services, a group of merchants and all the major branches of manufacturing. Below this level the range of functions diminished rapidly and settlements, even if larger than the normal run of kirk touns, were not truly urban.

In its preponderence of small centres Scotland most closely resembles Ireland or Scandinavia. Unlike Ireland, Denmark or Sweden, however, where the capital cities held high percentages of the total urban population, Edinburgh's dominance was reduced by the existence of major regional centres. The Danish and Swedish urban systems were influenced by the centralised nature of administration in these countries. The size and relative independence of regional centres in Scotland may in turn reflect the more decentralised pattern of control.

It is instructive to compare the distribution of the Scottish urban population among towns of different sizes with those of neighbouring countries (Table 10.3). The Scottish figures for 1639 mark a peak of urban prosperity, and probably population before the disruption of the Scottish Revolution. Comparison with figures for England c1600 show, not surprisingly, that Edinburgh held a much smaller percentage of Scotland's population than London did of England's but the rest of the Scottish urban hierarchy is unexpectedly strong compared with England. The proportion of Scotland's population living in centres with over 2,000 inhabitants in 1639 may have been as great or even greater than in England, even allowing for substantial growth of English towns between 1600 and 1639. Despite rapid growth in the later seventeenth century Dublin still held a smaller proportion of Ireland's population than Edinburgh did of Scotland's, although in Scotland middle-rank centres were weaker than in Ireland. Although the dominance of

Table 10.3 Comparative distribution of urban population in various countries

	Scotland		Ireland		England		Denmark
	1639	1691	1660	1680s	1600	1700	1672
Capital	2.7	4.5	1.5	3.5	4.5	10.6	8.8
Other towns over 10,000	3.5	2.7	0.8	3.8	1.3	2.6	0
5,000–9,999	3.3	1.6	0.5	2.3	1.9	2.7	0
2,000–4,999	2.6	3.1	2.3	3.1	1.0+	2.2+	4.7
1,000–1,999	?	3.5	2.0	?	?	?	3.7
500–999	?	?	1.6	?	?	?	3.4
Total in towns over 2,000	12.1	11.9	5.1	12.6	8.7+	18.1+	13.5

London over the English urban system contrasts with Edinburgh's smaller proportion of the Scottish population, at lower levels the English and Scottish hierarchies were not markedly different. In Denmark Copenhagen was about the same size as Edinburgh but held nearly twice the proportion of the national population. Denmark was devoid of other large towns and urban life, outside the capital, was dominated by smaller centres to a greater degree than Scotland.

No data are available from which population figures can be calculated for a range of towns at any time during the sixteenth century. The rankings of towns in the royal burgh taxation list from 1535 give an indication of economic success and decline. Sharp changes in tax assessment suggest that middle-rank towns experienced recurrent short-term economic crises against a background of longer-term difficulty.[3] Even major regional centres like Perth and Glasgow did not escape although they were more resilient than smaller towns. The high level of dependence upon the export of a limited range of primary products rendered Scottish towns particularly vulnerable to sudden shifts in the patterns of supply and demand. To what extent these ups and downs were accompanied by population changes has yet to be established. One group of prospering centres were the Fife burghs which increased their share of the tax contribution four times between 1535 and 1600. Economic growth, however, was not necessarily accompanied by population growth.

3. M. Lynch (ed.), *The Early Modern Town in Scotland* (London 1987), pp. 4–7.

Urban growth continued into the early seventeenth century then ceased. The period of the Scottish Revolution did not encourage urban growth. All towns were affected by social and economic instability, high taxation, and the quartering of troops. None of the burghs north of the Tay escaped dislocation in the mid-1640s. Among the larger towns Aberdeen and Dundee suffered badly from military action. Aberdeen was occupied by five armies in 1639 each making demands for supplies, quartering and finance. The town was also sacked by Montrose's army in 1644, before losing nearly 2,000 inhabitants in the plague outbreak of 1647. During the 1640s 32 merchant vessels belonging to Aberdeen were lost while large sums of money were spent on the defence of the town and on maintaining quartered troops. Aberdeen's population, perhaps around 9,000 in 1640 had fallen to around 6,000 by the 1650s. Dundee was stormed by Monck's forces in 1651 leaving up to 800 dead and causing enormous losses from plundering.

South of the Tay there was less direct damage due to war but the disruption of trade, high taxation and quartering took its toll. In such unsettled conditions there was growing reluctance to hold office in the burghs and many wealthy inhabitants fled the major towns to escape taxation or plundering leaving a growing tax burden to be shouldered by those who remained. Edinburgh continued to consolidate its hold over Scottish trade at the expense of other large towns until the collapse of the covenanting regime in 1649–50. Following this the grip of the capital slackened markedly. In 1670 the town's share of the royal burghs' tax assessment was lowered from 36 per cent to 33 per cent. The change may have been even more significant as the 36 per cent was probably a substantial underestimate of the city's pre-revolution trade and wealth.

For the later seventeenth and early eighteenth centuries Lynch has suggested that while Edinburgh and Glasgow continued to grow other large towns, notably Aberdeen and Dundee, stagnated or even declined and that there was a general decline of population in the smaller royal burghs.[4] Certainly the proportion of the population in towns with over 2,000 inhabitants seems to have remained about level between 1639 and 1691. While Edinburgh grew substantially the share of urban population in other large and medium-sized towns does appear to have fallen. To some extent this was balanced by the growth of certain smaller towns including baronial burghs.[5] Some were satellites of Edinburgh and Glasgow, such as Dalkeith and Musselburgh, Greenock and Hamilton. Others were specialised small ports like Culross, old established inland trading centres including Cupar, Forfar and Linlithgow, and Border burghs such as Jedburgh, Kelso and Selkirk which benefited from growing overland trade with England. Contemporary perceptions concerning whether towns were stagnating or

4. Ibid., and M. Lynch, Urbanisation and urban networks in seventeenth- century Scotland, *SESH*, 12, 1992, 24–41.
5. I.D. Whyte, The growth of periodic market centres in Scotland 1600–1707, *Scottish Geographical Magazine*, 95, 1979, 13–26.

expanding varied. Sir Robert Sibbald, writing in 1698, claimed that towns had grown generally and cited the example of Bo'ness: 'Ther was a gentleman died since the year 1660 who remembered that ther was bot one house wher now ther is the town of Borrostoness.' To set against the expansion of Bo'ness, one of the most successful baronial burghs, a report on the royal burghs in 1692 painted a dismal picture of declining trade and ruinous tenements in a number of middle-rank towns. Overall the urban system stagnated and may even have declined in the later seventeenth century.

During the first half of the eighteenth century Edinburgh and Aberdeen increased their populations only moderately but Glasgow doubled in size while Dundee grew by around 50 per cent. Some second-rank towns like Dumfries, Montrose, Perth and Stirling seem to have grown while others did not. By contrast baronial burghs like Alloa and Greenock may have expanded almost as fast as Glasgow. Growth in the urban sector at this period was still linked primarily to trade, and to service activities which had not yet filtered far down the urban hierarchy. The rapid growth of new industrial centres was still to come. In England the old urban hierarchy, inherited from medieval times, changed markedly during the eighteenth century. In Scotland the urban hierarchy was more stable; the most remarkable long-term change was the rise of Glasgow. Due to the lack of vigorous middle-order towns the old-established provincial centres were able to maintain their pre-eminence. Many of the fastest-growing towns of the later eighteenth century were effectively satellites of these regional centres, notably Paisley and Greenock.

Recent research on Scottish towns has tended to focus on the sixteenth and seventeenth centuries. The decades between the Union and the onset of large-scale industrialisation have received less attention. We have some knowledge about the development of Glasgow, the great success story of the first half of the eighteenth century, and the activities of the merchant communities of the larger burghs. But we know less about how urban economies and social structures developed during this period in either the larger or the smaller towns. An important aspect of the success of individual towns during the first half of the eighteenth century was how they coped with the problems and opportunities brought by the Union of 1707. The ways in which individual towns reacted to post-1707 trading conditions helped to determine their success later in the century. The positive effects on Glasgow's trade are well known. The impact on other towns was less beneficial. Jedburgh, close to the Anglo-Scottish border, went into a decline after 1707 and the effects of the Union were still being blamed for its moribund condition at the end of the eighteenth century.

The records of the Convention for the early eighteenth century present a picture, superficially, of widespread urban decline. A pessimistic interpretation would view this as a continuation of the prolonged urban decay of the seventeenth century, exacerbated by more recent economic difficulties. Sometimes this can be related to a specific industry like the collapse of the export of plaiding from Aberdeen or the drop in exports of coal, salt and ironware from Culross. In many cases economic activity was being redistributed rather than reduced. The demise of the ironware industry in Culross was largely due to competition from neighbouring manufacturers in Valleyfield. Other evidence of decline should also be treated with caution. Decaying harbours may have been the result of storm damage rather than a fall in trade. The poor state of public buildings in a burgh may indicate a crisis in urban finances but not necessarily an impoverished community. While the volume of official trade passing through some burghs was undoubtedly falling many of the inhabitants may have benefited from smuggling, which assumed large proportions in the early eighteenth century. The changes in the rankings of the royal burgh tax lists show Glasgow as having had the greatest increase in the early eighteenth century but Dumfries and Kirkwall, a staging post on the trans-Atlantic route, also improved their positions. By contrast a group of burghs in Fife including Burntisland, Crail, Cupar, Culross, Dysart, Inverkeithing, Kirkcaldy and St Andrews had their tax contributions reduced. This may represent the continuation of the decline which has been noted at an earlier period.

Scotland was not characterised by a single over-large primate city like England or Ireland in the seventeenth century. In the 1690s Edinburgh was little more than twice the size of the second city, Glasgow. The combined populations of Glasgow, Aberdeen, Dundee and Perth equalled or even exceeded that of the capital. This suggests that in Scotland the role of the major provincial centres was greater than in England, reflecting the strong element of localism within Scottish society. The dominance of the urban hierarchy by the 'four great burghs of Scotland', Edinburgh, Aberdeen, Dundee and Perth was maintained from the mid-fourteenth century to the mid-seventeenth.[6] Perth declined relative to the others, due in part to the silting of the Tay which cut its overseas trade and to the murder of James I there in 1437 which led to the court ceasing to use Perth as a residence. In 1535 the big four paid 52 per cent of burgh taxation and by 1613 54 per cent. By 1697, however, the pattern had changed with 55 per cent being paid by only two centres, Edinburgh and Glasgow, the former alone accounting for 40 per cent.

Regional patterns of urbanisation are also interesting. The Highlands were almost devoid of towns but many parts of the Lowlands, notably the south west, west and north east, had only a scattering of small burghs. On the other hand the area around the Firth of Forth was highly urbanised. By the later seventeenth century over 40 per cent of the population of this region lived in towns, a figure higher than contemporary East Anglia and comparable with parts of the Netherlands. Much of the activity which sustained smaller towns in this area was generated by Edinburgh but the functions of the capital changed during the seventeenth century. Early in the century Edinburgh had been a major entrepôt with a near monopoly on many sectors of Scotland's trade. In the second half of the century the city's economy moved decisively

6. Lynch, *The Early Modern Town in Scotland*, pp. 4–5.

to that of an administrative centre with a concentration of employment in the professions and the service sector. The impact of such changes on the surrounding region has yet to be properly assessed.[7]

Rapid urban growth in early-modern Scotland has many implications. The increasing urban population required feeding. That it *was* fed and that a substantial volume of grain was exported in most years during the later seventeenth and early eighteenth centuries suggests that Scottish agriculture was not as inefficient as has sometimes been suggested. The implication must be that productivity per head in agriculture was rising, albeit modestly, whether by the development of better techniques or improved organisation. To what extent the increasing demand for food from the urban sector generated greater prosperity for landlord and tenant has yet to be determined, or whether this in turn stimulated demand for urban goods and services. The supply of food to the growing towns must have had an impact on transport and internal trading.

Urban growth must have had major effects on agriculture in the immediate vicinity of the larger burghs. For the larger towns to grow as they did there must have been a steady influx of migrants from the countryside, especially young single people like apprentices and servants. It is easy, however, to forget the counter-current of people moving back to the countryside. In early-modern Scotland this must have included apprentices who had served their time. The poll tax records suggest that in the 1690s the four largest Scottish towns must have employed at least 12,000 female domestic servants. Many of these would have come from the countryside and some would have returned there to marry. This reverse movement also represents a flow of money from the towns to the countryside in the form of remittances or accumulated savings. Return migration from the towns must also have helped spread new ideas and fashions like tea drinking and the wearing of imported cloth. These appeared first in the larger towns and were transmitted into rural areas in the course of the eighteenth century.

SMALL TOWNS: THE CHALLENGE OF THE BARONIAL BURGHS

The foundation of large numbers of new towns, primarily as trading centres, is usually considered a feature of medieval Europe. In Scotland, however, new towns were still being established in the sixteenth and seventeenth centuries. Scotland had this in common with Sweden where the late sixteenth and seventeenth centuries was a period of vigorous urban foundation. The spread of baronial burghs in Scotland occurred much later than that of seigneurial foundations in England. The fact that new centres were being created in Scotland suggests a degree of immaturity in the urban system. Unlike Sweden, however, new towns were not founded as part of a policy to

7. Lynch, Urbanisation.

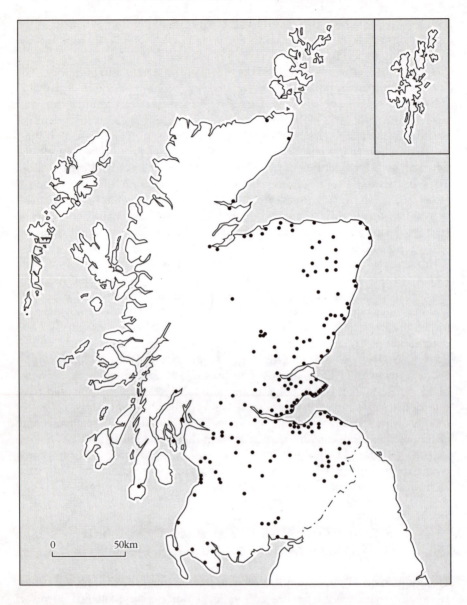

Map 10.1 Distribution of Market Centres in 1600

extend central control over peripheral areas. Nor were fortress and garrison functions important in Scotland as they were with many continental new towns. Little is known about the motives which led landowners to establish baronial burghs or the degree to which they provided capital for facilities and infrastructure. Moreover, the role and functions of these new centres within the developing urban system is still far from clear.

Between 1500 and the early eighteenth century around 270 new baronial

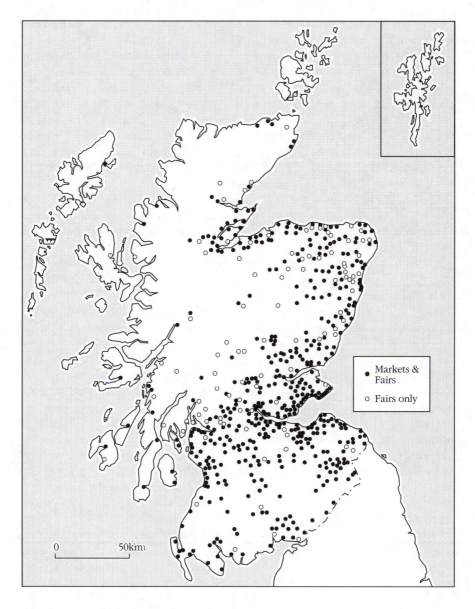

Map 10.2 Distribution of Market Centres in 1707

burghs were authorised in Scotland. The pace of foundation reached a peak in the decades after the Restoration before tailing off sharply after the Union of 1707. It is impossible to be precise about numbers because it is sometimes difficult to differentiate between new foundations and efforts to re-establish burghs which had declined or whose rights were not clearly defined. The establishment of so many new centres, even allowing for a high failure rate, suggests that internal trading expanded, particularly after the Restoration when over 40 per cent of the new foundations were authorised and a large number of non-burghal market centres were also licensed.[8]

In trying to establish how many of the new centres achieved genuine urban status various indices are useful including the development of corporate administrative structure, the existence of functioning markets and fairs, the possession of diversified occupational structures and a certain minimum population size. Population provides the best overall measure of success or failure. Only about a quarter of the burghs of barony founded after 1500 had reached a population of 500 by the later eighteenth century. These new centres tended to fill the lower levels of an urban hierarchy dominated by royal burghs and burghs of barony founded before 1500.

The high failure rate of baronial burghs is hardly surprising. Some of their charters were obtained due to rivalry between neighbouring proprietors. Other centres were founded in good faith but failed to prosper. Some foundations succeeded for a time then declined. Most proprietors who obtained a burgh charter were probably only seeking to attach market and fair rights to existing rural settlements without any intention of developing them as towns. The failure rate of post-1500 baronial burghs is substantially reduced if the existence of functioning markets and fairs rather than size or the possession of a corporate structure is used as a measure of success. In Aberdeenshire in the early eighteenth century there were at least a dozen baronial burghs which, although rural rather than urban in character, had active markets and fairs. Some baronial burghs, notably the coal and salt towns of the Forth, had an industrial base but most were established with the aim of generating or capturing trade.

There was no need for a landowner to invest a lot of capital in burgh development. By the early sixteenth century, however, landowners who obtained charters for baronial burghs had the right to establish burgesses and create institutions with a degree of self-government. The need to apportion land to burgesses entailed an organised land division and might initiate a new planned settlement. As with many later planned villages, proprietors passed on much of the cost of development to the inhabitants. With a coastal settlement the provision of a harbour was sometimes an important pre-requisite for success and required a more substantial outlay as at Fraserburgh, developed by Sir Alexander Fraser of Philorth. Providing harbour facilities was particularly useful where the main function of a baronial burgh was to act as an outlet for the export of estate resources. This was particularly the case with the coal and salt-producing burghs of the Firth of Forth. On the other hand, such infrastructure was not essential and landlord investment could be kept to a minimum.

Instances of large-scale capital investment by landowners are less common but the Earl of Winton at Port Seton, the Earl of Wemyss at Methil, the Duke of Hamilton at Bo'ness and Sir Robert Cunningham at Saltcoats were all involved in major industrial and urban developments. The Erskines of Mar

8. Whyte, The growth of periodic market centres.

turned Alloa from a squalid collier village into a thriving town as part of a programme of development which began with their adjacent mansion and grounds but extended to laying out new streets, rebuilding the houses, and financing a range of industries including sawmilling, rope-making, sailcloth manufacture, a woollen mill and brewing. The town became a major growth point for the upper Forth estuary attracting a good deal of trade away from Bo'ness.

The factors which encouraged some baronial burghs to succeed to a degree where they could be considered as real towns included a reasonable distance from competing royal burghs, a degree of landlord involvement, a range of functions which provided the basis for development and the ability to generate trade at more than a local level. One example of such a modest success story was Langholm in Dumfries-shire. The settlement grew from 10 plots of land feued by the Earl of Nithsdale in 1621. The feuars were required to build two-storey houses of stone and lime facing each other across a street at least 30 feet wide. By the early eighteenth century Langholm had grown into a small town with a range of crafts. It was the seat of the court of the regality of Eskdale, a function which helped to bring in business from the surrounding area. Its markets and fairs were handling a flourishing trade in local produce. At the other end of the country Thurso had received its charter in 1633. A century or so later it had a population of around 1,200 and the income from its tolls and market charges brought its patrons, the Sinclairs of Ulbster, a revenue of 500 merks a year. Thurso had captured many of the functions formerly discharged by Wick, the official sheriffdom centre, and had a thriving export trade in grain, livestock products and fish.

By the early seventeenth century the two-tier structure of burghs was becoming obsolete. There is a mounting body of complaint in the records of the Convention during the first 30 years of the seventeenth century against infringements of trade regulations by baronial burghs. The Revolution and Cromwellian occupation brought economic disruption to Scotland's major towns allowing the inhabitants of baronial burghs to encroach still further. Although the Restoration brought more stable conditions the status quo was never quite restored. It was understandable that many nobles, in financial difficulties after Cromwellian fines and taxation, should have sought to maximise the commercial potential of their estates. With the return of their influence at court and in government they were able to pursue their interests more successfully against the royal burghs.

The Act of 1672 which removed most of the monopolies on foreign trade possessed by the royal burghs was an important shift in economic policy. It represented a victory for the landowners who were able to impose a more realistic trading framework on the conservative royal burghs. Individual profit and ambition was probably involved too. The Act was pushed through with the support of the Duke of Lauderdale, Charles II's Secretary for Scotland. He also had a personal interest through his control of the large baronial burgh of Musselburgh. In 1661 he had succeeded in having Cromwell's old citadel at Leith erected into a separate burgh of regality outside the control of

Edinburgh. He blackmailed the city's authorities by threatening to develop it as a rival trading centre. Whether he could have done so is immaterial; Edinburgh's council panicked and bought him off. Whatever the motives involved, the 1672 Act helped create a more open network of trading centres. The royal burghs protested that the old system had facilitated the collection of customs and that any changes would imperil their ability to meet their share of national taxation. Supporters of the unfree burghs argued in turn that the more trading outlets there were the richer the country was likely to be.

As well as the spate of new baronial burghs after 1660 nearly 150 other centres were granted the right to hold markets and fairs without enjoying burghal privileges.[9] It is difficult to be sure to what extent such new centres reflected an expansion or merely a redistribution of trade. A significant number of new market centres were located within the southern and eastern Highlands or along their margins, in areas previously poorly supplied with marketing outlets. Such centres are likely to have encouraged a real growth of trade; the rise of the cattle trysts at Crieff is one example. Many new centres were authorised in areas already well supplied with trading outlets. Sir George Mackenzie, writing in 1669, considered that the creation of so many new centres was detrimental by spreading the existing volume of trade through too many small market centres. The protests against the activities of unfree traders and burghs which dominate the records of the Convention in the late seventeenth and early eighteenth centuries only tell one side of the story though. Many royal burgh merchants were effectively undermining the old system by operating through the baronial burghs and entering into partnerships with unfree traders.

The Act of 1672 did not result in a massive expansion in overseas trade by merchants in baronial burghs though a few in towns like Bo'ness and Kilmarnock are recorded trading abroad. The royal burghs lobbied for the restoration of their privileges but were fobbed off by Charles II's administration. James VII also refused to help. The royal burghs were more successful after the Revolution of 1688. They drafted an Act restricting the trade of baronial burghs and in 1690 it was passed though with less generous provisions than the royal burghs had hoped for. The import of foreign goods was to be restricted to royal burghs as well as the export of most manufactures but baronial burghs could export agricultural produce and raw materials. This was a sensible compromise but the royal burghs believed, correctly, that many baronial centres would continue to trade under the terms of the 1672 Act. The 1690 legislation marked the start of a long wrangle in which the royal burghs, resigning themselves to the baronial burghs' encroachments, tried to force them to accept 10 per cent of their taxation. The right to participate in foreign trade was granted to baronial burghs whose inhabitants would undertake to contribute to the royal burghs' tax burden. In doing so the Convention implicitly recognised that the old system had

9. Ibid.

changed for good. The baronial burghs were slow to co-operate but some 130 settlements eventually participated in the scheme, their tax contribution ranging from the 16 shillings in every £100 paid by Bo'ness to a mere penny per £100 from many of the smallest centres. The Convention had alternatively to coax and coerce baronial burghs to contribute their share of taxation, measures which met with varying, but never total, success. By 1728 the accumulated arrears were equal to four times the total annual tax contribution due by all the baronial burghs.

EARLY-MODERN SCOTTISH TOWNS: FORM AND FABRIC

Population growth, increases in prosperity for some sectors of the urban population, and changes in the economies and social structures of Scottish towns from the sixteenth to the eighteenth centuries had marked effects on their layout and appearance. Visitors, particularly from England, often commented on the small size and mean appearance of the many small burghs but the larger towns received some praise. Travellers were particularly impressed with Edinburgh. The length and width of the High Street excited admiration, as did the quality of its surface which was first paved in 1532; 'the most stately and graceful street that I ever saw' commented Sir William Brereton in 1636. Nearly a century later Defoe was even more effusive: 'perhaps the largest, longest and finest street for buildings and number of inhabitants in the world'. The height of the tenements lining the High Street was also a matter for wonder but the practice of facing them with timber boards was seen as a disfigurement. In 1600 the Duc de Rohan described the city as so densely packed 'that there can hardly be another town so populous for its size'. On the other hand, the dark, evil smelling closes filled with rubbish, and the general low standard of cleanliness of the inhabitants were universally condemned. Contemporary accounts of other regional centres are also favourable. One visitor in the 1660s considered Glasgow 'fair, large and well built ... somewhat like Oxford'. New public buildings like the tolbooth, Hutcheson's Hospital and the Merchants' Hall had enhanced the appearance of the town. Defoe described Glasgow as 'a very fine city; the four principal streets are the fairest for breadth and the finest built I have ever seen in one city together ... the cleanest, and beautifullest and best built city in Britain, London excepted'. He also considered Aberdeen and Dundee well-built and attractive.

A few Scottish towns were still walled. John Major, writing in 1521, claimed that the Scots put their faith in the prowess of their armies and not in defended towns. This was mere boasting; the real limiting factor was cost. Few towns could afford to adapt their medieval walls to the new, expensive technology of artillery fortification. Nevertheless, some towns upgraded their medieval walls, Edinburgh, Dundee, Perth and Stirling among them. The inhabitants of Peebles built an entirely new wall with towers and gun loops as late as the 1570s following attacks on the town by raiders from the Scottish side of the Border. Edinburgh's early defences were replaced during the first half of the sixteenth century by the Flodden Wall which enclosed a larger area to the south of the High Street, protecting the city on the west, east and south sides. The deep valley to the north was dammed to form the Nor Loch which served in place of a wall. In other towns, however, walls symbolised the desire of burgesses to defend their burghs against attack by unfree traders rather than armed aggressors. Walls allowed the movement of people and goods in and out of a town to be controlled. Tolls could be collected at gates or 'ports' which could be closed at night. Vagrants could be turned away and towns sealed off in time of plague. Most of the larger burghs marked their limits by some kind of boundary between burgh and landward, burgess and unfree trader.

There was rarely a sharp visual demarcation between town and country though. Bird's-eye views of Scottish towns in the sixteenth and seventeenth centuries show that most were not densely built up; they had plenty of open space occupied by gardens, orchards and smallholdings. The burgh courts of towns like Lanark and Peebles contain frequent Acts regulating the freedom of livestock within the built-up area. Beyond most towns lay the rigs of the burgh's arable land and the common muir where animals could be grazed under the supervision of the town's herd. In the sixteenth and seventeenth centuries population growth in the larger towns and increasing prosperity for at least some of the inhabitants influenced the character and density of housing. The demand for more accommodation encouraged the infilling of the rear of burgage plots with housing and workshops. Such structures were often flimsier and more of a fire risk than buildings along the street frontage while the presence of industries requiring the use of forges and kilns added to the danger. After a serious fire in 1652 the Glasgow candlemakers were banished to the outskirts of the burgh to join craftsmen like the fleshers whose slaughterhouses were too noisome to be allowed close to the town centre.

Pressure on space also led to encroachment on the streets and market-places. The owners of plots with street frontages might fill in the ground floor arcades with shops or allow wooden fore-booths to be erected against the building. In Gladstone's Land in Edinburgh the replacement of timber balconies by stone arcades in the early seventeenth century allowed the building line to be extended further into the High Street. Traders who were allowed to set up stalls in the market-place sometimes managed to replace them with more permanent structures. The colonisation of market-places in this way is especially evident in Haddington and Stirling where the original market area must have been impressively wide. In Edinburgh the clutter of shops between the tolbooth and St Giles, known as the Luckenbooths, which may have been built as early as 1386, reduced the High Street to a narrow lane. The mercat cross of a burgh was its legal caput, the place where proclamations were read, executions carried out and business transacted. Different areas within the market-place generally concentrated on the sale of particular commodities. Pressure on space within the main street and market-place of the largest towns led to the relocation of specialist markets into more scattered sites. By the sixteenth century Edinburgh had as many as 15 different markets and Stirling six.

Where there were no walls or restrictions population growth could be accommodated by outward expansion, as occurred in sixteenth- and seventeenth-century Glasgow. In walled towns like Edinburgh and Stirling, with steeply sloping sites growing population was more easily accommodated by building upwards. A feature of Scottish towns was the prevalence of apartment housing. Such accommodation can still be seen in some of the small burghs of Fife where it cannot simply have reflected a lack of space. Economy in the use of building materials and a tradition of lower housing standards in a comparatively poor country may provide part of the explanation. In Glasgow during the later seventeenth century the buildings lining the High Street ran to three, four and sometimes five stories. Gardyne's House in Dundee, a five-storey block built around 1560, shows that high-rise building was not confined to Edinburgh but tenements were especially characteristic of the capital where the population was particularly dense, confined by the city's walls, its awkward topography, and the lack of land within the burgh's royalty for further expansion. In the century after 1540 the population within the walls – a mere 140 acres (57 hectares) – doubled to produce one of the densest concentrations of urban dwellers in Europe.[10] The result was high-rise building on a unique scale.

In the early sixteenth century much of Edinburgh's housing was of timber-frame construction with thatched roofs. A combination of growing prosperity and increasing concern for the fire risk posed by these structures led to their gradual replacement by stone houses with slate roofs though these new buildings were often faced with timber boards and had projecting wooden galleries. John Knox's House is the only remaining example of this type. The change to stone as the main building material allowed construction to a greater height. The early seventeenth century saw the replacement of this first generation of stone houses by taller tenements, so that the upper part of the High Street became lined with buildings rising to six or seven stories. Those which were built into the steep slope leading down to the Cowgate in the area around Parliament Close had up to seven stories facing north on to the High Street and as many below facing south. Gladstone's Land in the Lawnmarket, built for a well-to-do merchant around 1620, is the best surviving example of this phase of tenement construction. With a frontage only 23 feet (7 metres) wide it had two shops protected by an arcade on the ground floor. A forestair at the side of the building gave access to the first floor from which an internal staircase led to five floors of accommodation. In the 1630s these housed two merchant and three other families. A further phase of rebuilding in the later seventeenth century created more stylish tenement blocks like Mylne's Court and Mylne's Square with greater uniformity of design and more elegance.

10. M. Lynch, *Edinburgh and the Reformation* (Edinburgh 1981), pp. 2–8.

The widespread rebuilding of houses in Scottish towns during the seventeenth century is best seen today in some of the small Fife burghs which were then at the height of their prosperity. Their buildings, differing in detail but with an overall consistency of style, vary from the solid and homely to the impressive. They represented a considerable improvement on earlier timber-frame housing, virtually none of which has survived. This phase of reconstruction parallels the rebuilding and extension of many country houses by the lairds and nobility. Together they constitute a revolution in housing comparable with the 'Great Rebuilding' of Tudor and Stuart England.

As elsewhere in Europe fire was a major hazard and an important agent of urban change. The preponderance of thatch and timber-frame construction in smaller towns made them particularly vulnerable: Dunfermline was virtually burnt out in 1624, Kelso in 1684. In the larger towns the greater density of buildings and of industries which posed a fire risk offset the fact that less flammable stone-built houses were more frequent. In 1652 a major fire in Glasgow destroyed about a third of the town and left 1,000 families homeless. Edinburgh suffered a serious fire in 1674. After both disasters the Dean of Guild courts which dealt with matters relating to building and land use required that rebuilding be done in stone and slate. In Edinburgh a coherent set of building regulations was developed, helped by a 17-year tax exemption on new stone and slated houses and a willingness to be ruthless and require the demolition of buildings which were considered unsafe. This led to improved construction standards. The dense concentration of buildings still posed a threat though and a major fire in 1700 destroyed many of the highest tenements around Parliament House.

Beyond the limits of the larger burghs were the suburbs. There were few of these before the sixteenth century. Perth, where the first suburb grew during the fifteenth century, was an exception. Several medium-rank towns developed unfree suburbs such as Nungate adjoining Haddington and Newton and Bridgend beside Ayr. Lying beyond the jurisdiction of the burghs, suburbs benefited from the proximity of towns while evading their regulations. Edinburgh had a series of suburbs clustered outside her walls. During the seventeenth century a good deal of effort and money was spent by the city's authorities in gaining control of them. The Canongate, which formed the lower half of the route between the Castle and Holyrood Palace, was a separate burgh in its own right. Its superiority was only acquired by Edinburgh in 1636. To the south were Bristo, Potterrow, and Portsburgh belonging to the barony of Inverleith. Edinburgh acquired control of them in 1648 and 1649 but they retained a distinctive sense of community long after they had been absorbed into the built-up area of the city. To the north were detached industrial villages like Calton and Dean while the port of Leith was the largest and often the most troublesome suburb, control of which was only obtained by Edinburgh after a protracted and expensive series of negotiations.[11]

11. Ibid., pp. 118–19.

At a small scale Edinburgh and other large towns with high-rise buildings had a vertical social stratification with better-off families living on the first floors and poorer ones higher up. Such towns also had larger-scale divisions into distinctive social areas. Some towns had a quarter dominated by the town houses of landed proprietors. The Canongate, adjacent to Holyrood Palace, developed into a well-to-do suburb of Edinburgh dominated by the town houses of the nobility who attended the court. Stirling had a similar area at the top of the High Street, close to the Castle. At one time, it has been claimed, houses belonging to 10 earls and six lords were located here. Argyll's Lodging, built about 1630 around a courtyard and surrounded by a high wall with strong gates, was a country mansion squeezed on to a restricted urban site. Both Stirling and the Canongate suffered from the removal of the court to London after 1603 but the tradition of the nobility maintaining town houses continued. Glasgow too had its affluent area around the cathedral at the head of the High Street where, in the sixteenth century, the stone houses of the clergy contrasted with the timber-frame houses of the burgesses in the lower town.

The first half of the eighteenth century saw new developments in town planning with the first residential squares being laid out on the south side of Edinburgh and the west side of Glasgow. Although small in scale compared with the new towns of the late eighteenth and early nineteenth centuries they indicate that new attitudes to urban development were in the air by the 1750s. In Edinburgh plans for a new town connected by a bridge across the valley of the Nor Loch to the medieval burgh were put forward in the 1670s when James, Duke of York, was resident in the city. Although plans for a new town were not approved until the 1750s new public buildings like the merchants' exchange which was finished in 1683 (and was destroyed in the fire of 1700) began to improve the city's appearance.

CHAPTER 11

URBAN ECONOMY AND SOCIETY
c1500–c1750

Only recently have the economic and social structures of early-modern Scottish towns been considered in any detail.[1] There has been an implicit assumption that the late survival of royal burgh monopolies fossilised not only trading patterns but also urban society. Glasgow, where society was considered to have been more flexible and fluid, was seen as an exception but elsewhere burgh institutions and society were thought to have been little altered through the sixteenth and seventeenth centuries. This view favours a watershed in the late seventeenth and early eighteenth centuries. In the larger towns there was a relaxation of controls on entry to burgess-ship and the merchant guilds. The most successful towns, typified by Glasgow, were considered to have been those which shook off the old restrictive frameworks fastest. But was Glasgow really so different from other Scottish towns? Many aspects of Glasgow business practices which were once considered to have been late seventeenth-century innovations can be traced back to the early seventeenth or even the late sixteenth century, and also existed in other towns. The old structures of monopoly and privilege could be manipulated and circumvented when it was advantageous to do so.

Michael Lynch has proposed an earlier watershed in the later sixteenth century and a distinction between the 'early-modern' burgh and the 'pre-industrial' town.[2] In the first the institutions of the medieval burgh came under pressure from a range of new influences and were forced to adapt. In the second the old limiting structures of burgh life became increasingly inadequate and were modified or abandoned. The timing of these phases, as well as their nature and effects, differed from one town to another but the labels are useful guidelines in trying to identify the processes which were at work in changing urban society.

The volume of evidence for the study of Scottish urban history increases greatly from the sixteenth century. In recent years this material has been exploited by a new generation of historians. Several studies have examined

1. M. Lynch (ed.) Whatever happened to the medieval burgh?, *SESH*, 4, 1984, pp. 5–20.
2. Ibid.

the major towns, notably Edinburgh, Glasgow, Aberdeen and Perth, while some middle-rank centres, such as Dunfermline, Dumfries and Stirling, have also received attention. We still know far less about the dozens of small burghs which formed most rural dwellers' experience of urban life. Research has focused on the period around the Reformation so that we have a clearer understanding of urban society at this time than during the early eighteenth century. While a good deal of research has been undertaken on the merchant communities of the major Scottish towns there has been a lack of work on other urban groups, notably the professions, or even a comparison of the activities of particular crafts over a range of towns.

THE MEDIEVAL BURGH UNDER PRESSURE

Population growth was a major force for change in Scottish towns in the later sixteenth and early seventeenth centuries. In England a period of urban crisis and difficulty has been identified between the late fifteenth and early seventeenth centuries. The causes of this were complex but one influence was the migration into the towns of large numbers of poor people in search of a livelihood which they could not obtain in the countryside. This produced problems for the maintenance of order in English towns, for systems of poor relief which were in any case disrupted by the effects of the Reformation, and for the welfare of existing townspeople who found themselves in competition with the incomers. It is harder to examine the idea of urban crisis for Scotland as the range of sources is more limited. The impression is, nevertheless, that problems for Scottish towns occurred rather later. Nevertheless, the population increases which occurred in the later sixteenth and early seventeenth centuries seem to have been caused mainly by in-migration, particularly in the larger burghs where mortality rates were probably higher than in rural areas. We do not know enough about conditions in the countryside to estimate how much of this movement to the towns was positive, with people migrating in search of advancement, or negative as a result of forces driving them from the land.

The middle and later sixteenth century were characterised by rapid inflation. While the wealthier merchants and craftsmen managed to maintain their living standards some poorer burgesses and the unskilled element of the labour force did not. Despite this, indications are that conditions for the urban poor were less difficult than in some English towns. One possible reason was the reaction of burgh authorities to the problem of poverty. Rather than trying to institute systems of poor relief they kept the prices of basic foodstuffs down. Direct financial aid, however administered, was inevitably selective but low food prices benefited everyone. As long as food prices were low and the poor could obtain some money from craft work, casual labour or charity the Scottish urban poor were probably better off than their English counterparts. The cheap food policy, naturally, produced protests from those incorporations whose members were threatened by price fixing; the baxters, maltmen and fleshers. The position of the poor may have deteriorated in the last two decades of the sixteenth century as rapid inflation, linked to the debasement of the coinage, forced burghs to abandon this approach. The early seventeenth century may have been a more difficult time for the urban poor – later in the century food prices were generally low.

Late-medieval burghs have often been portrayed as small, tight-knit communities. Even in the early seventeenth century many people still viewed burghs in these terms though increasingly perhaps as an abstract concept rather than a reflection of reality. Because of their small size, medieval Scottish towns did not require sophisticated institutions to regulate their affairs. Small size also limited the scope for social differentiation. Burgh society in the early sixteenth century, though by no means egalitarian, probably had fewer contrasts in wealth and status than in later times. The burgesses formed a relatively homogeneous group and distinctions between merchants and craftsmen were less marked than at a later date. Population growth and economic change made burgh society more sharply differentiated. In the larger towns wealth, status and power became increasingly concentrated in the hands of small elites. The burghs accommodated these changes within existing institutional frameworks, like burgh head courts, whose activities were nevertheless subtly transformed. This continuity, this ability of old frameworks to stretch in response to change, makes it harder to identify the transformations which were taking place in urban society.

There were significant variations in the administrative structures of the larger towns. Parliament and the Convention tried, without complete success, to standardise procedures such as the ways in which councils were elected. Small burghs often dispensed with much of the bureaucracy of bigger towns. Less than half the royal burghs had merchant guilds in 1560. Dumfries had no incorporated guilds until 1621, Brechin even later. In the larger towns administration was tending to become more hierarchical, authoritarian and oligarchic. In fifteenth-century Edinburgh all the burgesses had met at an annual head court. As population grew this became impossible; administration became more closed and remote. Burgh councils were forced to delegate more day-to-day business, some of it to the trades incorporations. Rather than devolving power to a lower level, however, this had the effect of drawing the wealthier members of the craft fraternity into the ruling elite and distancing them from their poorer guild brethren.

There were two stages to the development of this more authoritarian style of burgh government. First, following the incorporation of craft guilds in most burghs, a few members of the leading crafts were admitted to the merchant guild.[3] This involved the recognition of a craft aristocracy whose composition varied from town to town. Second, there was a growing demand for a say in urban affairs by groups which were not represented, including the lawyers and the unincorporated crafts. Having fought to raise their status the craft

3. Lynch, *The Early Modern Town in Scotland*, pp. 13–20.

aristocracies in the larger burghs then had to struggle to maintain it against pressure from below. The overall effect of these changes was to make burgh society more distinctly stratified. There was little difference in the rankings of the different occupational and social groups within the larger towns. The merchants, lairds and ministers formed an upper level along with high-status craftsmen such as goldsmiths. Below them came the main body of crafts with the weavers firmly at the bottom. Then came the unfree craftsmen and labouring poor.

Historians have been obsessed with the idea that burgh society in the sixteenth century was divided by a bitter power struggle between merchants and craftsmen. This view has been challenged by Lynch.[4] He has pointed out that individual burghs often differed in their proportions of merchants and craftsmen. The general occurrence of such tensions is also made less likely by differences in the occupational and social structure of the major towns. Perth, for instance, was a manufacturing centre whose craftsmen were as wealthy as the merchants. Glasgow, too, had a stronger manufacturing basis to its economy than most large burghs. In the early seventeenth century there were 361 craftsmen against 213 merchants. In Edinburgh and Aberdeen, by contrast, merchants outnumbered the craft masters. The real gulf in urban society was not between merchant and craftsman but between the burgesses and the unfree inhabitants. In the larger towns the merchant guilds contained men of widely varying status and wealth. In 1565 the lowest 505 of Edinburgh's merchants paid as much tax as the 12 wealthiest ones. There was a similar range of wealth within Edinburgh's craft incorporations. The lower half of the 496 craftsmen in Edinburgh in 1583 only paid 15 per cent of the tax, less than the six wealthiest craftsmen.

The composition of merchant and craft guilds varied between towns. Edinburgh had 14 craft guilds but most of the main towns only had around seven so that people with a variety of unrelated trades might be included within the same incorporation. In Glasgow the masons, wrights, coopers, slaters, quarriers and sawyers were grouped as a composite incorporation in 1551. With such marked variation the idea of universal conflict between merchants and craftsmen seems less probable. In practice differences within the two groups were probably as significant as those between them.

Conflict between merchant and craftsman has been inferred from what appear to have been craft riots in the major burghs in the later sixteenth century. Closer examination reveals that most of these were not general craft riots but specific protests by baxters (bakers) or fleshers (butchers) over the fixing of prices by burgh councils at a time of rapid inflation. Urban protests which were politically motivated have also been mistaken for craft riots. Some examples of genuine merchant–craft conflict did occur but they were far fewer than has been realised and were often related to specific local circumstances. Although the merchant guilds had effectively monopolised burgh administration by the mid-sixteenth century there was an increasing

4. Ibid., p. 26.

trend towards giving craftsmen some representation on the councils of the larger burghs. This has sometimes been seen as a move towards greater democracy. In Perth, where half the members of the council were craftsmen by the middle of the sixteenth century, this may have been true. Elsewhere, however, the new craft representatives were chosen only from the wealthiest members of the highest-status crafts.

Edinburgh's revised constitution of 1583 was more of a cosmetic exercise than a revolution in power. The middling ranks of burgesses could gain some influence in minor administrative posts such as elders of kirk sessions but the highest levels of urban administration were virtually closed to them. Edinburgh's example was widely copied. Aberdeen used it as a blueprint for changes in 1587. In Aberdeen in the early seventeenth century 17 out of 19 councillors were merchants and the two craft councillors were changed each year to reduce their power. There was token representation for a few leading craftsmen but ordinary craftsmen burgesses had no more say in the running of the town than before.

THE BURGHS AND CENTRAL GOVERNMENT

Another change in urban society was its slow integration into a more centralised framework of authority. In the fifteenth and much of the sixteenth centuries many burghs, even large ones, came under the influence of local nobles and gentry. These could offer protection but the price that towns often had to accept was interference in their affairs. Aberdeen formalised this process in 1463 by entering into a bond of manrent with the Earl of Huntly. With royal authority distant and the power of the Gordons in the north east so strong this was a sensible arrangement. The Gordons used it to install one of their client families, the Menzies of Pitfodels, as virtual hereditary provosts of Aberdeen until the end of the sixteenth century. The Menzies family sometimes treated the city, it was alleged, as if it was their own burgh of barony. At least Aberdeen managed to keep their patron at a distance and did not always accept his authority but in other burghs the relationship was closer and more direct. Larger burghs could resist attempts by local lairds and even magnates to ride roughshod over their rights but smaller burghs were more vulnerable. Towns could also become embroiled in local feuds between landowning families. Even Edinburgh was not entirely free from this: in the 1510s and 1520s the struggle between the Douglases and the Hamiltons to control the burgh through the office of provost was bitter. In 1520 this led to a major street fight, 'Cleanse the Causeway', in which the Hamilton faction was temporarily driven from the city.

There was a lessening of interest by landowners in burgh government in the later sixteenth century. In Aberdeen this was signalled by the ousting of the Menzies dynasty in the 1590s. A decline in magnate involvement in urban affairs elsewhere left a gap which was readily exploited by ambitious craftsmen and lawyers. In 1609 an Act was passed against landed outsiders holding office in burghs. This stopped, until the later seventeenth century, the practice of appointing nobles as provosts. At the same time the burghs were beginning to play a more important role in national politics and were becoming more closely involved with central government. The crown had problems in dealing directly with individual burghs because of the links they had with noble patrons. The development of the Convention of Royal Burghs provided a new mechanism for contact with the burghs as a group.

The importance of the burgh contribution to royal taxation led the crown to meddle increasingly in burgh affairs, as did the religious struggles of the later sixteenth century. The most marked encroachments came not under the personal rule of strong kings like James V but during minorities as part of faction fighting between rival groups of magnates. During the Reformation crisis the court removed entire councils in Edinburgh and other major burghs. The practice of placing royal nominees as provosts in strategic towns became more frequent. Edinburgh, due to its importance and its proximity to the court, was particularly susceptible to such activities. The government nominated the provosts of Edinburgh for 25 years after 1553 and occasionally interfered with lower levels of the town's administration. In 1583 Regent Arran purged Edinburgh's council and in 1584 its kirk session forcing himself on the city as provost into the bargain.

In the early seventeenth century the crown began to move from a position of defending burgh liberties to one where it was prepared to ride roughshod over their rights. In Edinburgh the conservative attitudes of the magistrates and their desire to steer clear of political factions led to generally amicable relations with James VI. When, following a riot in the city in 1596, the king threatened to remove the seat of government from Edinburgh the council grovelled. During James' reign town and crown came to expect more and more of each other. The crown demanded money and support, Edinburgh's merchants strong central government to encourage economic stability. During the reign of Charles I, however, the balance shifted so that instead of a reciprocal relationship the crown continued to take without giving concessions in return. By the time of James' death in 1625 heavy taxation and attempts at religious reform were starting to cause disaffection. This increased during the reign of Charles I, gradually leading the city's magistrates down a path leading to rebellion and the signing of the National Covenant in 1638. The problem of royal interference in urban affairs surfaced again during the brief reign of James VII and formed one of the main complaints in the Claim of Right in 1690.

Sharp increases in burgh taxation were another element in the growing involvement of central government with the towns. Burghs, like the rest of late-medieval Scotland, had been lightly taxed. The taxation of urban dwellers increased sporadically from the 1530s and became regular from the 1580s. In 1597 the first general duty on imports was levied, over 80 per cent coming from Edinburgh, Aberdeen, Dundee and Perth. Between 1601 and 1624 Edinburgh's burgesses were taxed 23 times, sometimes at a national level, sometimes for local reasons. In 1621 James VI threatened to impose new taxes on the provision of credit, one of the most important developments in the economy of Edinburgh's merchant elite. The threat was avoided but only at the price of an increase in conventional taxation. Charles I raised urban taxation still higher. In the first two and a half years of his reign Edinburgh was faced with a bigger tax bill than during the previous 25 years under James VI. During the reign of Charles I Edinburgh, as the capital, also had to find the resources for a new parliament house, two new churches and the conversion of St Giles into a cathedral at a time when the city was already committed to an expensive programme of public works. Much of this was financed by voluntary contributions from leading citizens. A slowing down in the rate of donations and a corresponding drop in building activity is evident in the 1630s due, one suspects, as much to a loss of enthusiasm by heavily taxed merchants as to the start of an economic slump. This was nevertheless only a prelude to more drastic impositions by the Covenanting and Cromwellian regimes. As well as rising taxation during the Bishops' Wars of 1639–41 there was pressure for donations from richer citizens. From 1644 excise duties were charged and in the crisis years of 1644 and 1645 forced loans, quartering of troops and requisitioning of supplies for armies in the field added to the burden of the towns.

Higher taxation widened the spectrum of urban taxpayers. In Edinburgh the number of taxpayers increased by a third in the 1560s. Between 1603 and 1635 they rose from 1,157 to 1,653 and increased again by around 50 per cent in the 1630s with lawyers, landowners who were part-time residents, and merchants from other burghs who spent part of the year in Edinburgh being taxed for the first time. In other towns with a narrower base of population which could be brought within the tax net difficulties may have been greater. By the 1630s the burghs were probably the most heavily taxed section of Scottish society.

URBAN ELITES: MERCHANTS AND CRAFTSMEN

Burgesses and their households formed about a third of the population in the larger towns. Within the burgess group the ratio of merchants to craftsmen varied between towns and through time. In 1558 Edinburgh had around 768 burgesses; 367 merchants and 401 craft masters. In Aberdeen in 1669 there were around 600 burgesses; about 350 merchants and 250 craftsmen. There was no fixed quota of burgesses and more might be admitted to raise money quickly, as in Edinburgh between 1560 and 1564 when the new Protestant regime was short of cash. Burgess-ship provided protection from competition, the right to have a say in urban affairs, and the avoidance of complete destitution in old age. It could be inherited, acquired by marriage, bought for a substantial fee or attained by apprenticeship. In Edinburgh in the early seventeenth century 37 per cent acquired burgess-ship by marriage, 28 per cent through their fathers, 23 per cent by payment of an entry fee and only 12 per cent by apprenticeship. Once registered as a burgess the further hurdle of guild membership had to be overcome. Many burgesses were mere journeymen working for master craftsmen in the hope of eventually being able to set up on their own. As time went on the size of this group increased and it became more difficult to move into the higher echelons of guild activity.

Burgh councils were dominated by small oligarchies of merchants. In Edinburgh only about a quarter of the merchants on the tax roll of 1565 sat on the council at some point in their careers. The wealthier a merchant, the more likely he was to hold high office. Following an Act of Parliament of 1469 the structure of elections ensured continuity on burgh councils and the perpetuation of the influence of small elites. In Edinburgh the trend towards oligarchy intensified during the later sixteenth century with fewer small and middling merchants winning seats on the council as the wealthier merchants held on to power for longer. Half of Edinburgh's 14 craft incorporations were virtually excluded from representation on the council. Craft council members were mainly drawn from the six wealthiest guilds; the hammermen, skinners, furriers, goldsmiths, tailors and barbers. The revision of Edinburgh's constitution in 1583 brought little real change. Six new craft representatives were admitted to the council but they were drawn from the same six guilds plus the cordiners (shoemakers), the only craft to have benefited significantly from the new charter.

The status of the various crafts in a burgh varied. Wealth and influence usually coincided so that the goldsmiths, apothecaries and tailors had a relatively high standing and less skilled or messier crafts; baxters, fleshers, candlemakers and weavers, had a low rating. In Glasgow the hammermen, an incorporation of metal workers which included everyone from goldsmiths to buckle makers, regarded itself as the premier incorporation as was the case in Perth and Stirling but in Aberdeen and Dundee they were not accorded such a high position. In Edinburgh the goldsmiths, who had hived off from the hammermen as a specialist group, held this place. The capital's demand for high-quality clothing meant that tailors were one of the wealthy, high-status incorporations in Edinburgh but in Perth they only ranked sixth out of the nine guilds.

The merchant guilds were the most powerful organisations in the main towns, often including among their membership professional men and wealthy craftsmen. To be eligible to join Aberdeen's merchant guild a man had to have at least £1,000 Scots worth of trading stock and pay a fee of 400 merks. In Glasgow only a third as much stock was required. Such figures probably represented absolute upper limits though; most people probably paid much less. Those who had served an apprenticeship received substantial reductions while sons of merchants and those who married merchants' daughters were admitted at a nominal rate. By the end of the seventeenth century burgess-ship and guild membership was becoming increasingly honorary. There was a rise in the percentage of burgesses becoming guild members from around a third in the early seventeenth century to a half towards the century's end. In 1696 the Dundee guildry agreed to admit new members for £12 rather than the old rate of £60 and after a three-year apprenticeship rather than five or seven years. In Aberdeen and Glasgow by the 1720s burgess-ship was becoming a social distinction rather than an indispensable qualification for trading. In Aberdeen and Dundee the practice of fining men for trading while not being a guild member had almost ceased by the turn of the eighteenth century. In all the main towns there was a fall in the length of apprenticeships and a drop in the number of new apprentices registered.

In Edinburgh or Aberdeen the burgh council and kirk session required between them about 50 office holders each year in the early seventeenth century, perhaps about a twelfth of the men who were eligible. The annual turnover of office holders in Aberdeen was around 60 per cent a year so that the holding of public offices was well spread throughout the burgess group. The institution of the Justice of the Peace court in 1657 widened the number of office holders required at any time from around 50 to about 75 providing more opportunities for small merchants and craftsmen to have a civic role.[5] Aberdeen was a town in which the ruling elite became more easily penetrated during the seventeenth century but other towns were less open with high office restricted to a much smaller group of merchants. In Edinburgh a core of about 25 families dominated the council, an oligarchy which was not closed but was nevertheless hard to penetrate, one which was increasingly distanced from the ordinary inhabitants of the city. Kirk sessions provided scope for lesser merchants, often ambitious men who were upwardly mobile, to hold office. Along with power, wealth was also highly concentrated. In early seventeenth century Edinburgh, 8 per cent of the taxable population paid half the total. In Aberdeen about 6 per cent of the taxpayers paid a quarter of the tax, a figure in line with many English towns.

The merchant elites who ran the larger towns were drawn from the limited sector of the merchant guild which engaged in overseas trade. In Aberdeen in 1696 27 merchants out of around 239 had trading stock valued at over 10,000 merks. Seven of these had estates outside the burgh. The provost, dean of guild and baillies of the burgh were all drawn from this small elite. Entry to the merchant community was achieved most frequently by son following father. By the early eighteenth century, however, only 46 per cent of Edinburgh merchant burgesses were being admitted in this way and 48 per cent in Dundee. This means that slightly more than half must have entered by marriage, apprenticeship or purchase without established family links. Upward mobility within the merchant group was possible. Inevitably the sons of existing merchants had the advantage in terms of resources and connections but even the elite was not entirely closed. This was particularly so in Glasgow where some of the most prominent merchants in the developing Atlantic trades in the first half of the eighteenth century came

5. G. Desbrisay, Authority and discipline in Aberdeen 1659–1700 (Unpublished thesis, Aberdeen 1989), pp. 365–76.

from outside the elite and even from outside the burgh.

Merchants ranged from petty stallholders and travelling chapmen to large-scale operators who traded abroad. Most merchants confined their activities to internal trading. Perhaps only a quarter or a fifth of Glasgow's merchants in the late seventeenth century were engaged in foreign trade and the proportion is likely to have been smaller in the other large towns. In smaller towns like Dumfries merchants were general dealers rather than specialists though they might diversify their activities into moneylending or renting urban property. As well as the merchant burgesses there was an unofficial low-status trading sector composed of non-burgesses whose activities are poorly recorded. Such people existed by buying goods from merchants for resale in the country and by selling commodities like fruit and vegetables which were beneath the dignity of a merchant burgess to trade in.

Urban craft incorporations developed from the mid-fifteenth century although they had existed earlier as unofficial associations. Edinburgh's skinners were the first to become incorporated in 1474. They shared many of the features of guilds elsewhere but, partly due to the slower development of urban institutions in Scotland, they continued to flourish during the sixteenth and seventeenth centuries when similar institutions were in decline in other European countries. Before the Reformation they had an important role as religious fraternities. Even after the Reformation they retained a strong religious element. They also acted as benefit societies for their members, providing support for aged, impoverished and disabled craftsmen, their widows and families. Nevertheless, although their religious and social aspects were important their economic role was paramount. The incorporations were designed to preserve the monopolies of a privileged group with the same general ethos as the merchants. Their monopolies allowed them to control quantity and quality of production. The limited demand for quality goods from the home market often resulted in a levelling downwards of standards except in a few areas of specialist luxury work. This discouraged initiative and innovation. Periodic efforts to introduce foreign workers to demonstrate new techniques for producing higher-quality cloth were met with indifference or hostility. The craft guilds could be more restrictive and exclusive than even the merchant guilds. The Perth skinners and baxters effectively maintained closed shops. Elsewhere the continuity of surnames within a craft from one generation to another hints at similar practices.

The key industrial sectors in late-medieval Scottish towns were wool and leather. Trade in the former was controlled by the merchants, in the latter by the craftsmen who handled an increasing quantity of exports. The skinners were among the earliest crafts to become incorporated in the larger towns in the late fifteenth and early sixteenth centuries and they tended to form an elite with the metalworkers. Skinners were allowed to join merchant guilds in some numbers enabling them to purchase raw materials in bulk as well as to engage in overseas trade. In Edinburgh, 15 per cent of the merchant guild were craftsmen in 1500, 27 per cent in 1640. In Perth the percentage was much higher. A craft aristocracy of employers and entrepreneurs can be seen emerging in the larger towns during the mid-sixteenth century, men who were members of the merchant guild as well as craft masters. Problems with overseas trade and the growing home market for manufactured goods in the seventeenth century helped to change the makeup of the craft aristocracy with the decline of the skinners and increasing prosperity for makers of luxury goods like the glovers, tailors and goldsmiths, and providers of services like stablers and horse-hirers whose numbers in Edinburgh increased by 50 per cent between 1650 and 1680, and apothecaries who doubled in number in the capital during the same period.

The craft guilds were controlled by annually elected councils headed by deacons. A high proportion of craft burgesses would have served on the council of their incorporation at some time in their career. A favoured few went on to higher office on the burgh council. The incorporations controlled entry into their trades by systems of apprenticeship. The training was long with several expensive hurdles which, if not overcome, would fix a man permanently in an underprivileged position. An apprentice might have to serve his master for seven years before becoming a journeyman. After two further years' service he could become a burgess. In many cases he was only eligible for guild membership after another four years so that 13 years could elapse between his entry to a trade and his final attainment of guild membership. Many men remained journeymen because they could not afford the burgess fee; the numbers of people in this position increased in the later sixteenth and seventeenth centuries. Many burgesses could not afford guild membership; fees were heavily weighted in favour of sons or sons-in-law of existing guild brethren. In mid-sixteenth-century Edinburgh an outsider had to pay ten times as much for entry to the skinners' guild as the son of a burgess. Journeymen were increasingly becoming a caste of underprivileged and exploited labour in the burghs with little hope of rising to a higher level.

The guilds were no longer expanding by the seventeenth century. Entry to the Glasgow hammermen ran at slightly under three per year in the first half of the seventeenth century and was only just over three a year in the later decades despite the rapid growth of the town. As well as rising numbers of burgesses who did not attain guild membership there were many unfree craftsmen in the suburbs of the larger towns. In theory the guilds had little control over the activities of unfree tradesmen who were allowed to sell their wares in the burghs on market day, though not at other times. The craft deacons could, however, confiscate their work if they considered it to be shoddy. Tradesmen from outside the town were sometimes disadvantaged by being restricted to selling at certain times during market day and at less attractive locations within the market-place. Burgesses and guild brethren could sell their manufactures from their booths and stalls on any weekday.

Although unfree craftsmen could only sell their goods in the burgh on market days there was nothing to stop the inhabitants from going to the suburbs and placing orders with them. In 1592 Parliament passed an Act which, if interpreted strictly, forbade unfree craftsmen in suburbs from operating at all. Most burgh authorities interpreted the Act more sympathetically by entering into agreements with groups of suburban craftsmen which allowed them to operate subject to supervision from the incorporations. The Glasgow weavers drew up such an agreement with the weavers of Gorbals in 1657 in which the latter were not to allow any more workers to settle without permission from the deacon of the Glasgow weavers. The Gorbals workers were to contribute some money towards the Glasgow guild and were allowed in return to send a representative to guild meetings. Accommodations like these meant that groups of unfree workers were being brought within the framework of guild control in a loose and flexible fashion. This allowed for growth and gave the guilds a measure of control without opening their ranks too widely to all comers. Many new activities within the service sector as well as a range of specialist trades which helped to diversify the occupational structures of the major towns in the later seventeenth century operated outside the traditional guild framework. Not all recognised trades were incorporated either. In Aberdeen, for instance, the barbers and surgeons, litsters (dyers) and periwigmakers were often burgesses but did not have separate guilds, while other associations, such as those of the advocates and the shore porters, lay outside the conventional craft framework.

THE UNFREE POPULATION

Some two-thirds of the inhabitants of Scottish towns were not burgesses and were classed as 'unfree'. This term included many professional people as well as the labouring poor. There was a considerable expansion of the professional sector in the larger Scottish towns during the sixteenth and seventeenth centuries. In Edinburgh they accounted for 8 per cent of households in 1635 but this proportion had doubled by the 1690s. There was a growing number of administrative posts associated with the local and state bureaucracy which, if limited compared with some European countries, was nevertheless expanding. In the fifteenth century posts in administration and justice were filled by churchmen. During the first half of the sixteenth century they were increasingly challenged by the laity. This change was most marked in the law where the size of the professional group grew rapidly. The establishment of the College of Justice and Court of Session in 1532 by James V encouraged this trend. As bloodfeuds gave way to what could be an equally aggressive pastime – pursuing one's neighbour at law – the size, standing and wealth of the legal profession grew. This was especially evident in Edinburgh with its central courts, Parliament and the Privy Council, but also occurred in other towns which were the centres of sheriffdoms and regalities.

In Aberdeen the lawyers joined the merchant guild in large numbers. In Edinburgh their influence was less direct and lower key. By the later seventeenth century the law had come to be respected as an eminently suitable career for sons of the gentry and nobility. In the towns with universities (Aberdeen, Edinburgh, Glasgow and St Andrews by the end of the sixteenth century) the staff of the colleges broadened the professional group as did the masters of burgh grammar schools on a smaller scale elsewhere. The medical profession also increased in numbers and status as physicians and doctors of medicine separated from apothecaries and surgeons. Medical practitioners enjoyed a rather lower status than lawyers, as did those employed in education. Many schoolmasters were divinity graduates waiting for a clerical vacancy who had only entered teaching temporarily.

Merchant and craft burgesses with their families probably accounted for around a third of the inhabitants of the larger burghs during the later sixteenth century. The families of resident landowners and professional men added to this figure but this still leaves something like half the urban population unaccounted for. We know little about the less advantaged sectors of the urban population. Not all of them were 'poor' in the sense of being at or below the poverty line, however defined, but it is within this group that most of the urban poor were found. The scarcity of references to them and the relatively small numbers of pensioners supported by urban kirk sessions has been interpreted as indicating that the proportion of the urban population in Scottish towns which could be classified as poor was lower than the 30–40 per cent which has been suggested for contemporary England. Nevertheless, a census of 1,175 poor by the kirk session of Perth in 1584, in a town whose population must have been around the 4,500 mark, is more in line with this sort of figure. Recent calculations for Edinburgh based on the poll tax for 1694 suggest that around a third of the resident families within the city were on or below the poverty line, to which can be added the unknown numbers of vagrant poor producing a figure comparable with those for larger English towns.[6]

Unfree inhabitants, though unable to vote in burgh elections, were not without rights. The most important of these was belonging to the burgh community. Officials were supposed to record the names and details of all incomers though it is doubtful how thoroughly this was done in the largest towns. To be counted as an 'indweller' in Aberdeen one had to have been born in the town, have at least one parent born there, or to have lived in Aberdeen for a minimum of seven years.[7] Recognised indwellers were eligible for poor relief and could not be expelled. Upward mobility from this group was possible. In Aberdeen about half the craftsmen apprentices were the sons of unfreemen though many came from outside the town.

There are indications of growing problems of poverty in the larger burghs in the later sixteenth century. Population growth, rising prices, political crises and periodic food shortages were underlying influences. The Reformation had wrecked the system of poor relief provided by friaries and poor

6. M. Dingwall, The social and economic structure of Edinburgh in the late seventeenth century (Unpublished thesis, Edinburgh 1989), pp. 482–540.
7. Debrisay, Authority and discipline, p. 163.

hospitals. In the immediate post-Reformation period reliance was placed on voluntary contributions made to kirk sessions. Craft and merchant guilds were increasingly encouraged to look after their own poor and the incorporations could also be surprisingly generous to non-members, unfree craftsmen and even vagrants. There was doubtless also a lot of unrecorded private charity. A regular poor rate was introduced in Edinburgh in the 1580s but in other towns this did not occur till much later. The establishment of poor hospitals, often continuations of pre-Reformation institutions such as ones on the sites of the Black Friars and Trinity College in Edinburgh, were some help. Poor relief, in the form of monthly and quarterly pensions or one-off payments, was much less than assistance provided by the guilds. Only a small proportion of the unfree population received help from the kirk session at any time; in a town the size of Aberdeen only about 120 people were on the poor roll in the later seventeenth century. Few could have lived solely on the aid they received; as in rural areas charity from friends and neighbours plus casual labour must have been important in sustaining the poor. Even so, people receiving regular aid from kirk sessions were visited periodically and their good behaviour and attendance at church as well as their material circumstances were carefully monitored.

Many people must have scraped a precarious living by manufacturing and trading without burgess status. The very frequency of burgh council acts against unfree craftsmen suggests the existence of a large 'black economy' over which burgh authorities had little real control, especially in the large towns. There was also a legitimate petty trading sector. The sale of commodities like vegetables, milk, fish and fruit was beneath the dignity of burgesses. This provided opportunities for unfree men and women who were supposedly allowed to trade only in the market-place on market day though trading outside market times was widespread. Keeping alehouses and lodging houses was another element in this hidden economy, often undertaken by women. Keeping small shops was also a source of female employment. In Edinburgh in the late seventeenth century the council complained periodically that female domestic servants were leaving their masters and mistresses to keep such shops. Brewing, too, was a female occupation, often done by wives of burgesses. In 1530 there were 280 female brewers in Edinburgh, and over 150 in Aberdeen in 1509. In 1596 the formation of the Society of Brewers in Edinburgh, supported by merchant capital, altered the structure of the industry and undermined the economic position of women, for brewing had been a valuable safety net for widows. Horse hiring and keeping urban dairies were also activities in which burgesses were not normally involved. The impression is that this non-burgess sector of the urban population, along with wage-earning workmen and labourers, was growing steadily in the larger Scottish towns between the late sixteenth and mid-eighteenth centuries.

URBAN OCCUPATIONAL STRUCTURES

In the sixteenth century most royal burghs depended to some extent on overseas trade, especially the export of staple commodities; wool, cloth, skins and hides along with fish, coal and salt. This dependence made the towns transhipment points rather than manufacturing centres to a greater extent than elsewhere in Western Europe. This helped to restrict to an unusual degree the range of industrial activities in many Scottish towns until well into the seventeenth century. English visitors in the late sixteenth century commented on the lack of manufactures even in the larger towns, a feature which is likely to have been increased by the prevalence in rural areas of local self-sufficiency in most basic manufactures.

There were significant differences in the occupational structures of the main regional centres in the late sixteenth and early seventeenth centuries.[8] Following the collapse of the wool trade in the 1320s the four leading burghs diversified their economies in different directions. Edinburgh monopolised the wool trade when it revived in the later fifteenth century. By the late sixteenth century Edinburgh handled most of Scotland's trade in wool and cloth. The wider base of Edinburgh's economy compared with major towns is suggested by the grant of incorporation to 14 crafts between 1473 and 1536 while most large burghs only had half as many. The sixteenth century also saw in Edinburgh the growth of the professions, and the rise of luxury trades such as the goldsmiths and tailors. Perth, whose overseas trade had been curtailed by the silting of the Tay, had an occupational pattern which was rare in Scotland, a craft town depending on inland rather than overseas trade, a category found more commonly in England. In Perth the craftsmen paid as much tax as the merchants. Dundee was pre-eminently a port but one which suffered increasing competition from Leith and whose merchants reacted by switching into coastal traffic. Dundee specialised in cloth manufacture more than any other large Scottish town but had a narrower manufacturing base overall than Perth. This, with a more restricted participation in overseas trade than Edinburgh, made Dundee vulnerable to economic shifts both at home and abroad.

Aberdeen had a higher proportion of merchants than Edinburgh and relatively few craftsmen, especially in the metal and leather trades. Like Edinburgh, Aberdeen's economy was dominated by retailing and distribution rather than manufacturing. The town was dominated by a small clique of merchant lairds who owned estates as well as engaged in trade. Aberdeen was a major exporter of plaiding until the later seventeenth century, but although the industry was controlled by the town's merchants most of the work was done by rural craftsmen; the town only had 23 weavers in 1637. In Glasgow merchants made up only 37 per cent of all burgesses in 1605. In

8. Lynch, *The Early Modern Town in Scotland*, pp. 8–12.

Edinburgh at a slightly earlier date the proportion was 43 per cent and in Aberdeen 74 per cent. Glasgow in the early seventeenth century had a small merchant community but a very broad manufacturing base, especially in clothing, textiles and food processing. In this period Glasgow had less than half as many merchants as Edinburgh but more cordiners, weavers and maltsters; the town was clearly a regional centre relying on inland rather than overseas trade.

The poll tax records of the 1690s allow comparison of occupational structures for a range of towns.[9] Edinburgh was distinguished by the prominence of the professions, particularly law and medicine. Lawyers made up nearly two-thirds of the professional group which substantially outnumbered Edinburgh's merchants. In addition, landowners formed a sigificant group in the capital including those who owned town houses and those occupying rented accommodation. Aberdeen also had important professional and landowning groups. Of the larger burghs those which were heads of sheriffdoms and regalities, like Perth and St Andrews, had higher proportions in the professions, especially law, and significant groups of resident landowners though the men classified in this group were small lairds and portioners rather than nobles. Some larger baronial burghs like Bo'ness, Dalkeith and Musselburgh were deficient in professional employment, though in others like Peterhead and Fraserburgh which were relatively distant from royal burghs this trend was less marked. In the case of the first group their nearness to the capital may have diminished their need for a wide range of professional services. In the smallest burghs, whether royal or baronial, one or two ministers, a notary and a schoolmaster comprised the professional element.

The merchant class in Edinburgh was not as large, proportionally, as in some towns but it was far wealthier. Merchant communities were also prominent in regional centres like Dumfries, Glasgow, Inverness, Paisley and Perth. Some baronial burghs like Fraserburgh, Peterhead and Greenock also had relatively large merchant communities. By contrast baronial burghs like Bo'ness, Dalkeith and Musselburgh had few merchants in relation to their size. All these burghs were close to the capital with their trade dominated by Edinburgh merchants and also, in Bo'ness, by merchants from Glasgow, Linlithgow and Stirling.

Male domestic servants made up nearly a quarter of the male pollable population in Edinburgh and were also significant in smaller social centres like St Andrews. The importance of this group has probably been under-estimated in previous studies of urban occupations partly because many sources fail to record them. Female domestic servants outnumbered their male counterparts in all the larger burghs but tended to be less numerous than male servants in the smaller burghs, a pattern similar to the countryside. Agricultural activities were found even in the largest towns; Edinburgh had its cow feeders and

---

9. I.D. Whyte, The occupational structure of Scottish burghs in the late seventeenth century, in Lynch, *The Early Modern Town in Scotland*, pp. 219–44.

market gardeners concentrated in the less densely built up Canongate. The importance of agriculture is probably underrated by the poll tax classifications, especially for the smaller towns where many burgesses had a share in the burgh's arable lands and common pasture. Even in Edinburgh a considerable proportion of the population left the city at harvest time to obtain temporary work in the countryside. Quite large towns still retained a strong rural character. In Dumfries the burgesses reared animals within the burgh and leased land outside the town for grazing and cultivation. Out of 66 Dumfries merchants' inventories between 1600 and 1665, 36 showed direct evidence of farming.

Elements of specialisation within the manufacturing sector can also be discerned. Edinburgh and Aberdeen had proportionally small manufacturing sectors though in the case of the former much craft activity probably went on in the suburbs. The number of weavers in Edinburgh had been falling since the late sixteenth century despite substantial population growth and by the late seventeenth century the city had fewer weavers than Glasgow or Aberdeen. Manufacturing was more dominant in the baronial burghs. Edinburgh, Aberdeen and Perth had relatively few textile workers, while Musselburgh and Paisley had larger than average proportions of their workforce in linen and woollen manufacture. By contrast Edinburgh had a high level of specialisation in clothing with seven times as many clothiers polling in the three highest wealth categories as Glasgow and 21 times as many as Aberdeen. Perth and Selkirk, adjacent to upland pastoral areas, had concentrations of leather workers. Edinburgh, as might be expected, had more workers in the luxury trades than other large towns; booksellers, furriers, goldsmiths, gunsmiths, jewellers, printers and watchmakers emphasised the city's role as a centre of education, culture and fashion. Outside Edinburgh such occupations are only represented sporadically; they were probably not absent in other large towns but existed as small-scale adjuncts to more basic activities.

Edinburgh had an impact on the occupational structures of other burghs within a radius of 20 miles (32 kilometres) or more. Satellites like Bo'ness, Dalkeith and Musselburgh were deficient in professional men and merchants. Their industries were closely tied to the needs of the capital, focusing on primary processing while Edinburgh specialised in the finishing trades. Glasgow appears to have had a similar relationship with nearby burghs like Paisley, Renfrew and Rutherglen. Most towns had a similar spread of employment in trading, services and basic industries such as clothing, textiles, leather, iron working, construction and food and drink. Some elements of functional specialisation can be identified; the coal and salt burghs of the Forth and some of the Fife fishing burghs for example but these were grafted on to a basic occupational structure that was fairly constant from one burgh to another. In general terms the occupational structures of Scottish towns were similar to those in England. The principal difference was the lower percentage of workers in manufacturing in the larger burghs; around 40–50 per cent instead of the two-thirds suggested for many English towns. This emphasises the extent to which Scottish burghs were trading rather than industrial centres.

During the eighteenth century signs of increasing functional specialisation begin to appear, particularly among smaller towns; spa and resort centres like Moffat and communications centres like Portpatrick. Some towns acted as social centres for the county gentry. Maybole, the only corporate town in Carrick, had developed in this way by the early eighteenth century. On a larger scale, towns like Dumfries consolidated their position as legal, educational and market centres for their localities. The development of newspapers, printing and publishing, stagecoach services and the establishment of coffee houses also emphasised their role as places from which news was disseminated. Other towns began to move from service provision towards manufacturing, particularly in west-central Scotland where a number of specialised textile-producing centres developed.

Edinburgh was by far the largest town in Scotland during the sixteenth and seventeenth centuries and the city's economic and social structure had some distinctive features. The area around the capital had an unusual concentration of relatively small estates. One commentator estimated that there were as many as 100 noble's and gentlemen's seats within half a day's ride of Edinburgh. This pattern of landownership made it far easier for the wealthy merchants and lawyers to purchase estates. It also meant that no local magnate was sufficiently strong to exert long-term influence over the city in the way that the Gordons did with Aberdeen. In the later seventeenth and early eighteenth centuries a range of source material, especially the poll tax records, makes it possible to examine Edinburgh's social structure in some detail. By this time the central part of the city was divided into eight parishes, including the Canongate, plus the two parishes of North and South Leith and West Kirk, the rural parish surrounding the city which contained several suburbs. This allows spatial variations in social and economic structure within the capital to be identified. A recent study by Dingwall has demonstrated many parallels between the social and occupational structures of Edinburgh and London emphasising the extent to which Edinburgh formed part of the European urban system.[10]

The percentage of apprentices among Edinburgh's population was similar to contemporary London. Comparison between apprentices listed in the poll tax records and those in the city's apprenticeship registers indicate a high drop out rate with only a small percentage of apprentices completing their training and becoming burgesses. The 5,500 or so households in the Edinburgh poll tax contained around 5,000 servants, male and female, who made up 23 per cent of the community overall and nearly 30 per cent in the wealthiest parishes. Fifty-one per cent of all households included servants rising to nearly three-quarters in city-centre parishes. Again these figures are similar to London. The preponderance of female domestic servants in all parishes was a major factor in producing a surplus of females in the capital.

10. Dingwall, The social and economic structure of Edinburgh.

There were only 76 men per 100 women in Edinburgh overall. The range of household sizes within the city was considerable with 73 per cent of households having 1–4 members and 5 per cent between 9 and 12. The largest households in the city were maintained by merchants, lawyers, some landowners and only a few craftsmen. Family and household structures demonstrate the rarity of extended families and the predominance of nuclear ones. Big households were mostly ones with lots of servants like that of Viscount Tarbat with 24 assorted servants including cooks, footmen and gardeners in addition to his family.

Resident gentry made up only 6–7 per cent of the households in most parishes and were heavily outnumbered by those in the professions which accounted for up to a third of all households in city-centre parishes. Up to a fifth of all households in the same central parishes were merchants. Craftsmen made up as many as half the households in the Canongate which, despite its reputation as an area dominated by the town houses and apartments of the gentry, appears more as a craft suburb with few merchants and a not unduly high proportion of gentry households. Some occupations were concentrated in the city centre such as the merchants and the legal profession. Although some craftsmen were found in the city centre craft activities were more characteristic of the suburbs. A few industries showed marked geographical concentrations like brewing which, needing a water supply, was located to the west of the city and in Leith but most crafts were widely dispersed. Overall the city had some 1,800–2,000 burgesses accounting for about 30 per cent of households but even in central parishes only two-thirds of the people in trade and craft activities were registered burgesses. Low-status crafts like weaving, where only 20 per cent of the people listed were burgesses, contrasted with high status ones like surgeons where 86 per cent were burgesses. Clothing manufacture and the metal trades were more prominent in London, the professions more dominant in Edinburgh, but otherwise the occupational structures of the two cities were remarkably similar.

There was a marked contrast in patterns of wealth between the prosperous city centre and the poorer periphery. Sixty-eight per cent of the households were in the lowest tax category and the remaining 32 per cent paid the bulk of the tax. There was a wealthy elite of just over 500 households, about 10 per cent of the total, the bulk of which were merchant (31 per cent), professional (37 per cent) and gentry (24 per cent) with only a few wealthy craftsmen including goldsmiths, glovers, tailors, pewterers and skinners. Within the merchant and craft categories there was considerable variation in wealth. Twenty-eight per cent of the merchants polled in the two lowest wealth categories but 25 per cent in the highest. Craftsmen were markedly less wealthy with 63 per cent in the lowest tax category and under 2 per cent in the highest one. There were contrasts in wealth between different crafts with a third of the goldsmiths and surgeons polling in the highest category but all the weavers and shoemakers in the lowest.

The legal profession formed 3.6 per cent of the workforce against the merchants' 4.1 per cent emphasising the extent to which Edinburgh had become a centre supplying professional services. There was a steady rise in the proportion of professional men in the city during the seventeenth century but less change in the manufacturing profile. Comparison between the poll tax lists and a stent (tax) roll of 1635 show a number of occupations which seem to have appeared during the intervening period including tobacconist, wigmaker, confectioner, and perfumer highlighting the rise of luxury trades. An analysis of Edinburgh's marriage registers suggests that there was little overall change in the occupational profile of the city during the first half of the eighteenth century. There were, however, some interesting developments in detail including a rise in the number of people employed in administration, whether connected with the city, business or government. Within the manufacturing sector a rise in the importance of the building trades was probably connected to the city's first phase of expansion beyond its medieval limits. An increase in the workforce employed in book production and printing is also evident.

Much of the recent research on Scottish towns has concentrated on late sixteenth and seventeenth centuries. There is, consequently, a gap in our knowledge regarding how urban societies and economies changed during the first half of the eighteenth century. In particular there has been no general study of how the main towns and smaller burghs adapted, or failed to adapt, to new conditions after the Union of 1707. The success story of Glasgow has received more attention than Edinburgh and a new study edited by Devine and Jackson is forthcoming, though Houston's work sheds considerable light on how society in the capital developed during this important period.[11] Nevertheless, the theme of Scottish towns in the decades before industrialisation is yet another neglected area where more work is badly needed.

11. R.A. Houston, *Social Changes in the Age of the Enlightenment, Edinburgh 1660–1760* (Oxford 1994).

CHAPTER 12

LAW AND ORDER, CRIME AND VIOLENCE

An enduring feature of Scotland's identity is a legal system which differs in many important respects from that of England. It has long been suggested that the maintenance of law and order, and the level of violence in society marked Scotland as essentially different from England. Yet there is a conflict between this image and the equally prevalent one of a Calvinist, God-fearing country within which the strong grip of the reformed kirk had produced a closely controlled and biddable society. It is impossible to understand Scottish society without appreciating the framework of law and order within which it operated and patterns of crime and violence.

THE SCOTTISH LEGAL SYSTEM

The Scottish legal system was decentralised in a way which has often been portrayed as weak and inefficient. More recent evaluations have suggested that it was better integrated and more effective than has sometimes been supposed.[1] The abolition of heritable jurisdictions in 1747 put an end to a complex pattern of royal, seigneurial, local and church courts and replaced them by a more centralised system. The machinery of justice in Scotland had, however, been evolving from late-medieval times and was already moving towards a more formal structure. Down to 1747 a distinctive feature of Scotland was the existence of extensive areas which effectively lay outside the jurisdiction of central government for all but a few serious offences. Much of the administration of justice was in the hands of local landowners through a mosaic of franchise courts within which the interpretation of justice depended on local custom rather than statute law. Much of the law of early-modern Scotland had evolved from within communities, tailor-made to fit their needs, rather than being imposed from above. Parliament served

1. S.J. Davies, The courts and the Scottish legal system 1600–1747: the case of Stirlingshire, in V.A.C. Gatrell, G. Lenman and G. Parker (eds), *Crime and the Law* (London 1980), pp. 54–7.

more to clarify and systematise the customs of communities rather than to impose a centralised code upon them.

Although the patchwork of jurisdictions may look confusing the different courts seem to have integrated with each other reasonably well. In particular, the lower levels of the church and secular courts reinforced each other. Each level of the judicial system had a clearly defined role and disputes over jurisdictions were uncommon. The system that they formed was loosely articulated by modern standards but worked nevertheless and while it had a built-in resistance to change it was far from static. The jurisdictions of regality and barony courts, sometimes huge sometimes tiny, are difficult to map. At the time of their abolition in 1747 there were nearly 200 regalities in Scotland and probably over a thousand baronies. English commentators on the Scottish judicial system were amazed at the hereditary character of the franchises and the extent of their powers. While English manorial courts still existed they were in decline during the seventeenth century and only dealt with minor civil actions and breaches of the peace.

Regalities and baronies, once created by royal grant, became permanent. Where they reverted to crown control they were known as stewartries and baillieries. Baronies were often small and compact but they could be scattered through several shires. In many smaller baronies the landowner was resident but where baronies were fragmented or formed part of a larger regality the baron was often a remote figure and the administration of the court was left in charge of a baillie. Regalities could also be fairly small but some, like Atholl or Argyll, covered huge blocks of territory. Regality courts had criminal jurisdictions comparable to the central High Court of Justiciary. Many could try every type of case except treason and so were effectively petty kingdoms. The extent of actively functioning regalities is uncertain but one estimate suggests that they may have covered half of Scotland. The granting away of rights on this scale has been seen as a sign of weakness on the part of Scottish monarchs but it was an effective way of ensuring that justice in some form was provided in more remote areas by people who were best placed to exert local control.

There was often, by the seventeenth century, a gap between the theoretical powers of the franchise courts and the offences they actually handled. Baronies could deal with cases of theft where the criminal was caught in the act or with the stolen goods in his possession, and with 'red handed' cases of slaughter as well as more minor assaults. Some baronies had the power of 'pit and gallows', the right to imprison and even execute offenders. Such rights were in abeyance throughout most of the Lowlands by the seventeenth century but were sometimes invoked within the Highlands. Lowland baron courts handled very few criminal cases apart from assault. Their activities were concerned mainly with pursuing petty debts, maintaining 'good neighbourhood', ensuring that rents were paid and that feudal obligations and services were discharged. Punishments were generally fines on a fairly standard scale; corporal punishment or banishment was rarely enforced. Baron courts were probably quite effective in maintaining good relations within the rural community as well as supporting the established social order.

The operation of some regality courts was barely distinguishable from baron courts despite their greater powers. On the other hand, larger regalities like Argyll, Dunfermline and Orkney had administrative structures modelled on the royal courts with justiciary courts trying capital offences and sometimes going on circuit. Regality courts could try the 'four pleas of the crown'; robbery, rape, murder and arson. Only treason and, after 1597, witchcraft lay outside their jurisdiction. The baronies within a regality handled routine business and passed on more difficult cases. In regalities like Atholl and Montrose offenders were still being executed for theft as late as the 1730s. Nevertheless, the standard punishment for crimes like theft, which supposedly carried the death penalty, was usually banishment from the regality. Regality courts also had an important commercial role, regulating prices, wages and markets. The regality of Falkirk in the early eighteenth century continued to enforce its commercial rights even though it had let many of its justiciary privileges lapse. By the 1740s many regality courts were letting the High Court of Justiciary encroach on their rights regarding criminal cases and were functioning primarily as co-ordinating bodies for groups of baron courts.

The secular franchise courts were reinforced by the church courts. As in early-modern England there was no clear-cut division between sins and crimes. Following the Reformation, as in other European countries, a range of sins became criminalised including adultery and blasphemy. In seventeenth-century Scotland the punishment of sin was thus not confined to the church courts, nor crime to the secular authorities. Kirk sessions can be found dealing with cases of assault while adultery, potentially a capital offence, was often dealt with by the highest criminal court, the High Court of Justiciary. The network of kirk sessions and presbyteries which was gradually set up after the Reformation represented a formidable machine for social control.[2] Church courts had existed before the Reformation but their surviving records suggest that they were mainly concerned with property transactions and drawing up contracts. By the 1620s virtually every Lowland parish had a kirk session. The state supported the kirk by criminalising a range of moral offences including Sabbath breaking, swearing, drunkenness, adultery and fornication. A substantial proportion of the population of a community was likely to appear before the kirk session at some point. In St Andrews between 1560 and 1600 around 1,000 cases of sexual misconduct were dealt with in a town whose population can only have been around 4,000.

The most frequent types of case which kirk sessions dealt with were sexual, especially fornication and adultery. Sabbath breaking, drunkenness, swearing and slander accounted for most of the rest. In operation a kirk session was a kind of tribunal before which people were called and interrogated regarding their alleged offences. There were no established rules of procedure but most

2. R. Mitchison and L. Leneman, *Sexuality and Social Control in Scotland 1660–1780* (Oxford 1989).

cases were straightforward and few people refused to acknowledge the sessions' authority. The elders usually had defined areas of their parish to keep under observation. As there was no financial gain from reporting someone to the session it is likely that most cases were generated by the vigilance of the elders who must have acted like a kind of moral police force.

In cases of fornication the normal procedure was for an unmarried woman to be summoned once she was obviously pregnant. She was asked to name the father who was then brought before the session and asked to admit his guilt. The power of the kirk sessions and the strength of their hold over society is shown by the fact that most men admitted paternity even though there was no means of proof if they denied it. If a stubborn (or innocent) man refused to admit his guilt he would be brought before the presbytery and required to swear his innocence under oath. If he did this he was deemed innocent and was discharged. This procedure usually broke all but the most recalcitrant of fathers but neither the session nor the presbytery could do anything with someone who remained obdurate. Where pregnancy had been followed by marriage kirk sessions were more lenient in their treatment of offenders. Unmarried couples were often put under considerable pressure to get married to ensure that child and mother would be adequately supported. Adultery attracted more severe penalties being seen as more sinful and a threat to family life. Persistent adulterers who refused to submit to kirk discipline risked being brought before the High Court of Justiciary with a far more severe penalty.

Less common cases like blasphemy and wife beating were also treated more severely. Cases of slander were dealt with by kirk sessions in some areas, baron courts in others. To ensure that accusations were not lodged lightly they had to be made in writing accompanied by a deposit of 40 shillings which was forfeited if the case was not proven. Penalties for sexual offences often involved fines, which usually went into the parish poor box. The major element, however, was a ritual of public humiliation designed to shame the culprit into better behaviour. This usually consisted of sitting on the stool of repentence in church on Sundays, the number of appearances being proportional to the seriousness of the offence. Minor offences might merely merit a public rebuke from the minister. More serious breaches of discipline could result in the culprit being forced to wear sackcloth and being placed in the jougs, an iron neck collar fastened to an outside wall of the church or churchyard, prior to sitting on the stool.

Presbyteries monitored the activities of groups of parishes. They were formed by ministers and, after 1638, by ruling elders elected from each parish. Their main task was to ensure the religious orthodoxy of their ministers but they also handled difficult cases passed on from the sessions including bigamy, incest, rape or verbal and physical assaults upon ministers. They could also impose the kirk's ultimate threat, excommunication. There were two kinds of excommunication; the lesser which involved a ban on attending communion, and the greater which amounted to virtual outlawry. The process of excommunication was long and complicated, more often initiated than completed. It was applied to murderers but also to persistent minor offenders such as drunkards or Sabbath breakers. The number of people who were excommunicated was fairly small. In Stirlingshire between 1640 and 1701 there were only four cases. In the handling of difficult cases, such as accusations of witchcraft, presbyteries can be seen trying to be fair in their questioning and sometimes attempting to defuse potentially explosive situations before they got out of hand and turned into major witch hunts.

The degree of social control exerted by kirk sessions probably reached a peak between the 1620s and the later seventeenth century. Their power was due to the readiness of the population to accept their authority and the close links which they had with secular justice. Some of their authority was lost after the Restoration when sessions and presbyteries were instructed not to meet until they had been authorised by the newly appointed bishops. This sometimes produced a gap of two or three years in their operation. A decline in the numbers of cases dealt with by kirk sessions from this time onwards suggests that they may have lost some of their efficiency. After the Revolution of 1688 and the re-establishment of a Presbyterian system numerous episcopalian ministers who would not conform to the new order were ousted and many parishes had no ministers for several years. After this further hiatus many kirk sessions never fully recovered their authority. Schism in the church increased from the 1730s with the growth of dissenting congregations at a time when many functions of kirk sessions were being taken over by Justice of the Peace courts. Kirk sessions continued, nevertheless, to exert considerable authority over the lives of their parishioners throughout the first half of the eighteenth century.

Sheriff courts were an Anglo-Norman institution introduced into Scotland in the twelfth century. Sheriffs were, potentially at least, the most powerful and effective local agents of the crown, their courts the king's courts in the localities. Their efficiency, however, depended on strong central control. Sheriffs were notionally royal officers but in practice they came to be independent of the control of central government, most of the offices becoming hereditary in particular families. Much of the active business of the courts was carried out by sheriff deputes. This helped maintain a reasonably efficient system for dealing with routine business though there was a temptation for sheriffs to use their powers to their own advantage. The sheriff and his depute were still, nevertheless, the central government's local representatives. It was through them that government proclamations reached the bulk of the population. They collected taxes and royal revenues, organised the election of shire commissioners to Parliament and were responsible for raising and leading the shire levies.

Sheriff courts had a range of functions and dealt with much civil work. They were closely in touch with both the franchise courts and kirk sessions within their jurisdictions. They exercised comparable criminal jurisdictions to regalities, serving as courts of appeal for the inhabitants of baronies. Cases of debt, spulzie (borrowing without the owner's consent), and assault were commonly dealt with. Assault was divided into bloodwyte, where blood was shed, or the less serious offence of riot. Sheriff courts enforced various penal statutes imposed by the government from the cutting of green timber and fishing for salmon out of season to the attending of conventicles (illegal religious gatherings). Cases of theft where the culprit was caught in the act or in possession of stolen goods were also dealt with though some were passed to the High Court of Justiciary. Slaughter (public killing) and murder (premeditated or concealed killing) were also handled, though rather infrequently. A high proportion of cases was dealt with by imposing a fine but for theft, scourging, branding, banishment or occasionally the death penalty might be applied.

Burgh courts were the urban counterparts of the rural franchises. Cases involving property, debt and economic matters tended to dominate their business but they also tried a similar range of criminal cases to sheriff courts. During the early eighteenth century burgh courts increasingly let their criminal and civil activities lapse, to be taken over by the Sheriff Courts and Justices respectively. Like baron courts, burgh courts worked closely with local kirk sessions sharing many of their personnel. Justices of the Peace had first been appointed in 1609 in emulation of the English system but their remit was restricted. This, and the lack of suitable people willing to fill the offices, meant that the system was ineffective until revived by Cromwell. After the Restoration the Justices managed to retain some of their enhanced powers, mainly in social and economic matters such as regulating servants' wages, prices, weights and measures. After 1707 they were given an authority more comparable with their English counterparts. The range of their business expanded during the early eighteenth century to include matters such as the maintenance of bridges and roads, checking weights and measures and enforcing customs and excise regulations but the system only developed fully after 1747 because there was insufficient room before the abolition of the heritable jurisdictions for another tier within the judicial system.

The Court of Justiciary formed the upper level of the Scottish criminal legal system having evolved, like the Court of Session which dealt with civil matters, from the earlier curia regis. The medieval Justiciar was a royal official who dealt with criminal cases. In the early sixteenth century there were two of them, dealing with areas north and south of the Forth. In 1514 the posts were united in a hereditary Lord Justice General though most of the work was done by deputes and the Lord Justice Clerk. The last hereditary Lord Justice General resigned in 1628 and thereafter the Lord Justice Clerk presided over the court. In 1672 the court was reconstituted as the High Court of Justiciary, sitting in Edinburgh as well as going on circuit. Prosecutions by the court were usually made as a result of letters sent to sheriffs asking for lists of crimes committed within their jurisdictions. Because the court tended to deal with particularly difficult cases many prosecutions were abandoned because of lack of evidence. Due to the efficiency of kirk sessions in notifying sheriffs many moral offences, especially adultery, came before the court which also dealt with cases of treason, religious dissent, sodomy, bestiality, witchcraft, forgery, major public disturbances and political offences. For serious offences the punishment was normally death or transportation and acquittals were rare. Minor offences like adultery were subject to heavy fines although from 1709 the operation of the court was revised so that the numbers of minor moral offences tried was greatly reduced.

Although the High Court of Justiciary was, in theory, the highest criminal court it and other courts were subject to the authority of the Privy Council. The Privy Council's particular concern was the maintenance of political stability and public order. Unlike its English equivalent it also functioned as a court which dealt with much routine civil and criminal business as well as acting as a court of appeal against judgements passed by inferior courts. Its jurisdiction overlapped with the Court of Justiciary and it is not always clear by what processes cases came to be tried by one court or the other. The Privy Council could, and did, intervene at every level of the judicial structure and its abolition in 1708 seriously weakened the old Scottish legal system.

The Act of 1747 which removed the regalities and curtailed the powers of baron courts dismantled a system of interrelated and mutually supporting courts which was more successful in maintaining an orderly society than has often been admitted. Much of the administration of justice was done by people who were amateurs, who might often have their own interests to pursue, but who were nevertheless closely in touch with local issues and attitudes. It was replaced by a more impersonal, centralised system whose success owed a good deal to the order imposed by the pre-1747 system. The 1747 Act hastened a shift from a system of justice that was community-based to one where justice was imposed from above by the state. The fact that this occurred later in Scotland than in some European countries does not necessarily indicate that the Scottish system was more primitive or less effective. It was certainly different from that of England but within its context it appears to have worked quite well.

BLOODFEUD AND KINSHIP

Another feature of the Scottish judicial system was that many cases never came before a court at all but were settled privately by arbitration. At the core of this process was the institution of the bloodfeud. The practice by which a murderer offered compensation to the kin and friends of the man he had killed was deeply rooted in Scottish society and survived down to the mid-eighteenth century in the Highlands, and it was expressed by bloodfeud. Late-medieval Scottish history has often been presented as a series of violent clashes between magnates and lairds. In fact down to the early seventeenth century bloodfeud was more widely distributed through Scottish society than has been realised but at the same time was often much less violent. Bloodfeud represented a traditional form of kin-based justice which was adopted and institutionalised by the Scottish legal system. It integrated well with the machinery of government and law and order because under the decentralised Scottish system it offered a realistic way of maintaining peace in the localities.[3]

Little information is available on the nature of the bloodfeud in Scotland before the fifteenth century. At this time it was found in both the Highlands and Lowlands. There was no distinction between the way that bloodfeud operated in the two regions until the later sixteenth century. By this time the courts were starting to become involved in what had previously been private affairs. During the fifteenth and sixteenth centuries royal justice grew stronger but still interacted with private kin-based justice. From the fifteenth century to the early seventeenth the custom is chronicled by over 800 bonds of manrent, formal articles of allegiance and mutual protection between magnates or between a lord and a lesser landholder. These contracts specify the mutual obligations and responsibilities of the two parties. Their significance is that they codify, between people who were not closely related, the relationships and responsibilities in relation to bloodfeud which existed within families but which were so uniformly accepted that they did not have to be written down.

There was no conflict between the private justice of the bloodfeud and public justice in situations where major landowners were responsible for maintaining law and order in their localities through franchise and sheriff courts. When private settlements proved impossible cases could go to law as a last resort but private settlements were faster and often fairer. A man who lost out in a settlement might be more prepared to accept a ruling against him when the decision came from his peers rather than a distant, anonymous court. The successful conclusion of a feud by these means required that both sides should find the settlement acceptable. If the loser was treated too severely then this was less likely to work so conciliation and compromise were normal. Curiously, a settlement following a murder was often easier to achieve because there was a mutual interest in preventing further bloodshed, while in a dispute over land there was a clear gainer and a loser. Settlements often involved formal public reconciliations as part of a religious service and sometimes a marriage between members of the opposing families to try and cement the peace.

It was acknowledged that compromise and compensation provided a more effective way of checking violence than the imposition of penal statutes. The crown gained rather than lost power by underwriting the justice of the feud and increased its influence in the localities for the magnates and heads of kin groups who were involved in private settlements were often royal officials as well. The two systems interdigitated, and efforts to strengthen royal justice were designed to supplement local justice rather than to undermine it.

In 1597 James VI urged his son to 'rest not until ye roote out these barbarous feides'. By the late sixteenth century the Privy Council was becoming more involved in trying to settle feuds, especially in the Borders, supervising the nomination of arbiters for each party and drawing up

3. J. Wormald, Bloodfeud, kindred and government in early-modern Scotland, *Past and Present*, 87, 1980, 54–97.

settlements. Feuds were gradually brought within the law and were increasingly being carried out by litigation rather than bloodshed to the great profit of the legal profession. Lawyers in the central courts did not oppose the justice of the feud; they merely absorbed it into their system. The decline of private bloodfeuds was hastened by the expansion of the legal profession during the sixteenth century which encouraged the gradual transfer of the bloodfeud into the courtroom. James VI passed legislation against feuds before 1603 but he pursued his campaign with greater success after the Union of the Crowns. Stray incidents of violence linked to feuds continued to occur in various parts of the Lowlands during the early decades of the seventeenth century but by the accession of Charles I feuds had largely died out. After 1603 the expansion of centralised justice, under the control of the Privy Council began to create a new ethos in which the ethics of the bloodfeud were seen as increasingly antiquated so that throughout the Lowlands by the later seventeenth century it had become an anachronism whose continuation in the Highlands was viewed by Lowlanders as a symbol of backwardness. The transition was still in progress in the early seventeenth century but by the end of the century the change had been completed. The collapse of magnate power during the Great Rebellion hastened the demise of the bloodfeud but this merely accelerated a trend which had been in progress for a considerable period.

CRIME, VIOLENCE AND PROTEST

Scottish society in late-medieval and early-modern times has often been portrayed as violent. Conflicts between monarch and magnate, or feuds between landed families, have been taken to indicate the ubiquity of violence at all levels of society. More recently, it has been suggested that the extent of magnate conflict has been exaggerated. It has also been pointed out that certain kinds of violence and protest, such as peasant uprisings, found in England and on the Continent were rare in Scotland.[4] There were no Scottish equivalents of the peasant revolts of seventeenth-century France or the food and enclosure riots of sixteenth-century England. The harvest crises of the late sixteenth century caused great distress but little recorded violence. The only enclosure riot, the Levellers' Revolt of the 1720s, stands out as an isolated anomaly. It was England, not Scotland, which experienced six changes of dynasty and numerous smaller-scale rebellions during the fifteenth century!

Conflict between monarch and magnate was a feature of most of Europe in the fifteenth and early sixteenth centuries, one which was gradually resolved in favour of the crown in England, France and Spain leading to more autocratic government but which in Scotland was dealt with in a different

---

4. A. Grant, *Independence and Nationhood, 1306–1469* (1984) pp. 57–8 and J. Wormald, *Court, Kirk and Community in Scotland 1470–1625* (London 1981), pp. 39–40.

manner. Scotsmen who travelled in England in the seventeenth century were surprised at the amount of aggression displayed by the lower levels of English society. In Scotland peasant aggression tended to reflect ruling-class splits in politics and religion emphasising the strength of vertical linkages in society. The dispersed nature of population in ferm touns rather than large villages may have limited opportunities for large gatherings leading to collective action. The lack of rural unrest has also been attributed to the close personal structure of Scottish society.

The idea that Scottish society was inherently violent is not borne out, for the Lowlands at least, by court records. Even assuming that these only list a proportion of violent crimes the impression is not one of a brutalised and intensely violent society. This paradox is similar to the one which Alan Macfarlane has highlighted for sixteenth- and seventeenth-century England. It can be resolved by suggesting that, magnate conflict and bloodfeud notwith-standing, Lowland society was less violent and more orderly than has often been portrayed. With the exception of the Borders there is no evidence for any dramatic re-orientation of society towards less violent more law-abiding attitudes. Popular protest did occur but it was more local, small-scale, short-lived and less well organised than in neighbouring countries.

As in contemporary England there are problems in defining crime. Official ideas regarding what constituted crime varied through time; a notable example, witchcraft, is discussed below. The perception of what was criminal, also depended on the social position of an individual. To Parliament or a landowner the cutting of green timber was a clear offence. To a tenant needing to shore up rotting roof timbers it was a perfectly acceptable activity, unjustly punished if one had the misfortune to be caught. Attitudes regarding criminal behaviour also differed from one area to another. Activities like cattle reiving which remained commonplace and, in a sense, socially acceptable in the Borders till the end of the sixteenth century would have been much less readily countenanced in a more regulated area like the Lothians.

It is difficult to estimate levels of crime and violence in early-modern Scotland due to the poor reporting and recording of offences. A high proportion of crimes are likely to have gone unrecorded, unpunished, even unreported. The Justiciary Court of Argyll tried only 86 cases between 1705 and 1742. In a region which contained some notably lawless districts this works out at under two cases per 100,000 inhabitants, far lower than modern crime rates and totally unbelievable. Surviving records, particularly of franchise courts, are often scrappy and may omit many of the cases which were considered. Prosecutions were often dropped if insufficient evidence or a lack of witnesses made conviction unlikely. Many cases were settled out of court. Indeed, taking a criminal case to court was often a last remedy. An out-of-court settlement might prove more profitable to the victim of a crime; hanged men paid no compensation. Bringing a criminal action was expensive, risky and uncertain so that private settlements were encouraged, not least by court officials. In Scotland, as in England, many crimes carried the death penalty but this was only regularly applied to a limited range including murder, arson, witchcraft, incest and sodomy. Sometimes, as with theft, the death penalty was imposed occasionally to make an example of some unlucky person, often a persistent offender or an outsider.

Information on the nature and treatment of crime improves through time as the central courts took over more of the work of the franchise courts. In the earlier part of the period crime was often not something that the state took responsibility for dealing with; it was up to an individual or kin group to pursue a criminal. The range of crimes over which the state took action widened from the sixteenth to the eighteenth century. Lacking modern forensic aids, the prosecution of many offences was difficult unless criminals were caught in the act. With theft of everyday items like livestock, butter or peat it might be hard to establish the ownership of suspected stolen goods. In Orkney in 1615 a man was convicted of stealing a sheaf of corn found in his house because it had been bound in a style which was recognised as being that of the pursuer. Such proof was fortuitous and must often have been lacking. When cases did come to court, however, offenders rarely escaped. In the Justiciary Court of Argyll of the 86 cases tried between 1705 and 1742 14 ended in hanging, 3 in branding, 10 with people being nailed by the ear to the public pillory, 26 in banishment and most of the rest with fines.

Witnesses or confessions were normally required to secure a conviction; circumstantial evidence was not usually admitted as in England, nor was torture used to obtain a confession as on the Continent. Imprisonment and a poor diet might break a person's health and encourage them to confess but their confession still had to be repeated in court. When there were no witnesses even a murderer might escape if he was prepared to perjure himself and swear his innocence under oath. This explains why so many crimes were never brought to court; it was a waste of time unless there was sufficient evidence to make the accusation stick.

Was society in Scotland more violent than in England? The slower decline in organised violence north of the Border may be seen as a function of the more limited power of central government in the localities compared with even Northern England. Remoteness from central authority and the *laissez-faire* nature of royal control allowed family feuding to survive later than in England. Nevertheless, by the later seventeenth century society over much of Lowland Scotland seems to have become fairly peaceable. The black and pessimistic view of interpersonal relationships in early-modern rural communities as being cold and hostile, characterised by hatred, malice and occasional mass hysteria seems as over-stated for Scotland as for England. The court book of the barony of Stitchill in the Merse records, on average, only one or two cases of minor assault each year. A blow was treated seriously enough but where actual blood was shed the more serious charge of bloodwyte was involved with a much higher fine, although many bloodwyte cases were less serious than the term might suggest. In 1663 one man was fined £50 for a bloodwyte caused by throwing a cup at a neighbour. This kind of violence is more suggestive of small-scale quarrels which got out of hand rather than a high level of endemic aggression and brutality.

In England the sixteenth century saw the emergence of a criminal stereotype in the vagrant. The association, in the official mind, of vagrancy and crime is reflected in increasingly harsh legislation designed to control vagrancy. Similar attitudes obtained in Scotland developing against a background of rising population pressure. Among vagrants gipsies were seen as a particularly dangerous deviant group and were singled out in national legislation as well by local courts. The importance of one's reputation in local society is emphasised by the trial of James MacPherson, the celebrated gipsy leader, at Banff in 1700. The fact that witness after witness could swear than he was 'halden and reput ane Egyptian' counted heavily against him. Hardened criminals existed, as in any society, though few can have rivalled in variety and determination the tinker who was brought before the sheriff court at Cromarty in 1676 charged with repeated stealing from corn stacks, breaking into two merchants' booths to steal 20 merks and merchant wares, stealing the communion cup of the kirk of Tarbat, false coining of money, poisoning his wife and committing adultery. For these offences he was secured in the prison of the castle at Cromarty while awaiting trial but he escaped by tunnelling through a thick stone wall and, light-fingered to the last, he made off with the contents of his cell; a pewter vessel and two blankets. Having been apprehended once more he was, not surprisingly, hanged.

Local society in the Lowlands seems then to have been able to maintain a reasonable level of order. In many sets of court records there is a decrease in the number of cases of violence occurring through the second half of the seventeenth century and into the eighteenth. Some of this may have been due to the atrophying of the activities of the franchise courts but it may reflect a real trend towards a better disciplined, more peaceful society. The decline in the use of force for settling disputes was marked in the landscape by the end of the construction of new tower houses during the second quarter of the seventeenth century and the spread of undefended lairds' houses and mansions. Within the Highlands, however, fortified houses continued to play a useful role for another century or so. That there was, by the early eighteenth century, a distinct difference in the level of violence between Highland and Lowland is also suggested by Leneman's observation on the kirk session records for the Lowland barony of Fossoway and the Highland barony of Blair Atholl, both on the Atholl estates.[5] In Fossoway the most frequent cause of Sabbath-breaking was drunkenness; in Blair Atholl it was getting involved in a brawl.

Lowland society in the later seventeenth and eighteenth centuries appears as stable, almost subservient, compared with England or Ireland.[6] This has been attributed to the control exerted by landowners and kirk sessions, and

5. L. Leneman, *Living in Atholl: A Social History of the Estates 1685–1785* (Edinburgh 1986), pp. 103–7.
6. C. Whatley, How tame were the Scottish Lowlanders during the eighteenth century?, in T.M. Devine (ed.), *Conflict and Stability in Scottish Society 1700–1850* (Edinburgh 1990), pp. 1–30.

the strength of vertical linkages within society cemented by paternalism, patronage and kinship. Levels of popular protest seem to have been lower than in England but lack of protest does not necessarily indicate social harmony. Signs of social tension can be discovered in lower-key forms of protest. Many baron court books provide examples of passive resistance and small-scale protest. Passive resistance may underlie the rent arrears which appear in many sets of estate accounts even when harvests appear to have been good. The assaulting of barony officers in the execution of their duty is often chronicled, usually by one or two individuals but sometimes by stone-throwing mobs including women as well as men. Cases of dyke-breaking, cutting green wood or poaching game may reflect challenges to encroachments on traditional rights by landlords.

After 1707 anti-Union or anti-English feeling caused more protests.[7] The most common cause of violence was the new customs and excise duties. These made smuggling more profitable and caused customs officials, some of them English, to be detested. Attacks on them became a popular bloodsport. Anti-English and pro-Jacobite sentiments may have been behind such activity but so may economic necessity. In the years after the Union the economy was stagnant while the price of some basic commodities like ale and salt rose as a result of the new duties. Many people's involvement in smuggling may have been from sheer necessity rather than a desire to make a profit. It may be significant that when economic conditions began to improve in the 1740s attacks on customs officers became less common. It has been estimated that around 60 people were killed in Scotland in the 1720s and 1730s as a result of mob violence associated directly or indirectly with taxation, a figure comparable to the number of deaths due to rural protests in Ireland between 1761 and 1790, in a country traditionally seen as much more violent. The whole topic of popular protest in eighteenth-century Scotland requires more research.

Food riots, so prevalent in England and on the Continent, also occurred. As with smuggling such protests were aspects of the struggle for survival and were more common than has often been appreciated; in 1709–10, 1720, 1727, 1740 and 1756–57 not only in large cities but also in smaller towns. These riots were often, but not invariably, related to years of shortage when grain prices were high. In 1720, when they followed a good harvest, fears of shortage may have been provoked by rising exports of grain. Food riots and attacks on customs officials were concentrated in the towns. Scottish urban mobs in the early eighteenth century have sometimes been considered as one-off events related to particular political circumstances; the lynching on Leith Sands of the luckless captain of the Worcester in 1705 (Chapter 16) the malt tax riots in Glasgow in 1725 or the Porteous riots in Edinburgh in 1736. They have not been related to longer-term undercurrents of urban protest but these undoubtedly existed, particularly in Edinburgh, and were similar to the mob violence found in other European cities. The Edinburgh mob was a

7. Ibid.

significant political force on a number of occasions in the sixteenth and seventeenth centuries but no one has yet assembled the evidence relating to the capital or to other large Scottish towns.

WITCHCRAFT

One of the most distinctive crimes in early-modern Europe was witchcraft. Scotland is notorious as a country where witch persecution was rife in the late sixteenth and seventeenth centuries. To appreciate why we need to consider witchcraft in a European context. Two kinds of witchcraft were widely believed in throughout Europe until the later fifteenth century as well as in primitive societies today; white witchcraft which involved healing and black witchcraft. From the late fifteenth until the early eighteenth century a third kind of witchcraft existed, one defined not by local communities but by churchmen, lawyers and social elites. This stressed the importance of the Demonic Pact and the association of witches in groups to worship the devil. The development of these theories elevated the prosecution of witchcraft from an isolated, random occurrence to a mania which was characterised by periodic waves of persecution or 'witch hunts'. As the powers of witches came from the devil and were inherently evil both white and black magic, charming as well as cursing, were liable to be prosecuted.

England escaped the worst of the witch craze because of a different legal system from Scotland and much of continental Europe. In England suspects were rarely tortured to generate the names of accomplices, the demonic pact was rarely invoked and the distinction between black and white magic was maintained. Scotland was closer to continental Europe in the scale of its witch hunts and the ways in which people accused of witchcraft were dealt with. Scottish witchcraft prosecutions form part of a wave of witch hunts which swept across Europe from the mid-sixteenth century, although it reached Scotland later than many parts of the Continent. Despite the fact that the number of executions in Scotland has been revised substantially downwards Scotland was still one of the major areas of witch persecution. Previous work on Scottish witchcraft has tended to chronicle the colourful details of some of the more famous trials like those of the North Berwick witches in 1590 and the Paisley witches in 1697 without trying to explain the social background of witch persecution. Larner has placed it firmly within a social context emphasising its distinctive features and the extent to which prosecutions in Scotland were part of a European pattern.[8]

Only a few pre-Reformation trials and executions for witchcraft are known. In Scotland witchcraft was a crime in statute law punishable by death from 1563 until 1736. The last recorded execution was in 1727. The main period of witch hunting was briefer, lasting for around a century from the 1590s until the 1690s, with relatively little activity after the 1660s. Most prosecutions were

8. C. Larner, *Enemies of God: The Witch Hunt in Scotland* (London 1985).

concentrated within a few limited periods. Only a few cases are known from the 25 years or so after 1563 though admittedly documentation is poor for this period. Not many of them resulted in executions. Beliefs concerning witchcraft, even among the clergy, were still relatively simple with no ideas about demonic pacts and night flying. The wording of the Act of 1563 suggests considerable scepticism about the very existence of witchcraft. Witch persecution only arrived in Scotland in the winter of 1590–91, a century after it had developed on the Continent. The first great witch hunt in 1590–91 was started by James VI. Another, perhaps the most widespread, occurred in 1597 and may have gained impetus from the publication of James' 'Daemonologie' in that year. A peak in 1628–30 coincided with one on the Continent. Further witch hunts occurred in 1649 and 1661–62. After this there were some local outbreaks as in East Lothian in 1678–79 and Renfrewshire in 1697. During the peaks of witch hunting as many as 400 cases might be dealt with in a year. In between were lulls punctuated by individual cases and some local purges. During the Protectorate, with the normal machinery for processing witchcraft accusations gone and more sceptical English judges in control, prosecutions fell sharply. The massive witch hunt of 1661–62, when over 600 cases were tried and some 300 executions carried out, may have represented in part the clearing of a backlog of resentment against individuals which had built up over several years during which prosecution had not been possible. Equally, the fall in prosecutions after 1662 may have been partly because most of the more obvious reputed witches had already been dealt with.

The rise in witchcraft prosecutions was related to a number of elements in European society. In particular, it has been argued that it was only with the Reformation and the Counter-Reformation that the European peasantry became Christianised. For the first time they were exposed to systematic Christian teaching and moralising by preaching in the vernacular, and to the idea that each individual was personally responsible for their own salvation. It was only within this context that the individual rejection of God and worship of the Devil could be accepted. The general nature of this process of Christianisation is of greater significance than the details of religious belief in any country or region. Other essential preconditions for witch prosecution were the existence of belief in witchcraft among the peasantry, a belief in the Devil among the educated elite, a rise in literacy, even if only second-hand through the medium of a better-educated clergy, and a change in law towards a more modern retributive system of justice in which there was much less risk of an accusation rebounding on the accuser. The passing of statutes against witchcraft in many European countries in the late sixteenth and early seventeenth centuries was often associated with the criminalisation of other religious and sexual offences such as blasphemy and adultery. Lacking any minority of heretics to prosecute, society in Lowland Scotland, attempting to conform to the new standards, turned inwards to persecute misfits and deviants. There is no clear link between the timing of the major periods of persecution and widespread disasters such as harvest failures or epidemics.

It is impossible to be precise regarding how many people were tried for witchcraft during this period and how many were executed. In particular the scale of the witch hunt down to 1597 is unclear because cases were handled by local courts whose records are scanty. Even after 1597, when a commission from the Privy Council was necessary to initiate a prosecution, coverage is far from complete. In particular, court records sometimes omit the final verdict. Nevertheless, making a reasonable allowance, Larner has estimated that around 1,500 people were executed for witchcraft between 1563 and 1736.[9] This is a substantially lower figure than previous estimates which have run as high as 30,000. Even so, it compares with around 500 executions for England, with a much larger population. The biggest individual English witch hunts involved less than a score of executions while in Scotland in 1649, 250 commissions for trial and burning were issued for the county of East Lothian alone.

A clear confession was normally required before a Privy Council commission was issued. On the other hand, there were few controls as to how a confession was obtained. Depriving the victim of sleep was a simple yet effective method, one which tended in any case to cause hallucinations. Confinement in poor conditions on a meagre diet, sometimes naked, might break a woman's spirit just as effectively. Pricking in search of a witch's mark, a spot impervious to pain, was a form of torture as well as a means of investigation. More straightforward torture with thumbscrews, tearing out fingernails, or crushing the legs in an instrument called the 'boots' was also used. The use of torture, sanctioned by James VI, was also employed against political prisoners but from the middle of the seventeenth century there was increasing concern about its use on suspected witches as a means of obtaining the truth.

From the 1670s the Council set its face more firmly against the use of torture and there was a rising proportion of acquittals. Few cases were coming up by the 1690s, making the 1697 outbreak in Renfrewshire all the more notable. Even then only seven out of 20 accused were executed. The last legal execution was at Inverness in 1706. The one at Dornoch in 1727 followed an illegal local trial. Nevertheless, the legal profession, inherently conservative, did not speak out strongly against the idea of witchcraft as a crime. The removal of the act was due not to any Scottish initiative but to a House of Commons amendment to the repeal of English witchcraft legislation.

The geographical distribution of cases was very uneven. Most of the Highlands, beyond the reach of the kirk sessions, as well as the far north, Orkney and Shetland, produced hardly any cases. The famous Brahan seer, burned at Fortrose in 1578, was one of the few Gaelic speakers known to have been executed for witchcraft. Witchcraft cases came overwhelmingly from the Lowlands with a marked concentration in the Lothians, the Merse, Fife and around Aberdeen. Within these districts some parishes produced only the odd case while in others, like Prestonpans or Tranent, instances

9. Ibid.

occur again and again. The link between high incidence of cases and fishing communities may relate to the suspected involvement of witchcraft in disasters at sea. Although detailed local studies may reveal structural elements in particular communities which predisposed them to outbreaks of witch hysteria it is probable in many cases that once a witch hunt had been initiated within a community, for whatever reason, its memory was enough to keep belief in witchcraft strong and to generate fresh outbreaks years later.

James VI derived his ideas about witchcraft from the Danish court. There is no evidence that he had any interest in the subject before he sailed to Denmark in 1590 to bring home his bride. The North Berwick trials of 1590-91 marked a dramatic change in attitude towards witchcraft in Scotland. What actually happened is not clear; whether there was a genuine conspiracy to kill the king, merely a scare, or whether the authorities deliberately tried to implicate the troublesome Francis Stewart, Earl of Bothwell, a cousin of James VI. It was alleged that large numbers of witches gathered to raise storms to destroy the king on his homeward passage from Denmark. Over 100 suspects were examined and some – it is not clear how many – were executed. This was the last of the old-style treason/witchcraft trials with political undertones which had occurred occasionally in the fifteenth and sixteenth centuries but also the first of the new witch hunts in which continental ideas regarding the Demonic Pact and gatherings of witches to worship the devil were a central feature. Such ideas seem to have been introduced to Scotland by James himself following his stay in Denmark where witch-hunting was endemic.

The North Berwick trials precipitated the most extensive of the general witch hunts. The number of prosecutions may have been increased by the activities of Margaret Atkin of Balweary, an accused witch who claimed to have a special ability to detect other witches on sight. She was taken from one community to another denouncing further victims. Her exposure as a fraud, and a general feeling that prosecutions were getting out of hand, may have been instrumental in persuading James VI to recall the Privy Council's general commission against witches. The damage was already done though with continental ideas regarding witchcraft firmly implanted in the minds of ministers, lawyers and landowners. The interest created by the North Berwick trials encouraged James to write his 'Daemonologie'. He did so in response to a book 'The Discoverie of Witchcraft' by Reginald Scot, which had been published in 1594 and was a scholarly, well-written attack on belief in witches. James' book, shorter and less authoritative, was partly a justification for his role in the North Berwick trials. James has been accused of initiating the Scottish witch hunt and sustaining interest in witchcraft through his book. In a sense this is true yet the preconditions for witch persecution already existed in Scotland and it is unlikely that witch hunts would have recurred decades after the North Berwick trials unless there had been a general belief in the existance of witches among the ruling elite.

The work of Macfarlane and other social historians has emphasised that in England witches were not randomly selected but had definite characteristics; they were old, poor, female, and generally of lower status than the neighbours who accused them.[10] Macfarlane has suggested that in England witch hunts reflected tensions in communities relating to social and economic changes, particularly the growing number of poor people, and a move towards a cash economy accompanied by a shift in emphasis from individual to official charity. These ideas do not fit as well in a Scottish context; the pace of social change was slower in Scotland during the period of the great witch hunts. Nevertheless, individual Scottish case studies often suggest a not dissimilar social context for witchcraft accusations. Scottish witches were not necessarily drawn from the very poorest classes of society as in England. They often appear to have been the wives or widows of small tenants or sub-tenants; women with a place in society but a precarious one, often dependent upon friends and neighbours to help make ends meet. Such a situation did not in itself produce a potential witch though. What was necessary in addition was for such a woman to have an aggressive, quarrelsome, ill-tempered personality and to lack the deference which was considered appropriate to someone in her position. Most allegations of malefice seem to have started as a result of a quarrel, often accompanied by a curse of the 'you'll be sorry' variety which may not have seemed threatening at the time but could be re-interpreted in retrospect.

The procedure for witchcraft prosecutions varied over time. Early trials like those of the North Berwick witches took place before special justiciary courts. During the 1590s most cases were handled by local courts under a general commission from the Privy Council. From 1597 the Council withdrew this and reserved the right to consider each application before deciding whether to issue a special commission to local landowners and officials. This became the standard way of dealing with witchcraft accusations although the Court of Justiciary also considered cases. Most accusations were initiated by complaints brought before local kirk sessions but sometimes official channels were short-circuited and an unknown number of witches were executed illegally without official warrant.

The prosecution of witchcraft in Scotland differed from England in several ways. In Scotland the crime was being a witch rather than, as in England, performing specific acts of witchcraft. Central to being a witch was the existence of a Demonic Pact whereby a person renounced their baptism, received the Devil's mark and dedicated their soul to his service in return for earthly advantages. The Demonic Pact does not figure prominently in English witchcraft trials. Because of the lack of belief in conspiracy theories of witchcraft in England there was no need to torture suspects to extract the names of accomplices. The lower level of religious intensity in England, where the Reformation was less of a sharp break with the past compared with Scotland, may also have been significant.

Popular belief in witchcraft did not develop suddenly after the Reformation though its nature may have changed with the spread of ideas from the Continent. It is extremely difficult to discover the popular beliefs which

10. A. Macfarlane, *Witchcraft in Tudor and Stuart England* (London 1970).

underlay the Scottish witch hunts. They are filtered through court records and have probably been altered and distorted in the process. The accusations of malefice which were made against individuals probably come closest to representing what ordinary people thought about witches and their powers. On the other hand, these accusations were undoubtedly selected and framed in ways which would secure a commission and facilitate a trial. A whole range of popular beliefs regarding witchcraft may have been omitted as irrelevant to the business of achieving a successful prosecution. The confessions of acknowledged witches present even greater problems as they were obtained under duress. Often they must represent an agreed story between victim and inquisitor which drew upon the beliefs of both. A certain form of confession, emphasising the existence of a Demonic Pact, was needed to secure conviction. The questions which were put to the accused may have been framed so as to produce the right kind of story and may reflect the ideas of the educated elite regarding witchcraft rather than popular beliefs.

Allegations of witchcraft often emphasise the importance of reputation, good or ill, in Scottish society. To have been 'halden and repute' a witch was in itself a powerful argument for conviction though not as strong as an actual confession. The incidents involved in an allegation had often taken place over a number of years. There must have been a strong tendency to reinterpret past events to suit the case. Even so it seems that it took time for a reputation for witchcraft to be built up and, as a result, many women reputed to be witches may have managed to escape prosecution and die in their beds. The details of the confessions in witchcraft cases reveal some distinctly Scottish elements. The Devil seems to have acquired adherents at minimum cost. Instead of promising wealth and riches his normal agreement with his servants was that they 'should never want'. This must reflect the constant anxiety of women in the lower levels of Scottish society over their ability to gain a bare sufficiency. Witches' meetings in churchyards, on open moors or around gallows have an equally simple quality to them. There are few stories of cannibalism, disinterring corpses, sacrificing infants or indulging in sexual orgies as occur frequently in some parts of Europe. Instead the focus of such gatherings was the eating and drinking of simple fare, music and dancing. The church, with its increasingly tight control over 'penny weddings' and other celebrations was making innocent gatherings of this sort rare and there is a sense of wistfulness in some of the confessions.

During the mass witch hunts many of the people who were charged were named under torture by women who had already confessed to being witches and were effectively already under sentence of death. Such circumstances must have offered opportunities for women to settle old scores by dragging down others with whom they were on bad terms. It is clear from the evidence that some women accepted their reputation and genuinely believed that they had special powers; some even revelled unrepentantly in their deviance. Others maintained their innocence even under torture, though this did not necessarily save them from execution.

The executions were great public spectacles. Some unfortunate victims were burnt alive. More commonly witches were strangled and their bodies burnt, but by the later seventeenth century it was normal to hang them. Scottish witchcraft prosecutions have sometimes been considered as foregone conclusions leaving no avenue of escape for the hapless victim. This was not entirely true. A woman accused of witchcraft before a kirk session could counter-attack by charging her accusers with slander. Flight before arrest or escape before trial offered other ways out. By the later seventeenth century defence lawyers in cases brought before the High Court of Justiciary were sometimes able to secure the dismissal of cases by pointing out inconsistencies in the accusations while some women who had confessed to being witches were discharged because it could be shown that they were feeble-minded. Where a verdict of guilty was arrived at a sentence of banishment rather than execution was sometimes imposed. A significant proportion of women were released from execution by premature death in custody from suicide, disease, hunger or injuries received under torture.

CHAPTER 13

CULTURE, EDUCATION AND LITERACY c1500–c1750

Images of early-modern Scottish culture are confusing and sometimes contradictory. On the one hand, there is a picture of a popular and a polite culture impoverished and ruthlessly repressed by the reformed church. The Scots are justly proud of late-medieval makars (poets) like William Dunbar (c1460–c1520) and Robert Henryson (c1420–c1490). By comparison Scotland's artistic and literary achievements in the late sixteenth and seventeenth centuries can seem limited. Yet from the same period comes an image of a system of education unusually effective for its time producing levels of literacy which were high by European standards. Scottish popular culture in the early-modern period is a difficult topic to discuss because the evidence is fragmented and has yet to receive systematic study. Nevertheless it is clear that the impact of the Reformation on popular culture was more subtle, less stultifying, than has sometimes been thought. The superiority of the Scottish education system over that of England in the past as well as in recent times has been one of the pillars of Scottish self-esteem. Recent research has, however, suggested that reality was somewhat different.

LOWLAND CULTURE, POLITE AND POPULAR

The Scottish court provided a focus for aristocratic culture and the spread of Renaissance influences during the sixteenth century, notably under James IV. During his reign in 1507 Walter Chapman, a wealthy Edinburgh merchant, and William Myllar, a bookseller, were granted a royal patent to set up Scotland's first printing press in Edinburgh. Despite the advent of printing most Scottish poetry and prose continued to circulate in manuscript form. Our appreciation of the variety and quality of late fifteenth- and sixteenth-century court literature is tempered by the realisation that much material has been lost. Dunbar's famous 'Lament for the Makaris' mentions a number of poets whose works only survive as fragments if at all. Much of the material that has come down to us from this period is derived from a mere handful of manuscript compilations.

William Dunbar, who was influenced by Chaucer, belongs in part to an older medieval Scottish literary tradition which includes James I and Robert Henryson. On the other hand, his sharp eye and tongue, his criticism of contemporary society castigating among others the idle courtiers who surrounded James IV and Edinburgh's profiteering merchants, anticipates later satirists. Gavin Douglas (?1475–1522), the third son of the Earl of Angus, also forms a bridge between the medieval makars and the Renaissance poets. His greatest achievement was the rendering of Virgil's *Aeneid* in Scots. This was the first full translation of a major classical text in Britain and so deserves a more important place in the history of European literature than it sometimes receives. Sir David Lindsay (1490–1555), a member of the royal household of James V, seems to have been responsible for organising royal entertainments and it was presumably in this context that he developed his flair for drama. His work was part of a vigorous tradition of theatre in sixteenth-century Scotland which drew on elements from religious mystery plays and popular pageants as well as courtly themes, a tradition that was extinguished after the Reformation. Lindsay's success was as a satirist and social commentator. He had anti-clerical views and a sense of natural justice which gave him a sympathy with the common people and a hatred of oppression not often found in ambitious courtiers. His talent was to criticise contemporary society at a level which provoked thought but did not give too much offence. His greatest success was the *Satyre of the Thrie Estaitis*, first performed before James V at Linlithgow Palace in 1540. The criticisms expressed by Lindsay were pointed, yet at the same time he was practical in his suggestions for social reform.

As well as poetry sixteenth-century Scotland also had a strong tradition of religious and court music which developed under a variety of influences. In the early sixteenth century, following the marriage of James IV to Margaret Tudor, England provided much of the inspiration. Later in the century there was a strong French influence at the courts of James V, Mary of Guise, Queen Mary and James VI after the arrival from France of his cousin Esme Stuart in 1579. By the early seventeenth century part singing was giving way in popularity to songs with lute accompaniment and a stronger English influence. The Reformation removed most of the glories of Scottish church music, replacing it with more modest settings of psalms. Nevertheless, manuscripts of pre-Reformation sacred music and secular songs continued to circulate. The Gude and Godlie Ballads, published in 1567, tried to harness contemporary secular songs to the needs of the Reformers, sometimes with (unintentionally) comic results. The song schools did not disappear immediately at the Reformation and indeed James VI made efforts to revive some of them.

After the political upheavals of the 1560s and 1570s a court circle of literati developed around James VI, who fancied himself as a poet as well as a patron of the arts. James was determined to create a new Scots poetic movement. This 'Castalian Band' of poets and musicians (named after the fountain of Castalia, sacred to Apollo and the Muses) was headed by Alexander Montgomerie (?1545–?1610), much of whose extensive output was not published until well after his death. His best-known work, *The Cherry and the Slae*, is deeply allegorical reflecting Montgomerie's dedication to Catholicism and his anger at the mercurial nature of his royal patron. The Reformation did not bring the tradition of the makars to an end immediately but it hastened the spread of English influences on Scottish society and culture encouraging writers to imitate English literary forms. Montgomerie and his contemporaries wrote in Scots but their language was considerably anglicised compared with that of Dunbar and Henryson. The use of English bibles from the sixteenth century had a major effect in bringing Scottish written style closer to that of England and the Castalians looked increasingly southwards for their literary models. The universal use of the King James Bible from the early seventeenth century was another powerful anglicising influence on Scottish culture.

The removal of the monarch to London in 1603 signalled the end of royal patronage for the arts in Scotland and of a tradition of poetry, music, song and dance based on the court and aristocratic ideals. During the seventeenth and early eighteenth centuries this tradition was gradually transformed into a more bourgeois, genteel one. James VI remained a patron of the muses after he left Scotland and literary hopefuls soon followed him southwards. Sir William Alexander (?1577–1640) and Sir Robert Ayton (1569–1638) were the two best-known figures. The former was strongly influenced by contemporary English verse while the latter wrote in French, Latin and Greek as well as English and Scots. Ayton's best work consisted of songs for lute accompanyment. Their near contemporary was William Drummond of Hawthornden (1585–1648) a man who, after the death of his fiancée, avoided public life and spent most of his time on his estates near Edinburgh. Despite a gloomy, depressive temperament he was keen to be taken seriously south of the Border. His style was essentially conservative, looking back to Elizabethan England.

Scots prose developed more slowly than poetry during the sixteenth century, as was the case with other European countries. Latin remained the language for major prose works such as Bishop Leslie's 'History of Scotland', published in 1570 and George Buchanan's 'Rerum Scoticarum Historia' of 1582. Nevertheless, Robert Lindsay of Pitscottie's 'Historie and Chronicles of Scotland', written in the mid-sixteenth century though not published until 1778, has an idiomatic and racy Scots narrative style. Even John Knox's 'History of the Reformation', biased and one-sided though it is, has a colourful and gripping vernacular style in places.

Scotland was far from being an intellectual wilderness in the late sixteenth and early seventeenth centuries.[1] The establishment of Edinburgh University in 1583, Marischal College, Aberdeen in 1593 and the publication of works like George Buchanan's History in 1583 testify to this. Buchanan (1506–82) was one of Europe's foremost Latin stylists and humanists. He produced a

---

1. G. Donaldson, Stair's Scotland: the intellectual inheritance, *Juridicial Review*, 1981, 128–45.

wide range of works and had an important indirect influence as tutor to James VI. Portrait painting also developed in Scotland at this time and there was a fashion for painted ceilings which can be appreciated from surviving examples such as those at Merchiston and Pinkie. The fusion of Renaissance architectural styles with traditional Scottish forms can be seen in late examples of tower houses like Crathes and Craigievar. In law Sir James Balfour of Pittendreich produced a compendium of the decisions of the Court of Session and Sir Thomes Craig (1538–1608) wrote the Jus Feudale, a major treatise on feudal law. John Napier of Merchiston (1550–1617), the inventor of logarithms, also designed a calculating device which was the ancestor of the slide-rule. The astronomer Duncan Liddell (1561–1613) was one of the first to teach the theories of Copernicus. Already in this period Scottish science had an applied slant with efforts directed toward problems such as the drainage of coalmines. Timothy Pont (c1565–1614), inspired by the work of Saxton in England but without the same official backing, produced a series of regional maps of Scotland including remote areas of the Highlands and Islands. His work was continued by Robert Gordon of Straloch (1580–1661) and his son John Gordon of Rothiemay (c1615–1686), who edited Pont's maps for publication as well as contributing original maps of their own. A number of Scots achieved recognition at home and abroad in the fields of medicine and science including John Craig, James VI's physician, and John MacCulloch (d1611) physician to the Duke of Tuscany.

Despite the Reformation a vigorous folk culture survived the seventeenth century in Lowland Scotland. The very frequency with which kirk sessions inveighed against celebrations at weddings, dancing, drinking, playing sports and the observance of seasonal festivals like Beltane, Yule or saints' days suggests that an active popular culture thrived despite efforts to ban it. The use of pre-Reformation feast days as a means of dating continued into the eighteenth century. Popular recreations in the seventeenth century included archery, fencing, golf and hunting for the better off, football, dancing, and animal baiting for those of lesser rank. The reformers were especially active in trying to ban 'penny weddings' where the guests clubbed together to provide entertainment on a scale that the newly-wed couple could never have afforded on their own.

Drinking played a major role in Scottish social life as it still does today. A visit to the alehouse must have been one of the few recreations available to ordinary people in early-modern Scotland, a welcome break from an existence which was often monotonous and hard. Brewing and selling ale was a widespread activity but one which was fairly tightly controlled by local authorities. Whisky, which is first mentioned specifically in 1494, was distilled on a small scale throughout the Lowlands as well as in the Highlands. As we will see in Chapter 15, wine was also consumed in quantity, not just in the higher levels of society. Many brewers and ale sellers were women. Their activities were often viewed in a poor light by landowners and kirk sessions concerned at the moral degradation they might bring to their customers. How often heavy drinking led to alcoholism and poverty is uncertain but it affected all social levels from Lady Wemyss, who in 1652 had a door made between her chamber and the wine cellar because of 'a great desire after strong drink', to Thomas Louthian in Fossoway, whose habitual Sunday recreation, instead of attending church, was to stay at home drinking himself paralytic while cursing and swearing at anyone who interrupted him. Even in the mid-eighteenth century visitors to Scotland commented on Edinburgh's tavern-centred culture, the heavy consumption of alcohol by professionals like lawyers and judges, and the curious blend of refinement and coarseness in language and manners exhibited by many intellectual figures which was often associated with heavy drinking.

Fireside socialising must have been the most widespread, but least well recorded, way of spending free time. Much popular culture revolved around meetings in houses, alehouses, church, and at markets. Men and women often worked together but women had their own distinct elements of popular culture, important for the preservation of oral tradition as they lagged behind in literacy. Women were also healers and midwives. Only gradually during the seventeenth century did the growing professsonalisation of medicine and its dominance by men begin to oust women from this role.

Scotland in the first half of the eighteenth century had a song culture which was so well established and so rich that it cannot have been a recent development. Anthologists and collectors like James Watson and Allan Ramsay took many of the examples that they printed from contemporary broadsides and chapbooks. The transmission of songs and the market for printed versions was by no means purely Scottish though. Chapbooks printed in Newcastle, York and London contained versions of traditional Scottish songs while Scottish printers reproduced English ones. English tunes and lyrics had been in widespread circulation in Scotland during the seventeenth and even the sixteenth century. Later eighteenth-century collections of traditional songs suggest that there was a wide repertoire of love songs, drinking songs, work songs and songs relating to occupations, including forerunners of the later bothy ballads about agricultural life, of which only a small part got into print and has come down to us.

One of the most famous elements of Scottish popular culture, ballads, began to be collected in the eighteenth century but what remains (sometimes 'improved' by early editors like Sir Walter Scott) is probably only a fragment of rich orally transmitted tradition. The problem of trying to date Scottish ballads which preoccupied early collectors is almost as misleading as the question of their authorship. Ballads were probably in circulation from at least the fourteenth century and continued to be recited, amended and composed into the late seventeenth century and after. Where ballads tell stories related to real historical events we have at least some indication of the earliest date that they were in circulation. The Complaynt of Scotland (1549) refers to ballads on the Battle of Harlaw, Chevy Chase and the Battle of Otterburn, versions of all of which have been preserved. But many ballads with romantic or supernatural themes are versions of stories known from other parts of Europe and may have circulated in various forms for centuries before being written down by collectors. Ballad composition seems to have flourished particularly in two regions, the Borders and the north east, areas where social tensions were greater in the sixteenth and early seventeenth century than elsewhere in the Lowlands, although the traditions of the two areas were by no means separate and ballads were widely sung elsewhere.

Regarding authorship, scholars have varied between the idea that ballads were produced by a whole series of people as gradual accretions from tales and folk memory or that they were the products of individual composers which then developed into variant forms as they were disseminated. Because of their economy of words and their use of stock phrases and epithets, ballads were easily memorised and passed on. Those which have survived in published collections are often misleading as it is likely that they were originally designed to be sung rather than spoken. The power of their imagery is often striking but there are indications that standards of composition were declining in the seventeenth century as the oral tradition faced a steady onslaught from the literate one, driving the oral ballad further down the social scale and making women, less literate than men, its principal repositories.

With the demise of the court tradition of poetry after 1603 it became increasingly difficult to distinguish between popular and polite poems and songs, especially in cases where new words were set to traditional tunes. The distinction between folk songs and 'art' poems was often blurred with courtly poems finding their way into the repertoires of popular singers and the productions of broadside printers. In the course of the eighteenth century it became common for traditional folk songs to be re-cast in more polite, genteel versions, an activity for which Allan Ramsay and Robert Burns were both noted.

During the sixteenth and especially the seventeenth century the culture of the printed word gained ground steadily over oral tradition. Although the patent for Scotland's first printing press was granted in 1507 Scottish printers remained relatively isolated, unambitious and small-scale with a limited range of titles. The reading public was slowly growing though and in the seventeenth century chapbooks often printed in England were sold by travelling chapmen. The impression from surviving material is that there was much less diversionary popular literature in Scotland than south of the Border in the seventeenth century. A high proportion of the books published in Scotland were devotional in theme. Most of the rest consisted of guides, almanacs and works on history or politics. The books found in ordinary households were mainly the Bible and psalm books. Only landowners and professional people had collections.

THE GAELIC TRADITION

Gaelic culture has been persistently ignored or undervalued in the past and is not easily accessible to the majority of Scots today. As with other Celtic languages such as Breton and Irish, Gaelic was systematically attacked and undermined by central authority over a long period. Nevertheless, Gaelic culture, little affected by the Reformation but by no means isolated from outside influences, remained vigorous and rich throughout our period. Unfortunately it was an orally transmitted culture and the amount of material which has come down to us in written form is limited.

In the Highlands the Reformed church made little progress before the eighteenth century while the Catholic church had assimilated rather than replaced pre-Christian beliefs. Consequently it is here that we find such elements surviving most strongly in popular culture although the supernatural element in many Lowland ballads indicates that this was not an exclusively Highland phenomenon. Many Highland festivals, despite Christian overtones, were thinly disguised celebrations of fertility, the winter solstice or attempts to ensure a good harvest, sometimes with watered down representations of what may originally have been human sacrifice. There was even a survival of idol worship into the eighteenth century at a cult centre at the head of Glenlyon where carved stone idols were brought out of their special house on the 1st of May and propitiated to ensure good pasture for the livestock and a good harvest, the idols being returned to their house for the winter after harvest was ended.

One of the best-known but least understood elements of traditional Gaelic culture is the work of the bards. The corpus of bardic verse which survives is small. Much of it comes from two manuscript collections, the fifteenth-century Book of the Dean of Lismore and the seventeenth-century Red Book of Clanranald. A number of surviving poems date from the later fifteenth and early sixteenth centuries, most of the rest to the later sixteenth and early seventeenth centuries. Bardic poetry often involved eulogies of clans or their leaders, and laments for the deaths of chiefs. Poems recounting the genealogy and history of clans were also popular, the roles of bard and sennachie (clan historian) often overlapping. Bards were also responsible for playing Brosnachadh Catha, incitements to battle. Irish bardic schools, and possibly Scottish ones too, taught the rules of metre and syntax for bardic composition. Bardic verse, especially praise poetry, had to be composed when occasion demanded. On the quality of such poetry depended a bard's patronage and fame but they were also free to write poems on other themes which were less hidebound by stylistic conventions. Until the suppression of the Lords of the Isles at the end of the fifteenth century their court was the premier focus for bards but there were many lesser courts among the major chiefs while clan leaders of more modest means who could not support a bard of their own gave hospitality to wandering ones. Failure to do so might incur the wrath of bards like Aonghis nan Aoir (Angus of the Satires) a sixteenth-century itinerant bard who was usually given a generous welcome because his satires and lampoons on stingy patrons were so vitriolic.

There was also a tradition of poetry produced by ordinary people, only a tiny proportion of which has survived in written form. Although less likely to be preserved in early manuscript anthologies than the bardic verse the folk tradition remained strong in the Highlands into the nineteenth century and even the twentieth century in more remote districts. Many songs collected in modern times clearly originate from before the eighteenth century. Such songs and poems reflected contemporary Highland society; conservative, relatively isolated, bound by ties of family and clan, and closely in tune with the local environment. Many songs celebrate particular places or historical events. Others were love songs or lullabies. Work songs formed another major category. Songs sung by women while waulking (fulling) cloth, with a chorus and refrain, and by men while rowing, were among the most popular types but songs were also fitted to the rhythms of spinning, weaving, milking, harvesting and other communal activities. The bardic and popular traditions cannot always be easily separated for both were essentially oral and they interacted to enrich each other. In addition there were the great heroic ballads. Some of those which have survived may have originated as early as the twelfth century and were still popular in the eighteenth. It was from fragments of such ballads that James MacPherson produced his 'Ossianic' selections in the 1760s. These poems have elements in common with traditional Lowland ballads but the heroes were generally Celtic ones. Such ballads were usually accorded the highest status in a person's repertoire and some of them survived in oral tradition into the twentieth century in parts of the Outer Hebrides.

Gaelic songs could be sung on their own or accompanied by the clarsach or celtic harp. Many harpers learned their skills in Ireland but the use of the instrument died out rapidly in Scotland during the early eighteenth century being replaced by the fiddle whose popularity increased rapidly throughout Scotland at this time. Indeed, many tunes written originally for the harp only survived as versions re-written for the fiddle. During the eighteenth century Highland and Lowland fiddle music increasingly converged as dancing became more and more popular in the Lowlands and the disapproval of the Kirk waned. But of all musical instruments it is the bagpipe with which the Highlands are most closely associated. The early history of the bagpipe in the Highlands is unknown; there are no certain records of its use before the sixteenth century. In late-medieval times the bagpipe was played widely throughout Europe but it declined in popularity during the sixteenth century surviving mainly in more isolated, peripheral areas.

In the sixteenth and seventeenth centuries pipers were found in every Highland community but official pipers to the great chiefs had the widest reputations. Their tasks included playing to wake the chief's household in the morning, and to honour the arrival and departure of guests. They composed pieces in praise of their patrons and laments for their passing, as well as tunes to rally clans in battle. During the seventeenth and early eighteenth centuries bagpipe music evolved into a high art form. There were two musical traditions in the Highlands, the ceol beg or little music of ordinary songs, dances, marches and rallying calls and the ceol mor or great music, a form unique to the region. Often called Piobaireachd (pibroch), which simply means 'pipe music', this was the classical music of the bagpipe. Pibrochs were compositions for solo bagpipe lasting up to 15 minutes or so. They had a carefully defined structure beginning with a relatively simple theme, the urlar or ground. A series of variations on the theme, the siubhal, was then developed, each variation more complex than the last and requiring more dextrous fingering, building up to a climax or crunluath, after which there was a return to the original urlar. As stirring war tunes or as laments pibrochs can equal the greatest of European music although they were composed and passed on entirely aurally. A well-trained piper might have been able to play up to 200 pibrochs from memory. The greatest exponents of pibroch were the MacCrimmons, hereditary pipers to the MacLeods of Dunvegan. The MacCrimmons appeared in Skye during the sixteenth century: their earlier origins are unknown. They dominated Scottish piping as composers, teachers and players until after Culloden and the banning of the bagpipe as a war instrument.

By the early seventeenth century classical bardic poetry was changing and later in the century it began to decline as aristocratic patronage started to dry up. Gaelic poetry began to appear which belonged to the bardic tradition stylistically but used different themes, often being composed by amateur poets rather than official bards. This type of verse was frequently concerned with the changing nature of clan society and its wider political context. Such poetry has sometimes been termed 'semi-bardic'. As the Highland clans became drawn into national politics so were the verses of the bards, their style becoming at the same time less formal and traditional. This is demonstrated in the work of Iain Lom (?1620–?1707), the most influential Gaelic poet of his day. Bard to the MacDonalds of Keppoch, he was present at the Battle of Inverlochy in 1645 when the Marquis of Montrose and Alasdair MacColla shattered the power of the Earl of Argyll. Iain Lom celebrated the defeat of the Campbells with venomous verses whose economical style and carefully selected detail reflected the harsh reality of battle. He was an active political figure himself, being responsible for inciting revenge after the murder of the young chief of Keppoch. Iain Lom continued to write poetry commenting on contemporary political developments down to the Union of 1707.

A contemporary of Iain Lom was Roderick Morison (?1656–?1714), known as An Clarsair Dall, the Blind Harper. He was both bard and harpist, one of the last of his kind. After being blinded by an attack of smallpox he travelled around the Highlands as an itinerant bard before settling for a few years with Iain Breac, chief of the MacLeods, at Dunvegan, one of the last chiefs to keep a full retinue of bard, piper and jester. When Iain Breac died in 1693 Roderick composed a song to him which turns, in its later verses, into a scathing attack on his son castigating his extravagance and adoption of a Lowland lifestyle. Bards had always been critical of the actions of their chiefs if these breached accepted codes of behaviour. This was usually done in a less overt way than Morison who highlighted the extravagance of the young chief by describing each newly acquired item of equipment and estimating how many farms' rent it had cost. Morison was Gaelic Scotland's last famous bard/harper and it is ironic that his best-known work attacks the influences which were to destroy traditional Gaelic society during the eighteenth century.

Although bardic poetry was a male preserve there was a vigorous tradition of women poets in Gaelic. Their themes were not necessarily confined to domestic affairs. They might write praise poetry for their chiefs while Catherine MacLean, who lived on Coll in the early eighteenth century, wrote scathing verse about the incompetence of the Jacobite commanders during the 1715 rebellion. Women's songs included laments for menfolk lost in battle or at sea. Women on St Kilda composed songs in memory of men killed in falls from the cliffs while collecting seabirds and eggs. The classical bardic tradition was dying out in the early eighteenth century. This may have enriched rather than eroded the Gaelic tradition as poets and musicians responded to changed circumstances by turning to simpler, less formal styles. Gaelic poets of the first half of the eighteenth century composed for a wider audience than the earlier bards and wrote less formally but although their range of themes was wider they continued to use stylistic elements drawn from the earlier bardic schools. The work of some Gaelic poets was published in the middle and later eighteenth century but despite the interest aroused by MacPherson's Ossian (published 1760–63) the audience for contemporary Gaelic poetry in print was limited. Because Lowlanders viewed Gaelic language and culture as primitive they considered that Gaelic poetry could only explain primitive emotions and ideas: hence the popularity of the 'ancient' epics of MacPherson's Ossian. The subtleties of contemporary Gaelic poets such as Duncan Ban MacIntyre were lost on them.

The most influential and innovative early eighteenth-century Gaelic poet was Alasdair MacMhaigstir Alasdair (c1695–c1770). The son of an episcopalian minister in Moidart, he studied for a while at Glasgow University but never graduated, becoming a schoolmaster until 1745 when he joined the Jacobite army. He wrote many poems on political themes including a number of pro-Jacobite poems which incorporated visions of a Gaelic resurgence free from the influence of Lowland manners and culture and emphasised the old warlike spirit of the clans. Some of his best poems were descriptions of nature. Gaelic poetry had always been closely in tune with the Highland landscape and environment and many surviving sixteenth- and seventeenth-century poems contain sharp descriptions of nature. But it was only in the eighteenth century that this emerged as an important poetic theme in its own right. MacMhaigstir Alasdair may well have been influenced by James Thomson's 'The Seasons', published between 1727 and 1730, but poems like 'Oran an-t Samhraidh' (Song to Summer) and 'Oran a'Gheamhraidh' (Song to Winter), while using the same broad themes as Thomson, are altogether less romanticised. 'Allt an t-Siucair' (Sugar Brook), written in the early 1740s, is a detailed description of a settlement in Ardnamurchan and the countryside around it. His most famous poem, 'Birlinn Chlann Raghnaill' (Clanranald's Galley) vividly recreates a voyage from the Hebrides to Ireland. The poem has a wealth of technical detail relating to the working of the galley but also a good deal of subtle human observation. He also wrote love songs and satires.

His poem 'Moladh Morag' (Praise of Morag) has a metrical pattern similar to the musical structure of a pibroch, a style of composition which was followed by other eighteenth-century Gaelic poets like Duncan Ban MacIntyre.

Robb Donn Mackay (1714–1778), an illiterate cattle drover from Sutherland, composed in a more restricted vein about everyday life in a pre-Clearance community. Growing up on the estates of Lord Reay, Robb's talents were recognised by the local tacksman who took him into his household and encouraged him. More than any other contemporary Gaelic poet Robb was able to convey the lifestyle of traditional Highland society with the ties and tensions that existed within small communities. Duncan Ban MacIntyre (1724–1812) was strongly influenced by MacMhaighstir Alasdair's work. He too was involved in the 1745 campaign, fighting reluctantly at Falkirk in the Argyll Militia, but most of his early manhood was spent as a gamekeeper in and around Glen Orchy. During this period he produced his most famous descriptive poems, 'Oran Coire a'Cheathaich' (Song to Misty Corrie) and 'Moladh Beinn Dobhrain' (In Praise of Ben Dorain). Although not literate he had a wide knowledge of earlier Gaelic poetry. His intensely focused observations of nature reached their best when describing the deer he was in charge of. There was nothing sentimental about his work: he could describe the graceful movements of the deer and then the weapons which would kill them with equal impartiality. MacIntyre was keenly aware of how the Highlands were changing in the mid-eighteenth century. In a later poem he revisited the Misty Corrie and described how it has been ruined through overgrazing by the newly introduced sheep which had driven away the deer.

EDUCATION AND LITERACY

The oral tradition of the Highlands contrasts with the increasingly literate one of the Lowlands which in turn reflects developments in education. It is often suggested that the system of parish and burgh schools which developed in Scotland during the later sixteenth and seventeenth centuries was entirely the work of the reformers. It is likely, however, that they built on foundations which had been laid well before the Reformation. This was certainly true in the burghs for there was a grammar school in every sizable town by 1500. The situation in rural areas is less clear. There are few references to pre-Reformation parish schools but given the sparsity of the surviving documentation it would be dangerous to infer that this indicates that they did not exist. Schools attached to abbeys, cathedrals and collegiate churches may also have provided some education for the laity.

Although schools in rural areas may have existed before 1560 the reformers saw a clear need for a greatly improved and standardised education system so that people could read scripture for themselves. A desire to provide education was common among the religious reformers of the sixteenth century. In Scotland, however, the church was able to enlist the support of the state for its educational programme in contrast to England where, until the nineteenth century, the system depended on charity and private fees rather than a regulated system of support. The First Book of Discipline proposed a carefully stratified system with a school in each parish providing elementary teaching of reading, writing and the Catechism to children from the age of five or six. At about eight some of the more able pupils would go on to grammar schools in their nearest burgh where they would be taught Latin. At 12 they might then transfer to colleges or high schools in the larger towns which would provide teaching in the classical languages, logic and rhetoric in preparation for university entrance at 16. As with the other aims of the early reformers these well-meaning plans were undermined by lack of finance.

Despite some state encouragement for the setting up of parish schools it is unlikely that much progress was made before the early seventeenth century. Most of the available resources were channelled into setting up the new parish ministry and education had to take second place except in a few parishes where the initiative was taken by enthusiastic landowners. In 1616 the Privy Council gave its support to the reformers' initiatives on education by passing an Act requiring that every parish should have a school and a suitably qualified master funded by the local inhabitants. The Act was ratified by Parliament in 1633. In 1646 it was repeated with the requirement that the costs of providing education in each parish should be met by the heritors. This Act was abolished after the Restoration and its mechanism for funding parish schools were only restored in 1696. The 1696 Act has been seen as a watershed in the development of Scottish education not because it legislated for a system of parish schools funded by landowners (who were allowed to recoup half the cost from their tenants) but because it included measures for enforcement. In parishes where heritors failed to come up with the necessary money it was possible for ministers to apply to Commissioners of Supply to impose a settlement by placing a stent on them.

Too much faith, though, can be placed in the efficacy of well-meaning legislation. The very fact that Acts authorising the establishment of parish schools had to be repeated so often indicates that their success was neither immediate nor universal. Even when schools can be shown to have existed their impact cannot easily be assessed. Nevertheless, although the Acts of 1616, 1633 and 1646 have been seen as ineffective because there was no way of enforcing them, the number of functioning parish schools throughout the Lowlands seems to have increased substantially during the seventeenth century. By the end of the century many Lowland parishes had a school and schoolmaster funded partly by landowners and partly by fees. There were also unofficial 'adventure' schools. References to their existence are usually incidental like one at Ceres in 1649 when a woman 'that learns the bairns' was recorded as receiving support from parish funds. Their number and overall impact has probably been underestimated. They were sometimes suppressed by kirk sessions or restricted as to who and what they could teach, being confined to younger children, to girls, and sometimes to the acquisition of purely practical skills such as stocking manufacture. In larger parishes they were useful in serving outlying areas. Farmers in such districts sometimes clubbed together to hire a teacher for several weeks over the winter, short-term informal instruction which probably provided most of the education than many children from poorer families received. Informal learning within the family may also have been more important than has sometimes been realised, particularly for girls for whom there was less incentive to invest money in education.

The burgh schools provided a second tier in the education system, taking children from the age of seven or eight, after two years or so of elementary education, teaching Latin and sometimes Greek. Some burgh schools, like those at Dalkeith and Perth, had reputations which attracted pupils from a considerable distance. By the early eighteenth century some of these schools were teaching subjects like book-keeping, geography and navigation in addition to the traditional curriculum. Scotland lacked large numbers of schools on the English model which had been endowed specifically for the benefit of poor scholars. Provision for poor children was made individually within existing schools. The major towns did, however, have some important charitable foundations. In Edinburgh the most famous was the one established from money left by the wealthy goldsmith George Heriot who died in 1623. In Glasgow, Thomas Hutcheson left a large endowment in 1641 for the education of poor and orphaned sons of burgesses. Further establishments of a similar kind were founded in the two cities in the later seventeenth century and the first half of the eighteenth.

Reform of the universities was another aim of the new church. Between 1574 and 1579 Andrew Melville instituted major changes at St Andrews and Glasgow. The original plan had been for the three St Andrews colleges to specialise, St Salvator's in arts and medicine, St Leonard's in moral philosophy and law, St Mary's in theology. These aims were not fully achieved. St Mary's did become a college of divinity but the teaching of law and medicine failed to develop. In 1582 a new college at Edinburgh received its charter and in 1593 Marischal College was established in Aberdeen, largely due to the slowness of the staff of King's College in supporting the Reformation. It had been an ideal of the Reformers that every large town should have its own college to teach higher education. The new college at Edinburgh was a positive achievement in this direction but elsewhere the need was met by the broadening of the curricula in burgh schools rather than the creation of new tertiary institutions.

It has been suggested that most Lowland parishes had schools by the end of the seventeenth century. In some areas this was undoubtedly true. In the Lothians during the 1690s at least 61 out of 65 parishes had schools, in Fife 55 out of 60 parishes. It is well known that schools were few in the Highlands during the seventeenth and early eighteenth centuries but even within the Lowlands schools were slow to spread in some districts. Provision varied depending on local circumstances such as the attitude of individual landowners, the size of the population and the nature of the local economy. In Wigtownshire at the time of the 1696 Act the only schools were in the burghs of Stranraer, Wigtown and possibly Whithorn. There were none in the rural parishes. The legislation of 1696 had little immediate impact in this area and half the parishes did not have a school established until the 1740s or even later. The situation was similar in neighbouring Kirkcudbrightshire. Even in the presbytery of Ayr 12 parishes out of 28 had no school in 1735. Despite the measures in the 1696 Act for compelling heritors to raise schoolmasters' salaries it was possible for landowners to delay the establishment of a school for years even when the minister was enthusiastic. Problems were created by non-resident heritors, lack of agreement on the level of the schoolmaster's salary, failure to provide funds for a school, and disputes over where in the parish it should be located. When a salary for a schoolmaster was agreed it was often too small to attract suitable applicants and was often not paid in full.

The provision of schools in the Highlands remained poor into the eighteenth century. In the early eighteenth century the need to improve education in the Highlands was associated with the desire to counter Catholic, Episcopalian and Jacobite sympathies. William III made a gift of £1,800 Scots a year for the use of schools in the Highland areas of Dumbartonshire, Perthshire and Stirlingshire. In 1709 the Society in Scotland for Propagating Christian Knowledge (SSPCK) was founded with the aim of establishing charity schools in the Highlands. By 1732, 109 masters were being financed by the society and by 1758 it had opened 176 schools. The results of their activity often fell short of initial expectations due to lack of co-operation from local landowners in the provision of adequate facilities. The standard of education provided in SSPCK schools was modest; the aim was to teach pupils to read sufficiently to allow them to follow the Bible themselves. Writing and arithmetic were probably only taught to a minority. Nevertheless, education at this level was freely available even to children from the poorest families.

The salaries for schoolmasters laid down in the 1696 Act were modest ranging from 100 to 200 merks but these were supplemented by fees from pupils and payments for acting as session clerk and precentor, entering proclamations of marriage, recording baptisms and writing testimonials. Many schoolmasters took on a range of other by-employments to make ends meet. The bulk of a schoolmaster's income was paid by the heritors of a parish in proportion to their valued rent. If proprietors were tight-fisted a substantial part of a schoolmaster's income might have been in arrears or even not paid at all. Mechanisms for compelling heritors to pay were lacking unless the schoolmaster himself was desperate enough to go to law. The consequences of this could be unpleasant as with the case of the schoolmaster of Comrie in 1707 who was beaten up and abused because he had resorted to legal action to try to recover his rightful salary. He and his family were forced to flee the parish as a result. It is not surprising that schoolmasters were sometimes difficult to recruit or that the educational standards of those who were obtained were often quite low. Although Scotland's educational system was distinctive in that it became subject to centralised control at an early date, legislation did not necessarily produce compliance at a local level even by the mid-eighteenth century. The differences between the education systems of Scotland and England may have been less than has sometimes been suggested.

Much of the research on Scottish education has concentrated on the provision of schools and schoolmasters rather than their impact on the population. How effective were schools in spreading literacy, especially in the Lowlands? Earlier generations of Scottish educationalists had no doubts that the achievements were substantial. In the mid-nineteenth century Lowland Scotland had a higher level of literacy than other parts of Britain. The Scottish model of education was seen as one to be emulated south of the Border. From this it was widely believed that the Scottish educational system had also been superior to that of England during the eighteenth and even the seventeenth century. This echoes Defoe's comment that Scotland had 'the most enlightened peasantry in the world'. It must be remembered, however, that this claim was produced at the time of the debate leading to the Union of 1707 when Scotland's good points were being extolled by pro-Union propagandists. Even so such opinions may reflect how contemporary Scots saw their education system for it appears to be from this time that some of the fundamental myths regarding it seem to have originated. The success of the educational system introduced by the reformers and its impact on literacy remains one of the great legends of Scottish nationalist sentiment. In the seventeenth and eighteenth centuries, it has been claimed, education was available to a broader spectrum of society than in England and Scotland had one of the most literate societies in Europe.

Education in Scotland during the seventeenth and eighteenth centuries was thought to have been cheap, universal and widely accessible to the lower levels of society promoting equality of opportunity and encouraging the selection of gifted individuals for upward social mobility. From this it was a short step to suggesting that the Scottish education system had made Scottish society not just different from that of England but better. It has been claimed that virtually everyone in the Lowlands could write by the mid-eighteenth century. Most statements about Scottish literacy have, however, been based on assumptions rather than facts.

A recent study by Houston has revised this picture by showing that educational ideals were a long way from reality in the seventeenth and eighteenth centuries.[2] Scotland did indeed enjoy a fairly high level of literacy but it was far from being exceptional. Measured by the ability of people to sign their names, Scottish literacy levels were poorer than in Sweden or New England and the achievements of the Scottish education system seem less impressive than have often been claimed. It is clear that the attainment of literacy was far from being universal but varied greatly with social status, between town and countryside, and between men and women. Literacy levels in Scotland were broadly similar to those of Northern England with

2. R.A. Houston, *Scottish Literacy and the Scottish Identity* (Cambridge, 1985).

about 75 per cent male illiteracy around 1640 and 35 per cent by 1760. For a small, relatively poor country this was nevertheless a considerable achievement. Scotland may not have had the very high levels of literacy of New England but the demand for serious religious historical and literary works does seem to have been spread more widely through society than in Northern England. It is important to remember, though, that such achievements were largely confined to the Lowlands. In the Highlands the population continued to remain largely illiterate into the nineteenth century.

Literacy levels in different societies can be compared by using the index of the ability of individuals to sign their names on documents. This may underestimate the reading ability of women more than men; reading was taught before writing and many Scottish women may have been able to read but not write. Nevertheless, it allows comparisons between different areas and over time. Signatures to the National Covenant of 1638 and the Solemn League and Covenant of 1643 have survived for a range of parishes from Aberdeenshire to Galloway. They suggest that adult male illiteracy in the mid-seventeenth century was only 32 per cent in Edinburgh and ranged between 46 per cent and 53 per cent for smaller urban centres. In rural areas it was around 80 per cent. Overall about 75 per cent of the population were unable to sign their names compared with c70 per cent for England. A study of witnesses in cases brought before the High Court of Justiciary in the later seventeenth century shows that landed and professional men were almost totally literate. Craftsmen and traders were 23 per cent illiterate, falling to around 13 per cent in the first half of the eighteenth century. Farmers had lower literacy levels than craftsmen but even so only 28 per cent were unable to sign their names. Servants, who were 70 per cent illiterate and labourers, 82 per cent illiterate in the late seventeenth century, had only improved their position marginally by the mid-eighteenth century. The main gain in literacy during this period was by the middling groups of society such as craftsmen and tenants, while literacy levels of cottars and labourers stagnated.

The markedly lower level of literacy of women stands out; about 28 per cent of men in the sample were illiterate compared with 80 per cent of female witnesses. Female illiteracy before the mid-seventeenth century may have been over 95 per cent in both Scotland and England. The profile of male versus female literacy in Scotland was broadly similar to that found throughout north-west Europe; women were slightly less literate than their counterparts in Northern England, men slightly more so. 'Open access' to Scottish education did not include women any more than the poor. Female literacy fell during the period but only slightly – from 88 per cent in the later seventeenth century to around 75 per cent in the mid-eighteenth century.

For particular occupational groups literacy levels were substantially higher in Edinburgh and Glasgow compared with smaller towns which in turn were more literate than rural areas. By the mid-eighteenth century, however, the gap between Edinburgh and Glasgow on one hand and smaller towns had been closed or even reversed while the rural–urban gap overall was widening. An influx of population into Scotland's two largest cities, particularly illiterate Highlanders, may provide the explanation and there are, for Edinburgh, indications of a sharp contrast in literacy levels between the wealthier central areas and the artisan suburbs. Edinburgh and Glasgow had only a slight lead in literacy levels over Northern English towns like Newcastle, Durham and Carlisle though they were better than York whose economy was stagnating. When the sample of witnesses was broken down by geographical origins literacy was highest in Edinburgh (15 per cent illiterate), the Lothians and the western Lowlands (26 per cent) and the Borders (18 per cent). Elsewhere in the Lowlands the figure was around 25–30 per cent but rose to 46 per cent in the North. Seventy-one per cent of women in Edinburgh were illiterate against 90 per cent from the North.

Indications are that literacy levels in Scotland were fairly stable between the mid-sixteenth and the mid-seventeenth centuries. There is no indication of the educational revolution which has been claimed for England during this period. The most marked improvement in literacy levels seems to have occurred towards the end of the seventeenth century. By the mid-eighteenth century male illiteracy in the Lowlands was around 35 per cent, similar to Northern England but slightly better than for England overall. In the Highlands, however, the figure was probably in excess of 60 per cent.

The Scottish education system produced levels of literacy no higher than in Northern England. Scotland was one of the better-educated countries in Europe but was no more advanced than Holland, England or Sweden. The differences in levels of literacy in Scotland between town and country suggest that economic rather than cultural forces provided the main spur encouraging people to learn to read and write. At its best the Scottish system was able to produce slightly better results than the English one – in terms of the proportion of people in certain social and occupational groups who could sign their names – but overall there was little to choose between the systems. By the mid-nineteenth century literacy levels were undoubtedly higher in Scotland than England but the bulk of this improvement must have come late.

Free education was available to only a tiny minority; most families had to pay. The need for children to undertake agricultural and domestic work often interrupted schooling for all but the youngest children. Education was often only part time for a year or two, long enough for children to learn to read but often not to write or count. The percentage of children at any period who attended school, even for only a short period, is unknown. It is possible that the chances of poor children acquiring some education were better in Scotland than in England though there is no evidence that the Scottish system was significantly better at catering for gifted children from poor backgrounds.

The need for literacy grew from the sixteenth to the mid-eighteenth century. Bureaucracy was spreading increasingly into the everyday life of ordinary people. Involvement with courts, which in Scotland tended to emphasise written procedures, the drawing up of agricultural leases, wills and testaments, marketing and the keeping of accounts all provided a stimulus for literacy. The role of the Church of Scotland in promoting literacy is less clear although its stress on making the scriptures available to everyone for personal study may have encouraged more widespread ownership and use of bibles than in England. The proportion of Scottish inventories which lists books is small; book owners were drawn overwhelmingly from the middling and upper ranks of society. In a study of testaments from the Northern and Western Isles during the late seventeenth and early eighteenth centuries, Shaw has shown that only 56 mentioned the ownership of books.[3] Of these 46 related to men and 10 to women. Thirty-eight came from Orkney. Of the men, 76 per cent were professional and 24 per cent were craftsmen and traders, mainly Kirkwall merchants.

Although the importance of literacy was growing it should not be assumed that those who were unable to read were cut off from literate culture. Reading often seems to have been done aloud, especially within the family. Literacy levels were probably high enough for all but the most remote and isolated communities to contain someone who could read and write. Notaries who could draw up formal legal documents were quite widely distributed in small burghs and market centres. The advantages of literacy may seem obvious in modern society but were not necessarily as clear in the past. The spread of literacy in Scotland was slowed by a widespread distrust of documents and visual symbols often retained a power which was lacking in print. Although the Register of Sasines was instituted in 1617 as a standardised record of land transactions the process of transferring property continued to retain as its central feature the placing of a clod of earth in the hand of the new proprietor. Repeated efforts by kirk sessions to ensure the attendance of children at parish schools may have reflected a reluctance on the part of parents to send their children to school as much as economic reasons. The widespread existence of private adventure schools which, presumably, were less concerned with social conformity, may reflect a distrust by the ordinary population of the establishment-orientated values of the official education system. This in turn may explain why many kirk sessions were eager to ban them.

A central function of education in seventeenth- and eighteenth-century Scotland was to produce ideological conformity. Adam Smith believed that the Scots were more law abiding than the English due to more widespread education. The provision of a centrally organised education system at an early date may have helped create a more docile and disciplined workforce, promoting social stability and reducing disruptive class conflict by teaching a shared set of values which encouraged conformity rather than independent thinking. The systems of rote learning, which were the main form of instruction, encouraged the acquisition of knowledge rather than the development of understanding and was geared for preparing pupils to accept a pre-ordained position in life rather than promoting social mobility.

It has been suggested that the Scottish education system was a major force in blurring social distinctions because pupils of all ranks from the very poor

---

3. F.J. Shaw, *The Northern and Western Islands of Scotland in the Seventeenth Century* (Edinburgh 1979), p. 189.

to the sons of landowners were taught together in the same classrooms. While lairds' and cottars' sons may have rubbed shoulders in the classroom there is no indication that this reduced the gulfs which existed within Scottish society. In practice children from higher-status backgrounds were often treated differently and taught more advanced material than their poorer classmates. In the sense that boys from humble backgrounds could compete on equal terms with those from the upper levels of society equality of opportunity did not exist.

As regards higher education, Scotland's position with respect to the proportion of people from poor backgrounds who were able to enter university was probably a little better than England but not outstanding in European terms. The number of students in Scottish universities in the early eighteenth century was only around 1,000. Perhaps about 1.5–2 per cent of boys in the appropriate age groups were able to attend university. The figure for England may have been between 1 per cent and 1.5 per cent. Scotland may have performed better in this respect than France or Germany but was on a par with Sweden and the United Provinces. When it is appreciated that a significant proportion of places in Scottish universities was occupied by students born outside Scotland openness of access seems even more of a myth despite the fact that it cost only a tenth as much to send a boy to Glasgow University as to Oxford or Cambridge.

By the later eighteenth century the view of the superiority of the Scottish educational system had crystallised around the idea that it was well geared to the promotion of social mobility by encouraging the advancement of gifted boys from impoverished backgrounds. The widespread belief in such an idea can be seen as a way of convincing the lower orders to conform by suggesting that the system allowed capable people to overcome inequality and implying that those who were not able to do this had only themselves, and not the system, to blame. The myth of the 'lad o' pairts' thus served to bolster the established social order. In practice social mobility by these means seems to have benefited very few and to have had limited impact on society. The highest position that a boy from a poor background who surmounted all the obstacles and graduated from a Scottish university could normally hope to obtain was a schoolmaster or minister. The system reinforced the dominance of the landed and professional elite over Scottish society, severely restricted upward mobility, and had no real commitment to equality of opportunity. The evidence for literacy suggests that we need to re-examine the belief that Scottish society in the eighteenth century was a very open one compared with England with less rigid stratification and a good deal of upward social mobility.

NATIONALISM AND LITERARY REVIVAL

After 1707, although the Scots were politically British, nationalist sentiments survived. This was partly due to English animosity and also to a sense that the Union was often working unfairly against Scotland. Inevitably, given the scale of popular opposition to the Union, there was an element of hurt pride in the years after 1707. One expression of this was a turning back to Scotland's literary past and the rediscovery of achievements from the days when Scotland had possessed its own distinctive literature. This re-assertion of Scottish culture had undertones of hostility to the Union and many of its exponents were Jacobites. The early eighteenth century saw the appearance of a number of patriotic histories of Scotland and the publication of earlier works like Gavin Douglas' sixteenth-century translation of the *Aeneid* and Blind Harry's 'Wallace'. Publishers like James Watson and Robert Fairbairn, both Jacobites, sought to revive Scottish vernacular literature. In 1706, at the height of the union debate, Watson produced the first volume of his *Choice Collection of Comic and Serious Scots Poems both Ancient and Modern.* Further volumes appeared in 1709 and 1711, marking the start of the eighteenth-century Scots literary revival. The collection was a strange rag-bag of sixteenth- and seventeenth-century verse, some popular, some from court poets like Montgomerie and including such diverse authors as the Marquis of Montrose, the Covenanter poet William Cleland and Sir George Mackenzie of Rosehaugh. It was perhaps a shaky foundation on which to rebuild the tradition of Scottish poetry.

The Scots vernacular tradition was continued by Allan Ramsay. Born in 1684, the son of a Leadhills mine manager, Ramsay was apprenticed to an Edinburgh wigmaker before becoming a writer and bookseller. At its best his own lively verse used contemporary Scots rather than self-consciously harking back to the language of the makars. Ramsay demonstrated that vernacular Scots still had literary potential. He also edited the Tea Table Miscellany, published between 1724 and 1727, a collection of traditional Scots songs and ballads. In the Ever Green, which appeared in 1724, he reproduced poems by late-medieval Scots poets like Henryson and Dunbar with editorial alterations designed to make the text easier for his readers to understand. This was a tacit admission of the extent to which Scots had declined as a literary language.

Strongly patriotic and anti-English, Ramsay was a romantic Jacobite who, when the crunch came, sensibly arranged to be elsewhere during the Jacobite occupation of Edinburgh in 1745. Nevertheless, there was an ambivalence in Ramsay's attitude to both England and the use of Scots. Some of his poems were clear imitations of English Augustan verse. A number of them are characterised by the use of what has been called 'sprinkled Scots', the use of occasional Scots words to give local colour to themes derived from English poetry. This watered-down Scots contrasts markedly with Ramsay's racy use of vernacular Scots in his poems of Edinburgh low-life. This can be seen as the start of a split between polite and popular culture in eighteenth-century Scotland, one which was bridged by some of the leading intellectual figures who wrote in English but spoke in Scots and sang traditional Scots songs and ballads at social gatherings. There was, however, a distinctive self-consciousness about the vernacular revival by Ramsay and his friends which suggested that the use of Scots in literature was considered more appropriate to the quaint, pawky, comic and burlesque than to serious themes. A similar dichotomy can be found in Burns. It was a dilemma, a crisis of identity which Professor Daiches has called a kind of national schizophrenia, which goes a long way to explain the failure of Scots writers to develop a distinctively Scottish 'high' literary style in the eighteenth century.

Many of the poems included in collections by Ramsay and others had originally been songs and were published without any indication that they had originally been set to music. Nevertheless, the first half of the eighteenth century also saw an awakening of interest in traditional Scottish tunes. Just as Ramsay had 'improved' the verses he had edited so others gentrified the old Scottish airs they collected to make them more acceptable to contemporary taste. The first collection of traditional Scots song tunes, *Orpheus Caledonius*, appeared in 1725. It was followed by Alexander Munro's *Collection of the best Scots Songs* (1732) and William McGibbon's *Collection of Scots Tunes* (1742–55). Some of the sets of words accompanying the tunes in Orpheus Caledonius were traditional, others modern, many a mixture of both, so that it is difficult to separate the truly traditional from the pastiche and the contemporary. Such work led on to later eighteenth-century antiquarian collectors like James Johnson's *Scots Musical Museum* and was magnificently continued by Robert Burns. During this period, however, the Jacobite movement was creating a wealth of vernacular songs, some entirely new others adapted from older ones, at a time when such traditions were disappearing in other countries. At the same time many traditional dance tunes began to be recorded, some of them originally song tunes going back to the seventeenth century or earlier but with a faster tempo to make them suitable for dancing. As with the verse collected by Ramsay and others there was a tendency to make dance settings less rustic and more elaborate to suit contemporary genteel tastes. During the same period other musical traditions flourished in Scotland. Classical music was firmly linked to European trends and was frequently performed in the main towns. There was a strong tradition of performing and composition among landowners and professional men. Sir John Clerk of Penicuik and Thomas Erskine, sixth Earl of Kellie, were both talented composers. Clerk was a pupil of Corelli but on inheriting the family title the arts took a back seat in favour of a career in politics. At a more popular level the revival of dance and traditional songs caused fiddle music to flourish, the greatest exponent being Neil Gow (b1727). But the folk tradition and the classical were closely interwoven though; Gow, for instance, was also an admirer and an accomplished performer of the works of Corelli.

CHAPTER 14

HIGHLAND SOCIETY AND ECONOMY c1500–c1750

The distinctiveness of the Scottish Highlands in terms of its landscapes, society and economy has long been recognised. Youngson,[1] writing of the area's geology, has suggested that the Highlands 'could scarcely be more geologically different from the rest of Britain if they were part of another continent, and in some areas ... they look as if they might be part of another planet'. The inhabitants of this region were viewed in similar terms, during the sixteenth and seventeenth centuries, by the few English visitors who came into contact with them and by most Lowland Scots.

THE HIGHLAND/LOWLAND DIVIDE

In Scotland, consciousness of the distinctiveness of the Highlanders seem to have developed by the mid-fourteenth century. John of Fordun, writing in the 1380s, was the first author to suggest that Highlanders were socially and culturally inferior to Lowlanders. His tone was echoed with varying shades of scorn and contempt for the next 350 years. Highlanders were seen as different, first in terms of their language. They were noted for their military prowess, notorious for their lawlessness. They were distinguished by a pastoral economy which allowed a more indolent lifestyle, and by the general hardness of their existence. Modern commentators tend to add that the clan system made Highland society different but this did not strike Lowlanders during the sixteenth century as being significant. By the eighteenth century Highlanders were also set apart by their dress. The plaid, an all-purpose garment in which people could wrap themselves at night as well as wear by day, was worn universally. Highlanders in turn viewed their Lowland neighbours as alien intruders, racially different, soft and effete, a useful pretext for driving off their cattle.

Recent historians have tended to view contrasts in social structure between the Highlands and the Lowlands as ones of emphasis and chronology rather than as fundamental differences of kind. This has been most clearly

---

1. A.J. Youngson, *After the Forty Five* (Edinburgh 1973), p. 4.

expressed by Smout who has suggested that Highland society was based on kinship modified by feudalism, Lowland society on feudalism modified by kinship.[2] The balance between Celtic traditions and feudalism varied within the Highlands with a distinct gradient from the more feudalised east and south towards the north and west. To talk of a 'clan system' implies a uniformity that is misleading. This gradient was recognised by James VI when he wrote that Highlanders were divided into two groups; those of the mainland 'that are barbarous for the most parte yet mixed with some shewe of civilitie' and those living in the Isles who were 'totally barbarous'.

Highland society perpetuated institutions like the bloodfeud and bonds of manrent which were fast disappearing from the Lowlands by the seventeenth century. An element of the Lowlander's derision of Highland society may have stemmed from the subconscious realisation that the Lowlands had only recently shed similar patterns of behaviour. The declining importance of kinship, the social control imposed by the kirk, the rise of middling groups like the lairds and the professions and the growth of towns were among the influences which helped to distance Lowland from Highland society in the sixteenth and seventeenth centuries.

The extent of the Gaidhealtachd, the area of Gaelic speech, provides a means of delimiting the Highlands as a cultural province between c1500 and c1750.[3] Gaelic had been spoken as far south as the Tweed and the Solway in the eleventh century. Between the mid-eleventh and late sixteenth centuries it retreated from the Lowlands and English advanced, spearheaded by Anglo-Norman landholders and their followers in the countryside and English-speaking merchants in the burghs. Gaelic may have survived in parts of lowland Aberdeenshire into the sixteenth century and in Galloway into the seventeenth but apart from these isolated pockets the boundary between Gaelic and English stabilised. It followed closely the topographic boundary of the Highlands in the south. Parishes astride the Highland line like Aberfoyle or Port of Menteith contained distinct areas of English and Gaelic speech. In the east English penetrated the Angus glens and the Dee valley but the intervening upland areas remained Gaelic-speaking. Inverness was a bilingual town and English maintained footholds further north in the Black Isle and eastern Caithness but otherwise all inhabitants north of the Great Glen (excluding the Northern Isles) spoke Gaelic. Once this linguistic boundary had become fixed, the use of Gaelic served to define the Highlander. In the eleventh and twelfth centuries Gaelic had been referred to as 'Scottis' but by the later fourteenth century this term was being used to describe the Scottish version of English speech and Gaelic was becoming known as Erse or Irish. The dismissal of Gaelic involved the rejection of a culture that was rich yet different from the Lowlands, notably in music and poetry (Chapter 13).

The contrast between Highland and Lowland was probably sharpest in the

2. T.C. Smout, *History of the Scottish People 1560–1830* (London 1969), pp. 312–20.
3. C.W.J. Withers, *Gaelic in Scotland 1698–1981: The Geographical History of a Language* (Edinburgh 1984).

late sixteenth century. Clans developed as a response to increasing lawlessness but to Lowlanders clanship was a cause rather than a product of violence. They had some justification in this view because violence and plundering seem to have been endemic in the Highlands for much of the sixteenth and seventeenth centuries and at times clans became warrior societies in which heroic virtues dominated. To the Lowlander the Highlander was increasingly a figure of fun and ridicule, but the Highlands were not an isolated backwater. The very poverty of the area forced many of its inhabitants to look elsewhere for a living and to develop international contacts. The region was an important source of mercenary soldiers; for wars in Ireland in the sixteenth century and on the Continent in the seventeenth. Many Highland chiefs, from the seventeenth century at least, were educated in the Lowlands and had cosmopolitan tastes. Within the Highlands an increasing cultural gulf was opening from the mid-seventeenth century between chiefs with their broader outlook and increasingly expensive lifestyles and ordinary clansmen. Some historians have attributed change in the Highlands to the impact of external forces but much of the transformation of the economy and society of the Highlands between the seventeenth and later eighteenth centuries was accomplished by internal adjustments set in motion by the chiefs themselves. Before looking at how this happened we need to understand the broader structures of the region's society.

HIGHLAND SOCIETY

In the past Highland history has tended to be written from the top downwards, emphasising the concerns of the chieftains rather than those of the ordinary people. This is an understandable result of the lack of documentation for much of the area before the eighteenth century. As Richards has indicated, the ordinary inhabitants of the Highlands down to the mid-seventeenth century are no better documented than contemporary African peoples.[4] It is this which makes it so difficult to determine just how much Highland society differed from the rest of Britain and to what extent there really was a distinctive type of social organisation based on the clan. Highland clans have generated a vast literature (much of it romantic rubbish) but we still know little about how they evolved and functioned. Clans were not survivors of a primitive Celtic tribalism. They seem to have developed from the fourteenth century when the spread of feudalism into the Highlands was checked by the declining power of the monarchy. Clans arose from a need for local leaders to protect themselves and their followers without the support of central authority. Protection meant, effectively, aggressive expansion. This could be legitimised by various means including ones based on feudal authority or on kinship.

4. E. Richards and M. Clough, *Cromartie: Highland Life 1650–1914* (Aberdeen 1989), pp. 26–7.

A clan was, in theory, a patrilineal kindred whose members could trace their descent from a common ancestor. In the West Highlands clans often traced their ancestry back to early Celtic or Norse leaders like Somerled. Where the common ancestor was patently invented he was sometimes changed periodically as clans sought more distant or imposing origins. In the eastern Highlands many clans were feudal in origin, their chiefs descended from Anglo-Norman families, established on their lands by feudal charter, who had seen the benefits of 'going native' and augmenting their feudal powers by kinship structures based on local customs.

Clan chiefs had obligations as well as powers; to provide land, protection, welfare and hospitality for their clansmen. Chiefs might give livestock to those whose animals had died or take elderly people into their own households. Within a clan there was usually a group of people with close kinship links to the chief; his advisors in peace, his lieutenants in war, a gentry class known as 'daoine uaisle' and later as 'tacksmen' who held land from the chief on a hereditary basis in return for rent and services. Chiefs were supposed to take the advice of the daoine uaisle who, in the earlier part of our period, might elect a chief from rival candidates or depose an unsuitable one. By the seventeenth century the clan gentry were increasingly being required by the chiefs to hold their lands by formal leases or tacks. This was the origin of the term 'tacksmen' by which they were generally known in the late seventeenth and early eighteenth centuries. The possession of a tack distinguished them from ordinary clansmen who mostly held at will by verbal agreements. Tacksmen collected rents from their sub-tenants which were substantially greater than those which they passed on to the chief, the difference providing them with the income to maintain a suitable lifestyle. The extent of their appropriation appears to have varied. On the Argyll estates in the early eighteenth century the tacksmen collected about 30 per cent more rent from the sub-tenants than they passed on, as well as extracting labour services, but in other areas it has been claimed that the sub-tenants paid two or three times what was rendered to their chiefs. The tacksmen were able to accumulate capital which could be re-invested in helping sub-tenants by the system of 'steelbow' where under-capitalised farmers were provided with livestock, seed corn and implements. They also acted as middlemen and by the later seventeenth century many of them were involved in the cattle trade.

Most ordinary clansmen were not directly related to their chief but the idea of such a relationship was a useful fiction which helped clan unity. Clans were usually divided into branches; 'septs' or 'sliochdan' containing smaller kin groups or 'cloinne' (singular 'clann'). A clann might inhabit a single township. Occupation for three generations was considered to confer 'duthchas', a customary right of tenure similar to the Lowland concept of 'kindness'. At the heart of a clan was the relationship between the chief and the tacksmen heading the various septs, some of which had once been independent clans in their own right.

Kinship was an important unifying element within a clan but it was not the only one. A contemporary description of clans being united by 'pretense of blude or plaice of thair duelling' neatly expresses the mixture of genuine kinship and geographical propinquity which fostered unity. The sense of loyalty to the chief and the clan often transcended blood ties. Clans have sometimes been seen as military machines, geared to war and to perpetuating lawlessness; certainly this was how contemporary Lowlanders viewed them. Clan power was measured by the number of fighting men a chief could raise. This produced a vicious circle in which the maintenance of excessive populations on meagre resources precipitated subsistence crises, which encouraged raiding and warfare with other clans, which in turn made it important to maintain large numbers of fighting men.

Less is known about the degree of social differentiation that existed in Highland society below the level of the tacksmen. The people who leased lands from the tacksmen frequently sublet tiny plots of arable with grazing rights to cottars who may, as in the Lowlands, have formed a majority of households in many communities. In such a poor society, with population often thinly scattered, it is not surprising that there was less division of labour than in most Lowland areas. Any information we have about occupational structures suggests that specialist craftsmen and tradesmen were far fewer in number. The Highland tenant or cottar was a jack of all trades and even in the later eighteenth century it often proved difficult to establish specialist craftsmen on Highland estates because of an ingrained reluctance to pay them for work which could be done at home, however crudely.

Clans have been viewed by historians as contemporary outsiders saw them; archaic and outdated systems fossilised into a structure dating from the Celtic Iron Age and which had survived due to the area's isolation. The idea that Highland clans were dynamic structures capable of evolution and of adjusting to external and internal influences is a recent one. Work by Dodgshon, using theories about the nature of chiefdoms developed by anthropologists, has shed new light on the organisation and development of Highland clans emphasising their composite character and showing that they were dynamic social systems capable of responding to changing circumstances.[5] Kinship links within clans were often based on alliances rather than genuine family relationships producing a structure in which ideologies of unity were as important in holding a clan together as kinship ties.

Dodgshon believes that kinship structures in the Highlands were a response to the need to control access to subsistence, the tenure of particular areas of land being based on the fact that specific ancestors had occupied them. Given the limited extent and fragmented distribution of arable land within the Highlands it is easy to see competition for land as the basic mechanism for producing such kinship groups. The functions of the descent-group were gradually broadened to include other social and political processes such as

5. R.A. Dodgshon, Pretense of blude, and, Place of their dwelling: the nature of highland clans, in R.A. Houston and I. D. Whyte (eds) Scottish Society 1500–1800 (Cambridge 1989), 169–98.

the bloodfeud. Changes in the circumstances surrounding the occupation of land could produce corresponding changes in the nature of clans which could prove to be adaptable rather than conservative.

Work on chiefdoms in other parts of the world has emphasised the impact on such societies of population growth. When population pressure was low family groups constantly broke away from the main stems as new settlements were formed. When pressure on resources grew social structures adjusted by evolving into descent-groups linked across several generations, focused around a chief who could organise the tribal economy in a more intensive manner. Research by anthropologists has indicated that chiefdoms followed an evolutionary cycle, developing from simple forms towards more complex structures and then collapsing again. At the start of a cycle there were many small chiefdoms the leaders of which competed for status to enhance their power. This was done through feuding and by displays of conspicuous consumption at feasts. Those who succeeded extended their influence by conquest and marrying their sons into surrounding chiefdoms, creating expanding webs of alliances. In time, though, such chiefdoms become too large and complex to be sustainable, collapsing into a chaotic pattern of small competing chiefdoms from which the cycle began once more.

This provides a useful model for interpreting aspects of Highland society between c1500 and c1750. Before the sixteenth century the main complex chiefdom in the Highlands was the Lordship of the Isles. Its break up in the 1490s, and its replacement by a number of small clans vying with each other for power in a welter of feuding, fits the pattern closely. The continuation of the cycle by the build up of another great chiefdom during the seventeenth century was arrested by external forces, notably the extension of government control, although the growth of the Campbell empire fits the model to some extent.

As kinship structures may have altered to suit the changing circumstances of individual clans it cannot be assumed that all clans were organised in the same way. Dodgshon suggests that three types of kinship structure existed.[6] The first, linked with larger clans, involved a single family or chief holding large blocks of land. This was not achieved simply by the chief overriding the rights of his clansmen but by a range of strategies including inheritance, conquest, marriage and grants from the crown. Such territories were often built up rapidly creating problems of how to control them. This was done by granting portions of the newly won land to members of the chief's family. The chief's kinship ties gradually spread as new land came within his control. These sub-chiefs and tacksmen would establish their own family groups working downwards through society, gradually displacing local families which had once held authority. The expansion of clan Donald, which eventually came to have 17 separate branches, is a good example.

The growth of lesser clans was limited by the availability of land leading to greater prestige and importance being attached to feuding and feasting as, within the tighter compass of a small clan, these would have been harder to

6. Ibid.

afford and sustain. The spoils of successful feuding provided the means for feasting and the maintenance of fighting men. The status of a chief could be measured by how many days' eating and drinking a feast could occupy; a week or more was not uncommon like the famous celebration which the MacGregors provided for James IV in 1506. Obligations to provide hospitality for a peripatetic chief and his retinue survived into the seventeenth century and helped strengthen personal contacts between chiefs and their followers. Feasting and giving prestige gifts helped cement alliances with neighbouring chiefs. Prospects for territorial expansion by such groups were limited and many were forced to accept the protection and overlordship of larger clans. While large clans tended to diverge as kin groups much of the growth of smaller clans was achieved by individual families creating their own opportunities through marriages and leases rather than by their chiefs undertaking major expansions of territory. In such situations women often tended to marry within the clan, men outside it, a system which helped the clan hold on to its existing land and increased its chances of acquiring new areas.

A third type of kinship structure was linked to hereditary service. Within many clans there were families serving as pipers, harpists, bards, doctors, armourers or smiths to the chiefs receiving land free or at a reduced rent in return for their services. The MacCrimmons, hereditary pipers to the MacLeods, are among the most famous of such families. The MacMhurich family of bards can be traced back for some 14 generations to the thirteenth century and remained bards to the chiefs of Clanranald into the eighteenth century. Within such families the appropriate skills and training were passed down from father to son and were jealously guarded.

The spread of feudal rights attached to individuals rather than descent groups did not remove the value of kinship; it merely incorporated it within a different framework. From the sixteenth century most Highlanders were tenants in a feudal sense but kinship, real or assumed, still gave them a right to hold clan land so that Highlanders often considered that they had a hereditary right to their holdings, their chief being the guardian rather than the absolute owner of the clan territory. This widespread belief in customary rights encouraged a focus on people's descent which established their position and rights within a township.

A focus on rights to land linked with descent might be considered to have produced a stable and immobile population. Inter-clan warfare and the expansion and contraction of clan territories, however, caused considerable turnover of population in some areas. This must have prevented widespread identification of descent with the occupation of particular holdings making absolute unity of kinship in many areas impossible. The operation of this process can be seen in the adoption of new clan names by smaller kinship groups which were absorbed by expanding rivals. By these means people could be absorbed into new clans on the basis of their geographical proximity and their adoption of pretended kinship ties as is shown by Simon Fraser, Lord Lovat, who made gifts of oatmeal to those of his tenants who would change their name to Fraser. In the process the expanding clan became larger but more composite in structure. The acceptance of a different clan name involved the recognition by an individual of the necessity of having an established place in the social order, trading allegiance against the need for security and access to land.

As a result many clans, particularly the larger ones, were united not just by kinship but by common interest. Control over land was essential; a clan without land was a broken clan, like the MacGregors. Availability of land allowed a chief to reward kinsmen and supporters. Food rents could be used to cushion the clan against crop failure emphasising the interdependence of clan and chief. They supported the chief's household; his piper, harpist and other retainers whose presence gave him status. Food rents maintained a nucleus of fighting men for defending clan territory and pursuing feuds, as well as allowing chiefs to provide feasts and hospitality which emphasised their generosity. Rents in cattle provided the tochers or dowries with which marriage alliances were cemented.

In the past it has been suggested that the spread of Anglo-Norman feudalism into the Highlands helped undermine the clan system. Clanship and feudalism have been seen as incompatible, the stresses between them causing most of the trouble that occurred in the Highlands during the late sixteenth and seventeenth centuries. Feudalism, based on property, has been seen as alien to clanship, based on people. It is unlikely, however, that such considerations bothered Highland chiefs; power was exercised by whatever means were available. The two systems probably reinforced each other more often than they clashed. By the later sixteenth century most chiefs held their lands by feudal charters. If there had originally been a concept of clan lands as communal property it had disappeared. Selection of new chiefs from among the most suitable candidates still occurred in the early sixteenth century but had given way to primogeniture by c1550. Feudal lords found the kinship ties of clanship, real or putative, a useful device while clan chiefs could strengthen their position by means of feudal grants and powers. Chiefs who conquered new territory invariably tried to get their control legitimised by a charter from the crown.

Conflict was sometimes evident where feudal superior and clan chief did not correspond. This was a principal cause of unrest during the seventeenth century. Where this happened loyalties were sometimes pulled in two directions and it was frequently clan loyalty which proved stronger, not least because the chief represented power locally while the feudal superior was often a more distant figure. The example of Morvern, held by the Dukes of Argyll in the early eighteenth century but effectively under the control of the chiefs of Clan Cameron, illustrates this point.

Some Highland landowners were feudal magnates pure and simple like the Murray earls and dukes of Atholl. There was no clan Murray, the inhabitants of the Atholl estates being mainly Stewarts and Robertsons. The powers of the Dukes of Atholl within their regality were no different from those of many major Lowland proprietors yet they were exercised in the context of a different society. This explains Daniel Defoe's awe at the princely lifestyle of the first Duke and his description of him as, potentially, the most powerful man in Scotland because he could raise an army of 6,000 men from his own lands. It was the feudal tenure of wardholding which allowed Highland landowners to mobilise their men for war in 1715 and 1745. This explains why after Culloden the abolition of wardholding and heritable jurisdictions was the most important and far-reaching measure taken to curb the power of the clans.

An important question regarding Highland society, clans and feudalism apart, is whether for the ordinary sub-tenant or clansman life was any different from that of his Lowland counterpart. Visitors to the Highlands were struck by the stark poverty of the ordinary people. Yet one doubts whether the existence of many Lowland cottars was any better. Lack of material possessions did not necessarily mean that the average Highlander was closer to starvation than the average Lowlander though there are indications that this may have been the case. Given the physical environment of the Highlands it is difficult to believe that crop failure was not more common than in the Lowlands; certainly subsistence crises continued to a later date. Violence was an additional cause of hardship and poverty while Highland livestock were especially susceptible to severe weather conditions and diseases due to the lack of winter fodder. On the other hand, the strong element of paternalism which existed within some clans may have made the distribution of available food supplies more equal in times of crisis than on many Lowland estates. Most of the region had no formal system of poor relief but there are plenty of instances of chiefs giving out meal and livestock to needy clansmen in a way in which some Lowland landowners during the 1690s conspicuously failed to do. So it should not necessarily be assumed that life in the Highlands was worse than in other parts of Scotland. Shaw, in her study of the Northern and Western Isles during the seventeenth century, contrasts unfavourably the position of tenants on the crown lands in Orkney and Shetland with their Hebridean counterparts.[7] The crown lands in the Northern Isles were granted to tacksmen on short leases for which they had to bargain hard. The tacksmen in turn pressed the ordinary tenants for their rents. There were few concessions to those who were unable to meet their rents in full. Hebridean sub-tenants, though living in a society which may have been more violent, received more consideration and had more effective security of tenure.

THE HIGHLAND ECONOMY

Between c1500 and c1750 there are two recurrent themes relating to the Highland economy. First, the narrowness of the region's resource base with an environment mostly ill-suited to arable farming. Second, there were pressures caused by the growth of population. Dodgshon has detected

7. F.J. Shaw, *The Northern and Western Islands of Scotland in the Seventeenth Century* (Edinburgh 1979), pp. 184–201.

indirect signs of population growth in the Highlands from the sixteenth century with an expansion of the arable area by the creation of outfield and an intensification of cultivation, especially the substitution of hand cultivation for animal-drawn ploughs.[8] Highland farming townships had, below the level of the tacksmen, many similarities with their Lowland counterparts. Townships were generally leased from the tacksmen by groups of tenants who often held the land in common and were jointly responsible for the rent. The lands of individual cultivators were scattered in runrig and sometimes subject to periodic re-allocation. The complexity of plot subdivision which could occur comes out in Peter May's surveys of some of the Annexed Forfeited Estates in 1755. In Coigach, where arable land was especially scarce, there were sometimes 100 plots within a single acre. As population increased during the late seventeenth and early eighteenth centuries numbers of cottars rose many having only an acre or so of land plus some grazing.

As in the Lowlands arable land was divided into infield and outfield. Bere and oats were the main crops though some rye was grown on sandy soils. One important difference from Lowland practice was that in many parts of the Highlands cereals were harvested by being pulled up instead of cut with sickle or scythe. Also the grain was extracted by burning away the husk and most of the straw. As a result there was little straw for winter fodder, no stubble for animals to graze after harvest. The livestock were maintained almost entirely by pasturing on the outfield and the rough grazing beyond. The infield did not always receive the high inputs of manure which characterised Lowland farming, reducing crop yields. As the carrying capacity of the land depended on the number of livestock which could be wintered and little provision was made to conserve additional winter fodder the stocking density of animals as well as their quality, was low. Only during the eighteenth century, with an increased emphasis on commercial livestock rearing, did this situation improve.

From the sixteenth century, Highland townships accommodated population growth by a range of strategies including the intensification of infield cultivation, the creation and expansion of outfields, the use of a range of fertilisers drawn from beyond the arable area such as seaweed, shell sand, peat and turf, the adoption of hand cultivation and the use of the potato. Dodgshon has made some ingenious calculations on the nutrient budgets of sample Highland townships in the eighteenth century, estimating the input of nitrogen and phosphorous from manures and fertilizers and losses from the system in the harvested crops.[9] Because many assumptions have to be made regarding farming practices the results are tentatative but intriguing. In the four sample areas manure from cattle formed a variable but important source of nutrients but on Lochtayside the input of nutrients from turf recycled from fold dykes and thatch was particularly important. In Barrisdale, on the far

---

8. R.A. Dodgshon, *Land and Society in Early Scotland* (Oxford 1981).
9. R.A. Dodgshon and E.G. Olsson, Productivity and nutrient use in eighteenth-century Scottish highland townships, *Geografica Annaler*, ser. B. 70, 1988, 39–51.

north-west coast, 30 per cent of the nutrient input came from seaweed. Farming at Barrisdale made optimum use of available nutrients by garden-style cultivation with spade and foot plough, lazy beds and seaweed fertiliser. The arable area was tiny, however, less than 1 per cent of the township, insufficient to maintain the inhabitants who must have derived a significant proportion of their food intake from fish and livestock products. On Lochtayside the farming system was less efficient, supporting only 40 per cent more people on thirteen times as much arable land. These inland areas, however, had greatest scope for absorbing extra population.

Highland touns generally consisted of extensive tracts of rough grazing and limited areas of arable land. In southern and eastern areas the proportion of arable land was greater but in the far north and west it could be tiny. Arable land in steep-sided, flat-floored Highland valleys was particularly vulnerable to flooding, a danger which probably increased as the build up of population encouraged more low-lying haughland to be cultivated. The amount of cultivated land per family fell as population pressure built up bringing more families to the margins of subsistence. In Sunart in 1723 and Ardnamurchan in 1727 each family had only 3 acres (1.2 hectares) of arable land to sustain it. In Barrisdale in 1755 the area was under 1.5 acres (0.6 hectares). The position of the cottars with their tiny plots or that of the completely landless must have been precarious indeed. Pressure of population led to the extension of cultivation on to hillsides where only spade cultivation was possible, and around shielings which often led to their conversion to new permanent settlements.

Although large numbers of sheep were kept it was cattle around which the Highland economy revolved by the seventeenth century. They were the main source of wealth, often being substituted directly for money in dowries and the repayment of loans. Their mobility allowed them to be driven into the mountains in time of danger but also made them the principal object of inter-clan raiding. As in other primitive cattle-rearing societies, their value as an indication of wealth led to overstocking and poor quality which, with the lack of winter fodder made them vulnerable to hard winters and late springs. This could bring severe hardship to the population helping to de-stabilise an area.

Industrial activity beyond purely local needs was limited. Growing interest in the development of timber and metallic ores is evident in the late seventeenth and early eighteenth centuries (Chapter 15) but operations were scattered, small-scale and usually short-lived. In the past it has been suggested that commercial exploitation, beginning in the seventeenth century and accelerating in the eighteenth, was the principal factor behind the deforestation of the Highlands. Nevertheless, the Military Survey of 1747–55, shows that at this time, before the supposed peak of commercial forestry, only around 5 per cent of the Highlands were wooded. Commercial felling of pine forests occured in areas like Rannoch, upper Deeside, Speyside and parts of the west coast. Coppice management of deciduous woodland, which was particularly widespread in the south-western Highlands, was also being practiced on some estates by 1700. Far from stripping the Highlands of timber, coppicing to produce bark for tanning and charcoal for iron smelting increased the area under woodland in some districts. The role of charcoal blast-furnaces in denuding the Highlands of timber has been wildly exaggerated. Less than a dozen iron-making plants have been recorded over a 250-year period. Many, like the blast-furnace set up on Cameron of Lochiel's lands by Loch Arkaig in the late 1670s, the one at Invergarry which operated intermittently between 1729 and 1736, and the York Buildings Company's site at Abernethy (c1728–c1734), were short-lived ventures which cannot have had a major environmental impact.

Textile manufacture provided additional income. Cloth had always been woven throughout the Highlands for local use but during the first half of the eighteenth century the spinning of linen yarn for Lowland manufacturers spread through the southern and eastern Highlands. It became a major source of cash for paying rents and also caused a minor revolution in the use of labour, forcing men to spend more time working in the fields in place of their wives. Fishing offered an alternative source of food and income to agriculture but outside the Northern Isles, where the white fishery for cod and ling was important, it remained a small-scale part-time occupation. The unreliability of the herring shoals in West Highland waters, as well as lack of capital and skills, may account for the reluctance of the inhabitants to specalise in fishing.

The Highland economy was far from being a closed one. From the sixteenth century and probably earlier there was a two-way trade across the Highland line, cattle and horses being exchanged for meal. Grain-producing districts like the Spey and Tay valleys traded meal into adjoining upland areas. In the seventeenth century the growth of Glasgow began to channel an increasing amount of traffic towards the Clyde, animals being driven to Glasgow overland and boats from the West Highlands bringing fish, skins, hides, plaiding, butter and cheese in exchange for meal and manufactured articles. Within the Highlands certain areas like Caithness, Lewis, Tiree and Islay, noted for their fertility, were normally self-sufficient in grain and had a surplus to exchange in most years. Many other districts, such as the north-west mainland, were perennially short of grain and had to import it.

While most Highland tenants obtained little more than a bare subsistence they were not completely isolated from the market. Indeed, while their Lowland counterparts still paid rents mainly in produce tenants even in more remote areas of the West Highlands were paying cash by the end of the seventeenth century. The growing involvement of Highland landowners in a wider society increased their cost of living and encouraged the commutation of rents in kind to money. The cattle trade operated on the basis of many small tenants selling animals to raise money for their rents. The droving of cattle to the Lowlands from areas as distant as Skye is recorded from the early sixteenth century. Pacification of the Borders after 1603 encouraged the development of droving to England. In the first half of the eighteenth century the potential of the cattle trade as a source of cash led to structural changes in farming in some areas. Some tacksmen, notably on the Argyll estates, began to operate large cattle ranches under their own direct management. The profits from specialist cattle rearing allowed the rents of some estates to be increased substantially before the advent of commercial sheep farming.

During the first half of the eighteenth century the traditional role of the tacksman came increasingly under threat. They began to be seen by Lowlanders, and some Highland proprietors, as obstacles to progress who rack-rented and oppressed the small tenants. Because they creamed off a higher surplus from the tenantry than they paid to the chiefs the removal of the tacksmen on an estate could give the proprietor additional income without necessarily raising the rents paid by the tenants. By the end of the seventeenth century tenurial systems characterised by direct proprietor–tenant relationships without intermediate tacksmen had begun to appear. The removal of the tacksman system is seen most dramatically on the Argyll estates during the first half of the eighteenth century. The initiative taken by the Dukes of Argyll in estate re-organisation and improvement has sometimes been couched in heroic terms as an example of forward-looking, progressive estate management. More recent research suggests otherwise. There is no sign in the correspondence of the second Duke that he was interested in economic improvement on his estates for its own sake; he was merely concerned to squeeze more money out of his tenants. The changes were designed to increase estate income providing the Dukes of Argyll with an ostentatious lifestyle which, under the third Duke, became focused on the massively expensive rebuilding of Inveraray Castle, the improving of the surrounding parklands and the creation of a new town nearby.

The second Duke of Argyll began removing tacksmen from around 1710 in Kintyre.[10] The rents which the tacksmen paid were already rising. In Mull the total rental had risen from £668.13.4 sterling in 1703 to £1,300 by 1736. On Tiree the increase had been from £130 sterling in 1674 to £200 in 1706 and £325 by 1727. The rises were inevitably passed on by the tacksmen to the sub-tenants. This began to alter the tacksmen's relationship with the bulk of the population, making them identify more with the landlord and his estate administration and less with the interests of the ordinary people. In 1737 Duncan Forbes of Culloden re-organised tenures in Mull, Morvern and Tiree for the second Duke. The tacksman system was abolished and written leases were offered direct to the former sub-tenants, mostly at higher rents, but without the labour services that had been due to the tacksmen. About a quarter of the leases (but three-quarters of the land) went to the tacksmen who, instead of their former extensive estates, mostly leased small groups of farms with only limited scope for sub-letting. The tacksmen, with their accumulated capital, were able to bid for larger farms and groups of farms and retained their dominance over local society; only now it was based on economic rather than traditional sources of power. The removal of the tacksmen created an administrative gap which necessitated the appointment

---

10. E. Cregeen, The Tacksmen and their successors; a study of tenurial reorganisation in Mull, Morvern and Tiree in early eighteenth century, SS, 13, 1969, 93–145.

of local estate factors – most of whom were recruited from the ranks of the former tacksmen.

By removing the key group which had linked the house of Argyll with the ordinary clansmen these reforms virtually dismantled the clan system. Finance rather than family was the basis on which land was now to be allocated, competition rather than clanship was the principle in the granting of tenancies. Kinship and traditional loyalties continued to exert some influence on estate management but to a more limited degree than before. Competitive bidding pushed up rents substantially. Argyll's own chamberlains, closely in touch with the economic reality of the West Highlands as the Duke was not, were against the proposals. In their view moderate rents fully paid were preferable to high rents and high levels of arrears. The Duke chose to view this as obstruction and preferred to listen to Forbes who, though owning estates on the fringes of the Highlands, had a strangely intense prejudice against tacksmen.

The reforms were pushed through at an unfavourable period when the cattle trade was in the doldrums. Within a couple of years arrears were rising rapidly. Bad weather in the early 1740s caused heavy losses of livestock and many bankrupt tenants abandoned their holdings. When the third Duke succeeded in 1743 he showed a greater appreciation of the nature of the crisis by making modest but vital reductions in rents in some parts of the estates. For a while the possibility of re-establishing the tacksmen was even considered. The removal of the tacksmen as figures of authority and the erosion of the traditional values of clanship on the Argyll estates goes a long way to explaining the failure of the Campbells to mobilise against the Jacobites in 1745: the clan had been virtually destroyed by commercialisation, a process which was soon to spread more widely through the Highlands. It is not clear how far this process had gone elsewhere in the Highlands by the 1750s but it is unlikely that the Argyll estates were unique in trying to remove their tacksmen. There are indications that they were being undermined and eased out on the Cromartie estates in the far north during the 1730s and this may have been happening elsewhere too.

THE HIGHLANDS IN A WIDER WORLD c1600–c1750

Political changes during the seventeenth and eighteenth centuries led to the increasing interaction of the Highlands with the Lowlands and with a wider world beyond. Attempts by Scottish monarchs to extend control over this area included James IV's forfeiture of the Lordship of the Isles in 1493. The Lordship had been, effectively, an independent state extending from Lewis to Islay, covering large areas of the West Highland mainland, and penetrating far to the east. Its destruction ended any threat to the Scottish crown but it precipitated a period of bitter feuding among contending clans. Having removed the threat of the Lordship the monarchy then proved incapable of controlling the region.

Throughout the sixteenth and seventeenth centuries the crown sought to extend its influence in the Highlands by using powerful families in particular regions as their instruments. The rise of the Campbells in the south west, the Gordons in the north east and the Mackenzies in the north partly reflects the aggrandisement which such positions allowed. The policy was a source of trouble in that the families selected as crown representatives also had their own interests to pursue. It was not unknown for the Campbells or the Mackenzies to manipulate events by encouraging disorders among their neighbours, intervening to crush them in the name of the government and then picking up the spoils. Royal policy sometimes focused on specific groups which were seen as particularly troublesome, such as the MacGregors who had become notorious for theft and violence on the southern fringes of the Highlands in the late sixteenth century. The clan MacGregor was proscribed in 1603 and the very use of the name forbidden. Charles II restored their name but not their ancestral lands which had been absorbed by the Campbells. In 1693, however, the ban on their name was re-imposed.

Clan Campbell and the House of Argyll benefited especially from co-operation with the government. In the late fifteenth and early sixteenth centuries they had been the crown's instrument for destroying Clan Donald, the Campbell's bitter rivals. Their reward was a major slice of MacDonald territory. They took over Kintyre in 1607, Ardnamurchan in 1625. The Campbells of Cawdor, a cadet branch with their base in the north east, received Islay in 1614. Some of the success of the Campbells was due to their unscrupulous use of credit to take over other estates. By buying up debts and then foreclosing on the borrowers they took over the lands of the MacLeans of Duart in Mull, Morvern and Tiree. They also extended their influence by discharging debts in exchange for feudal superiority over the debtors. Such actions inevitably provoked ill feeling. The MacLean inhabitants of Mull resisted Campbell annexation. Argyll had to mount a full-scale invasion of the island in 1674 and fight a series of campaigns there before the island was finally subdued in 1679.[11] Morvern, a Cameron stronghold, did not come under full Campbell control for decades. Incoming Campbell tacksmen faced a campaign of intimidation, robbery, arson and cattle maiming until the Argyll estate administration gave in and sublet the land to native Camerons. Effective control of Morvern remained with Cameron of Lochiel and despite Campbell overlordship proved a good recruiting ground for the Jacobites in 1745.

Newly acquired territory like the MacLean lands was settled by Campbell colonists from the core of their estates, tacksmen from cadet families. The terms of their tacks required them to evict resident MacLeans and forbade them to sublet to anyone with that surname. In the political and religious crisis of the mid-seventeenth century the close relationship between the Stewarts and the house of Argyll broke down and gave way to a new alliance with the Presbyterian cause and later the Whig party and the House of

11. P. Hopkins, *Glencoe and the End of the Highland War* (Edinburgh 1986), pp. 39–71.

Hanover for which services the 10th Earl of Argyll received a dukedom in 1703. The Campbells, as the chief representative of the Whig interest in the Highlands, were a natural focus for resentment grounded on earlier clan rivalries. Arguably it was the domination of the Campbells that cemented the opposition among the western clans which made the Jacobite rebellions possible, though the role of anti-Campbell feeling can be exaggerated and there were Campbells on the Jacobite side in 1715. The Jacobitism of clans on the margins of Campbell territory like the Stewarts of Appin, the Camerons, the Macdonalds and the MacLeans, was based as much on hatred of the Campbells as affection for the Stewarts.

In the sixteenth century, while Lowland magnates tried to take over and manipulate central government, Highland chiefs ignored it as far as possible, paying lip service to the idea of the monarchy but preferring to focus on their own local issues rather than becoming involved in national politics. James VIs policies towards the Highlands created a framework within which later governments operated. In 1597 James ordered all chiefs to produce feudal charters for the lands they held and to be answerable for the behaviour of their men. He may have hoped to forfeit lands whose occupiers had no written title and to plant Lowland colonies on them. Recognising the difficulty of imposing direct central control on the area, James made the clans responsible for policing themselves, getting chiefs and landowners to subscribe to bands in which they agreed to answer for the conduct of their clansmen and tenants.

James' hatred of the Highlanders was tempered by the more pragmatic attitude of the Privy Council and it was due to this that the compromise proposals of the Statutes of Iona were produced. In 1608 Lord Ochiltree, the king's lieutenant, mounted an expedition to the Isles. A group of prominent West Highland chiefs was tricked into capture and imprisoned for some months in the Lowlands. They were then forced to attend a conference on Iona in 1609 and to agree to a range of proposals. Chiefs would be responsible for their clansmen and would appear regularly before the Privy Council in Edinburgh to account for their conduct. They also agreed to help spread the Reformed church in the Highlands. The Statutes, and further legislation in 1616 attempted to impose curbs on the chiefs' traditional lifestyle including the sizes of their households, the number of war galleys they maintained, feasting and drinking, carrying firearms and exacting hospitality from their followers. Bards, troublemakers whose heroic poetry was liable to incite violence, were to be suppressed. Landowners in the Isles worth 60 cows or more were to have their eldest sons (in the 1616 Act all their children) educated in the Lowlands and taught English.

The details of the Statutes show that the government had a clear idea of the role of feasting and feuding in the clan system.[12] By trying to limit conspicuous consumption and the maintenance of retainers they were endeavouring to undermine the ideology of the clan. The Statutes have been

12. Dodgshon, Pretense of blude.

seen as marking the beginnings of effective central control over the Highlands, an important preliminary step in the decline of the clan system. Many of the stipulations were unenforceable but by making chiefs responsible for their men and bringing them to Edinburgh with some regularity the legislation increased contact between the leaders of Highland and Lowland society, developing in chiefs a desire for more ostentatious and expensive lifestyles. Despite the fact that the incomes of Highland chiefs were likely to have risen with more settled conditions and the growth of the cattle trade, many were soon in financial difficulties. Some chiefs were forced to raise large sums of money as security for their good behaviour or to meet fines imposed for misdemeanours committed by their clansmen. Policing their territories to keep the peace was an additional drain on resources as was the cost of having sons educated in the Lowlands, as some chiefs began to do.

From the mid-seventeenth century Highlanders were mobilised in support of the Stewarts. Highland support for Charles I was based on negative rather than positive reasons. Charles was seen as less likely to meddle in their affairs than the aggressively Protestant Covenanting regime. In addition, the identification of the house of Argyll with the Covenanters automatically inclined many clans towards the king. The campaigns of Montrose and Alastair MacColla between 1644 and 1647 demonstrated the potential of the Highlanders as a fighting force.[13] MacColla developed the tactic of the Highland charge which, in an age of slow-loading firearms, gave Highlanders a tactical advantage over all but the most experienced troops. This, plus MacColla's core of seasoned Irish fighting men, was fundamental to the success of the campaigns of the Marquis of Montrose. Montrose's initial victory at Tippermuir was the first occasion for over 200 years that Highlanders and Lowlanders had clashed in a major battle, inaugurating a century of periodic Highland military involvement in British affairs and intensified Lowlanders' perception of the Highlanders as barbarous savages.

The Cromwellian occupation imposed on the Highlands for the first time effective centralised rule but after the Restoration there was a return to more distant, ineffectual control by a government preoccupied with quelling opposition to its religious settlement within the Lowlands. This encouraged lawlessness on a new scale. The rise of the cattle trade provided new targets in the increasingly large cattle droves. Raiding into the Lowlands also continued into the eighteenth century. The worst of the trouble seems to have been concentrated in specific areas and to have been the work of limited groups; the Camerons, Keppoch and Glencoe MacDonalds and MacGregors had particularly bad reputations, often raiding far south of their own territories to the very margins of the Highlands. Local watch schemes by both Highland and Lowland communities and protection rackets, operated on a poacher-turned-gamekeeper basis by men like Rob Roy MacGregor, had

13. D. Stevenson, *Alastair MacColla and the Highland Problem in the Seventeenth Century* (Edinburgh 1980).

some effect and were countenanced by the government for want of anything better.

Large-scale clan conflict was dying out by this period. Indeed, major inter-clan conflicts in which neither party could claim a legal right or government support were increasingly rare from the early seventeenth century. The last great 'clan battle' at Mulroy in 1688 was fought between the MacDonalds of Keppoch and the Mackintoshes. The latter, however, had official support in the form of a contingent of government troops.[14] Feuds were increasingly being pursued by law rather than by the sword. Raids were now rarely led by chiefs in person. The upheavals of the mid-seventeenth century had displaced many groups of Highlanders creating bands of 'broken men' and robbers outside the framework of clanship but whose operations often had the tacit approval of local chiefs. It was this minor robbery and raiding which was the problem for law and order in the Highlands in the later seventeenth and early eighteenth centuries rather than inter-clan warfare.

The relationship between the chiefs and the crown gradually changed during the seventeenth century. Under James VI they merely wanted the freedom to live as they pleased without reference to central authority. Gradually the relationship became closer. The alliance between certain Highland clans and the Stewarts was first made in the 1640s out of expediency. James VII, when Duke of York had, during his period of rule in Scotland, worked hard to ensure the future support of those clans which had aided his brother and father, especially by trying to curb the power of the Campbells. After 1689 loyalty to the cause of the exiled dynasty, cemented in part by a hatred of the Campbells, became a potent force which turned a regional problem into a national one. Abolition of the Privy Council in 1708 weakened control over the region and did much to foster conditions under which armed rebellion was possible in 1715, 1719 and 1745. The existence of the Highlands as a focus of Jacobite activity was due in part to the fact that the nature of clan society made this the only area of Britain in which a force of trained fighting men could be readily mobilised. The danger that this represented to central authority led to increasing government involvement in the Highlands at first in purely military terms but, especially after the 1745 rebellion, with social and economic dimensions.

The start of the process by which the Highland clans were destroyed has been placed on a cold April morning in 1746 when the Jacobite cause was finally defeated on Culloden Moor. The battle has sometimes been presented as a clash between a traditional society which had survived with little change from the Celtic Iron Age, and the inexorable military machine of an increasingly imperialist power. This ignores the fact that social and economic change within the Highlands had been occurring steadily over the previous century and a half. While the two generations after Culloden were to witness the destruction of the institutional structure of the clan system much of this change would have occurred if the 1745 rebellion had not happened.

14. B. Lenman, *The Jacobite Clans of the Great Glen* (London 1984), p. 41.

Nevertheless after Culloden government control over the Highlands greatly increased.[15] Raiding and violence diminished markedly. There was more concern for the social and economic development of the region with the aim of integrating it more closely with the rest of Britain. The abolition of wardholding and heritable jurisdictions in 1747 and a sustained attack by the government on the structure of clanship aimed to destroy the political separateness of the Highlands and impose an ideology of improvement. A disarming Act, more rigorously enforced than earlier ones, was imposed in 1746. Wearing Highland dress was forbidden in 1747. Despite these measures it was economic change rather than political action which undermined traditional Highland society.

A good deal of attention has been focused on the activities and supposed achievements of various official bodies in the Highlands in the later eighteenth century. The example of the Annexed Forfeited Estates demonstrates the need to examine critically the work of such organisations.[16] After the failure of the 1745 rebellion 41 forfeited Scottish estates were taken over by the Barons of Exchequer. Most were auctioned off to pay creditors but 13 were annexed to the crown in 1752. Three years later a body of commissioners; crown officials, lairds, nobles and lawyers, was appointed to oversee their management which continued for some 25 years. The Highland estates in their care were spread over 30 parishes from near Stirling to Coigach in the far north.

The aims of the Board were philanthropic as well as economic. The welfare of the inhabitants of the estates was always a prime consideration and improvements could only be carried out with their co-operation and agreement. The Commissioners included several peers, some of whom were noted improvers or on the Board of Trustees for Manufactures (Chapter 16) as well as members of the legal establishment. They were, however, unpaid and their attendance at meetings was often poor. The administration of the Annexed Estates was highly centralised and bureaucratic. Commissioners seldom visited the estates to assess conditions for themselves. They relied on surveys and reports from factors who were frequently summoned to Edinburgh at considerable expense. Work was hampered by the slow reponse of the government in London to proposals for projects. At a lower level the factors also had their hands tied: tenants found that they could easily obstruct unpopular changes. Agricultural improvement was the most sustained of the Commissioners' activities but the pace of change was slow, results uneven. The more accessible southern estates benefited most. Efforts to encourage industry, especially linen manufacture, were a failure. Other schemes to develop fishing and aid the establishment of craftsmen also enjoyed only limited success. The Commissioners did more useful work in contributing to road and bridge building schemes but this was done in an unco-ordinated, piecemeal fashion.

15. Youngson, *After the Forty Five*.
16. A. Smith, *Jacobite Estates of the Forty Five* (Edinburgh 1982).

The Board was constantly hampered by a shortage of funds. Like many other bodies operating in eighteenth-century Scotland ambitious aims were not matched by a sufficiently large budget. The assumption was that without proprietors to cream off the rents, income could be ploughed back into improvements. In reality much of the income was absorbed in meeting management costs and debts which the estates had accumulated before forfeiture. Much of the well-intentioned paternalism of the Commissioners had little effect. In terms of achieving improvements its estates were no more advanced than those of the average Highland estate under ordinary management. The Board was the first in a series of bodies with the aim of promoting regional development in the Highlands which came to grief through insufficient funds, ill-judged policies, and the intractable nature of both the environment and inhabitants. Instead of putting them in the vanguard of improvement the Commissioners' policies had little effect compared with the slow but more widespread changes which were taking place throughout the Highlands as a result of growing commercial links with the rest of Britain.

It is easy to focus on well-documented organisations like the Annexed Forfeited Estates and to underestimate the importance of more gradual, less obtrusive changes. Attempts to transform the Highlands from outside were rarely as effective as those that were generated internally. In social terms there was a gradual shift within Highland society from a chief-clansman to a landlord–tenant relationship. Aspects of both existed until after our period but there was a steady change of emphasis from the first to the second as chiefs came to define clan lands increasingly as economic resources. The Highlands in the 1750s were poised on the brink of major developments. The region had finally been brought under political control. Its inhabitants, arguably, were becoming more prosperous as the region's economy became more closely integrated with the rest of Britain. Agricultural improvement, the spread of the potato, the expansion of the cattle trade, the spinning of linen yarn, fishing, mining and forestry all generated additional income as did increasing seasonal employment in the Lowland harvest. This modest prosperity was precarious though and proved to be short-lived, being wiped out by population growth in the second half of the century. Disaster was staved off temporarily by expedients like kelp burning and increasing reliance on the potato but the crisis which was building up proved to be all the greater through being delayed.

CHAPTER 15

TRADE AND INDUSTRY IN THE SIXTEENTH AND SEVENTEENTH CENTURIES

The pattern of trade which characterised late-medieval Scotland continued through much of the sixteenth century. Scotland's export trade was heavily dependent on wool, woollen cloth, hides and fish. From a low level in the early sixteenth century Scottish trade expanded in the 1530s, slumped during the English invasions of the 1540s, then grew in the second half of the century to reach a peak during the 1620s and 1630s. The evidence for this expansion is fragmented but the overall trend is clear. The rapid rise in coal exports, especially from the 1590s, was paralleled by the growth of the salt industry. Production of lead ore, though far smaller in quantity, may not have been far behind coal in terms of value. An expansion of industrial output is also demonstrated indirectly by rising imports of raw materials like iron, timber and flax. Shipments of iron from the Baltic more than trebled between the 1570s and the 1630s while those of flax and hemp doubled.[1]

The influences behind this expansion included greater internal stability during the personal rule of James VI. Population growth increased both the size of the home market and the workforce. Rapid inflation, while resulting in a fall in living standards for those who depended on money wages, benefited some sectors of Scottish society like feu-holders whose rents were fixed and may also have lowered production costs in some industries. It has been suggested that the Reformation provided more favourable conditions for economic development but, as was discussed in Chapter 6, this is hard to accept. More important for trade were closer links with England following the Reformation and the Union of 1603.

THE PATTERN OF TRADE

Scottish trade in 1550, 1600 and even 1660, retained the structure that had characterised English trade at the end of the fifteenth century, resting on the

---

1. S.G.E. Lythe, *The Economy of Scotland and its European Setting 1550–1625* (Edinburgh 1963), pp. 142–69.

export of the primary products of agriculture, fishing and mining, along with some low-grade manufactures like linen and woollen cloth. In return Scotland imported a wide range of manufactures and luxury items as well as basic raw materials. Scotland's main trading partners still lay around the North Sea, tried and tested markets which minimised the element of risk to Scottish merchants.

Scandinavia and the Baltic supplied many essential commodities on which the development of Scottish manufacturing depended. For a country almost denuded of forests, except in remote Highland districts, Norwegian timber was vital for every form of construction from barrels to houses. One cargo in three coming into Dundee in the late sixteenth century was from Norway, almost all of it timber. The Baltic also provided iron, as well as flax, hemp, pitch and tar. In return Scottish salt, fish, skin, leather and cloth found a ready market. In the 1560s and 1570s around a million skins and hides were being sent to the Baltic each year. The balance of trade was severely disrupted in years of dearth when emergency imports of grain had to be paid for in coin. As a result, in the long term the Baltic trade was probably a net drain on the Scottish economy. Scotland's trade with Sweden developed from the 1570s and imports of iron rose steadily. Recorded shipments of iron from Sweden totalled 103 between 1590 and 1599 and 462 between 1630 and 1639. Between the same two periods shipments of hemp and flax rose from 90 to 196. In return the export of cloth to Sweden rose from 250 ells in 1681–86 to 9,300 in 1607–15. Average annual sales of salt to Stockholm rose to nearly 900 tons in the early seventeenth century while herring exports also increased rapidly.

Trade with France benefited from the friendly glow of the 'Auld Alliance' in the decades after Flodden. In some parts of France Scottish traders were exempt from most customs duties and they enjoyed preferential treatment more generally. Entente between the two countries reached a peak in 1558 with the marriage of Mary to the Dauphin, Scots being granted the full privileges of French citizenship. The Reformation marked the start of a cooling of relations with France. Decline in trade, relative rather than absolute, was more marked after the Union of 1603, particularly following the Anglo-French war of 1626 into which Scotland was unwillingly dragged. Northern France was a source of manufactures and luxury items ranging from cloth to weapons. From south-western France came salt and wine. The scale of the wine trade was remarkable given the small size of Scotland's population. Average consumption of wine per person was little lower than in England, a far richer country. By 1600 well over half a million gallons of wine were imported from France each year, about half being consumed in and around Edinburgh. Imports on this scale suggest that wine drinking had spread well down the social hierarchy and was not exclusively a pleasure of the rich. Wine was a luxury, the cost of which to the Scottish economy was criticised by some contemporaries but salt was a necessary commodity. Although the scale of imports was reduced with the rise of salt manufacture at home, Biscay salt was favoured for curing fish rather than the less pure

Scottish salt. The rise of production from salt-pans around the Forth eliminated much of the demand for French salt in eastern Scotland but it was still preferred by the fish curers of the Clyde. In return the French bought Scottish fish, skins, hides, coarse cloth and wool. It is difficult to be sure where the balance of profitability lay in the trade between the two countries but it has been suggested that rising wine prices in the later sixteenth century were making the trade less attractive to Scottish merchants.

Trade with the Low Countries put Scottish merchants in direct contact with the world's greatest commercial centres. The Dutch provided Scotland with a wide range of manufactures, cloth, dyestuffs and provisions. In return they took skins, hides, wool and fish as well as coarse cloth, hose and linen yarn for which Scotland was a low-cost producer, as well as increasing quantities of salt and coal. Much of the trade was with Leith and, with the rise of coal and salt exports, other Forth burghs. In some years in the early seventeenth century as many as 50 vessels laden with Scottish coal arrived at Veere alone. The profits from the Dutch trade, directly and indirectly, probably subsidised deficits in other sectors.

Scotland's other main trading partner, growing rapidly in importance in the later sixteenth century, was England. Over the same period trade with France may have become relatively less significant while trade with the Low Countries probably continued to grow. The Reformation and the Treaty of Edinburgh in 1560 had converted the 'auld enemy' into an ally, not completely trusted but with increasingly converging interests. From the 1590s there were regular exports to England of salt, fish, coal, skins and hides, linen cloth and yarn, knitted hose, and some grain and wool. By the time of the Union of the Crowns England was competing with the Low Countries and France as Scotland's major source of high-quality manufactures. In the early seventeenth century exports of coal and salt to England rose and by 1615 London was taking over 3,000 tons of Scottish coal in peak years.

At a time when the horizons of European traders were widening to include the New World, Africa and the East Indies those of Scottish merchants were firmly fixed on the North Sea. One or two voyages to the Mediterranean are recorded in the early seventeenth century and some trade with Spain, but there are few signs of a wider outlook at a time when English merchants were pioneering contacts with Russia and renewing trade with the Mediterranean. Scotland's only successful colonial venture was close to home; the plantation of Ulster. The settlement of Scots in Ulster began in 1609 and migration seems to have continued at a steady rate into the 1630s. The spin off from this was increased trade with Ireland which benefited Glasgow and other west-coast ports. There was also an attempted trans-Atlantic venture which showed that Scotsmen were not unaware of the opportunities of a wider world. Pamphlets encouraging colonial ventures to the New World both reflected and encouraged interest in the 1620s and led to Sir William Alexander's attempt to establish a Scottish colony, Nova Scotia, in North America. Small groups of settlers left Scotland in 1622, 1623, 1627 and 1629. James VI supported the scheme by creating Nova Scotia baronetcies; each new baronet, in return for his title, had to furnish 3,000 merks towards the venture. As a way of purchasing hereditary titles at bargain prices the scheme was a huge success but it did little to help the colony which fizzled out in the early 1630s.

ECONOMIC AND INDUSTRIAL POLICY

Expansion of trade and economic growth in the later sixteenth and early seventeenth centuries occurred without the support of any coherent government policy. Economic legislation lacked direction and often demonstrated a near-total failure to understand how the Scottish economy worked. This reflected the ignorance of James VI who had little interest in, or knowledge of, trade. When in 1608 he proposed a ban on the export of timber from Scotland he had to be tactfully reminded that no timber had been sent out of Scotland in living memory. Part of James' lack of interest in trade stemmed from the fact that royal receipts from customs were small, being derived mainly from a modest levy on exports of staple goods. Annual revenue on exports remained at around £3,000 Scots a year down to the 1590s when, with expanding trade, it rose to £6,000 and eventually £12,000 in 1599. Given the rate of inflation, receipts were falling in real terms while trade was expanding. A growing crisis in royal finances precipitated the introduction of a general import tariff in 1597. Official economic policy was muddled. It worked best in short-term crises, grappling belatedly with the problem of famine by banning grain exports, prohibiting hoarding and imposing price controls. The government blew hot and cold on the export of wool and the import of cloth depending on customs receipts and which pressure group – the Convention or major landowners – was able to shout loudest. Economic legislation sometimes paid lip service to the idea of protecting the home market and, more urgently, to trying to achieve a net inflow rather than an outflow of coin but no clear mercantilist policy had yet been formulated.

Industrial growth occurred in spite of rather than because of official initiatives which relied mainly on the granting of monopolies to individuals. Some 24 attempts to establish manufactures or purchase monopolies are recorded between 1587 and 1642 ranging from paper and pottery to glass and gunpowder, soap and sugar. Production was short-lived and of little consequence in most cases. Sir George Hay's glassworks at Wemyss and Nathaniel Udward's soapworks at Leith were more successful than most. Initiative regarding industrial policy still lay largely with the Convention whose attitude was conservative and rigid, more concerned to maintain traditional privileges and resist competition than to innovate.

Economic development in the later sixteenth century took place against a background of inflation, the scale and impact of which has yet to be evaluated in detail. Price rises had affected Europe from the late fifteenth century, reaching crisis level in many countries in the mid-sixteenth century.

In Scotland the impact of inflation came later. Price rises seem to have been relatively modest before the 1560s but between then and 1600 the cost of many basic commodities rose three, four, or even six times. Wages appear to have increased in the first half of the sixteenth century, then stabilised. They lagged behind price rises until the 1590s before accelerating again to reach a plateau by about 1615 after which they altered little until the mid-eighteenth century. The amount of bread that a day's labour could buy fell during the last 60 years of the sixteenth century before rising modestly until around 1620 then stabilising.

Prices were rising in England too but not so fast. As a result the rate of exchange of the Scots pound against the English one shifted from around 4:1 in 1560 to 12:1 by the time of the Union in 1603. Harvest failures in the late sixteenth century, population growth and the debasement of the Scottish coinage all contributed to the problem. Taking in old money and re-issuing new was profitable for the government but was a prime cause of inflation. The situation was worsened by the bewildering range of foreign coins circulating in Scotland. Even the Scottish coinage was varied and bore no fixed relation to its accounted value.

The Union of 1603 did not mark a major watershed in economic relations between England and Scotland, merely a further stage in the slow process of integration. One solid result of the Union, the pacification of the Borders, allowed landowners in this region to turn their attention to commercial livestock farming. The Union also involved costs for Scotland; ties with France were loosened, while incomes which might have been spent in Scotland began to be drawn to London. James VI was keen on promoting a full economic union between the two countries but this was unacceptable to the English Parliament and was not welcomed north of the Border either.[2] Proposals for commercial union were not prominent, compared with political, legal and religious issues, in the various tracts and treatises for and against a fuller union which appeared in 1604 and 1605. Opposition to the idea of free trade between the two countries came mainly from England. Rational economic debate was submerged by national prejudice. The English feared that the Scots would undercut them in both manufacturing and trading – Scottish labour costs were lower – and unleash on England a plague of poor pedlars and other undesirables. Scotland would gain access to the wealth of England providing only poor fish and worse cloth in return. English grain would flow north to needy Scotland bringing dearth to the south. English commentators resented the Scots' position in France where their naturalisation let them buy Bordeaux wine direct from the suppliers, cutting out the middlemen with whom the English were forced to deal. Overall the incentives for economic union were not great. After 1603 the Scots traded with England on terms which were slightly more favourable than before – they had the benefit of being exempt from the additional customs tax on

2. B. Galloway, *The Union of England and Scotland 1603–8* (Edinburgh 1986).

aliens – while English merchants could trade in Scotland without payment of some customs duties. Scots and English born after 1603 were treated as subjects of either country but Scots born before 1603 were only given full rights in England after James had agreed not to give his countrymen undue preferment in appointment to offices in England.

INDUSTRIAL DEVELOPMENT

Among efforts to encourage industry particular attention was directed at improving the quality of textiles. In the first decade of the seventeenth century a group of Flemish weavers was brought to Scotland to teach the manufacture of the fabrics known in England as the 'new draperies'. Progress, in the face of opposition from the conservative urban craft guilds, was limited. More general attempts to encourage textile production were made in the 1640s. An Act of Parliament in 1641 was designed to encourage the manufacture of fine woollens by freeing foreign wool and dyestuffs from import duties and removing taxes on the cloth that was produced. Manufactories were started at Bonnington near Edinburgh, at Ayr and at Newmills near Haddington. They seem to have enjoyed modest success but they faced the problems which blighted all attempts to develop high-quality textile production in seventeenth-century Scotland: high costs, lack of a skilled workforce, insufficient capital and a limited home market.

There were also developments in mineral extraction. The discovery of various metallic ores stimulated a wave of prospecting and mining in the Lowlands.[3] The Scottish crown was perennially short of bullion and the discovery of gold on Crawford Muir in upper Clydesdale was especially welcome. In 1540 the Scottish coins known as 'bonnet pieces' were minted from Clydesdale gold which also furnished metal for the Scottish Regalia. Because of a lack of native skill in prospecting and mining the crown engaged foreign experts; Dutch, German, Flemish, French and English, to try their luck. The most famous was an Englishman, Bevis Bulmer. He was engaged in the 1590s by Thomas Foulis, an Edinburgh goldsmith who had leased the right to mine gold on Crawford Muir. Most of the gold was extracted from alluvial deposits rather than veins and Bulmer employed up to 300 men washing the river gravels. In one year gold worth £100,000 sterling is claimed to have been taken from this area by Bulmer. In 1606 a vein of silver was discovered at Hilderstone in the hills south of Linlithgow and 60 miners were soon at work there with a smelter first at Leith and then near the mine.

Lead mining was beginning to make a useful contribution to Scottish exports in the early seventeenth century. In 1611–14 the value of lead ore exported nearly equalled that of coal and was almost twice that of linen. Although small-scale working at a number of sites including Islay and

3. Lythe, *The Economy of Scotland*, pp. 51–7.

Lismore produced a fluctuating output, the principal mining field lay around Leadhills on the watershed between Clydesdale and Nithsdale. Some lead had been mined there in the late sixteenth century. In 1638 the mines came into the possession of Sir James Hope and production was stepped up. By the mid-seventeenth century some 50 workers were producing 3–400 tons of ore a year. Much of it was exported unprocessed to the Low Countries due to the difficulty of obtaining fuel for smelting on site.

The Scottish iron industry was hampered by a lack of suitable ore as well as fuel. High-grade haematite occurred in only a few localities and although the clayband ores of the Carboniferous strata were first used in the early seventeenth century the richer blackband ores were not exploited until much later. This explains the substantial imports of Swedish iron. There was still timber in the Highlands where bog ore was widely smelted on a small scale using primitive bloomery forges. Possibilities for developing larger charcoal blast-furnaces in the Highlands were being considered in the early seventeenth century. This prompted an Act of Parliament in 1609 forbidding the setting up of 'yrne mylnes' in the region to prevent the destruction of forests. Sir George Hay, one of the 'adventurers' who had made abortive attempts to settle a Lowland colony in Lewis, appears to have done a deal with Mackenzie of Kintail in which, in return for transferring all his rights in Lewis, Hay got access to woods around Loch Maree. He used his interest at court to obtain exemption from the 1609 Act and by 1610 a blast-furnace, the first in Scotland, was operating on the shores of the loch, aided by English technology and possibly also English capital. In a pattern which was to become a model for later industrial developments in the Highlands skilled workers were brought from north-west England. Cumbrian haematite and clayband ore from Fife were shipped to Poolewe. The history of the venture is obscure but the smelter still seems to have been operating in 1626. Hay's scheme, surprisingly successful in its day, was nevertheless ahead of its time. It was not until the early eighteenth century, when the Highlands were more settled, that further large-scale ironmaking ventures were undertaken there.

Less glamorous than the hunt for gold and silver but more important for the economy was the mining of coal. Coal had been worked in Scotland in medieval times but only on a small scale. The later sixteenth and early seventeenth centuries saw a major increase in production. Mining technology remained primitive. Throughout the seventeenth century most mines were small, the coal being worked from surface outcrops or by shallow bell pits and levels. By the early seventeenth century improved technology from England and Flanders was being applied at some collieries allowing deeper working. The most famous example was Sir George Bruce's mine at Culross, one of the wonders of its day. Before Bruce took over the colliery in 1575 it had been worked to a shallow depth by Cistercian monks and then abandoned due to drainage difficulties. Bruce had the mine extended nearly a mile under the Firth of Forth. Problems of drainage and ventilation were tackled by horse-driven pumps and by the ambitious scheme of sinking a shaft from an artificial island at the lowest level of the foreshore. At high tide the top of the shaft was surrounded by the sea, allowing the coal to be wound up and loaded directly on to vessels moored at an adjacent pier. The mine was linked to 44 salt-pans making it one of the largest integrated industrial units in Scotland. Unfortunately the great storm of 1625, which wrecked salt-pans and collieries around the Forth, submerged the island and flooded the mine so that it had to be abandoned.

While Bruce's mine was advanced for its day others along the Fife coast were also being extended under the sea and were using improved drainage technology. Elaborate systems of dams, reservoirs and channels were built to operate water-powered pumping equipment. Such pumps could raise water from a depth of up to 30 fathoms. Large collieries are also recorded from the upper Forth around Alloa in the early seventeenth century, some of them financed in part by Edinburgh merchant capital. Nef has estimated that the export of coal from Scotland rose from around 7,000 tons a year in the 1590s to 60,000 in the 1630s. The figures are questionable but there is no doubt that the increase was substantial. Export duties on English coal from 1599 helped make Scottish coal competitive abroad and it also began to find a market in England, particularly London.

Closely linked to the expansion of coalmining was the development of the salt industry.[4] In the sixteenth century, Scotland imported a good deal of French salt but the dislocation of this trade stimulated production at home while exports of Scottish salt to the Baltic and Low Countries also rose. The dross from the coalmines was used for evaporating sea water in large shallow iron pans to produce sea salt. Salt-making was widespread around the shores of the Forth. Scottish salt exports were only a tiny fraction of the European trade but Scottish producers were quick to take advantage of market opportunities. The collapse of the Dutch salt trade with Spain as a result of the outbreak of the Dutch Revolt in 1566 created conditions which gave Scottish high-cost, low-quality producers a chance to increase their exports. The volume of salt exported increased eight times in the early 1570s. Sir William Brereton, visiting Scotland in the 1630s when production was at its peak and the value of exported salt exceeded that of coal, described the pans around the Forth as 'innumerable'. Generally favourable conditions for export persisted until the early 1640s.

Scotland was richly endowed with fisheries but not with the resources to exploit them effectively. Much fishing was supplementary rather than specialised, part of a range of subsistence activities engaged in by coastal communities. Salmon formed a useful additional source of income on many estates; the Tweed, Tay and Dee were particularly important. In 1614 salmon accounted for about a third of the value of fish exported from Scotland; the rest came mainly from herring. The Scots were disadvantaged in the herring fishery compared with the Dutch by their lack of capital. Although from time to time grandiose plans were floated for establishing companies with

4. C.A. Whatley, *The Scottish Salt Industry 1570–1850* (Aberdeen 1987).

sufficient money to finance fleets of large fishing vessels the industry remained local and small scale, depending on open boats operating in inshore waters. Such vessels brought their summers' catches to centres like Anstruther, Crail, Dunbar or Greenock for salting and sale. The main exception was the Clyde herring fishermen who operated in West Highland waters with a fleet of hundreds of boats.

Fishing was significant in the economy of Orkney and especially Shetland where it was an almost universal occupation.[5] Many ordinary families owned or at least had shares in a four-or six-oared yole. Shetland landowners were also beginning to be involved in commercial fishing, some of them owning several boats and employing fishermen as wage-earners. The local white and herring fisheries around the Northern Isles declined during the seventeenth century due to over-exploitation. In the 1630s some 500 large Dutch vessels were operating off Shetland each year as well as fishing boats from Fife and local yoles. By the end of the century fish were no longer as plentiful among inshore waters and local fishermen were having to go further out for their catches. Merchants from Bremen and Hamburg arrived in Shetland in May or June and stayed till September, setting up booths as trading bases where they bought fish and other local produce. Their trade remained significant, though declining, until the Union of 1707 when stricter regulations on the use of foreign salt for fish curing and higher duties on imported foreign salt killed the trade.

Despite the expansion of trade and industry it would be dangerously optimistic to talk of a transformation of the Scottish economy in the late sixteenth and early seventeenth centuries. Increases in production in industries like coal and salt were often spectacular in proportional terms but started from very low baselines. One cannot even talk about an 'industrial sector' in an economy which was still so overwhelmingly agrarian. Most coal-mines and salt-works were still adjuncts to estates where the bulk of the income came from agriculture.

THE EDINBURGH MERCHANT ELITE IN THE EARLY SEVENTEENTH CENTURY

In the later sixteenth and early seventeenth centuries the domination of Edinburgh over Scottish trade was even greater than that of London over English commerce. As early as 1480, Edinburgh had accounted for 54 per cent of Scotland's export revenues. By 1578 this had risen to 75 per cent. Over the period 1460–1600 Edinburgh handled the export of 76 per cent of Scotland's wool, 73 per cent of the cloth, 80 per cent of the sheepskins, 83 per cent of the hides and much of the trade in fish, hosiery, plaiding and grain. During the first four decades of the seventeenth century more and more of Scotland's

5. H.D. Smith, *Shetland Life and Trade 1550–1914* (Edinburgh 1984).

trade came into the hands of a small elite of Edinburgh merchants.[6] The scale and range of this group's activities has only recently been appreciated. Their business methods became increasingly sophisticated involving the use of joint-stock companies, especially for imports where the element of risk was greater, and the employment of factors in foreign cities providing rudimentary banking services.

As their wealth increased Edinburgh's elite diversified into new enterprises. They beame increasingly active as shipowners. Vessels, or shares in ships, accounted for 26 per cent of the value of their inventories. Patrick Wood, who died in 1638, owned shares in at least 36 vessels although these assets accounted for only 16 per cent of the total valuation of his inventory. Some merchants speculated in grain futures by the advance purchase of crops for agreed sums. Of more general importance was their investment in industry including lead mining, coal and salt production, herring curing, brewing, rope making and cloth manufacture. Several merchants owned salt-pans around the Forth and the boom in salt production in the early seventeenth century may have been due to injections of Edinburgh merchant capital. A herring curing factory at Dunbar, which had come into the hands of William Dick, greatest of Edinburgh's merchant princes, was valued at 60,000 merks in 1642. In 1597, 18 Edinburgh merchants set up the Society of Brewers whose plant was worth 40,000 merks in 1618. It too was taken over by Dick who also had a soapworks in Leith.

Edinburgh's wealthiest merchants were deriving an increasing proportion of their income from moneylending by the 1630s, prompting royal attempts to impose a direct tax on interest in 1621. Over half the city's richest merchants were involved in moneylending as an integral part of their activities. The rates that they charged often seem to have exceeded the legal maximum. Another outlet for Edinburgh merchant capital was investment in urban property. Population growth in Edinburgh encouraged a boom in tenement construction, especially in the 1630s, financed by the richer merchants, of which Gladstone's Land in the Lawnmarket is a surviving example. By 1635 over half the city's wealthier merchants were deriving income from urban property.

Edinburgh's merchant elite also invested in rural property. This did not usually involve the purchase of estates with the aim of social climbing. It was done mainly for business purposes. Much of the money that they lent was on wadset giving them control of land and its products in lieu of rent. It has been suggested, on the strength of the limited mercantile involvement in land during the later seventeenth century, that Scottish merchants had little interest in rural property. From the 1590s, however, their activities in this sector expanded rapidly. In the charters of the Register of the Great Seal for the early decades of the seventeenth century 60 per cent of the transactions involved merchants, the bulk of them from Edinburgh.

6. J.J. Brown, The social and political influence of the Edinburgh merchant elite 1600–1638 (Unpublished thesis, Edinburgh 1985).

Involvement in land by Edinburgh merchants in the early seventeenth century was spread throughout Scotland. Thirty-six per cent of transactions concerned land in the Lothians, 13 per cent in Fife, 13 per cent in west-central Scotland, 14 per cent in the south west, 14 per cent north of the Tay and 10 per cent in the Borders. There was a concentration on arable areas suggesting links with the grain trade, much of which was in the hands of the elite. Although merchants were not directly involved in crop production it is possible that their capital lay behind the mini-agricultural revolution in the Lothians in the early decades of the seventeenth century with the widespread adoption of liming and substantial increases in both crop yields and rents (Chapter 8).

DISASTER AND RECOVERY: THE ECONOMY IN THE MIDDLE AND LATER SEVENTEENTH CENTURY

The economic boom which saw the rise of Edinburgh's merchant elite was ending by the mid-1630s. When Charles I visited Scotland in 1633 he was greeted by complaints about the decay of towns and trade. There was a drop in imports into Leith from 1636. Although problems already existed the outbreak of the Covenanting wars in 1638 heralded the start of a 15-year period of disaster for the Scottish economy.[7] Both town and countryside suffered from attack, plundering, military occupation, heavy taxation and the casual levying of additional funds. Trade was disrupted and vessels were seized. Outbreaks of bubonic plague in the mid-1640s added to the social and economic dislocation. Following the Cromwellian occupation in 1650–51 a period of stability, if not prosperity, ensued.[8] Taxation was high but not as ruinous as under the Covenanters. Economic revival was delayed by the effects of the First Dutch War of 1652–54 and by serious dearth in the North. Devine[9] has detected signs of recovery and a revival of trade in Aberdeen between 1652 and 1660 based on the evidence of expenditure on harbour works and the Shore Work Accounts which can be used to provide figures for the number of vessels entering and leaving the port. Nevertheless, Desbrisay[10] has urged caution in this interpretation suggesting that expenditure on the harbour was less evidence of revival than a desperate attempt to prevent inadequate facilities from deteriorating further due to storm damage and silting. A report from Thomas Tucker, an English customs officer who

7. D. Stevenson, *The Scottish Revolution 1637–44* (Newton Abbot 1973), and *Revolution and Counter-Revolution in Scotland 1644–51* (London 1977).
8. F. Dow, *Cromwellian Scotland 1651–60* (Edinburgh 1979).
9. T.M. Devine, The Cromwellian union and the Scottish burghs: the case of Aberdeen and Glasgow 1652–60, in J. Butt (ed.), *Scottish Themes* (Edinburgh 1976), pp. 1–16.
10. G. Desbrisay, Authority and discipline in Aberdeen 1650–1700 (Unpublished thesis, Aberdeen 1989), p. 27.

surveyed Scotland's ports in 1656, makes dismal reading and provides few indications of a revival in trade. On balance it looks as if the economy had stabilised at a low level of activity by the later 1650s and was barely beginning to expand by the Restoration.

After Cromwell's invasion, Scotland was treated at first as a conquered province but English attitudes were gradually tempered by the realisation that some kind of accommodation with the Scots was necessary.[11] Scotland was incorporated into the Commonwealth of England, Scotland and Ireland in 1653. The settlement was imposed rather than negotiated. Not surprisingly it had little popular support. Scotland was described by one contemporary as having been merged with England 'as when the poor bird is embodied into the hawk that hath eaten it'. Under the new system Scotland had the right to send 30 members to the new parliament but was nevertheless still under military rule. The occupation had its positive side, at least for dealers in provisions and whores in the towns which held major garrisons, but taxation was heavy. Military rule provided order and firm, impartial justice but was extremely expensive. General Monck was ordered to levy £10,000 sterling a month from the Scots but although this figure was soon lowered even the reduced sum proved impossible to raise. Many of the nobility had been ruined by fines and the sequestration of their estates. The occupation of Scotland was a heavy cost to the English exchequer and as late as 1658 Cromwell described the Scots as 'a very ruined nation'. Scotland had the benefit of freedom of trade within the Commonwealth, a measure resented by English traders, but her merchants lacked the resources to benefit from it and few tears seem to have been shed when the union was dissolved in 1660.

The recovery of the Scottish economy after the Restoration was slow.[12] The Dutch wars of 1665–7 and 1672–4 were setbacks to progress. The English Navigation Act hampered Anglo-Scottish trade while increasingly protectionist policies by the French affected one of Scotland's most important traditional markets. It is unlikely that economic recovery was sufficient to restore the level of prosperity reached in the 1630s but the scale of expansion was still impressive. The later 1670s in particular were a boom period marked by a great increase in the volume of Scottish shipping as merchants and skippers took advantages of the opportunities offered by British neutrality amidst European conflict. This boom in trade provided spin off into other aspects of the economy including harbour construction schemes and the development of new industrial enterprises around Edinburgh and Glasgow. The 1680s were less prosperous. Higher overseas tariffs on Scottish grain and coal caused problems as Scotland's trading partners increasingly imposed protectionist policies. Plaiding lost most of its established markets in France, Sweden and Holland in the late 1680s and early 1690s. Nevertheless, there were still good years such as 1685 when a glut of Scottish grain was matched by higher prices abroad.

11. Dow, *Cromwellian Scotland*.
12. T.C. Smout, *Scottish Trade on the Eve of the Union 1660–1707* (Edinburgh 1963).

The stubbornly conservative pattern of trade in the later seventeenth century confirmed the fears of many who were concerned about Scotland's long-term economic development. In such a poor country the domestic market was limited and could not be expanded rapidly. As a result prosperity depended upon developing overseas markets. The increasing difficulties faced by the Scottish economy in the later seventeenth century were partly due to the fact that while foreign trade was vital to Scotland its contribution to European trade was marginal. The vessels used by Scottish merchants were small. Scotland lacked harbours that could accommodate the larger vessels which were becoming vital to trade elsewhere. Leith, Aberdeen and Dundee, the principal east-coast ports, had poor facilities and were difficult to use.

Scottish merchants were small-scale operators by European standards. Normal practice in trading ventures was to spread the risk by a number of merchants owning shares in particular vessels. While informal partnerships between merchants were normal, true joint-stock companies remained rare. Most Scottish trade, unlike that of England, was handled by Scottish vessels, an indication of the importance of foreign trade to Scotland and its insignificance to her partners. Such ships were not necessarily Scottish-built though. Shipbuilding had declined since the days of James IV and the Great Michael. Risk of loss or damage of goods by storm, shipwreck or piracy was always present but the use of tried and tested markets reduced the economic risks of trading. No Scottish merchant in the Restoration period could match the scale and diversity of operations of Edinburgh's merchant princes of the early seventeenth century. Memory of their dramatic downfall may have cautioned their successors against over-expansion. Yet it was from these late seventeenth-century merchants that the increasingly successful Scottish business class of the eighteenth century was to evolve.[13] The traditional view is that only towards the end of the seventeenth century did Scottish merchants start to introduce innovations like long-term credit mechanisms and business partnerships as well as investing in other sectors like industry. This, it was thought, transformed the antiquated medieval trading system allowing the Scottish business community to face the post-1707 economic situation with growing confidence. It is now clear, however, that these 'innovations' were actually the re-introduction of business practices which had been normal before the Covenanting wars.

In the later seventeenth century many landowners were active in trade and industry. Those in Galloway and the more accessible areas of the Highlands were involved in cattle droving. East-coast landowners from East Lothian to the Moray Firth and beyond handled grain, sometimes shipping it directly overseas if prices at home were low. Proprietors around the Forth developed coalmines and salt-works on an increasingly large scale. The Earl of Winton employed Peter Bruce (Breusch), a German engineer, to build a harbour at

---

13. T.M. Devine, The Scottish merchant community 1680–1740, in R.H. Campbell and A.S. Skinner (eds), *The Origins and Nature of the Scottish Enlightenment* (Edinburgh 1982), pp. 26–41.

Port Seton to facilitate the export of coal and salt. The Earl of Wemyss at Methil and the Duke of Hamilton at Bo'ness had similar integrated coal, salt and harbour schemes as did Sir Robert Cunninghame at Saltcoats in Ayrshire.

Although quantities are elusive Scotland's main exports in the later seventeenth century can be ranked approximately by value. There were some significant changes from the early part of the century when hides and skins, followed by herring, and then linen and woollen cloth had been the most valuable exports. By the end of the century linen occupied first place followed by cattle and wool (during those periods when the export of wool was permitted) with coal, salt, fish, woollens and grain of lesser importance but still significant. Trade with France was increasingly hit by protectionist policies but remained considerable until the outbreak of war in 1689. Leith continued to receive the bulk of imported wine but trade with France was of proportionally greater importance to the Clyde ports. Voyages to Iberia were no more frequent than they had been early in the century but ventures to the Canaries and Madeira by Glasgow ships were a new development during the 1690s. The staple at Veere still functioned but was declining in importance. The commodities designated as 'staple goods' – skins, hides, woollens, salmon, tallow and beef – were less prominent exports than they had been earlier in the century. The decay of the staple was also due to the Convention, from 1661, allowing the Conservator to be chosen by the king. The Conservator became an agent of the crown rather than the Convention and was often less than vigorous in discharging his duties. In addition, the growth of Rotterdam was turning Veere into a backwater.

Trade with England after 1660 was handicapped by the English Navigation Act and by substantial tariffs on many commodities, notably coal, linen, salt and cattle. The Scots retaliated in 1661 with their own navigation act but this was an empty gesture. A good deal of cloth, as well as cattle and sheep, was sent overland to England but Scottish east-coast ports had regular contacts with many English towns, particularly London. By the end of the century tobacco was one of the most valuable imports from England; over 2 million pounds entered Scotland in 1700. Although linen was, along with cattle, Scotland's major export to England a good deal of finer cloth came north in return.

An important development in the later seventeenth century was the rise of Glasgow. In 1656 Thomas Tucker noted that Glasgow vessels had already ventured to the West Indies. The Glasgow port books indicate that by the 1680s a number of Scottish vessels were trading with the Caribbean and the North American mainland. By this time Glasgow merchants were combining to make such ventures more feasible. In 1668 a company of 107 merchants was formed to trade with America. This contravened the English Navigation Act but the Scottish Privy Council seems to have turned a blind eye. Between 1680 and 1686 over 40 voyages to the New World are recorded in Scottish port books, many of them in Glasgow-owned ships. Sugar and tobacco were the main imports with linen and woollen cloth, yarn, hosiery, shoes and hardware among the exports. The dynamic approach of the Glasgow merchant community is shown by the establishment in 1667 of a new harbour down-river at Port Glasgow. Glasgow was accessible only by small craft but the new outport could accommodate the largest seagoing vessels. Beside the harbour a new town with customs house and warehouses was soon under construction, an ambitious scheme for its day.

Towards the end of the seventeenth century exports of woollen cloth from Scotland declined but this was partly compensated by an expansion of the grain trade. The peak year was 1685 when over 160,000 bolls were exported from east-coast ports. More assured food supplies at home had led to a gradual change in attitudes to the export of grain from the early seventeenth century policy of banning exports. From the 1620s a compromise was adopted allowing exports when prices fell below a certain level and banning them when they rose too high. In 1669 this gave way to allowing export at any time unless the Privy Council intervened. In 1671 the import of grain was forbidden unless with the Privy Council's permission. Norway was the best market but the Scots faced increasing competition there from Baltic suppliers. Holland was also a useful customer, particularly in years when the Scottish harvest was good and the Baltic one poorer, but the English market was closed to Scottish grain. Towards the end of the century it became harder to sell grain abroad due to tariff restrictions.

Another significant trend was the rise of the droving trade to England, principally in cattle but also in sheep.[14] Scottish cattle and sheep had been sold to England before 1603. The traffic was irregular due to the instability of the frontier zone but the livestock trade was evidently growing in the 1580s and 1590s. Following the Union of 1603 there was a time-lag while the areas closest to the Border quietened down and livestock rearers moved to a more commercial footing. An isolated record of livestock crossing into Cumberland by the Western March between November 1617 and November 1618 shows that the trade was already significant with 5,641 cattle and 3,752 sheep recorded as entering England across only part of the Border. There was a steady increase in demand for meat from England's growing urban markets and for the navy. In 1662, 18,574 cattle from Scotland are recorded as having passed through Carlisle although an unknown proportion of these may have been Irish animals shipped to ports like Stranraer and driven through the Solway Lowlands. Irish animals were larger, heavier and readily distinguishable from Scottish beasts giving them a clear advantage in English markets. In 1663 it was estimated that as many as 61,000 Irish cattle were being brought into England by various routes. An Act of 1666 excluded Irish livestock rearers from the English market and gave a boost to Scottish producers. By the end of the century several estates were sending 400–500 cattle across the Border each year. Records for the Border customs precincts between 1680 and 1691 show that in some years around 30,000 cattle and rather more sheep were crossing to England though the number of animals which evaded the tolls is unknown.

14. I.D. Whyte, *Agriculture and Society in Seventeenth-Century Scotland* (Edinburgh 1979), pp. 234–42.

An important aspect of the cattle trade with England was the rise, in the later seventeenth century, of droving from the Highlands. Its continued development in the early eighteenth century added a new commercial dimension to the Highland economy but even before the Union its impact was considerable. The origins of this trade are uncertain but it was probably mainly a post-Restoration phenomenon. By 1692 the trade had elevated Crieff, created a burgh of barony only 20 years earlier, into one of the most important market centres in Perthshire. The south-west Highlands seem to have taken a lead due to the stability of the rule of the House of Argyll and the area's more southerly location but by the end of the century more distant parts of the Highlands like Skye were involved in droving. By the end of the century all the elements which characterised the droving trade in later times had emerged; the involvement of the Highlands as well as the Borders and Galloway, the growth of the great cattle trysts at Crieff, and the long route across the Border to destinations as far south as East Anglia from where, after fattening, the animals made their last journey to the slaughterhouses of Smithfield in London.[15]

In the later seventeenth century coarse woollen plaiding was widely made in the north east (Map 15.1) but output does not seem to have recovered to much more than half that of the 1630s peak while prices were also lower. Linen manufacture was also widespread, to some extent in the towns but mainly in the country with concentrations of production around the Firth of Tay and in the western Lowlands centred on Glasgow (Map 15.1). During the seventeenth century the quantity of linen exported from Scotland grew dramatically. In 1599–1600 18,000 ells of linen had been sent to London. By 1700 the figure was around 650,000 ells with total exports to England probably being somewhere between 1.2 and 1.8 million ells. Wool was a more variable export. In the 1660s and 1670s little Scottish wool was exported because the domestic woollen industry was thriving. Later in the century, with the decline of home woollen manufacture, considerable quantities were exported but these included unknown amounts of English wool which had been brought across the Border.

Nef has estimated that Scottish coal production had risen to around 475,000 tons a year by the 1680s.[16] Between 300 and 400,000 tons came from the Lothians and Fife, up to 100,000 tons from Lanarkshire and a mere 25,000 tons or so from Ayrshire. These figures are probably substantial over-estimates. Most collieries remained small although some large, integrated coal, salt and harbour schemes were capital-intensive. The salt industry was an important consumer of coal with between six and eight tons being required to produce a ton of salt. Nef estimated that by the end of the seventeenth century the salt-pans were consuming 150,000 tons of coal a year but Christopher Whatley has recently suggested a lower figure of around 50,000 tons.[17] About half the vessels leaving Scotland in the 1680s carried

15. Ibid.
16. D.U. Nef, *The Rise of the British Coal Industry*, vol. 1, (London 1932), pp. 42–52.
17. Whatley, *The Scottish Salt Industry.*

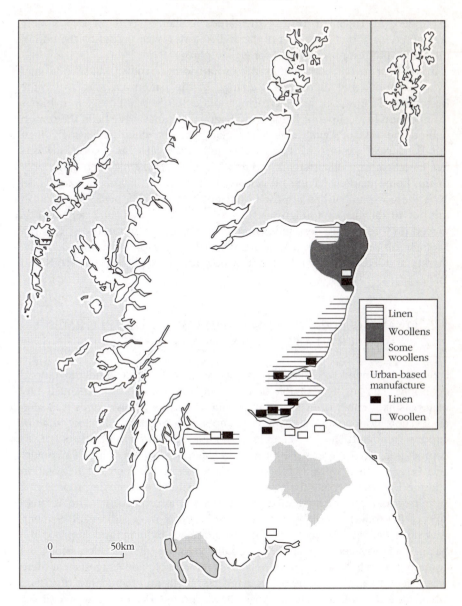

Map 15.1 Distribution of large-scale textile industries in the late seventeenth and early eighteenth centuries

coal. It has been suggested that exports rose from around 16,000 tons in 1615 to perhaps 30,000 tons in the 1680s. Coal exports began to fall in the 1690s. The Dutch, who were already reducing coal consumption by the use of coke, began to impose tariffs. Markets in Norway and France were also hit by rising duties and by increasing competition from English coal. On the other hand, home consumption, particularly for the salt-pans and the larger towns, expanded. At Tulliallan, one of the largest collieries, coal for export only accounted for about 7 per cent of the 15,000 tons a year output by the end of the 1670s; the rest provided fuel for 20 salt pans.

In the later seventeenth century the production of Scottish salt held up and even expanded but there was a change in the pattern of sales. After the Restoration Scottish salt was increasingly difficult to sell in European markets. Competition from superior French and Spanish salt may have been the reason behind the loss of Dutch and Norwegian markets while increasingly high duties caused exports to England to fall drastically. As export markets declined Scottish saltmasters moved to achieve an almost complete monopoly of the home market, having previously neglected it in favour of exports. In 1661 the government had imposed duties of 15 shillings a bushel on Scottish salt but 40 shillings on foreign salt. In 1665 a further duty of £12 per boll was placed on foreign salt, despite vociferous complaints from salt users. This put Scottish salt producers in an almost unassailable position regarding the home market and led to the establishment of new salt works during the 1660s and 1670s.

ECONOMIC POLICY AND INDUSTRIAL DEVELOPMENT IN THE LATE SEVENTEENTH CENTURY

Scotland continued to exhibit the classic weaknesses of an underdeveloped economy. The inability of the domestic economy to furnish essential raw materials like timber or even all but the most basic of manufactures was seen as a major shortcoming by many contemporaries. Scotland's limited range of exports rendered her vulnerable to shifts in overseas markets or to competition from larger-scale producers. Members of Scotland's Parliament and Privy Council were aware of these problems. Between the Restoration and the Union they passed a series of Acts which, taken together, represent a sustained and co-ordinated attempt at economic improvement. (The agrarian side of this policy, perhaps in its modest way the most successful element, was discussed in Chapter 8.) Efforts to stimulate industry and improve the balance of Scotland's trade were equally vigorous, if less successful. The continuity which underlay these policies is remarkable and suggests that there was a broad consensus embracing magnates, lairds and merchants, regarding what needed to be done to improve the economy. The policy was a classic mercantilist one of conserving bullion by developing the domestic economy and trying to exclude imports which were a drain on foreign exchange while encouraging the export of manufactures where possible. The basic assumptions were that Scotland was short of money and economically backward with an unfavourable balance of trade. This analysis was accurate enough. The desire to imitate successful neighbours like England and Holland was understandable. The methods used to try and generate economic growth were, however, unrealistic. There was a persistent hope that suitable legislation would, on its own, create the necessary conditions for economic growth. In fairness to the legislators though it must be admitted that the difficulties of achieving growth were enormous.

Periodic attempts were made to ban the import of luxury items. More positively, efforts were made to encourage new industrial ventures. A statute of 1661 re-enacted earlier legislation offering naturalisation to foreigners who brought new skills and capital to the development of industry. As well as tax exemptions for 19 years on new industrial ventures the formation of joint-stock companies was encouraged and such concerns were allowed to export their products direct without being dependent upon the merchants of royal burghs. In addition, most of the new industrial enterprises which were started in the later seventeenth century benefited from import bans on the products which they were trying to develop.

Over a dozen manufactories were set up following this encouragement of which the most successful were the first two sugar houses in Glasgow in 1667 and 1669. In 1681, after the tax exemptions of the 1661 Act had run out, another Act prohibited the import and wearing of certain kinds of foreign cloth and materials such as cambrics and calicoes. Further efforts were made to encourage people with capital and skills to come to Scotland and establish new industries or improve existing ones. Imports of raw materials were to be admitted duty free, products relieved of duty for a further 19 years and capital invested in manufactories was exempt from taxation. It is no accident that this Act was passed at a time when mercantilist policies by many European countries were imposing restrictions on trade. Other legislation aimed at improving commercial conditions by facilitating the provision of credit.

More than 60 manufactories were established between 1681 and 1707 as a result of this legislation.[18] Most appear to have been small in scale and survived for only a few years but lack of documentation may have led to the importance of some of them being underestimated. Among the most notable were ones concerned with producing higher quality textiles. Some manufactories were moderately successful as long as their products had protection on the home market but they were vulnerable to even slight shifts in economic conditions. The largest woollen manufactory may have been one established in Glasgow in 1699, financed by a group of partners including the Principal of the University, a distiller and several shipowners. It had up to 1,400 employees, most of them presumably outworkers, and was regarded as Scotland's premier cloth manufactory in 1704.

Better known because of the publication of a selection of its records was a woollen manufactory at Newmills near Haddington. One of the main promoters was the English entrepreneur Sir James Stansfield whose estate included the buildings from a cloth manufactory of the 1640s. The company was established in 1681 and was soon active with skilled workers being brought in from Yorkshire and south-west England. The manufactory suffered from the disadvantage of having to import fine wool from Spain and England. As a result production costs were higher than English cloth of comparable

18. G. Marshall, *Presbyteries and Profits* (Edinburgh 1980).

quality. Stricter measures by the Privy Council to ban imports of foreign cloth helped the company to compete more successfully on the home market for a few years but after the Revolution of 1688 this legislation was increasingly flouted. An Act of 1701 renewed the prohibition on the wearing of imported foreign cloth but following the Union of 1707 English cloth could be freely imported. Newmills and other Scottish woollen manufactories, were unable to compete. The enterprise struggled on until 1713 but by this time most of the other fine cloth manufactories had already been wound up.

A range of other manufactures was started under the aegis of the 1681 Act including the production of glass, gunpowder, hardware, leather, linen, paper, porcelain, rope, sailcloth, soap and stockings. Most of the manufactories were located around Edinburgh and Glasgow whose merchants provided much of the capital. Few details are available concerning the operation of most of these companies although it is clear than only a handful survived the Union. Two more sugar mills were established in Glasgow in 1696 and 1700. Sugar refining and the associated distilling of rum was one of the few new industries which was consistently profitable and which continued to expand after 1707. Sugar manufacture provided the basis of the first of Glasgow's great mercantile fortunes.

Efforts to increase the scale of units of production can be seen in other industries. The brewery established in Leith around 1670, another of Sir James Stansfield's ventures, may have been the largest integrated industrial unit in Scotland before the Industrial Revolution and had close links with the nearby glass works.[19] Factories on this scale were exceptional though. The scale of production in most industries is highlighted by the example of the brewing industry in Fife. In 1700 a petition complaining of the wrongful imposition of excise duties produced signatures from no less than 522 separate brewers in the shire. St Andrews alone had 70 and even tiny burghs like Falkland and Pittenweem had more than 20 each.

That efforts to develop the economy did not succeed should not obscure the important fact that they were being made at all. There were evidently influential men who saw the problems facing Scotland and who were trying to formulate policies to solve them. Their failure was partly due to the fact that the measures were too advanced for the primitive Scottish economy, allied to the difficulty faced by the authorities in making legislation stick. An optimistic interpretation is that aspirations for economic growth existed and that Scotland was ready for, and capable of, expansion when other factors, such as some form of political accommodation with England, provided a more stable framework.

19. I. Donnachie, *A History of the Brewing Industry in Scotland* (Edinburgh 1979).

CHAPTER 16

THE UNION OF 1707 AND ITS IMPACT:

THE SCOTTISH ECONOMY IN THE FIRST HALF OF THE EIGHTEENTH CENTURY

The revolution of 1688 marked the start of a period of increasing difficulty for the Scottish economy. Scotland was dragged into wars with France which lasted from 1689–97 and 1701–13. Loss of French markets was accompanied by the depredations of French privateers which disrupted Scotland's coasting as well as overseas trade. Protection of Scottish merchant vessels by English warships was limited while war also brought Royal Navy press-gangs and higher taxation. A slump in textile production contributed to the widespread impoverishment of the population. Scotland faced increasing problems as more and more of its trading partners adopted mercantilist policies and erected tariff barriers. The Scots desperately needed international trade but international trade did not need the Scots. Scotland's population was less than a fifth of that of England and a twentieth of France. When such large countries were extending protectionist policies the Scots could do little in retaliation.

The autumn of 1695 brought the first of a series of disastrous harvests followed by severe famine (Chapter 7). Emergency grain imports had to be paid for in cash which created a shortage of specie at home. This in turn disrupted systems of credit and created an economic slump which was exacerbated by the collapse of the domestic market for manufactured goods caused by high food prices. Of the 47 Scottish manufactories operating in the early 1690s only 12 seem to have been active by the end of the decade. Scotland was not unique in experiencing food shortages during this period but conditions were worsened by the political situation following the Revolution. Poor relief throughout the Lowlands was disrupted due to the dislocation of the church. The Highland War of 1689–92 had wrecked the cattle trade causing widespread destitution before the famines struck.

Many of these difficulties were clearly temporary but the long-term outlook for the economy looked bleak. Trade with England suffered from increasing tariffs at a time when tariff barriers were rising across Europe and Scotland was being squeezed out of many traditional markets. The export of linen and cattle to England became more important as other sectors of trade contracted.

All these disasters had arisen from events largely outside Scottish control. To them was now added a classic example of ill-judged enterprise, the Darien Scheme. The idea of forming a company for trading to the East and West Indies, modelled on the English East India Company, may have been circulating among Scottish merchants for some time but an Act of Parliament in 1693 encouraging the formation of trading companies provided the spur. In 1695 plans for a Company of Scotland Trading to Africa and the Indies matured among a group of London-based Scots led by William Paterson and merchants in Glasgow and Edinburgh. They secured a charter for the company and began to raise finance in London and Scotland. The Scottish merchants had in mind realistic schemes for voyages to Africa. The London merchants had grandiose plans for challenging the East India Company. They proposed raising £600,000 sterling, half in London half in Scotland, nearly twice the amount the Scottish directors had in mind. They underestimated the strength of the opposition, particularly from the East India Company whose threats of retaliation removed any possibility of raising capital south of the Border. If the venture was to go ahead then all the money would have to come from Scotland. Anti-English feeling overcoming a traditional Scottish sense of caution, £400,000 sterling was raised, an astonishing amount for so poor a country. Nearly half came from landowners, a further 22 per cent from Edinburgh and Glasgow merchants and smaller proportions from merchants in other royal burghs and Edinburgh lawyers, a good indication of who had wealth to invest.

Instead of starting modestly the enthusiasm of the directors ran riot and they opted for William Paterson's half-baked scheme for establishing a Scottish trading colony at the isthmus of Darien in Central America. The idea of an entrepôt through which both Pacific and Atlantic trades could be channelled ignored realities such as the unhealthy location of the site and the fact that it already belonged to Spain. William III, anxious not to give Spain an excuse to ally with France, prohibited English colonies in the Americas from aiding the Scots. The size and resources of the colonising venture were insufficient. The first expedition sailed in 1698, another the following year, but by 1700 it was clear that the operation was a total diaster. Disease, Spanish attack and death on board ship during the return voyages wiped out most of the colonists. The expenditure, vast for a small, poor country, had all been for nothing. Feelings ran high; clear-thinking Scots who saw that the failure was due to the nature of the project combined with mismanagement did not dare express their views in public. The Earl of Seafield, who did his best to represent to the king the scale of the loss suffered by Scotland, had his house in Edinburgh burnt by an angry mob.

The result of the Darien disaster cost nearly 2,000 lives and a huge amount of money; as much as a quarter of Scotland's liquid capital according to one estimate. In the disillusionment which followed, the Scots conveniently overlooked the impracticality of the scheme, focusing their hatred on William, who they believed had sabotaged the venture, and on England in general. The strength of anti-English feeling was shown by the trial and execution in

March 1705 of Captain Green and two of the crew of an English East Indiaman, *The Worcester*, on trumped-up charges of piracy against a ship belonging to the Darien Company. The failure of the Darien Scheme concentrated the minds of many Scots on the problems which faced the country's economy. There was a growing feeling that the Union of the Crowns was proving unworkable. Smout has suggested that more than any other factor the Darien disaster created an atmosphere in which the possibility of closer union with England was considered seriously.[1] Whether people favoured an incorporating union, some kind of federal system or a complete separation of Scotland and England there was general agreement that Scotland's existing position was untenable.

THE UNION AND ITS ECONOMIC BACKGROUND

In 1702 negotiations towards a parliamentary union were started but neither the English commissioners nor the English Parliament were fully committed to the project. Nothing came of the talks apart from increasing the sense of disillusionment north of the Border. This encouraged the Scottish Parliament of 1703 to adopt a tough independent line which forced England to take the question of union more seriously. Since 1689 the Scottish Parliament had become increasingly assertive. In 1703 and 1704 it passed several pieces of legislation which alarmed English politicians. The Act of Security and Succession imposed major conditions on Scotland accepting the Hanoverian succession. The Act Anent Peace and War required the consent of the Scottish Parliament before war could be declared or treaties negotiated, allowing Scotland effectively to pursue an independent foreign policy. The wine Act legalised the import of French wine and challenged England's embargo on the trade although Scotland was nominally at war with France. An act allowing the export of wool from Scotland re-opened the round-about route by which English wool could be smuggled abroad. This legislation does not appear to have been designed to force an immediate split between the two countries but English politicians believed that this was the Scots' ultimate intention.

As a result English politicians revised their views on the desirability of political and economic union with Scotland. At first the objective of English ministers was to ensure the Hanoverian succession within the framework of the Union of 1603. When it became clear that this would not be acceptable the case for a closer union was considered. With the Scots taking such an independent line it did not seem likely that a loose federal system would be workable. The only feasible option was a full incorporating union. To achieve this it would be necessary to grant significant concessions to the Scots. The prospect of how the Scottish economy would fare in the event of a total breach with England helped persuade many moderate Scots to look seriously

1. T.C. Smout, *Scottish Trade on the Eve of Union* (Edinburgh 1963), p. 253.

at union with England. The Scots were also influenced by England's response to the Scottish legislation of 1703–4. In March 1705 the English Parliament passed an Alien Act which stated that unless the Scots agreed by Christmas 1705 to start talks on negotiating an incorporating union, or had accepted the Hanoverian succession within the framework of the existing union, all Scots resident in England would be treated as aliens and their lands would be liable to seizure. The import of Scottish linen, coal and cattle into England would be banned and a blockade imposed to prevent Scottish trade with France.

This crude but effective blackmail was directed particularly at the Scottish nobility. A number of them had acquired estates in England through marriage and many more were active in the cattle trade. The Act was repealed in November 1705 but this scarcely mattered; it could always be reinstated. After the initial outbreak of fury in Scotland, which led to the execution of the crew of the Worcester, more careful consideration of the various options followed. This was highlighted by a flood of pamphlets for and against union. There was general agreement about the depth of the economic crisis which Scotland was facing and that this was due to the country's unfavourable balance of trade. The pro-union faction saw unhindered access to English markets, especially for cattle and linen but also for grain, salt, coal and wool, as the only means of reversing economic decline. Their propaganda emphasised the degree to which Scotland was dependent on English markets and minimised the importance of trade with other European countries. The anti-unionist group rightly queried the figures of Daniel Defoe and other pro-union writers but they could not deny the importance of Scotland's trade with England. Their view was that Scotland needed to improve its competitiveness in European markets by cutting down on unnecessary imports and improving the quality of its exports so that it could regain European markets and make itself independent of England.

There is little doubt that the economic understanding of the pro-unionists was sounder, despite their over-optimistic figures. The anti-union arguments were flawed in terms of practicalities. It was all very well to suggest that Scotland should improve the quality of its exports but this had already been tried with little success. Moreover, they made few constructive comments regarding how, in the current political situation, continental markets could be regained. In the more favourable climate of the 1670s it had been difficult enough to make such policies work. Thirty years later it was almost impossible.

The union of 1707 is one of the most controversial topics in Scottish history. Not only did it end Scotland's history as an independent state; many people have also viewed it as a major economic and social watershed. Much of Scotland's economic history during the seventeenth century has been viewed, with hindsight, as leading inexorably towards amalgamation with England. As far as the eighteenth century is concerned the union is often presented as an inevitable and necessary foundation for the economic and social progress which untimately led to the Industrial Revolution. Most controversial of all has been the debate concerning the motives which prompted the Scottish commissioners and parliamentarians to support or oppose the union. There have been two main schools of thought in recent years. One has emphasised Scotland's economic situation at the start of the eighteenth century as a force which influenced the detailed discussions of the union debate. The other approach, by political historians, has focused on the role of parties and political management in bringing about the union and has relegated economic questions to the sidelines.

Those who have viewed the economic background as a key influence, notably Smout, have emphasised the low state of the Scottish economy at the start of the eighteenth century and the major threat posed by the English Alien Act.[2] As markets abroad declined the importance of trade with England grew until, by the end of the seventeenth century, about half of Scotland's exports were directed to England. This emphasises the scale of the threat posed by the Alien Act but it had already been foreshadowed by tariffs on coal and salt imposed in 1698 and an increase in duties on Scottish linen. A tightening up of restrictions from 1696 made illegal Scottish trade with the American colonies much more difficult. It has sometimes been implied that the Scottish economy was close to collapse at this time. Recent interpretations have suggested that many of the difficulties were merely temporary rather than a prelude to a major disaster which could only have been avoided by union. Perhaps this was so but it was not necessarily evident to contemporaries.

Smout believed that the bribes of money and preferment offered to prominent Scots parliamentarians in return for their support for the Union treaty were of little significance against this pressing economic background. He has also suggested that the economic issues were foremost in the pamphlet war of 1705–6. The nobility in particular, with their direct interests in the export of coal, salt, grain, cattle and linen, recognised Scotland's need to retain access to English markets. This view has been challenged, notably by William Ferguson who has pointed to the widespread anti-union feeling in the session of the Scottish Parliament of 1704.[3] At that time the ministry led by the Marquis of Tweeddale was attempting to secure the Hanoverian succession within the framework of an independent Scotland. Ferguson suggests that the shift of opinion over the next three years was the result of shrewd political management directed from England and aided by lack of unity among Scottish opponents of union. This view emphasises the importance of short-term political manoeuvring; economic issues were only significant in terms of how they were used to manipulate support.

This is not the place to discuss the complex system of political management regulated by patronage, influence and self-interest by which the Act of Union was brought about. But to ignore the fact that the support of many Scottish parliamentarians for the pro-Union cause was bought by pensions and

2. Ibid., pp. 253–6.
3. W. Ferguson, *Scotland's Relations with England: A Survey to 1707* (Edinburgh 1977).

payment of arrears of salary for present and past offices (with the implicit threat that such legitimately earned sums would not be forthcoming if support was withheld) is to ignore the reality of the political life of the period. To the charge that many of the sums were too paltry to have influenced the recipients' voting behaviour it may be pointed out that a lot of money changed hands without being properly accounted for and that it is hard to be certain how much some key figures received in return for their support. Even Ferguson admits that the politicians who pushed through the Act of Union against the wishes of the bulk of Scotland's population were fully aware of the importance of the decisions they were making and of the background issues involved, including economic ones.[4]

One effect of this new emphasis on the political background to the Union has been a re-evaluation of the economic setting. It has been appreciated that many Scots were reluctant to lose control over their economic affairs and that from one point of view Scotland's close trading links with England were the principal cause of its economic difficulties rather than a means of salvation. Despite the problems which the Scottish economy faced, pressure for an incorporating union rather than a federal solution came almost entirely from England. As a counter to the political school of thought it has been pointed out by Mitchison that over-reliance on the private correspondence of key political figures in the Union debate may be misleading.[5] Operating over short timescales they may have taken the background economic issues as given and focused instead on the minutiae of party politics. Given the threat of the Alien Act the Scots had little choice but to accept discussions for union and there was little scope for debate on the broader economic issues.

Economic factors also had a more direct and positive role to play in the Union debate. Fifteen of the 25 Articles of Union were directly economic in character. The advantages of the union were manifest for the cattle trade and linen manufacture. Arguments concentrating on the advantages of open Scottish access to English markets have, however, tended to overlook the other side of the coin; the internal problems faced by the Scottish economy. The advantages of access to England were evident to most members of the Scottish Parliament but they also appreciated the need to safeguard vulnerable sectors of the Scottish economy from English competition. This was particularly true of the salt and coal industries. It was once believed that coal and salt producers stood to benefit from the Union by gaining access to English markets. Recent research by Christopher Whatley casts doubt on this.[6] Relatively expensive to produce and of poor quality, Scottish salt had an increasingly limited foreign market. In the later seventeenth century the Scottish salt industry had increasingly catered for the home market and had benefited from protection against imports of better quality English rock salt.

4. Ibid.
5. R. Mitchison, *A History of Scotland* (London 1970), pp. 314–15.
6. C.A. Whatley, Salt, coal and the Union of 1707: a revision article, *SHR*, 66, 1987, 26–45.

As a result of restrictions on imports the domestic market for Scottish salt rose from around 40 per cent of production in 1670 to nearly 75 per cent by the time of the Union. The eighth Article of Union protected the salt industry from English competition by exempting it from duty for seven years and then fixing duties on it at a lower rate than for imported salt. After the Union, the salt industry maintained its output and even expanded.

Coal production was closely tied to salt manufacture. By 1700 about twice as much coal was being used to fire salt-pans as was exported and many collieries were producing almost exclusively for the salt industry. Exports of coal were declining in the face of English competition and many of the most accessible seams were nearing exhaustion. The Forth collieries could not compete with those on Tyneside where reserves of easily accessible coal were greater and more capital was available for constructing waggonways to open up new deposits. Salt is sometimes considered to have taken up a disproportionate amount of time during the union debate. Coal and salt were, however, important sources of income for many landowners, one of the main ways in which estate income could be augmented given that agricultural prices and rents were static.

It was the prospect of unrestricted trade with England and not with her overseas colonies which was the main attraction of the union for most Scotsmen. The Darien disaster may have cooled enthusiasm for exotic foreign ventures but in any case, with the economy so backward and capital in such short supply, the Scots could not rapidly develop a colonial trade. When capital was available it was not difficult for Scottish vessels to trade with America and there was little that England could do about it, something that was well appreciated by Glasgow's merchants who, despite their experience of trans-Atlantic trade, were solidly against the Union.

The commissioners and many parliamentarians involved in the union debate were landowners with a range of economic interests; cattle and corn, coal and salt, linen and woollens, salmon and herring. Riley has painted a cynical picture of the competition for position and office by Scottish magnates and their followers in the years after the Revolution of 1688.[7] He suggests that magnate wealth was not founded on coal, salt or cattle but on the direct and indirect profits of office. It is possible to argue this case either way because of the difficulty of producing a balance sheet setting income from estates against that from political office. Nevertheless, men like the Earl of Seafield, who owed their rise entirely to political office, were still in a minority. The perquisites of office might be considerable but they could not be relied upon. Estates not only conferred the prestige which enabled magnates to exert political influence; they were vital sheet anchors in times of difficulty and periods out of office.

Some specific economic bribery was applied to get the treaty through the Scottish Parliament. Six pro-Union Members of Parliament got private concessions exempting them from general conditions of the treaty such as

7. P.W.J. Riley, *The Union of Scotland and England* (Manchester 1978).

export duties on coal. Broader in scope was the promise of £2,000 sterling a year for encouraging industry. A bigger bribe, aimed particularly at the nobility, was the repayment of the money lost by the Darien investors with 5 per cent interest in return for the liquidation of the company. Taken together the measures amounted to a package of economic concessions designed to placate many who saw their interests threatened. The provisions were, considered impartially, fair overall and even generous in places. Compensation for shouldering a part of England's national debt and bearing an increased tax burden took form of the payment of a sum known as the Equivalent, £398,085. 10/- plus an Arising Equivalent, any increase in Scottish customs and excise over the original calculations due to the expected increase in trade after the Union. In the event public revenues diminished rather than increased after 1707 so that the Arising Equivalent produced nothing. From this money had to be paid the public debts of Scotland, some £200,000, much of which had built up due to the maintenance of a wartime military establishment which the Scots would happily have done without. The Equivalent also had to finance repayments to the Darien investors as well as the official 'expenses' of the commissioners. The Equivalent was insufficient to meet these demands. The most powerful men were paid off first and when the money ran out lesser men were given debentures, promises by the government to pay at some undisclosed date in the future. Many of them were re-sold by needy Scots to speculators at far less than their real value.

THE IMPACT OF THE UNION

The Union did not remove the distinctive national identity of either partner. Scotland and England were too different in their social structures and levels of economic development to be easily and completely integrated. Many of the provisions of the treaty were conservative in that they shielded Scottish institutions from rapid change. The Union offered a new framework for Scottish economic growth but no guarantee of success. There were high, if unrealistic, hopes for immediate and dramatic spin-off from the treaty. Disillusion set in rapidly, however, when the Union failed to generate the promised economic miracle and its disadvantages became evident. Some of the problems were caused by high-handed action by the new British Parliament (effectively still English with limited Scottish representation) which soon began to flout the spirit and even the letter of the treaty. It had been envisaged that the Scottish Privy Council would be retained until it could be replaced by something more effective. In 1708, however, it was abolished without any other institution being created. The Council had been able to respond rapidly to any threat to law and order. The lack of any effective executive body in Scotland was to be felt keenly in times of crisis, such as the 1745 rebellion.

The rights of the Church of Scotland were also ignored in 1712 when lay patronage, which had been abolished in 1690, was restored and an Act of Toleration was passed giving freedom of worship to anyone who was willing to pray for Queen Anne and take an oath of loyalty to the government. This angered Presbyterians and encouraged pro-Jacobite Episcopalians. Payment of the Equivalent (however belated) was seen by the British Parliament as giving it the right to tax Scotland as it wished. In 1711 a new duty was imposed on linen which made it harder for Scottish producers to compete in colonial markets. In 1712 the government announced its intention to levy roughly equal duties on malt in Scotland and England. The Union Treaty had exempted Scotland from any duty on malt while the war with France lasted and it was still continuing. The government approved the legislation but decided not to apply the tax to Scotland immediately after Seafield, one of the architects of Union, introduced a motion to dissolve the Union into the Lords which was only narrowly defeated. In 1725 major riots in Glasgow resulted from Walpole's determination to impose a tax of 3 pence per bushel on Scottish malt, half the rate that some MPs wanted to bring in. There was widespread resentment of the new customs and excise system. Smuggling had been a problem for the Scottish authorities throughout the seventeenth century but it developed on an altogether grander scale in the years after the Union. The greatest disadvantage of the Union, however, was that it did not immediately solve Scotland's economic problems. The pro-Union propaganda had been too optimistic and had raised expectations unduly.

On a longer-term view a case can be made for the Union having provided the foundation for Scottish economic growth during the eighteenth century. As well as giving access to English and colonial markets it provided political stability, diminishing the likelihood of Anglo-Scottish conflict. It assured the political and religious settlements of the Revolution of 1688. It allowed easier flow of capital, skills, technology and ideas northwards to combine with Scottish mineral wealth and cheap labour. It is hard to assess the impact on trade as after 1707 goods sent to England for internal consumption were no longer exports and were not recorded but the greatest benefit of the Union was undoubtedly the opening up of English markets. Less tangibly, greater contact with England after 1707 encouraged emulation and a fashion for improvement. Scottish landowners and the legal profession, lacking the pre-1707 avenues of political influence within Scotland, began to channel their energy into economic and cultural improvement.

The Union has been heralded by some historians as the dawning of a new era for Scotland but this remained only a prospect for some decades. The 'increase of trade' referred to in the treaty failed to materialise initially making the Union a constitutional rather than an economic watershed. Sir John Clerk of Penicuik, an enthusiastic pro-unionist, recorded in 1730 his impressions of Scotland's progress since 1707. Even he had to admit that the Union had brought little benefit to Scotland. For 30 or 40 years after 1707 there is little evidence of significant economic growth. This was hardly surprising; the Scottish economy was still basically agrarian and far from commercialised. The stimulus of the English market was not significant until it experienced substantial expansion, something which did not occur until the second half of the century. The Scottish economy seems to have been stagnant until the

1720s and only began to expand more rapidly in the 1740s. In between was a period when modest growth began to be evident, a period which could be considered to have started in 1727 with the foundation of the Royal Bank of Scotland and the establishment of the Board of Trustees for Manufactures.

The first two or three decades after 1707 showed that although the Union had disadvantages they were not as dire as some had predicted. Taxation rose. The fine woollen industry was almost wiped out by English competition but it had been in severe difficulties anyway. The manufacture of coarse woollens survived and producers were gradually able to open up new markets in the American plantations and the Caribbean. The absenteeism of Scottish magnates seeking places and fortunes in London which had occurred before 1707 was merely accentuated. On the positive side the need for higher rents to sustain more costly London lifestyles stimulated improvements and structural changes on some estates.

In the short term – until the 1740s – how much did Scotland gain? The growth of the tobacco trade might seem to have been founded on the Union. Even so, while the Union provided a framework within which the tobacco trade could expand the real cause of growth was the entrepreneurship of Glasgow's merchants. As will be discussed below, the tobacco trade was mainly an entrepôt one with little direct spin-off at first to other sectors of the Scottish economy. The cattle trade and linen manufacture certainly grew during the first half of the eighteenth century but these fitted into the traditional economy and could be expanded without any major structural changes. Numbers of cattle driven to England rose from around 30,000 a year in the early eighteenth century to perhaps 80,000 in the 1750s while producers also benefited from rising prices. It was only in the 1740s that the increased scale of linen production began to cause the industry to separate from its agricultural origins.

Nevertheless, Scotland did not sink into a position of dependency, a mere supplier of agricultural produce, raw materials and cheap labour with little scope for economic development, as happened to Ireland. England had no great interest in trying to exploit Scotland; the Union had been pushed through for political rather than economic reasons. The backwardness of the Scottish economy provided effective protection against the more advanced economy of England. On the other hand, trying to maintain a stable and docile Scotland sometimes involved positive government intervention in the Scottish economy such as the establishment of the Board of Trustees for Manufactures in the wake of the malt tax riots of 1725. In the short term the impact of the Union was marginal. In the longer term it was a basic influence behind economic growth but only because Scottish society already had, and continued to develop, the ability to exploit the opportunities which it offered. If the basic causes of modernisation of the Scottish economy after the 1740s did come from indigenous factors, the Union at least provided a context for them to develop successfully. Prior to the Union Scotland, in a mercantilist environment, had tried to compete with England's stronger economy. Success had only come in areas like sugar refining which were complementary:

competitive sectors like fine woollens did not survive the union. Campbell has pointed out that the Union pushed the Scottish economy in the direction of developments which complemented rather than competed with England; but this may have been less a benefit than a response born of necessity.[8] The Union was no automatic guarantee of success.

THE SUCCESS STORIES: LINEN AND TOBACCO

One of the success stories of the Scottish economy in the first half of the eighteenth century was the linen industry.[9] Ultimately, it was cheap labour which made Scottish linen so competitive. Much home-grown flax was of poor quality. Skills in spinning and weaving were low producing poor cloth while quality control was minimal. As long as the industry was merely an adjunct to agriculture serving mainly local needs this was not a major problem but it hindered the development of exports. The progressive mechanisation of the many time-consuming and labour-intensive stages of preparing the flax helped to separate the industry from its domestic origins. Before it could be spun flax had to be cleaned of seed, a process known as rippling, and retted or steeped in water to separate the fibres from the woody outer part. The next process was scutching, beating the fibres with wooden mallets to remove the bark. The fibres then had to be heckled or combed out for spinning. The first lint mill for scutching flax was built in 1729 by James Spalding after a visit to Holland; by 1770 around 250 were in operation. Other mechanical innovations included the thread twisting mill (1722), the Dutch press for folding cloth (1730) and the inkle loom for making tape (1732). The Irish method of bleaching, more suited to coarser cloth, was in use by the 1730s using water power for washing. The rubbing of the cloth between wooden boards was mechanised in the 1740s and beetling, or beating the cloth with hammers to give it a smooth surface, from the 1750s.

The Scots were deficient in the technology of bleaching linen. In the early part of the century fine linen was sent to Holland for bleaching. The Dutch process involved steeping the cloth alternately in alkaline and acid solutions and then laying it out to be bleached by the sun for periods of several weeks. By 1745 at least 25 bleachfields had been set up and many more were established in the next 15 years. Small bleachfields serving purely local needs gradually gave way to much larger concerns. While lint mills could be financed by a small-scale operator bleachfields required a larger capital outlay; subsidies were available from the Board of Trustees but were only payable retrospectively. The use of sulphuric acid for bleaching which greatly speeded the process was also introduced from Holland and became established during the 1750s.

8. R.H. Campbell, Scotland Since 1707: the Rise of an Industrial Society (Edinburgh 1985), pp. 2–5.
9. A.J. Durie, The Scottish Linen Industry in the Eighteenth Century (Edinburgh 1979).

Various organisations were concerned with the development of the industry including the Convention of Royal Burghs and the Society of Improvers in the Knowledge of Agriculture, founded in 1723. They produced pamphlets on growing better quality flax and improved bleaching techniques, urging the need to attract Dutch bleachers to Scotland. They also pressed the government to encourage Scottish industry in general and linen manufacture in particular. The result was the setting up of the Board of Trustees for Fisheries and Manufactures in 1727. Although it was belated and indirect the Board was one of the most positive examples of economic action to arise from the Union. With many influential and enlightened landowners, lawyers and merchants as members the Board was better placed than the Convention, with its narrower vested interests, to encourage the development of the linen industry though its policies in many respects were simply continuations of those of the seventeenth century.

The Board was allocated £6,000 a year, mainly from money which had been set aside at the time of the Union but which had not so far been applied to Scottish development. Nearly half was directed towards improving the linen industry. The Board tried to improve each stage in the process of manufacture. A high priority was given to improving the quality of yarn by setting up spinning schools. By 1731, 10 had been established and by 1752 24. Foreign weavers and bleachers, especially from Holland, were brought to Scotland to demonstrate improved techniques. Scottish scientists were encouraged to examine the industry's problems. The practical element of Scottish university education was demonstrated by the willingness of academics to undertake research in this field. Premiums were offered for mechanical and chemical innovations, subsidies for the growing of flax by large-scale producers under instructions prepared by the Board and £50 per acre for the establishment of bleachfields. Fifty stampmasters were appointed to ensure that cloth met specified standards.

Some of the Board's activities, such as paying premiums for the growth of flax were of little value. Its work was hampered by limited funding but despite this it encouraged a new spirit of improvement and enterprise in the linen industry. Members of the Board, including Lord Milton, the Earl of Ilay's political manager in Scotland, also took an interest in financing the industry and in marketing. Milton had an interest in a linen manufacturing company in Edinburgh and in 1746 this was expanded by a new charter into the British Linen Company, a large-scale concern which imported flax and operated an extensive putting-out system. Its activities were financed with the company's own notes issued by local agents who soon began to operate almost as branch banks. The Company eventually gave up manufacturing and went into finance in a big way providing badly needed capital for development.

Government attitudes towards the Scottish linen industry were ambivalent before the 1740s and 1750s. There was initial discouragement due to a new duty on the export of Scottish linen from 1711. This did not affect the home market but a duty on all printed linen from 1715 did. Export duties on linen were lifted in 1717 but only after 1742, when bounties were paid on exports of linen, did the Scots begin to compete more successfully in colonial markets with German and Austrian cloth. The importance of the bounties was demonstrated when they were temporarily withdrawn in 1754 and production fell sharply. Only then did the government move to provide positive protection first to the fine linen industry which was under most pressure from foreign competition and later on all exported linen.

Because of the introduction of a system of stamping linen, output data are available from 1728, the most complete run of production figures for any Scottish industry in the first half of the eighteenth century. The quantity of linen stamped each year rose from 3.5 million yards in 1728 to 9 million in the mid-1750s. Total output was higher as it included unstamped linen produced for household and local use. Exports of plain linen to America rose from 92,715 yards in 1744 to 468,640 in 1751 and 2,055,563 in 1760. The manufacture of Osnaburgs, coarse cloth imitating linen made in the German town of Osnabruck, began in the mid-1740s and rapidly became a major export item and a staple manufacture of the Tayside area. Output of finer linen also increased substantially in the late 1740s helped by protection of the British home market against French cambrics and lawns. Output of higher-priced linen, around 11,000 yards in 1730, rose to 147,000 yards in 1747 and 444,000 yards in 1750. Growth of production led to structural changes in the industry. Elements of regional specialisation had been evident at the end of the seventeenth century with a tendency for finer linen to be manufactured in west-central Scotland and coarser cloth in Fife and Angus. This trend became more marked during the first half of the eighteenth century.

The spinning of yarn was much more widely distributed than weaving. Spinning was a vital source of income to women throughout the central Lowlands and the north east. As the industry expanded the supply of female spinners began to dry up – it required five spinners to keep a weaver fully occupied – and in the 1730s and 1740s spinning began to spread into the Highlands. Some spinners worked up their own flax, selling the yarn to local weavers or travelling packmen. Those who did not have flax of their own got it from a dealer and worked it up at an agreed price. As spinning spread into new areas reliance upon imported flax grew along with the practice of putting out. Although women provided an important element in the rural labour force they experienced more seasonal underemployment than men and they had every incentive to augment their income from spinning yarn.

Outside the towns most weavers were cottars who only wove cloth on a part-time basis. Textile manufacture thus fitted comfortably into the Lowland farming economy. Agriculture and rural textile production in Lowland areas became separated when the cottar system was replaced by one where landless labourers were employed full-time for money wages. This only began to occur in the second half of the century. Under the traditional system weavers depended on local families handing over their yarn for making up. Demand was often seasonal, slack in summer and picking up after harvest when more money was in circulation. This seasonality of demand allowed weavers to provide a reservoir of farm labour. In the early eighteenth century it may have been difficult for weavers tied to local markets to obtain more than six months work in any year. As the industry grew, however, rising demand led not only to an expansion of the labour force but also to a growing time commitment by established weavers, an increasing number of whom became almost full-time industrial workers severing their links with agriculture apart from a period of work at harvest time. The development of factories was first evident in the fine linen sector where quality control was most important. By the 1740s the size of firms was increasing steadily with up to 70 looms in operation in a single building in one or two cases. Such factories were exceptional though and most weavers still operated from home. Even here though they came increasingly under the thumb of urban merchants and their agents. Customary weavers producing cloth on demand for purely local markets still existed in the mid-eighteenth century but their numbers were declining steadily.

The other spectacular growth area in the Scottish economy was the tobacco trade.[10] The first brief burst of prosperity at the time of the union, due partly to customs evasion, was followed by stagnation. Of tobacco, 6.5 million pounds were imported in 1722 but only 3.75 million in 1726. The level of imports rose rapidly from the 1730s to reach 15.2 million pounds in 1755 and 25.6 million in 1758. Much of this was re-exported; in 1755 over two thirds of the tobacco brought into Scotland. By this time tobacco formed, in terms of value, nearly half of Scotland's imports from outside the United Kingdom. Imports into Glasgow were starting to exceed those for all English ports put together. A number of factors lie behind this remarkable expansion. Growth was favoured by the shorter, safer passage from the Clyde and the possibility of supplying goods needed in the plantations such as cloth, tools, guns, fish, leather from manufacturers in central Scotland. Most important of all was the entrepreneurship of Glasgow merchants. Instead of sending vessels across the Atlantic to wait, sometimes for weeks, until enough tobacco to form a return cargo had been accumulated, Scottish merchants established stores with resident agents who bought the tobacco and sold goods exported from Scotland. Vessels arriving from Scotland thus usually had full cargoes awaiting them and with the quicker turnaround it became possible to fit two trans-Atlantic voyages into a season instead of one.

The tobacco trade initially produced little direct spin-off for the Scottish economy but by the mid-eighteenth century many of Glasgow's tobacco merchants were buying most of their export cargoes in Scotland. A number of Glasgow tobacco merchants were beginning to diversify their activities, investing in industry, mainly in the Glasgow area but not always directly concerned with supplying goods for the plantations. They also began to purchase estates around Glasgow and several were active in developing coal deposits on their lands.

10. T.M. Devine, *The Tobacco Lords* (Edinburgh 1975).

STAGNATION OR MODEST GROWTH: IRON, COAL AND SALT

In contrast to the spectacular growth of linen manufacture and the tobacco trade other sectors of the economy barely expanded during the first half of the eighteenth century. This can be seen in the iron, coal and salt industries. Iron smelting remained small-scale, reliance still being largely upon imported iron. Following the failure of the 1715 rebellion there was renewed interest in the Highlands by English ironmasters wishing to exploit sources of charcoal. As demand for iron in England rose many traditional iron-producing areas like Furness were reaching the limits of their fuel supply and the Highlands, more peaceful and accessible than before, looked increasingly attractive. Nevertheless, the difficulties of operating a relatively capital-intensive industry in what was still a remote area with poor communications ensured that most ventures were short-lived. In 1723 an iron mill was set up at Achray near Aberfoyle using scrap brought in from Port Glasgow and ore from Fintry. In 1730 the York Buildings Company established a smelter at Abernethy on Speyside using ore brought by packhorse from near Tomintoul, 20 miles (32 kilometres) away. Neither furnace lasted for more than a few years. A similar fate befell the blast-furnace set up at Invergarry in the Great Glen by the Cumbrian Backbarrow Company and an ironworks in Glen Kinglass by Loch Etive. More successful was one on Loch Fyne built by a partnership between the Duke of Argyll and a Lake District company. The longest lasting of these charcoal iron smelters was Bonawe Ironworks, established in 1753 by a group of Lakeland ironmasters which continued to produce around 700 tons of iron a year using local charcoal and Cumbrian ore into the later nineteenth century.

Locational disadvantages aside, another reason why Highland blast-furnaces tended to operate only intermittently was that demand for iron within Scotland was static. Such smelters were tied to English markets and even there demand was sluggish until the 1750s. English iron production began to expand and limitations of charcoal supply encouraged the smelting of iron using coal. In Scotland larger-scale production in the metal trades using imported Swedish bar iron was developing with forges and slitting mills like the Smithfield company near Glasgow in 1732 and the Cramond Ironworks near Edinburgh from 1752. A radically new development in the history of Scottish industry was the founding of the Carron Ironworks near Falkirk in 1759. The Carron Company provides a good example of how English technical expertise and entrepreneurship could be successfully combined with Scottish business sense. It was launched by a partnership of Samuel Garbett, a merchant and manufacturer from Birmingham, John Roebuck, an English chemist, and William Cadell, a merchant from Cockenzie. Garbett and Roebuck had already collaborated in establishing a plant to make sulphuric acid at Prestonpans in 1749. Here they met Cadell who had interests in the Baltic iron and timber trades.

The site of the new ironworks at the mouth of the River Carron was chosen carefully. It was close to carboniferous ironstone, an ore never previously used for ironmaking in Scotland. The site had ready access to coal and sufficient water power, while its location facilitated the transport of raw materials and the marketing of finished products. From the start Carron was conceived as an integrated operation on a scale hitherto rare in Britain. The plan was for four blast-furnaces, three finery forges, a boring mill and slit mill. The company handled every part of the production process from mining the coal and iron ore to selling the products. More than any other development in mid-eighteenth-century Scotland Carron heralded the coming of the Industrial Revolution. It is easy to over-emphasise Carron's importance though. It remained the only ironworks of its kind in Scotland until the 1780s and during its first 20 years of operation it barely survived a series of financial crises.

The demand for coal was no more buoyant than that for iron in the first half of the eighteenth century; prices remained static and output only rose slowly. As a result there were few technological innovations in Scottish collieries. Steam engines were slow to be adopted for mine drainage, waterwheels and horse gins continuing to suffice in most mines. The first steam engines are recorded in Scottish mines around 1719–20 but by the 1730s only a handful of Newcomen engines were in use in Scotland and not many more by the 1760s. On the other hand, technical developments included the cutting of some long-distance drainage levels in the Lothians and Fife. The first colliery waggonway, at Tranent, was constructed in 1722 by the York Buildings Company which had bought the Earl of Winton's forfeited estate after the 1715 rebellion. Like the steam engines which appeared about the same date, it was an innovation in advance of its time.

Much coal production was still associated with salt-works and, as agricultural improvement began to get under way, with lime kilns. Mines remained mostly small and shallow. Underground working continued to be conducted by the wasteful pillar and stall system in which a substantial proportion of the coal was left untouched; the more efficient longwall system of working was only introduced from England in the second half of the century. Although production figures and profits from individual collieries are difficult to calculate data for the Loanhead mines owned by Sir John Clerk of Penicuik suggest that a well-organised colliery could show a consistent, if modest, profit in most years during the first four decades of the century, rising in the 1750s. Coalmining was not an automatic road to wealth though. The salt industry did not benefit from access to English markets after the Union but lower duties on Scottish salt guaranteed its domination of the home market. Production fluctuated from year to year but remained fairly steady at between 250,000 and 300,000 bushels throughout the first half of the century. Salt remained an important source of cash for landowners, often cross-subsidising coalmining by providing the capital for driving new levels or sinking new shafts.

BANKING AND FINANCE

An achievement of the first half of the eighteenth century which was crucial to Scotland's economic expansion, was the creation of a banking system.[11] Scotland's business techniques and credit structures were primitive by the standards of Europe's more developed nations at the end of the seventeenth century. The main way of borrowing and lending money was by private contracts or bonds the most common type being the heritable bond secured on landed property. The use of bills of exchange had become common in foreign trade though more traditional merchants still preferred to deal in bullion. In their debates on how to improve the economy the men who framed the legislation of 1661 and 1681 do not seem to have considered the creation of a better banking system as a prerequisite for development.

The idea for establishing a Bank of Scotland came from London-based Scots. William Paterson, who was involved in the Darien Scheme, had founded the Bank of England in 1694. Thomas Deans, a banker, and a group of fellow Scots brought in John Holland, an Englishman with suitable experience, to draw up plans for a Scottish bank and the charter for the Bank of Scotland was granted in 1695. The Bank of Scotland was unusual in that it was purely private, unconnected with the state and, unlike the Bank of England, expressly forbidden in its charter to lend money to the government. Although the idea for a bank had been initiated in London; at least two-thirds of the shares had to be held in Scotland, a precaution designed to prevent an English takeover. The bank obtained a monopoly for 21 years. Loans were made on the security of land in the form of heritable bonds, on personal security and on the value of commodities. This last type of loan often involved discounting bills of exchange. The bank faced early competition from the Darien Company's excursions into finance and attempts to establish branches in Aberdeen, Dundee, Glasgow and Montrose failed. The early years of the bank were marked by a series of crises that it was fortunate to survive and which illustrate the problems faced by the Scottish economy. In 1704 an outflow of bullion to pay for Marlborough's campaign caused a run on the bank forcing it to suspend payments for several months. The invasion scare of 1708 and the Jacobite rebellion of 1715 caused similar problems. The bank's 21-year monopoly expired during the 1715 rebellion and the directors failed to apply for its renewal possibly because, with the bank's suspected pro-Jacobite leanings, it might have been refused.

A new challenge to the bank arose in the 1720s. The holders of the Equivalent debentures, a substantial proportion of them now in London, formed themselves into a company to facilitate the payment of interest by the government. Behind this was a scheme to use the company and its capital for

11. S.G. Checkland, *Scottish Banking: A History 1695–1975* (Glasgow 1975).

banking. The result was the foundation of the Royal Bank of Scotland in 1727, supported by powerful Whigs who were interested in promoting economic development in Scotland, part of the same drive which established the Board of Trustees for Manufactures in the same year. The debentures were tied up, earning a fixed income, and the bank had limited liquid assets. Nevertheless it mounted an immediate attack on the Bank of Scotland aimed at driving it out of business or forcing an amalgamation. By collecting up its notes and presenting them for payment it made the Bank of Scotland suspend operations but it survived nevertheless. Both banks coped with short-term crises of this sort by using an option clause which allowed them to defer payment of cash for notes, when presented, for up to six months with a payment of 5 per cent interest. The Royal Bank received as one of its first deposits £20,000 from the government as income for the encouragement of industry and fisheries by the Board of Trustees. The loss of the Bank of Scotland's monopoly and the foundation of the Royal Bank led to a different banking structure in Scotland compared with England where the Bank of England maintained its exclusive privileges.

The two public banks were not directly concerned with providing finance for trade and industry. This was done indirectly through private banks which borrowed from the public ones. The two banks provided credit for businesses on a fairly short-term basis, working rather than fixed capital. The need for working capital varied seasonally and to meet this need they provided credit more cheaply than private sources which tended to lend over longer timespans. In the early eighteenth century, with the Bank of Scotland pursuing a very conservative policy regarding the provision of credit, bills of exchange, changing from hand to hand, were being used effectively as bank-notes.

The Royal Bank's approach to lending was more flexible than its older rival including an early form of overdraft facility. After the initial period of antagonism competition between the two banks was beneficial as both were forced to improve and diversify their services. By the mid-1740s Scotland had a small but quite advanced banking system. The two public banks discounted bills of exchange drawn on London but not inland ones within Scotland so that outside Edinburgh people had to rely on private bankers for finance. From the 1740s, however, the Scottish banking system developed rapidly, becoming the most efficient in Europe and ready to respond to the challenges of economic growth. Banknotes increasingly replaced coins as the circulating medium. To the two public banks was added a third, the British Linen Bank. This developed from the British Linen Company, founded in 1746, which rapidly developed the financial side of its activities, issuing notes from 1750. The provision of credit by the British Linen Company for the linen industry was particularly important as there were long time-lags between the giving out of raw materials and the sale of the finished cloth. In addition there were perhaps 15–20 major private banks in Edinburgh.

Provincial banking firms developed due to dissatisfaction with the services offered by the Edinburgh banks which were reluctant to discount the trade bills of Glasgow's tobacco merchants.[12] The first, the Banking Company of Aberdeen, founded in 1749, was driven out of business by the two Edinburgh banks in 1753. In Glasgow the Ship Bank, initially encouraged by the Bank of Scotland and the Glasgow Arms Bank, promoted by the Royal Bank, (both banks were named from the devices used on their notes) were founded in 1750, financed largely by merchants engaged in the tobacco trade. They were encouraged by the main banks in Edinburgh which hoped to keep them in a subordinate position and use them to develop their links with Glasgow merchants. Although the public banks in Edinburgh sank their differences in order to combine against the Glasgow upstarts, the two west-coast banks survived the challenge and flourished. The development of an efficient banking system was one of the keys to economic development in Scotland. Economic changes in the first half of the eighteenth century were, however, matched by and closely associated with important developments in Scottish culture.

12. C.W. Munn, *The Scottish Provincial Banking Companies 1747–1861* (Edinburgh 1981).

CHAPTER 17

TOWARDS IMPROVEMENT AND ENLIGHTENMENT

From the 1740s a group of Scots based mainly in Edinburgh and Glasgow gained increasing recognition in a range of fields including philosophy, history, law, science, medicine, literature, economics, and what were to become the social sciences. This achievement, unmatched in England, was of major importance in European terms and has become known as the Scottish Enlightenment. It is often associated with the writings of its two greatest figures; David Hume, perhaps Britain's most original social philosopher, and Adam Smith who established the discipline of economics. But Hume and Smith did not work in isolation. They interacted with other writers whose works, although little read today, were important in their time. Adam Ferguson and John Millar established modern sociology while William Robertson, a historian with a strong sociological interest, was eclipsed in his day only by Gibbon. Together these and other men created a close-knit scholarly community.

TOWARDS THE ENLIGHTENMENT

It might seem surprising that such an intellectual revolution should have occurred in a small, poor country where Calvinism remained strong. This begs the question: was the Enlightenment a sudden phenomenon or did it have deeper roots in the seventeenth century? Superficially its debt to the seventeenth century might appear to be limited. This period has been seen as a dark age in Scottish culture, preoccupied with arid theological controversy and torn by political faction. This ignores significant intellectual achievements and institutional developments in the church, the law and the universities which provided a foundation for the Enlightenment.

Smout has viewed the Enlightenment more positively as the result of intellectual energy being liberated from the restrictions of theology by a gradual secularisation of society.[1] On the other hand, Campbell has

---

1. T.C. Smout, *History of the Scottish People 1560–1830* (London 1969), pp. 470–83.

considered that there was no fundamental gulf between Calvinism and the ideas of the Enlightenment.[2] He argues that Scottish Calvinist theology was in itself the supreme social science. In the eighteenth century Calvinism was gradually re-orientated, paving the way for the development of secular social science. If continuity between seventeenth-century Calvinist thought and the attitudes of the Enlightenment is accepted it allows us to consider as precursors seventeenth-century intellectual developments which were set within a Calvinist mould.

During the later seventeenth and early eighteenth centuries intellectual stimuli reached Scotland from England and the Continent in areas such as philosophy, law, medicine and science. Scotsmen like William Carstares, who returned to Britain with William of Orange, had often been resident in the Low Countries for years while in the early eighteenth century Jacobites who had made their peace with the authorities came home with ideas which had been circulating in France, Italy and Scandinavia as well as the Netherlands. In the later seventeenth century as in the eighteenth intellectual progress was centred on Edinburgh. The city experienced a cultural flowering stimulated in part by the patronage of James, Duke of York, during his period of residence in Scotland.[3]

Some of the patronage was directed at the aristocrats who formed a mini-court around James at Holyrood. More significantly, however, intellectual developments were also linked to a group of Edinburgh lawyers and doctors, reflecting the rising status, and the growing intellectual aspirations, of Edinburgh's professional classes. The interest in science which characterised Restoration England spilled over into Scotland. A Physic Garden, forerunner of the Royal Botanic Garden, was established at Edinburgh in the 1670s with the support of the burgh council. Under royal patronage medicine also received considerable encouragement. Before this period the provision of medical training in Scottish universities was limited and most students had either to train under an established practitioner or go abroad. The Royal College of Physicians was founded in 1681 following pressure from Edinburgh's doctors for a professional organisation to defend them against encroachments by the surgeon apothecaries who had long dominated the practice of medicine on the city. In 1685 three chairs in medicine were established in the town's College which was elevated to the status of a university to allow the professorial appointments to be made. The opening of Surgeons' Hall in 1697 saw the start of the first systematic teaching of anatomy under the auspices of the Royal College of Surgeons. In 1725 the teaching of anatomy was transferred to the university under Alexander Monro primus, professor of anatomy. The Royal Infirmary opened in rented premises in 1729 and from 1741 in a specially constructed building, leading to the introduction of clinical teaching as part of the medical curriculum. Medical

2. R.H. Campbell and A.G. Skinner (eds), *The Origins and Nature of the Scottish Enlightenment* (Edinburgh 1982), pp. 23–5.
3. H. Ouston, York in Edinburgh: James VII and the patronage of learning in Scotland 1679–1688, in J. Dwyer, R.A. Mason and A. Murdock (eds), *New Perspectives on the Politics and Culture of Early-Modern Scotland* (Edinburgh 1985), pp. 133–55.

teaching developed more slowly at Glasgow but progress was nevertheless made in the early eighteenth century with St Andrews and Aberdeen following more slowly.

During the same period important developments were also occurring in law. The legal profession in Edinburgh was becoming increasingly dominated by the upper levels of landowning society. By the early eighteenth century an overwhelming majority of advocates came from landed backgrounds. The absence of the court in Edinburgh after 1603 had created a social vacuum which was increasingly filled by the city's legal establishment. A career in law could lead to political advancement and the intellectual training that it gave was seen as a good liberal education. The volume of legal business had increased steadily during the Restoration period as had the status of lawyers in general. Edinburgh's lawyers, and their professional associations, the Faculty of Advocates and Society of Writers to the Signet, dominated the city's society and wielded considerable political influence. In turn the spending power of the lawyers became a key element in the city's prosperity. In seeking to understand why lawyers and the study of law contributed so much to intellectual life in Scotland and was such a prominent element in the Enlightenment it is important to appreciate the much wider interest in law among Scotland's educated classes and its more pervasive role in Scottish society compared with England.

The two leading legal figures of the later seventeenth century were Sir James Dalrymple, first Viscount Stair, Lord President of the Court of Session and Sir George Mackenzie of Rosehaugh, Lord Advocate. Stair's 'Institutions of the Law of Scotland' (1681) represented the first major codification of Scots civil law. Stair aimed not merely to systematise Scots law but to show that it formed a coherent, logical and practical system. As a result of Stair's achievement Scots law developed into a rational discipline based on philosophical principles which were clearly linked to European ideas of natural or universal law, and which contrasted markedly with the system of precedents that formed the basis of English law. Stair's work made Scots law more cosmopolitan in outlook and more receptive to change, as well as allowing the Scottish legal tradition to make a distinctive contribution to the Enlightenment. Stair was, nevertheless, a staunch Presbyterian, differing from continental writers on natural law who believed that a rational theory of law could exist independent of theology. Stair believed that God acted according to reason, that His law was rational and that law was founded primarily on His will. Sir George Mackenzie's 'Laws and Customs of Scotland on Matters Criminal' (1684), although of lesser weight, was nevertheless an important development in Scots criminal law. Together these two works provided the foundation on which the legal writers of the Enlightenment were to build. Mackenzie was the prime mover behind the foundation of the Advocates' Library in 1682. From the start it was designed to be a collection for the use of scholarship in general, not exclusively for the study of law, and within a decade or so of its foundation half the collection consisted of books on non-legal topics.

Cultural developments in Restoration Scotland were still dominated by aristocratic dilettantes who formed a group of royalist intelligentsia around James during his stay in Edinburgh. But as the professions gained in status and authority their members, often drawn from laird families, began to make increasingly important intellectual contributions. It was this group which in the mid-eighteenth century was to create the Enlightenment. The shift in domination of Scottish culture from the nobility towards the professionals became more marked in the first half of the eighteenth century. Some aristocrats contributed to cultural development as private and political patrons but the key figures of the Scottish Enlightenment were mostly professional men; ministers, lawyers and professors. Direct patronage by the nobility was rare though several men who later achieved international fame, including Adam Smith, spent some time as tutors to the sons of nobles. Patronage operated more broadly through control of entry to the professions. There were more educated men in early eighteenth-century Scotland than there were professional posts available. The church, with around 900 benefices, was the largest employer but at this period the system was clogged up with ministers who had been appointed after the restoration of Presbyterianism in 1690. Many intending ministers had to wait years for a parish while working as schoolmasters or private tutors. There were not so many opportunities in law; it took time and contacts as well as ability to build up a successful advocate's practice and there was keen competition for the 100 or so posts as Lords of Session, judges, or sheriffs, the income from which made the difference between getting by and living comfortably. The universities offered even fewer openings. Even men with the right connections did not necessarily get easily the positions they were seeking. Adam Ferguson served as an army chaplain for several years before obtaining a parish. William Robertson, Adam Smith and John Millar all had to wait some time for suitable employment after completing their professional training while David Hume spent eight years after graduation without a permanent post.

The transition from Calvinist ideas to more liberal ones is seen most clearly in the teaching of Francis Hutcheson. Born in 1694, he was the son of Scottish Presbyterian parents living in Armagh. His Calvinist background gave him the interest in moral issues which came to be a distinctive element of Scottish Enlightenment philosophy, leading to the broader consideration of human society and its relation to other themes such as history and economics. Educated at Glasgow University, he returned there in 1729 as professor of moral philosophy. His ideas have been seen as marking the beginning of the Scottish Enlightenment, starting the trend towards analytical discussion and liberal enquiry which so characterised it. Hutcheson brought together ideas which were current in early eighteenth-century Scotland, many introduced from England and Europe, and incorporated them into a philosophical framework which was later to form the basis of the views of the Moderate Party of the Church of Scotland. His ideas contained elements which were more radical than those of many of his successors. His approach to moral philosophy was based on the empirical study of human nature but his aim was to use this to illuminate God's purpose for man, not to replace it. His view of mankind was more optimistic than those of traditional Calvinist thinkers and led directly to the work of David Hume and Adam Smith. His work embraced fields which today would be called economics, politics and psychology. He believed in man as a social, caring creature whose humane feelings, rather than logic, encouraged him to act for the 'greatest happiness of the greatest number' but his beliefs were still essentially Calvinist.

Hutcheson's work, marking the real start of a serious tradition of Scottish moral philosophy, was taken up and magnificently developed by David Hume who in 1739 published his *Treatise of Human Nature* in which the study of human nature was seen as a pre-requisite for a wider understanding of society. Hume aimed to apply the experimental philosophy of Newton to the study of man and to discover the psychological characteristics in man which explained social relationships. His ideas represented a development of those of Locke, Shaftesbury and Hutcheson in stressing the empirical evidence of personal experience but he went further in seeing the Christian faith as undermining the basic principles of human logic, encouraging man to believe in what was completely contrary to his experience. Hume was the most brilliant figure of the Scottish Enlightenment but in many ways the least characteristic and the most isolated, censured by the church for his scepticism which exposed the weak foundations of much contemporary theology and barred from appointments to university chairs because of his extreme views.

THE NATURE OF THE ENLIGHTENMENT

The Scottish Enlightenment remains an enigma, particularly regarding its origins and causes. There has been little agreement among modern scholars over its definition or timespan. Narrow definitions restrict the Enlightenment to advances in moral philosophy, historical sociology and political economy embodied in the works of half a dozen writers: Adam Ferguson, Francis Hutcheson, David Hume, John Millar, William Robertson and Adam Smith, as well as to a relatively brief period from the 1750s to the 1780s. Wider definitions encompass achievements in the fields of medicine, science, art, architecture and literature. Some historians have broadened their scope to include the social, political and economic milieu within which these men operated, stretching the span of the Enlightenment from the Union of 1707 to the 1830s.

Too broad a definition of the Enlightenment, thematically and chronologically, blunts its impact and makes it too diffuse. Nevertheless, narrow definitions based on the works of a handful of figures fail to set their achievements in context. They ignore lesser contributors and those people who did not publish but who interacted with and influenced those who did. A consideration of the social and cultural context in which men like Hume and Smith lived and worked is essential for a proper understanding of their achievement. Neither can the intellectual advances of the period be divorced from their economic background and concerns such as agricultural improvement or industrial development. The distinction between the ethos of Improvement and Enlightenment is hard to make at times especially when both were pursued by the same person, like Lord Kames who was as keen to be thought of as an agricultural improver as a philosopher. The Enlightenment involved not only abstract thought but also the development of attitudes which saw man as being able to influence his environment to an increasing degree. Such attitudes were important in influencing entrepreneurship and economic development.

The causes of the Enlightenment are difficult to pinpoint. The occurrence of so many men of ability within such a small country and brief space of time could be dismissed as a random fluke. On the other hand, genius is unlikely to flourish unless appropriate preconditions exist to encourage it. In Scotland this was not the case before the 1730s. David Hume would not have had the freedom, in the 1690s, to express his views in the way in which he was able to do half a century later. One clear influence on Scottish intellectual life was the complex relationship between England and Scotland in the years following the Union. After 1707 English influences on Scottish society inevitably increased, evident by the growing popularity of London literary periodicals such as *The Spectator* and *Tatler* among Scottish readers. Some historians have seen the Union as precipitating a crisis of identity in a nation that was no longer a nation state. There was widespread admiration of English prosperity and economic achievement among the leaders of Scottish society. A sense of inferiority is reflected in the strenuous efforts made by men like David Hume and William Robertson to purge their prose style and speech of Scotticisms. In the later seventeenth century Sir George Mackenzie had defended Scottish speech but this view commanded less support from Scotland's educated classes as the eighteenth century progressed. To men like Hume, Scots was no longer a language with a respectable pedigree going back to the days of the makars but merely a corrupt dialect form of English. It was readily appreciated that nobody would be taken seriously as a literary figure south of the Border unless their spoken and written English was acceptable. The great works of the Scottish Enlightenment were all written in standard southern English. The desire to imitate English manners, speech and literary style was only one facet of a more general drive to achieve social and economic development which would bring Scotland alongside its wealthier, more developed partner.

One influence which has been seen as encouraging the Enlightenment was the political stability fostered by the Union. Others include economic development from the 1740s, the diversion of intellectual energy away from the political and religious strife of the seventeenth century, improvements in education following the 1696 Act, changes in the burgh schools and the Scottish university system, the expansion, rising prosperity and increasing status of the urban middle classes, growing liberalism in the church with the decline of hard-line Calvinism, and the distinctive character of society in eighteenth-century Edinburgh. The Enlightenment was only one element in the wider development of eighteenth-century Scotland. It has to be considered in the context of closer post-Union contacts with England coupled with a growing appreciation not only of Scotland's backwardness but also of the realisation that this could be changed. Given this, it is not surprising that the Enlightenment's leading thinkers were so concerned with social progress, with the ways in which the form of economic development influenced the nature of societies and their institutions. Nevertheless, even when the entire setting of the Enlightenment is considered its causes remain elusive. Certainly the broader frameworks of economic and social change in mid-eighteenth century Scotland provided the setting. Without them the Enlightenment would not have been possible: but this is not the same as saying that these influences actually caused it.

The second quarter of the eighteenth century saw an intellectual awakening which led into the Enlightenment. It was marked by the teaching of Francis Hutcheson and the appearance in 1739 of David Hume's *Treatise of Human Nature*. The first generation of Enlightenment intellectuals, including Francis Hutcheson, Lord Kames, Colin MacLaurin and Alexander Munro primus, was born in the 1690s. The major figures of the Enlightenment were born in the 1710s or 1720s; Robert Adam, Joseph Black, Alexander Carlyle, William Cullen, Adam Ferguson, David Hume, James Hutton, John Millar, Thomas Reid, William Robertson, and Adam Smith. They went to school, attended university, and began their professional careers in the 1720s, 1730s and 1740s.

This prompts one to examine the influences in early eighteenth-century Scottish society which helped to form their outlook and opinions. Camic has considered the early lives of Ferguson, Hume, Millar, Robertson and Smith, while Sher's overlapping study examines a group of ministers; Hugh Blair, Alexander Carlyle, Adam Ferguson, John Home and William Robertson.[4] It is possible to identify common elements in the childhood, education, adolescence and early professional experiences of these men which, while in no way unusual, taken in combination helped to give them attitudes which encouraged a different outlook from that of traditional Calvinists. They all came from devout Calvinist backgrounds; the fathers of many of them were ministers. Several of them, however, had an unusual degree of freedom in childhood and adolescence. Camic emphasises the lack of parental control at an early age: Hume lost his father when he was two, Smith before he was born, while Millar escaped parental control at an early age. Camic also pinpoints the varied social origins of pupils in the burgh schools, most of them they attended as a broadening influence. Next came the liberating effects of attending universities in which the old system of regenting had been replaced by a professorial structure, encouraging higher standards of teaching and scholarship, and their early struggles to obtain professional posts. The danger of this micro-scale approach, however, is that it restricts the

4. C. Camic, Experience and Enlightenment (London 1983), R. B. Sher, *Church and University in the Scottish Enlightenment* (Princeton 1985).

Enlightenment to a handful of individuals and ignores the broader social contexts within which they operated.

EDINBURGH SOCIETY AND THE ENLIGHTENMENT

The key intellectual developments in law, medicine and other spheres which led into the Enlightenment were centred in Edinburgh and to a lesser extent Glasgow. The study of the origins of the Enlightenment is in great measure the study of the development of culture and society in Edinburgh during the late seventeenth and early eighteenth centuries. In the late seventeenth century the city developed as a social centre for the nobility and gentry. Losses incurred in the Darien venture which prevented landowners from travelling abroad were one factor which encouraged the development of a winter social season in Edinburgh with concerts, dances and other activities. A new charter granted by James VII in 1688 envisaged a large-scale programme of civic improvement with government aid for new public buildings and streets. Although these ideas only came to fruition in the second half of the eighteenth century it is significant that they were circulating as early as this. The city continued to develop as a social centre during the early eighteenth century. The Assembly Rooms for dances opened in 1710. The Musical Society of Edinburgh, founded in 1728, held weekly concerts for much of the year and despite its expensive subscription had a lengthy waiting list. This period also saw the appearance of Scotland's first newspapers; the Edinburgh Evening Courant in 1718 and the Caledonian Mercury in 1720. In 1739 the Scots Magazine, a substantial literary journal, was started, an important source of information on politics, society, and new publications. Allan Ramsay's circulating library, dating from 1725, was the first in Scotland. The Copyright Act of 1709 allowed the Advocates' Library to develop into a major reference collection by receiving a copy of every work published in Britain. The censure of the church still caused problems though. Allan Ramsay's attempts to open a theatre in Edinburgh in 1736 were thwarted by a combination of disapproval from the town's magistrates and the kirk.

The take-off of the Enlightenment in Edinburgh during the 1750s occurred against a background of plans to improve the city which developed into the creation of the New Town. These expressed a sense of inferiority regarding the appearance of Edinburgh in relation to London and continental cities, just as many of the Enlightenment's main figures were motivated by a desire to show how much a supposedly backward country could achieve. The improvement of Edinburgh involved careful calculation by members of the town council who saw it as a means of bringing prosperity to the city through increasing its attractiveness as a social centre. George Drummond (1687–1766), who began his first term as Lord Provost in 1725, saw the expansion of the university as part of the plan for the development of the city. Drummond engineered the appointment of the first Alexander Monro as

Professor of Anatomy and helped him to establish the Royal Infirmary.

An important feature of the generation which grew up to produce the Enlightenment was its sociability. The major figures all knew each other, many since childhood or their student days. In Edinburgh they came into contact with each other in their professional lives through the General Assembly, the courts and the University as well as in formal and informal social gatherings centred on Edinburgh taverns. Tavern-based clubs often had a wide social range among their membership; in them men from different backgrounds and women too could interact to a greater degree than at more formal gatherings. Some clubs and societies were purely literary in character like Allan Ramsay's Easy Club (1712). The earliest one with more philosophical aims was the Ranken Club, established around 1716 and named after the Edinburgh tavern in which it met. Its members included William Wishart, Principal of the University and Colin MacLaurin, the mathematician. The Medical Society of Edinburgh, established in 1731, was the forerunner of the city's Royal Society. Founded by the Edinburgh medical professors led by Alexander Monro primus, it soon extended its interests into areas like physics and antiquities, and was re-named the Philosophical Society. The Select Society of 1754 included among its members the leading Moderate ministers and lawyers like Lord Kames and Lord Monboddo, as well as academics such as William Cullen and Adam Smith. It aimed to encourage philosophical enquiry in a range of areas including the sciences, arts, agriculture and industry. Such societies were less prominent in Glasgow although the Political Economy Club, established in 1743, counted Adam Smith and Sir James Steuart as members along with many of the city's leading merchants. Aberdeen was too small and remote, with insufficiently large legal and medical groups, to be a major intellectual centre though some of its professors made significant contributions to the study of moral philosophy.

With the exception of David Hume there were no professional men of letters in early eighteenth-century Scotland. There was not a sufficiently large market for literature within Scotland to support them. Writing remained a part-time activity by men engaged in the professions. The fact that the Enlightenment was the product of a group of professional men rather than the nobility made its focus on Edinburgh inevitable. It has been suggested that the city was large enough to offer a wide range of lucrative professional posts and a rich social life but at the same time still small enough for all the literati to be closely acquainted, unlike contemporary London or Paris. It was the attractiveness of this close-knit conviviality which made William Robertson refuse to settle in London and Hume, feted in Paris, to long for the 'plain roughness' of the Poker Club.

CHANGE IN THE UNIVERSITIES

The Enlightenment could not have occurred without major changes in the universities and the church. A significant development during the early eighteenth century was the reorganisation of the universities, particularly Edinburgh but also Glasgow and, more belatedly, Aberdeen and St Andrews. Scottish universities after 1560 had the tasks of training the ministers and schoolmasters required to spearhead literacy and the spread of the reformed church and producing the lawyers who were increasingly needed in a less violent but more litigious society. The universities were thus not isolated from Scottish society but were responsive to external influences and demands. They could not easily escape the narrow-mindedness and factionalism of seventeenth-century religion and politics though, suffering periodic purges during the swings between episcopalianism and Presbyterianism. For much of the seventeenth century higher education in Scotland was in a poor state and the nobility and gentry often went abroad to study. During the Restoration period, however, the situation improved, especially regarding the teaching of science and medicine at Edinburgh. Before this the Scottish universities had hardly concerned themselves with science at all.

Developments in medicine at Edinburgh in the later seventeenth century have already been noted. The Restoration period was also marked by advances in the Scottish universities in mathematics and the physical and biological sciences. St Andrews established its first chair in mathematics in 1668 with James Gregory as professor. In 1674 he moved to Edinburgh to a new chair founded specially for him. He introduced the work of Kepler, Galileo and Descartes and Newton into his teaching and established the first astronomical observatory in Britain in 1673. His work was continued at St Andrews by his pupil William Sanders, Professor of Mathematics 1674–88. At Edinburgh his nephew David Gregory became Professor of Mathematics in 1683 and made Edinburgh the first university in Europe to teach Newton's *Principia*. At Glasgow George Sinclair, the first Professor of Mathematics, was appointed in 1691.

Newtonian ideas were circulating widely at Edinburgh by the 1680s. Glasgow was more conservative although Newton's theories were being taught in the early years of the eighteenth century. St Andrews and Aberdeen stood somewhere between Edinburgh and Glasgow. Student notebooks and theses suggest that Newtonian ideas were more widespread at this time than university authorities might have admitted, perhaps treading warily for fear of censure from the kirk. Colin MacLaurin, a brilliant mathematician and one of the most distinguished Newtonians of his day, was appointed to the Edinburgh chair of mathematics in 1725, largely due to Newton's personal influence. John Stevenson, Professor of Logic at Edinburgh from 1730, introduced Locke's ideas into the curriculum while George Turnbull, Professor of Philosophy at Marischal College, Aberdeen in the 1720s, was the first to suggest that Newton's approaches could be applied to the study of human society. The spread of Newtonian ideas is only one way to gauge progress in the sciences. From the 1660s there was increasing interest in the experimental approach to science including the work of Robert Boyle and other English scientists connected with the Royal Society.

By the 1720s Edinburgh, under the influence of contacts with Utrecht and

Leyden, was emerging as a leading medical centre. Provost Drummond and other members of the burgh council worked to create new medical appointments within the university. In 1726 four new chairs were established. The development of medicine acted as a stimulus to sciences such as botany and chemistry which had originally been ancilliary subjects but which now began to emerge as areas of academic study in their own right. By the mid-eighteenth century chemistry had developed as a distinct subject. William Cullen began lecturing in chemistry at Glasgow in 1746, moving to Edinburgh 10 years later. He established a research programme at Glasgow which was continued by his brilliant pupil Joseph Black who developed the theory of latent heat. There was a strong empirical streak in their work with practical applications in agriculture, mining and textile production. Black's applied work with alkalis led to his discovery of 'fixed air' or carbon dioxide.

The arts curriculum, and the ways in which it was taught, had not changed markedly from late-medieval times. The curriculum comprised Latin and elementary Greek in the first year, followed by a year each of logic, and rhetoric, with moral and natural philosophy in the final year. Teaching was mainly by lectures, in Latin, often taking the form of dictation of set texts to large classes although there was some individual tuition and instruction. The philosophical basis of the curriculum was still mainly derived from Aristotle down to the 1660s, but thereafter student notebooks and theses begin to reflect ideas drawn from Descartes, Locke and especially Newton.

Intellectual advance in Scottish universities was restricted by the system of regenting under which a single member of staff took a class through the entire four-year curriculum. In the late seventeenth and early eighteenth centuries there was growing criticism of standards of education in Scottish universities, and their role in relation to society. There was increasing readiness to challenge the centrality of ancient languages in the curriculum. Classical learning was accepted as necessary for the professions but in teaching it was increasingly seen as dull and inefficient. In the later seventeenth century Edinburgh's links with Leyden and Utrecht were particularly strong. Among those who were impressed by the structure of the Dutch professorial system was William Carstares who returned to Britain with William of Orange in 1688 as his advisor on Scottish ecclesiastical affairs. Carstares became Principal of Edinburgh University in 1703. His brother-in-law, William Dunlop, was already Principal of Glasgow University. At the end of the seventeenth century Scottish universities were poorly endowed. Carstares and Dunlop persuaded the government to contribute more money to their institutions. Edinburgh's town council, mindful of the benefits which would accrue to the city in terms of prestige and economic spin-off, were also vigorous in promoting their university.

Carstares instituted far-reaching improvements in the administrative and teaching structure of Edinburgh University. In 1708 he abolished regenting and replaced it by a professorial structure. This permitted much more specialisation and the teaching of a wider range of subjects. Over the next three decades the impact of these reforms was wide-ranging. Under the new system the income of professors depended substantially on fees contributed by students attending their courses. There was thus a considerable incentive for them to be innovative in the content of their courses and effective as teachers. In 1727 Glasgow also abolished regenting. St Andrews followed in 1747 though Aberdeen's two colleges retained the old system until the end of the eighteenth century. This gave Edinburgh and Glasgow Universities a lead which they never lost making them the key centres of the Scottish Enlightenment. Though Aberdeen had an important regional role in Scottish intellectual development in the eighteenth century the St Andrews colleges stagnated.

Academic specialisation was encouraged by the establishment of more chairs at Glasgow and especially Edinburgh University. At Edinburgh new chairs were created in mathematics (1674), botany (1676), ecclesiastical history (1694), three chairs in medicine (1685), and one in public law (1707). The abolition of regenting in 1708 created further chairs in Latin, Greek, logic, metaphysics, moral philosophy and natural philosophy while other chairs were added in natural law (1710), chemistry (1713), universal history (1719), anatomy and Scots law (1722). A similar trend, on a smaller scale, was evident at Glasgow. The appointment of professors depended on patronage, family connections and also on political and religious views. At Glasgow appointments to chairs were in the hands of the appropriate faculty. At Edinburgh they were made by the town council, but with the approval of the political establishment. There was also a good deal of nepotism which established academic dynasties in some subjects, such as the three generations of Alexander Monros who held the chair of anatomy at Edinburgh from 1720 until 1846. The remarkable thing is that despite these constraints people of major intellectual stature were appointed.

These developments, though often piecemeal and unco-ordinated, had a major effect in enhancing the reputation of the two institutions. Glasgow had a stronger bias towards science and technology than Edinburgh. Some of the most distinguished scientists of eighteenth-century Scotland, such as Joseph Black and William Cullen, began their careers at Glasgow before being drawn to Edinburgh by the higher incomes available there. Edinburgh and Glasgow Universities grew steadily in size, attracting a small but significant percentage of their students from families of English dissenters who were barred from attending Oxford and Cambridge. Protestant Ulstermen tended to go to Glasgow and English students had a slight preference for Edinburgh. By 1725 Edinburgh had around 600 students compared with 400 at Glasgow, 300 at Aberdeen and 150 or so at St Andrews.

In the early eighteenth century students commonly entered Scottish universities at 14 or 15, graduating at 19, sometimes earlier. This early age of entrance was not uncommon elsewhere, including at Oxford and Cambridge. Admission standards were minimal, a basic grounding in Latin being the principal requirement. Students were more varied socially than in other European countries. There was a substantial proportion from the middle ranks of society and a smattering of poor scholars. Fees, though still impossibly high for children from the poorest backgrounds without financial assistance, were low compared with neighbouring countries. Fletcher of Saltoun calculated in 1694 that it was cheaper to train a graduate than a shoemaker or a weaver. This was not necessarily an advantage as low fees kept down regents' incomes and prevented good scholars from being attracted to Scottish university posts. St Andrews operated a system in which students were graded by social class and their fees assessed accordingly. Elsewhere there was less overt social differentiation but wealthier students nevertheless obtained better food and could afford additional private tuition.

Changes in education were not confined to the universities. The high schools in the larger towns taught an increasing range of post-elementary subjects such as French, navigation, mathematics, book-keeping and geography. Such subjects did not always form a compulsory part of their curriculum but were often taught privately as additional options with financial support from burgh councils. Emphasis on them grew as the pace of commercial development began to quicken with pressure from merchants and professional men for teaching to be practical and relevant. Such changes were already under way before the Union and the threat of competition from the burgh schools was one reason why the authorities of Edinburgh and Glasgow Universities were so ready to undertake reforms and to consider the relevance of their teaching to the needs of society.

CHURCH AND SOCIETY IN THE FIRST HALF OF THE EIGHTEENTH CENTURY

The strength of traditional Calvinist views in the Church of Scotland in the late seventeenth century is shown in the ratification by the Scottish Parliament in 1695 of an old Act making blasphemy a capital offence. This was followed in 1696 by the execution of a student, Thomas Aikenhead, for expressing heretical views on the divinity of Christ which he was prepared to recant. The era of narrow-minded intolerance had not yet passed. The church remained the focus of local society over much of the country and religious absenteeism was synonymous with crime, heresy and immorality. Calvinist attitudes continued to pervade society well into the eighteenth century. This was seen in many aspects of everyday life such as the way in which people were still prepared to submit to the discipline of the kirk sessions.

Between the rigid Calvinism of the seventeenth century and the religious Moderates of the mid-eighteenth was a generation of learned and more liberal-minded ministers the most notable of whom included Francis Hutcheson and his pupil William Leechman (1706–85), who was appointed to the chair of divinity at Glasgow and later became Principal there, Robert Wallace (1696–1771) and the two William Wisharts, father and son, both of whom became principals of Edinburgh University. They were more interested in spirituality, charity and tolerance than dogma. Hutcheson and Leechman urged students to avoid theological speculation in their sermons and to concentrate instead on personal conduct, living a godly life through their relationships with others. The controversies raised by these men and others helped the kirk to re-assess its attitudes to its doctrines and its relations to contemporary philosophy, paving the way for the even more liberalising atmosphere of the Enlightenment.

The first half of the eighteenth century was marked by a lessening of religious tension after the upheavals surrounding the religious settlement of 1690. The Revolution settlement, though welcomed by the majority of Presbyterians, could not hope to embrace all the shades of belief which existed within the kirk. Attempts to confine theological thinking within what was increasingly seen as a restrictive framework became more and more unrealistic. The General Assembly's annual reiteration of the need to maintain a pure doctrine by requiring ministers to sign the Westminster Confession emphasises that the church was under pressure. Two pieces of legislation passed in 1712 proved particularly controversial. One granted religious tolerance to the Episcopalians. The other, imposed in disregard of the Treaty of Union, removed the system instituted after 1690 under which ministers were appointed by all the heritors and elders of a parish and restored the earlier system whereby they were nominated by a single patron, generally a substantial landowner. This led to problems where patrons tried to install ministers who were not approved of by the bulk of their congregation though proprietors only began to exercise their rights to patronage frequently from the 1730s. Services at parish kirks had been gatherings where social distinctions were minimised. During the early eighteenth century, however, social differentiation became more apparent as landowners began to distance themselves from the rest of the congregation by constructing 'lairds' lofts' for themselves and their families. Proprietors increasingly claimed the right to annex a percentage of the floorspace in their local churches equivalent to the proportion of land they held in the parish. They then erected their own pews and allocated the seats in them.

The kirk faced a number of challenges during the first half of the eighteenth century with increasing uncertainty about its role in a society characterised by accelerating economic and cultural development. It gradually became more receptive to alternative viewpoints but the process was a slow one. The Arminian view that salvation was open to all believers leading a Christian life only gained ground gradually. In 1715 John Simson, Professor of Divinity at Glasgow, was brought before the General Assembly on charges of heresy. He admitted that he had put forward new ideas but insisted they could not be rejected without consideration: unless it was assumed that knowledge of divinity was complete and perfect there was surely scope for further exploration and debate. He encouraged his students to think for themselves rather than merely transmitting a given body of facts and ideas. He considered that the truths of the Calvinist faith were unalterable but the ways in which they were explained could be refined. The General Assembly found against him but there was increasingly restlessness of thought within the church which could not be stopped. Simson's vigorous defence of his views encouraged pupils like Francis Hutcheson. By the 1730s there were clear signs of a move away from Calvinism towards ideas stressing ethical teaching and morality rather than theological doctrine, particularly under the influence of Hutcheson and Leechman. As late as 1738, however, Hutcheson was brought before the Presbytery of Glasgow and accused of teaching false and dangerous doctrines.

An increasing need was seen for strength, unity and order within the church. After the death of William Carstares in 1715 there was no church leader of sufficient stature to achieve this. The failure of the 1745 rebellion ended any threat of an Episcopalian restoration but in making the Presbyterian church secure this helped to expose the divisions within it. The open, democratic structure of the kirk, compared with the hierarchical system of the Church of England, tended to weaken unity as there was less of a clear-cut structure of authority. A wave of evangelicalism swept through Scotland, reaching a peak in 1742 when tens of thousands flocked to open-air meetings at Cambuslang to hear the preaching of William McCulloch and George Whitefield. The emotional and mystic atmosphere of such meetings was attacked by Calvinists who were scared of a return to the fanaticism of the seventeenth century.

Another challenge came from secession raising the spectre of more and more splinter groups breaking away from the kirk and weakening its authority. In the 1730s and 1740s patronage became an increasingly vexed issue within the kirk. It caused the first major secession with Ebenezer Erskine, minister at Stirling, and his followers refusing to accept the influence of the landed interest. Their opposition was less to the Act of 1712 itself than to one passed by the General Assembly in 1732 which provided that if a patron did not act to replace a minister within six months, a new minister should be appointed not by free election but only by the heritors. After an outburst attacking the General Assembly's decision, Erskine was rebuked by his synod and then by the Assembly itself. He and three other ministers left the church to form the Associate Presbytery, which itself split into two distinct groups in 1747.

In a number of cases when clashes arose over the installation of a new minister presbyteries refused to obey rulings by the General Assembly on grounds of conscience. During the 1740s a group of young ministers was increasingly troubled by the rising tide of disputes within the church and the ease with which the authority of the General Assembly could be flouted. In May 1751 a number of them, including Hugh Blair, Alexander Carlyle, John Home and William Robertson, met in an Edinburgh tavern with some influential lay elders including Provost George Drummond. Out of this group the Moderate Party within the kirk was formed. It was solidly Whig and pro-Hanoverian; several of the ministers had seen active service on the government side during the 1745 rebellion.

In 1751 the Moderates fought a test case in the General Assembly over the parish of Torphicen where the minister put forward by the patron had not proved acceptable to the congregation and the Presbytery of Linlithgow had refused to induct him. The Moderates tried to get members of the Presbytery suspended for defying the General Assembly. They were defeated but the following year they fought another campaign over a similar issue in the parish of Inverkeithing and won. In the process William Robertson drafted a document which effectively became the manifesto of the Moderate Party.

The Moderates emphasised the need for order and subordination to authority within the Kirk suggesting that while individual members might disagree with decisions passed by the General Assembly they were not entitled to defy it on grounds of conscience. Why should a minister whose conscience would not allow him to obey the ruling of the church continue to draw a stipend from it? No matter whether it was desirable or justifiable patronage should be accepted as the law of the land to prevent confrontation with the government. This was the price which had to be paid for an independent church continuing to occupy a central place in national life. They were concerned to maintain the kirk's independence by reducing government intervention. The government was represented strongly at meetings of the General Assembly, not only by the Royal Commissioner but often by the Lord Advocate and other crown officers plus a number of judges sitting as ruling elders. Before the rise of the Moderates the kirk had been 'managed' by leaders closely attuned to the political interests which controlled the Scottish administration. The power which the Royal Commissioner could exert over the General Assembly was shown in 1749 when demands by the clergy for a long overdue increase in their stipends were quashed. If the government had agreed the increase would, of course, have come from the pockets of the heritors who supported them. The Moderates wanted the church to be in full control of its own affairs but to achieve this it had to demonstrate to the political establishment that it was responsible and unified. The church would co-operate with the state on equal terms in return for freedom from political manipulation.

At a broader level the Moderates saw the good order of society as essential with the church having a key role in achieving this. The involvement of the Moderates in literature and philosophy was a sign of their desire to integrate the church with a society which was becoming markedly more secular in its concern with matters like economic development rather than theological issues. They realised that there was little future in a church which remained negative, backward-looking and rigidly dogmatic. They opposed the severity of traditional Calvinism which frowned on activities such as dancing, theatrical performances, drinking and gambling.

The Moderates who gained control over the kirk during the 1750s were to dominate decision-making within it during the second half of the century. They were always in a minority compared with the hard-line Calvinist ministers who, because they had a greater level of grass-roots support, became known as the Popular Party. The Moderates were skilful organisers and orators as well as being in favour with the political establishment and they were able to manipulate the General Assembly to their advantage. Under their direction the kirk became more open to outside influences, more broad-minded and liberal. They aimed to replace the stereotype of the Scottish Presbyterian minister as intolerant, fanatical and ignorant with an image which emphasised style, refinement and good taste. They were accused of emphasising moral preaching at the expense of doctrine. They were superbly caricatured in 1753 by John Witherspoon with a satire which enumerated the characteristics of a Moderate minister in an exaggerated form. These included putting off all appearances of devotion, showing good will to all heretics, drawing texts from classical writers rather than scripture, and cultivating the airs and manners of a gentleman. Witherspoon's lampoon emphasised the close association of the Moderates with polite society, and also their literary ambitions. Moderate ministers were beginning to hold private parties during the General Assembly at which ministers mixed with lay intellectuals, including the notorious sceptic David Hume. Moderate ministers were prominent as founder members of the Select Society in 1754 along with Hume and Adam Smith. They were also leading lights in the short-lived *Edinburgh Review* of 1756, a publication which was designed to demonstrate the intellectual advances which were being made in Scotland by critically reviewing all important new works published in the country. The *Review* also provided a useful platform from which the Moderates could criticise the writings of opponents.

The rise of the Moderates did not go unchallenged. In 1755–56 a campaign was waged to censure the writings of David Hume and Lord Kames as heretical. The Moderates succeeded in getting the charge watered down into a more general resolution rather than one specifically attacking the two writers. One of Hume's bitterest opponents was George Anderson. His death in 1756 marked the end of an era. He had been the last of the old school of narrow-minded, intolerant ministers so prominent in the seventeenth century. His campaign against Hume had not received the widespread support that he had hoped for indicating that the kirk was slowly moving towards a more liberal standpoint.

This did not occur without a struggle though as the affair of Home's play *Douglas* showed. John Home, minister of Athelstaneford in East Lothian had written a play, *Agis*, with a classical theme in the 1740s which had been rejected for the London stage by David Garrick. Home's next effort was *Douglas*, a play with a patriotic Scottish setting. When Garrick turned it down Home's friends urged him to stage it in Edinburgh. There were legal problems regarding this, never mind the attitude of the church, for the law prohibited professional theatrical performances outside London without a special licence which, with the influence of the Kirk, was impossible to obtain in Scotland. Theatre-going, and even more the idea of a minister actually writing a play, was still regarded as sinful by a great many ministers and laymen.

Home would never have got the play performed without the backing of the Duke of Argyll, Scotland's political manager, and his agent Lord Milton. It was first performed in December 1756 and was received so enthusiastically that it was later successfully transferred to the London stage. In the meantime the

Presbytery of Edinburgh condemned Home for having produced the play, for attending a rehearsal and for consorting with actors. Moves were made to punish other ministers who attended performances including the minister of Liberton who was suspended for six weeks, his sentence being reduced because he tried to conceal himself from the rest of the audience by sitting behind a pillar. A vigorous pamphlet war ensued with Alexander Carlyle and Adam Ferguson as well as Home providing defences against attacks which varied from the hysterical to John Witherspoon's more measured 'Serious Inquiry into the Nature and Effects of Stage Plays'. Home resigned his parish in 1757 and embarked on a career as a professional playwright. Alexander Carlyle had the misfortune to be in the hard-line Presbytery of Dalkeith and was prosecuted for attending the play. Carlyle took the case to the synod and then to the General Assembly where his Moderate friends secured an effective victory by having the Assembly's resolution so watered down that it was rendered ineffectual.

The successful defence of *Douglas* by the Moderates marked an important watershed ensuring that the kirk, and Scottish society as a whole, would henceforth be more liberal, more open to new cultural and intellectual trends. After this the kirk ceased to block Enlightenment ideas and actively began to support them through the writings and preaching of the Moderates. The Edinburgh literati, especially those who were ministers, were now free to write and publish with far less fear of censure. The next few years were marked by prominent Moderates gaining more complete control over the kirk, by their professional success, and also by various literary triumphs which were recognised throughout Europe of which the greatest was the publication of William Robertson's *History of Scotland* in 1759. Its favourable response throughout Britain showed that a minister could make a name for himself in the world of letters without compromising his principles or his calling.

SCOTLAND c1750: TOWARDS IMPROVEMENT AND INDUSTRIALISATION

Scotland in 1750 was still a poor country, economically backward compared with England. Many features of Scottish society had only changed marginally during the previous century. The average Lowland cottar or Highland sub-tenant was little better clothed, fed, or housed in the mid-eighteenth century than in his great grandfather's time. Yet change was in the air. Scotland was poised on the threshold of major economic and social developments though this was not necessarily apparent to contemporaries. Developments which were unspectacular in the 1740s became more widespread in the 1750s, accelerated in the 1760s and were of major significance by the 1770s. The period from c1750 to c1780 has been called an age of improvement. This term was not confined to agriculture but embraced a wide range of economic and cultural changes which interlinked and reinforced each other in such a complex pattern of interactions that it is hard to isolate and evaluate the importance of the elements which were at work. Accelerating economic growth in the third quarter of the eighteenth century was an indispensable prelude to the onset of industrialisation from the 1780s. During this phase, Mitchison has suggested, Scotland achieved almost as much economic growth as England had in the previous two centuries.[1] Scotland in 1780 was still a predominantly rural country, still markedly poorer than England. Nevertheless, during the previous 30 years the pace and direction of economic and social change had begun to differentiate Scotland from its European neighbours and place it far closer to England. Scotland's ability in the late eighteenth and early nineteenth centuries rapidly to adopt innovations from England and then to improve upon them would have been impossible without the phase of pre-industrial expansion which was under way by the 1740s and 1750s.

One marked change which was occurring by the 1750s was accelerated population growth. Although no one could have realised it at the time the years 1739-41 marked a crucial watershed. For the first time a severe harvest failure had occurred without a correspondingly serious mortality crisis.

1. R. Mitchison, *A History of Scotland* (Edinburgh 1970), pp. 348–9.

Improvements in grain supply, more effective poor relief and more efficient transport and marketing systems shifted the balance from a society which, as in the 1690s, was unable to cope with bad harvests to one which could surmount such obstacles without major difficulties. Webster's census of 1755 suggests that Scotland's population at this time was growing by around 0.4 per cent per annum, a rate perhaps twice that of the seventeenth and early eighteenth centuries. This was the start of what has been called the 'mortality transition' with an improvement in the mortality of infants and children. Following European trends death rates in Scotland fell from around 35 per 1,000 before 1755 to under 30 per 1,000 by the 1790s. This was higher than in England but it represented a significant improvement. Population growth, which may have begun to quicken from the 1740s, was starting to affect grain prices by the 1760s. Between 1755 and 1801 the average rate of growth was around 0.6 per cent per annum, less than half that of England. This was fast enough to generate increased demand at home and to increase the supply of labour but not rapid enough to outstrip economic growth.

Wages do not seem to have risen at all in real terms during the first half of the eighteenth century and only rose modestly between 1750 and 1775. Nevertheless, additional earnings from the spinning of linen yarn may have boosted the income of many families. Any increase in the buying power of ordinary families, however marginal, is likely to have resulted first in greater consumption of food, including more meat and dairy produce and then in the more frequent and widespread purchase of clothing and household items, including linen. If living standards for ordinary people only improved slightly indications are that the incomes of middle-class and landowning families rose more markedly. This is evident in a revolution in lifestyles and tastes which had ramifications throughout the economy as it started to spread down the social hierarchy. By the 1740s tea drinking had become normal among the middle classes and was starting to become an occasional luxury even among the urban poor. Rising standards of living among Edinburgh's bourgeoisie are highlighted by the fact that between 1750 and 1770 the quantity of wheat ground at Edinburgh mills nearly doubled while the population of the city grew by less than a quarter.

In the 1750s the balance between population and agricultural production also began to alter decisively. Scotland moved from being a net exporter to an importer of grain. Prior to the 1750s with agricultural output rising ahead of population there had been relatively little incentive for large-scale agricultural improvement. Grain prices were static and the substantial exports which were normal in most years were, as in the late sevententh century, a reluctant reaction to a glutted home market. These conditions hardly encouraged investment geared at raising productivity on the land. From the early 1760s, however, grain prices began to rise and by the 1770s higher prices were providing a major stimulus to agricultural improvement. Cattle prices seem to have increased more than grain during the first half of the eighteenth century while numbers of cattle sent to England may have risen from about 30–37,000 in the early 1720s to around 40,000 c1740 and over

60,000 by 1770. On the other hand, the growth of the droving trade did not necessarily encourage major structural changes in agriculture. While incomes for some Galloway and Highland proprietors certainly rose, overall agricultural rents were stable until the 1750s before starting to rise markedly in the 1760s. Despite the improvements which had been made in some eastern lowland areas by the mid-eighteenth century the bulk of agricultural change still lay ahead. Nevertheless, the increasing tempo of change in the countryside is highlighted by three indices. The first is the foundation of planned estate villages. Two were developed in the 1740s, 15 in the 1750s, 45 in the 1760s. The number of divisions of commonty rose from eight in the 1740s to 23 in the 1750s and 40 in the 1760s. In the 1730s hardly any land surveyors were at work in Scotland. By the first half of the 1750s, however, there were 20 at work and by the mid-1770s 65 are known.

Increasing links overseas and with England undoubtedly encouraged the Scottish economy but the influence of the expanding home market was also significant. The continued growth of Edinburgh and Glasgow during the first half of the eighteenth century along with rising standards of living among the urban middle classes had effects on agriculture in central Scotland which have yet to be fully evaluated. As Edinburgh developed its role as a social centre rents from all over Scotland were spent here to the benefit of Lothian farmers. The importance of the Edinburgh food market helps to explain why the Lothians were the leading area in terms of agricultural improvement in the mid-eighteenth century.

The tobacco trade grew decisively in the 1740s as Glasgow merchants finally began to compete on more than equal terms with traders in Bristol, Liverpool and Whitehaven. The spin-off from the tobacco trade was slow at first but by the 1750s tobacco merchants were buying much of their exports from within Scotland. In addition, the rapid growth of the tobacco trade led to a transformation of the Scottish banking system which benefited the economy as a whole.

The initial multiplier effects of the tobacco trade were largely confined to west-central Scotland. More important as a widespread agent of economic growth and social change was linen manufacture, particularly from the early 1740s with improvements in quality and the payment of bounties on exports. Production of linen, which had been static in the decade before 1742, doubled in the following 10 years. Home demand and sales to England were more important in total than exports and even marginal improvements in the living standards of substantial sectors of the Scottish population may have greatly increased home demand for handkerchiefs, shirts and household linen. The numbers of people engaged in spinning linen yarn and weaving linen cloth can only be guessed at but it has been suggested that one person in every second or third family in the country was involved in linen manufacture. Much of this was part-time labour, but as output rose and demand increased more and more workers became virtually full-time producers and severed their links with agriculture. By the 1750s some linen manufacturers at least had established factory-sized units of production.

These developments in agriculture, trade and industry had a profound effect on Scottish banking. Scotland was undoubtedly short of capital but the increasingly efficient banking system made the most of what was available. The assets of Scottish banks increased 10 times between 1744 and 1772 and the issue of notes 15 times. Economic growth was occurring over a wide range of sectors, influenced both by internal and external demand.

The intellectual changes which were involved in the secularisation of Scottish society and which can be summarised under the themes of 'enlightenment' and 'improvement' also had a major if less directly measurable impact on economic development and social change. A key feature of intellectual development was that it occurred in a context which was socially and politically conservative. Political and social stability was an essential precondition for intellectual advance as well as economic development. The ideas of enthusiasts for improvement and the Enlightenment literati served to confirm the status quo rather than challenge it. The values of Edinburgh's intellectual elite were those of landed society. After the Union and the abolition of the Privy Council the role of landowners in society, whether at a local level or nationally, was enhanced rather than reduced. Most of the leaders of the Moderate party in the church, the legal establishment and the universities were solidly behind the Hanoverian regime. Even Hume, the most intellectual radical of the Enlightenment's major figures, was not a social or political radical; he was a firm supporter of the establishment.

It would be easy to present Scotland in 1750 as having recently emerged from civil war and only starting to recover from deep social divisions created by the persistence of the Jacobite movement whose supporters have been portrayed as inherently conservative in outlook. On this interpretation political stability was only achieved after Culloden. This is misleading. Lenman has shown how marginalised most of the support for the Jacobites was in 1745.[2] Moreover, it is clear that during the 1720s and 1730s the majority of Scots of all political persuasions thought that the Jacobite cause was dead. The 1745 rising, seen from this perspective, seems more a short-term aberration, interrupting briefly, then in its aftermath accelerating, trends within the Highlands which were already well established. It is a mistake to assume that all Whig landowners in the Highlands during the first half of the eighteenth century were progressive, all Jacobite ones stubbornly traditional. Nothing underlines this more than the example of Mackintosh of Borlum who emerges from most accounts of the 1715 rebellion as a stereotype Highland warrior – tough, fierce and uncompromising. Yet after the rising, from his prison in Edinburgh Castle, he wrote a treatise on agricultural improvement. The chiefs of the Camerons of Lochiel, one of the most staunchly Jacobite clans, had interests in West Indies plantations during the 1730s.

2. B. Lenman, *The Jacobite Rising in Britain 1689–1746* (London 1980).

The military occupation of the Highlands after Culloden did not bring immediate peace; indeed cattle stealing was more rampant in the dislocated social conditions immediately after the battle than before the rising. While military patrols and outposts helped curb cattle rustling more important was the increasingly commercial attitudes which flourished among Highland landowners of all political persuasions once the threat of disorder was removed. By the mid-1750s the government had begun the process of rehabilitating and reintegrating the families of forfeited Jacobites into British society. Simon Fraser (Lord Lovat) was the last peer to be executed for supporting the Jacobites. In 1750 his son, who had been forced by his father to lead the Clan Fraser in the rising, was pardoned. Six years later he was given the command of a new regiment raised for service in America from clansmen on the forfeited Fraser estates. The Frasers spearheaded the attack on the Heights of Abraham which allowed the capture of Quebec. Highlanders, who had been feared on battlefields from Killiecrankie to Falkirk, were now being mobilised in the service of the expanding British Empire. The image of the Highlander, scorned by Lowlanders and English alike in 1745, was soon to be rehabilitated and turned into a potent national myth.

Well before the 1745 rebellion the Highlands were beginning to change and there were signs of a growing ideological contrast between the traditional and the new. Emigration from the Highlands to the Lowlands and across the Atlantic was already under way by the 1740s, spearheaded by tacksmen who were leaving not because of poverty but because of the loss of their social position. The Highland economy was changing, too, as the vogue for improvement spread from the Lowlands. The potato first reached the Outer Hebrides in South Uist in 1743; by the 1760s it was a staple item of diet.

If the pace of change in Scotland during the 1750s was only slightly faster than in previous decades signposts pointing in the direction of major transformations were already in place. Among the examples may be mentioned the opening of the sulphuric acid works at Prestonpans in 1749, the publication of plans for Edinburgh's new town in 1752, John Smeaton's report on the possibilities for deepening the Clyde in 1755, and the founding of the Carron Company in 1759.

This book began with Macbeth, Scotland's most notorious murderer. It is appropriate that it should end with Scotland's most famous poet. The year in which the Carron Company was founded also saw the birth of Robert Burns. Burns' life typifies the ambivalence and restlessness of Scottish society in the mid-eighteenth century. His romantic Jacobite leanings led him to look back at the Union of 1707 and condemn the 'parcel of rogues' who had caused Scotland to be 'bought and sold for English gold'. At the same time, like the Edinburgh literati who encouraged him, he wrote in English rather than Scots when he was trying to impress most. His unsuccessful career as a farmer was influenced by the changes in agriculture and rural society which were affecting Ayrshire by the 1770s. His later post as an exciseman was gained by shrewd use of the system of patronage. By the time Burns died in 1796 the

Scottish and English economies were rapidly becoming so closely integrated that they cannot be considered in isolation. As this book has tried to show, Scotland's path to industrialisation was distinctive and very different from the one followed by England. So was Scotland's contribution to the Industrial Revolution, but that is a story which must be left for future volumes in this series.

GENERAL MAPS

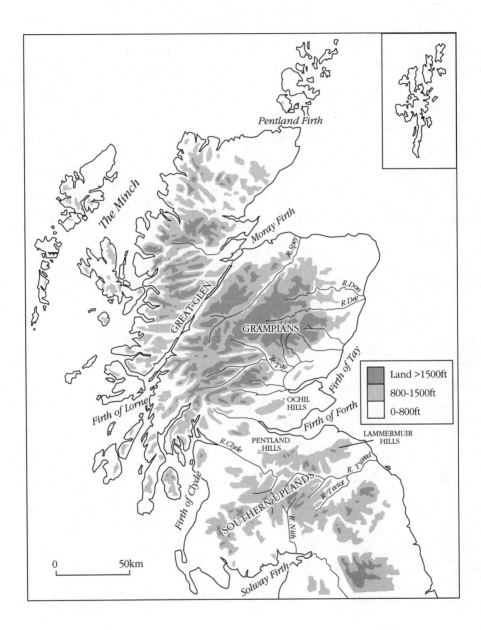

General Map 1 Scotland: Physical Features

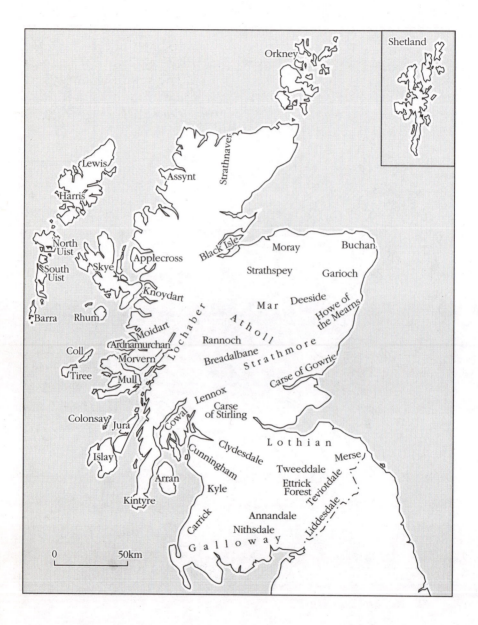

General Map 2 Scotland: Localities

General Map 3 Scotland: Sheriffdoms and Counties

GLOSSARY OF TERMS

Specialist terms are explained in the text where they first occur but some, which occur frequently but which may be unfamiliar to readers without a Scottish background, are listed below.

barony A legal jurisdiction or franchise granted to a landowner by the crown, incorporating a baron court and acting as the lowest level of the legal system.

bere A hardy four-rowed variety of barley.

bloodwyte An assault where blood was shed.

bond of manrent A written contract of allegiance and mutual support between two men, usually a lord and a laird.

bonnet laird A proprietor who was an owner-occupier, working his land in person.

clachan A term for a hamlet cluster, normally relating to settlement in the Highlands.

collegiate church A church established by a landowner in which a college of clerks held votive masses for the souls of the patron and his family.

commonty An area of rough pasture possessed jointly by two or more proprietors and grazed in common by their tenants.

cordiner A high-class shoemaker.

cottar A sub-tenant allocated grazing rights and often a small share of arable land by a tenant in return for providing labour.

crannog A hut or settlement constructed on an artificial island in a lake.

factor An estate manager or steward.

ferm toun A Lowland hamlet cluster.

feuar A proprietor holding land by feu ferme tenure.

feu ferme A hereditary tenure under which the feuar, in return for a substantial initial cash payment and an annual feu duty, had considerable security of possession.

grassum A lump sum paid on entry to a feu or a lease, or for the renewal of a lease.

hammerman A metal worker in a burgh.

heritor A landed proprietor (used from the later seventeenth century stressing property rather than feudal superiority).

infield-outfield A system of farming under which a limited area of the best land (the infield) was cultivated intensively, supplemented by a more extensive, less heavily cropped outfield.

kindly tenant Tenants with an acknowledged customary right to the possession of their holding based on kinship with the previous occupier.

kirk session The lowest level of church courts, comprising the minister of a parish and a group of elders, concerned with enforcing moral discipline and allocating poor relief.

kirkton A hamlet cluster grouped around a parish church.

laird A landed proprietor, usually below the level of the nobility.

liberty The defined hinterland of a royal burgh within which the burgh's merchants had various exclusive trading privileges.

litster A dyer.

mains The home farm of an estate, usually worked by the proprietor but sometimes leased to tenants.

Mounth The main east/west watershed of the Grampians which divides the lowlands of Strathmore and the Mearns from those of north east Scotland.

ploughgate The amount of land which could be kept in cultivation by a plough team of eight oxen.

policies The enclosed ornamental grounds around a castle or mansion.

regality A legal jurisdiction or franchise made up of a group of baronies. Regalities were possessed with wide powers and lay outside the jurisdiction of central government for all but a few serious offences.

runrig A system of allocating shares of arable among cultivators within a farm or settlement according to the quality as well as the quantity of land, producing fragmentation of holdings into scattered strips and parcels.

shieling Summer grazings for livestock, especially dairy cattle, usually in upland areas. Also applied to the temporary huts associated with them.

steelbow A lease which included the granting of seed corn, draught animals and farming equipment to the tenant.

tack A lease.

tacksman A term used in the Highlands in the seventeenth and eighteenth centuries to describe members of the clan gentry, with close kinship links to the chief, holding their lands on a hereditary basis in return for rent and services.

teinds Tithes.

thirlage A feudal obligation under which the inhabitants of an estate had to grind their grain at the proprietor's mill.

wadset A form of loan under which a proprietor borrowed a sum of money secured on an area of land which the lender held rent free, in lieu of interest, until the loan was repaid.

A GUIDE TO FURTHER READING

This bibliography aims to guide the reader towards some of the most important books and articles which have been published in recent years as well as to some of the older literature. Space does not permit an exhaustive bibliography, particularly of journal articles. Annual bibliographies of publications are produced in *Scottish Economic and Social History* and *Scottish Historical Review*. These journals also review recent books while SESH lists recently completed theses. Together they provide a good start for a more detailed literature search.

ABBREVIATIONS

BAR	*British Archaeological Reports*
JHG	*Journal of Historical Geography*
PSAS	*Proceedings of the Society of Antiquaries of Scotland*
SESH	*Scottish Economic and Social History*
SGM	*Scottish Geographical Magazine*
SHR	*Scottish Historical Review*
SS	*Scottish Studies*

GENERAL WORKS

The best starting-point for further reading remains T.C. Smout's *History of the Scottish People 1560–1830* (London 1969). Immensely readable as well as scholarly, its conclusions have inevitably been challenged in many areas by more recent work for which it served as an inspiration. Of one-volume economic histories B. Lenman, *An Economic History of Scotland 1660–1976* (London 1977) covers only the end of the period while S.G.E. Lythe and J. Butt, *An Economic History of Scotland c1100–1939* (London 1975) deals superficially with medieval times. A range of social themes are covered in R.A. Houston and I.D. Whyte (eds), *Scottish Society 1500–1800* (Cambridge 1989). The most recent one-volume general history of Scotland is M. Lynch,

Scotland: A New History (London 1991). Still useful is R. Mitchison, *A History of Scotland* (London 1970), especially for the seventeenth century. The *New History of Scotland* published by Edward Arnold covers Scotland to c1750 in five volumes: A.P. Smyth, *Warlords and Holy Men: Scotland AD80–1000* (London 1984); G.W.S. Barrow, *Kingship and Unity 1000–1306* (London 1981); A. Grant, *Independence and Nationhood, 1306–1469* (London 1984); J. Wormald, *Court, Kirk and Community in Scotland 1470–1625* (London 1981); R. Mitchison, *Lordship to Patronage, Scotland 1603–1746* (London 1983). The treatment of social and economic themes between these volumes is variable. P. MacNeill and R. Nicholson, *An Historical Atlas of Scotland c400–c1600* (St Andrews 1975), soon to be replaced by an expanded, updated edition, has useful summaries on many key topics as well as maps. I.D. Whyte and G. Whittington (eds), *An Historical Geography of Scotland* (London 1983) provides a geographical perspective.

CHAPTER 1 THE MAKING OF MEDIEVAL SCOTLAND

A.A. Duncan, *Scotland: The Making of the Kingdom* (Edinburgh 1975) covers the early period in great detail. Smyth, *Warlords and Holy Men*, provides challenging new interpretations on Pictish society and kingship. A more traditional approach is given in M.O. Anderson, *Kings and Kingship in Early Scotland* (Edinburgh 1973). For an anthropologist's interpretation of Pictish symbol stones see A. Jackson. *The Symbol Stones of Scotland* (Stromness 1984). The Picts are dealt with in F.G.P. Friell and W.G. Watson (eds), *Pictish Studies, BAR,* 125, Oxford 1984, and A. Small (ed.), *The Picts: A New Look at Old Problems* (Dundee 1987). For a recent study with an archaeological emphasis see L. and J. Laing, *The Picts and Scots* (Stroud 1993). G.W.S. Barrow, *The Kingdom of the Scots* (London 1973) brings together a number of earlier publications on themes including rural settlement, multiple estates and land denominations. Similar ground is covered more comprehensively in R.A. Dodgshon, *Land and Society in Early Scotland* (Oxford 1981). W.F.H. Nicolaisen, *Scottish Place Names* (London 1976) is the standard work on Anglian, British, Pictish and Scottish place-names. G. Whittington, Placenames and the settlement of Dark Age Scotland, *PSAS,* 106, 1977, 99–110 provides a model for the geographical study of place names. I.A. Morrison, *Landscape with Lake Dwellings* (Edinburgh 1976) looks in detail at crannogs. The Norse settlement is covered by B. Crawford, *Scandinavian Scotland* (Leicester 1987), usefully supplemented by A. Fenton and H. Palsson (eds), *The Northern and Western Isles in the Viking World* (Edinburgh 1984). A number of L. Alcock's excavations of early historic sites have been published in *PSAS* in recent years: L. Alcock, E.A. Alcock and S.M. Foster, Reconnaissance excavations on Early Historic fortifications and other royal sites in Scotland 1974–84: 1. Excavations near St. Abb's Head, Berwickshire, 1980 *PSAS,* 116, 1986, 255–80, L. Alcock and E.A. Alcock, Reconnaissance excavation on Early Historic fortifications and other royal sites in Scotland, 1974–84: 2,

Excavations at Dunollie Castle, Oban, Argyll, 1978, *PSAS*, 117, 1987, 119–48, L. Alcock, E.A. Alcock and S.T. Driscoll, Reconnaissance excavations on Early Historic fortifications and other royal sites in Scotland: 3, Dundurn, *PSAS*, 119, 1989, 189–226, L. Alcock and E.A. Alcock, Reconnaissance excavations on Early Historic fortifications and other royal sites in Scotland, 1974–84: 4, Excavations at Alt Clut, Clyde Rock, Strathclyde, 1974–75, *PSAS*, 120, 1990, 95–150, and, L. Alcock and E.A. Alcock, Reconnaissance excavations on Early Historic fortifications and other royal sites in Scotland, 1975–84: 5, A. Excavations and other fieldwork at Forteviot, Perthshire, 1981: B. Excavations at Urquhart Castle, Inverness-shire, 1983: C. Excavations at Dunnottar, Kincardineshire, 1984, *PSAS*, 122, 1992, 215–88. Economic aspects of the period are highlighted in L. Alcock, *Economy, Society and Warfare among the Britons and Saxons* (Cardiff 1987). S.T. Driscoll and M.R. Nieke (eds), *Power and Politics in Early Medieval Britain and Ireland* (Edinburgh 1988). J.C. Chapman and H.C. Mytum, Settlement in north Britain 1000BC–AD1000 (*BAR*, 118, Oxford 1983) contains important chapters on early historic settlement and society. F.J. Byrne, *Irish Kings and High Kings* (London 1973) and R.B. Warner, The archaeology of early Irish kingship, in Driscoll and Nieke, *Power and Politics*, 47–68 provides interesting material for comparison with Scotland. The text of the Senchus, with a commentary, is given in J.W. Bannerman, *Studies in the History of Dalriada* (Edinburgh 1974).

CHAPTER 2 THE INTRODUCTION OF ANGLO-NORMAN FEUDALISM AND CHAPTER 3 MEDIEVAL ECONOMY AND SOCIETY

Barrow, *Kingship and Unity*, and Duncan, *Scotland: The Making of the Kingdom* provide a good general framework. G.W.S. Barrow, *The Anglo-Norman Era in Scottish History* (Oxford 1980) is the most recent survey of the Anglo-Norman settlement and makes interesting reading alongside R.L.G. Ritchie, *The Normans in Scotland* (Edinburgh 1954). W.E. Kapelle, *The Norman Conquest of the North: The Region and its Transformation 1000–1135* (London 1979) looks at Norman influences in southern Scotland. Many aspects of the upper levels of society in the twelfth and thirteenth century are covered in K.J. Stringer (ed.), *Essays on the Nobility of Medieval Scotland* (Edinburgh 1985). Stringer's detailed study, *Earl David of Huntingdon 1152–1219* (Edinburgh 1985) provides the most detailed 'biography' of a Scottish magnate from this period and considers the problems of cross-Border landholding in detail. Dodgshon, *Land and Society* and Barrow, *Kingdom of the Scots*, looks at rural settlement. D. Pollock, The Lunan Valley project: medieval rural settlement in Angus, *PSAS*, 115, 1985, 357–401 provides a detailed case study of landscape remains while I.D. Whyte, The evolution of rural settlement in Lowland Scotland in medieval and early-modern times: an exploration, *SGM*, 97, 1981, 4–15 covers broader themes. Duncan, *Scotland: The Making of the Kingdom*, considers social structure. M.L. Parry, Secular climatic change and marginal agriculture, *Transactions of the Institute of British Geographers*, 64, 1975, 1–14 is a pioneering study of climatic influences on medieval and later cultivation limits. See also J.M. Gilbert, *Hunting and Hunting Reserves in Medieval Scotland* (Edinburgh 1979). The foundation of religious houses is chronicled in I.B. Cowan and D.E. Easson, *Medieval Religious Houses in Scotland* (London 1976). The essays in N.H. Reid (ed.), *Scotland in the Reign of Alexander III* (Edinburgh 1990) provide a badly needed re-assessment of Scotland's economy and society in the later thirteenth century. M. Lynch, M. Spearman and G. Stell (eds), *The Scottish Medieval Town* (Edinburgh 1988) contains a lot of material on medieval trade. The development of the money economy is discussed in W.W. Scott, The use of money in Scotland 1124–1230, *SHR*, 58, 1979, 105–31. D.M. Metcalf (ed.), Coinage in medieval Scotland 1100–1600 (*BAR*, 45, Oxford 1977) is far more wide-ranging on the medieval Scottish economy than the title suggests. The career of Thomas of Coldingham has been analysed by J. Donnelly, Thomas of Coldingham, merchant and burgess of Berwick upon Tweed (died 1316), *SHR*, 59, 1980, 105–25.

CHAPTER 4 MEDIEVAL TOWNS

The key volume is M. Lynch et al., *The Scottish Medieval Town*. E. Ewan, *Townlife in Fourteenth-Century Scotland* (Edinburgh 1990) provides an overview of society in the burghs. Duncan, *Scotland: The Making of the Kingdom*, has a good chapter on towns while B. Dicks, The Scottish medieval town, a search for origins, in G. Gordon and B. Dicks (eds), *Scottish Urban History* (Aberdeen 1983) pp. 23–51 considers the problem of urban origins in Scotland. The potential for analysing the evolution of Scottish town plans is brought out by N.P. Brooks and G. Whittington, Planning and growth in the medieval Scottish burgh: the example of St Andrews, *Transactions of the Institute of British Geographers*, NS 2, 1977, 278–95. J.B. Hunter, Medieval Berwick on Tweed, *Archaeologia Aeliana*, 10, 1982, 107–24 looks at the evidence for the layout and functions of this important centre. Stringer, *Earl David*, looks at the rise of the contrasting centres of Inverurie and Dundee. Many reports of excavations in Scottish towns are contained in recent volumes of *PSAS* but several important ones remain unpublished. More general summaries of the findings for Aberdeen and Perth have been produced: J.C. Murray (ed.), *Excavations in the Medieval Burgh of Aberdeen 1973–81* (Edinburgh 1982) and P. Holdsworth (ed.), *Excavations in the Medieval Burgh of Perth 1979–81* (Edinburgh 1988). J.S. Smith (ed.), *New Light on Medieval Aberdeen* (Aberdeen 1985) is also worth reading. See also W.B. Stevenson, The monastic presence in Scottish burghs in the twelfth and thirteenth centuries, *SHR*, 60, 1981, 97–118.

CHAPTER 5 LATE-MEDIEVAL SCOTLAND: ECONOMY AND SOCIETY IN TRANSITION

Grant, *Independence and Nationhood*, and Wormald, *Court Kirk and Community*, span this period and contain many challenging new interpretations. The upper levels of society are considered in A. Grant, The development of the Scottish peerage, *SHR*, 57, 1978, 1–27 and R. Mason, Kingship, tyranny and the right to resist in fifteenth-century Scotland, *SHR*, 66, 1987, 125–51. R.G. Nicholson, *Scotland: The Later Middle Ages* (Edinburgh 1974) is more traditional. J.M. Brown (ed.), *Scottish Society in the Fifteenth Century* (London 1977) contains a wide-ranging selection of essays on late-medieval Scotland including Brown's article, Taming the Magnates, which started off the revision of ideas on the relations between late-medieval Scottish kings and their magnates. For bonds of manrent see J. Wormald, *Lords and Men in Scotland: Bonds of Manrent 1442–1603* (Edinburgh 1985). N. Macdougall's biographies of *James III* (Edinburgh 1982) and *James IV* (Edinburgh 1989) continue this new approach. Lynch et al., *The Scottish Medieval Town*, contains considerable material on late-medieval trade as do articles in T.C. Smout (ed.), *Scotland and the Sea* (Edinburgh 1992) and G.G. Simpson (ed.), *Scotland and Scandinavia 800–1800* (Edinburgh 1990). The pattern of Scottish exports has been analysed by I. Guy, The Scottish export trade 1460–1599, in T.C. Smout (ed.), *Scotland and Europe 1200–1850* (Edinburgh 1986), pp. 62–81. Problems of the coinage are examined in W.W. Scott, Sterling and the usual money of Scotland 1370–1415, *SESH*, 5, 1985, 4–22 and in Metcalf, *Coinage in Medieval Scotland*. The feuing movement is discussed in detail in M.H.B. Sanderson, *Scottish Rural Society in the Sixteenth Century* (Edinburgh 1982).

CHAPTER 6 THE REFORMATION AND ITS IMPACT

Research on the Scottish Reformation has been dominated by the work of Gordon Donaldson. His short book, *Scotland: Church and Nation Through Sixteen Centuries* (Edinburgh 1972) is a useful introduction to the broad themes. Some of his more detailed essays have been collected in *Scottish Church History* (Edinburgh 1985). His standard work, *The Scottish Reformation* (Cambridge 1960) and the collection of detailed essays in D. McRoberts (ed.), *Essays on the Scottish Reformation 1513–1625* (Glasgow 1962) are basic texts, usefully supplemented by I.B. Cowan, *The Scottish Reformation* (London 1982) which takes a more social approach. New perspectives on the Reformation are explored in Wormald, *Court, Kirk and Community*. Among recent detailed studies are F.D. Bardgett, *Scotland Reformed: The Reformation in Angus and the Mearns* (Edinburgh 1989) and M. Lynch, *Edinburgh and the Reformation* (Edinburgh 1981). M.H.B. Sanderson, *Cardinal of Scotland. David Beaton c1494–1546* (Edinburgh

1986) is an interesting modern assessment of the life of one of the Scottish Reformation's most controversial figures. M.H.B. Sanderson, *Mary Stewart's People* (Edinburgh 1987) charts the careers of a wide range of people during the period of the Reformation. G. Marshall, *Presbyteries and Profits* (Edinburgh 1980) is a good example of what can be gained by applying sociological theories to historical problems, in this case re-examining the Scottish Reformation from the standpoint of Weber's ideas on the Protestant work ethic. The development of the church after the Reformation can be followed in G.R. Hewitt, *Scotland Under Morton 1572–80* (Edinburgh 1982); D.G. Mullan, *Episcopacy in Scotland: The History of an Idea 1560–1638* (Edinburgh 1986); W. Makey, *The Church of the Covenant 1637–51* (Edinburgh 1979); J. Buckroyd, *Church and State in Scotland 1660–81* (Edinburgh 1980); I.B. Cowan, *The Scottish Covenanters 1660–88* (London 1976).

CHAPTER 7 POPULATION c1500–c1750

The standard work is M. Flinn (ed.), *Scottish Population History* (Cambridge 1977), a book of major importance for Scottish scholarship but soon to be updated by a new study. Some of its conclusions have been questioned: for example in R. Mitchison, Webster revisited: a re-examination of the 1755 'census' of Scotland, in T.M. Devine (ed.), *Improvement and Enlightenment* (Edinburgh 1988), pp. 62–77. R.A. Houston, *The Population History of Britain and Ireland 1500–1750* (London 1992) reviews the latest ideas on population structure and dynamics in the seventeenth and eighteenth centuries and sets them within a British context. S.G.E. Lythe, *The Economy of Scotland in its European Setting 1575–1625* (Edinburgh 1963) looks at the evidence for famine in the late sixteenth century. T.C. Smout, Famine and famine relief in Scotland, in L.M. Cullen and T.C. Smout (eds), *Comparative Aspects of Scottish and Irish Economic and Social History 1600–1900* (Edinburgh 1985), pp. 21–31 looks at the seventeenth and eighteenth centuries. Changes in Scottish diet are discussed in a preliminary statement on a major research project, A. Gibson and T.C. Smout, Scottish food and Scottish history 1500–1800, in Houston and Whyte (eds), *Scottish Society*, pp. 59–81. The impact of the famines of the 1690s at a regional level is discussed in R.E. Tyson, The population of Aberdeenshire 1695–1755: a new approach, *Northern Scotland*, 6, 1984–5, 113–31. For comparisons with Northern England see: A.B. Appleby, *Famine in Tudor and Stuart England* (Liverpool 1978). Scottish marriage patterns are covered in T.C. Smout, Scottish marriage, regular and irregular, 1500–1940, in R.B. Outhwaite (ed.), *Marriage and Society* (London 1981), pp. 204–36. R.A. Houston, Age at marriage of Scottish women c1660–1770, *Local Popopulation Studies*, 43, 1984, 63–6. Marriage formation and domestic industry: occupational endogamy in Kilmarnock, Ayrshire 1697–1764, *Journal of Family History*, 8, 1983, 215–29. Illegitimacy has been the subject of important work by R. Mitchison and L. Leneman, which is brought together in *Sexuality and Social Control in Scotland 1660–1780* (Oxford 1989). The life expectancy of one particular social group is covered by R.A. Houston, Mortality in early-modern Scotland: the life expectancy of advocates, *Continuity and Change*, 7, 1992, 47–69. Migration and population mobility has been the subject of a number of recent studies. General surveys include: R.A. Houston, Geographical mobility in Scotland 1652–1811, *JHG*, 11, 1985, 379–94, R.A. Houston and C.W.J. Withers, Population mobility in Scotland and Europe 1600–1900: a comparative perspective, *Annales de Demographie Historique*, 1990, 285–308. I.D. Whyte. Population mobility in early-modern Scotland, in Houston and Whyte (eds), *Scottish Society*, pp. 37–58. More detailed studies of particular types of migration include A.A. Lovett, I.D. Whyte and K.A. Whyte, Poisson regression analysis and migration fields: the example of the apprenticeship records of Edinburgh in the seventeenth and eighteenth centuries, *Transactions of the Institute of British Geographers*, NS 10, 1985, 317–32; A.G. Macpherson, Migration fields in a traditional Highland community 1350–1950, *JHG*, 10, 1984, 1–14.

CHAPTER 8 THE COUNTRYSIDE c1500–c1750
AND
CHAPTER 9 LOWLAND RURAL SOCIETY c1500–c1750

Sanderson, *Scottish Rural Society in the Sixteenth Century*, I.D. Whyte, *Agriculture and Society in Seventeenth-Century Scotland* (Edinburgh 1979), M.L. Parry and T.R. Slater (eds), *The Making of the Scottish Countryside* (London 1981) and Dodgshon, *Land and Society*, provide the best introductions. The last of these brings together material from a wide range of papers published by Dodgshon on Scottish settlement, field systems, tenure and farming practices. Rural settlement is covered in I.D. Whyte and K.A. Whyte, *The Changing Scottish Landscape 1500–1800* (London 1991). The intensification of infield-outfield farming in the Lothians is examined in I.D. Whyte, Infield-outfield farming on a seventeenth-century Scottish estate, *JHG*, 5, 1979, 391–402. Early eighteenth-century improvement is considered in I.D. Whyte, George Dundas of Dundas: the context of an early eighteenth century Scottish improving landowner, *SHR*, 60, 1981, 1–13. Crop yields are discussed in I.D. Whyte, Crop yields on the Mains of Yester 1698–1753, *Transactions of the East Lothian Antiquities Society*, 22, 1993, 23–30. For agricultural and social changes in the Borders see R.A. Dodgshon, Agricultural change and its social consequences in the Southern Uplands of Scotland 1660–1780, in T.M. Devine and D. Dickson (eds), *Ireland and Scotland 1600–1850* (Edinburgh 1983), pp. 49–59. A. Bil, *The Shieling 1600–1840* (Edinburgh 1990) looks in detail at one aspect of the traditional rural economy. For rural society see Sanderson, *Scottish Rural Society*; Whyte, *Agriculture and Society*; I.D. Whyte and K.A. Whyte, Continuity and change in a seventeenth-century Scottish farming community, *Agricultural History Review*, 31, 1981, 151–69 and Debt and credit, poverty and prosperity in a seventeenth-century Scottish rural community, in P. Roebuck and R. Mitchison (eds), *Scotland and Ireland: a Comparative Study of Development* (Edinburgh 1988), pp. 70–80 look at aspects of life on the Panmure estates in Angus. K.M. Brown, Aristocratic finances and the origins of the Scottish Revolution, *English Historical Review*, 104, 1989, 46–87 and Noble indebtedness in Scotland from the Reformation to the Revolution, *Historical Journal*, 62, 1989, 26–75 provide insights into the economic position of proprietors in the late sixteenth and early seventeenth centuries. Geographical and secular variations in landownership are considered by R.F. Callander, *A Pattern of Landownership in Scotland* (Aberdeen, 1987) and L. Timperley, The pattern of landholding in eighteenth-century Scotland, in Parry and Slater (eds), *The Making of the Scottish Countryside*, pp. 137–54. W. Makey, *The Church of the Covenant* (Edinburgh 1979) contains some challenging ideas regarding changes in rents and their differential impact at a regional scale. For the Levellers' Revolt see J. Leopold The 'Levellers'' Revolt in Galloway in 1724, *Scottish Labour History Society Journal*, 14, 1980, 4–29. The structure of industrial communities is examined in R.A. Houston, Coal, class and culture: labour relations in a Scottish mining community 1650–1750, *Social History*, 8, 1983, 1–18; C.A. Whatley, A caste apart ? Scottish colliers, work, community and culture in the era of 'serfdom' c1606–1799, *Scottish Labour History Society Journal*, 26, 1991, 3–20; C.A. Whatley, *The Scottish Salt Industry 1570–1850* (Aberdeen 1987). R.K. Marshall, *The Days of Duchess Anne: Life in the Household of the Duchess of Hamilton 1656–1716* (Edinburgh 1973) looks at aristocratic lifestyles. R.A. Houston, Women in the economy and society of Scotland 1500–1800, in Houston and Whyte (eds), *Scottish Society*, pp. 118–47, is the first serious study of the role of women in early-modern Scottish society and the workforce. For poverty see R. Mitchison, The making of the old Scottish poor law, *Past and Present*, 63, 1974, 58–93 and North and south; the development of the gulf in poor law practice, in Houston and Whyte (eds), *Scottish Society*, pp. 199–225. For the characteristics of vagrants see I.D. Whyte and K.A. Whyte, Geographical mobility in a seventeenth-century Scottish rural community, *Local Population Studies*, 32, 1984, 45–53, and The geographical mobility of women in early-modern Scotland, in L. Leneman (ed.), *Perspectives in Scottish Social History* (Aberdeen 1988), pp. 83–106.

CHAPTER 10 URBAN DEVELOPMENT c1500–c1750
AND
CHAPTER 11 URBAN ECONOMY AND SOCIETY
c1500–c1750

The best introduction to recent research is M. Lynch (ed.), *The Early Modern Town in Scotland* (London 1987). The European background to urbanisation is presented in J. de Vries, *European Urbanization 1500–1800* (London 1985). Scottish urbanisation is debated in I.D. Whyte, Urbanisation in early-modern Scotland: a preliminary analysis, *SESH*, 9, 1989, 21–37 and M.

Lynch, Urbanization and urban networks in seventeenth-century Scotland, *SESH*, 12, 1992, 24–41. Studies of individual towns include M. Lynch, *Edinburgh and the Reformation* (Edinburgh 1981). The growth of small market centres is discussed in I.D. Whyte, The growth of periodic market centres in Scotland 1600–1707, *SGM*, 95, 1979, 13–26. A number of important PhD theses on social and economic aspects of Scottish towns have remained unpublished including J.J. Brown, The social and political influence of the Edinburgh merchant elite 1600–1638 (Edinburgh 1985), G. Desbrisay, Authority and discipline in Aberdeen 1650–1700 (Aberdeen 1989), H.M. Dingwall's thesis, The social and economic structure of Edinburgh in the late seventeenth century (Edinburgh 1989), is to be published by Leicester University Press. The legal profession is considered in G. Donaldson, The legal profession in Scottish society in the sixteenth and seventeenth centuries, *Juridical Review*, 1976, 10–19. N.T. Phillipson, The social structure of the Faculty of Advocates in Scotland 1661–1840, in H. Harding (ed.), *Law Making and Law Makers in British History* (Edinburgh 1980), pp. 146–56. The occupational structure of Scottish burghs is examined in I.D. Whyte, The occupational structure of Scottish burghs in the late seventeenth century, in Lynch (ed.), *The Early Modern Town*, pp. 219–44.

CHAPTER 12 LAW AND ORDER, CRIME AND VIOLENCE

S.J. Davies, The courts and the Scottish legal system 1600–1747: the case of Stirlingshire, in V.A.C. Gatrell, B. Lenman and G. Parker (eds), *Crime and the Law* (London 1980), pp. 54–79, provides a good review of the hierarchy of courts and their operation. Mitchison and Leneman, *Sexuality and Social Control* look at kirk sessions. Bloodfeud has been studied in detail by J. Wormald, Bloodfeud, kindred and government in early-modern Scotland, *Past and Present*, 87, 1980, 54–97 and *Lords and Men in Scotland: Bonds of Manrent 1442–1603* (Edinburgh 1985), also by K. Brown, *Bloodfeud in Scotland 1573–1625* (Edinburgh 1986). Popular protest is considered by C. Whatley, How tame were the Scottish Lowlanders during the eighteenth century? in T.M. Devine (ed.), *Conflict and Stability in Scottish Society 1700–1850* (Edinburgh 1990), pp. 1–30. Space has not permitted a consideration of that well-known theme, lawlessness on the Borders but see A.P. Bradley, Social banditry on the Anglo-Scottish Border during the later middle ages, *Scotia*, 12, 1988, 27–43 and T.I. Rae, *The Administration on the Scottish Frontier 1513–1603* (Edinburgh 1966). C. Larner, *Enemies of God. The Witch Hunt in Scotland* (London 1985) presents a major reinterpretation of Scottish witchcraft from a sociological perspective. A. Macfarlane, *Witchcraft in Tudor and Stuart England* (London 1970) considers the evidence for England.

CHAPTER 13 CULTURE, EDUCATION AND LITERACY
c1500–c1750

D. Daiches (ed.), *A Companion to Scottish Culture* (London 1981), R. Watson, *The Literature of Scotland* (London 1984) and M. Lindsay, *History of Scottish Literature* (London 1977) provide a general introduction. H.M. Shire, *Song, Dance and Poetry at the Court of Scotland Under King James VI* (Cambridge 1969) covers the Castalians in detail. For seventeenth-century cultural developments see G. Donaldson, Stair's Scotland; the intellectual inheritance, *Juridical Review*, 1981, 128–45. For Gaelic culture see D. Thomson, *An Introduction to Gaelic Poetry* (London 1974) and D. Thomson (ed.), *The Companion to Gaelic Scotland* (London 1983). T. Crawford, Society and the Lyric: A Study of the Song Culture of Eighteenth-Century Scotland (London 1979) and W. Donaldson, *The Jacobite Song* (Aberdeen 1988) look at popular song. Some aspects of popular culture have been considered in E.J. Cowan (ed.), *The Peoples' Past* (Edinburgh 1980). The development of Scottish education is considered by J. Scotland, *The History of Scottish Education*, Vol. I (London 1969). R.A. Houston, *Scottish Literacy and the Scottish Identity* (Cambridge 1985) provides challenging new interpretations. Book ownership in the Northern and Western Isles is considered in F.J. Shaw, *The Northern and Western Islands of Scotland in the Seventeenth Century* (Edinburgh 1979).

CHAPTER 14 HIGHLAND SOCIETY AND ECONOMY
c1500–c1750

For overall discussion of the development of the Highlands see C.W.J. Withers, *Gaelic Scotland: The Transformation of a Culture Region* (London 1988) and A.J. Youngson, *After the Forty Five* (Edinburgh, 1973). The distinctive features of Highland agriculture are considered in R.A. Dodgshon: The ecological basis of Highland peasant farming 1500–1800, in H.H. Birks, H.J.B. Birks, P.E. Kaland and D. Moe (eds), *The Cultural Landscape, Past, Present and Future* (Cambridge 1988); Farming practice in the Western Highlands and Islands before crofting. A study in cultural inertia or opportunity costs, *Rural History*, 3, 1992, 173–89; Strategies of farming in the western highlands and islands of Scotland prior to crofting and the clearances, *Economic History Review*, 46, 1993, 679–701; and R.A. Dodgshon and E.G. Olsson, Productivity and nutrient use in eighteenth-century Scottish Highland townships, *Geografiska Annaler*, Ser. B, 70, 1988, 39–51. One aspect of Highland agriculture is examined in detail by A. Bil, *The Shieling*. R.A. Dodgshon's ideas on clanship are discussed in 'Pretense of blude and plaice of thair dwelling', in Houston and Whyte (eds), *Scottish Society*, pp. 169–98. The Gaelic language is the subject of an important study by C.W.J. Withers, *Gaelic in Scotland 1698–1981: The Geographical History of a*

Language (Edinburgh 1984). Social and economic studies of particular areas include L. Leneman, *Living in Atholl: A Social History of the Estates 1685–1785* (Edinburgh 1986). F.J. Shaw, *The Northern and Western Islands of Scotland in the Seventeenth Century* (Edinburgh 1979); E. Richards and M. Clough, *Cromartie: Highland Life 1650–1914* (Aberdeen 1989) are two detailed regional studies. E Cregeen, The tacksmen and their successors; a study of tenurial reorganisation in Mull, Morvern and Tiree in the early eighteenth century, *SS*, 13, 1969, 93–145 looks at changes on the Argyll estates. The management of the Annexed Forfeited Estates after 1745 has been studied by A. Smith, *Jacobite Estates of the Forty Five* (Edinburgh 1982). The political background to Highland society is examined in D. Stevenson, *Alastair MacColla and the Highland Problem in the Seventeenth Century* (Edinburgh 1980). For the later seventeenth and early eighteenth centuries see: P. Hopkins, *Glencoe and the End of the Highland War* (Edinburgh 1986); B. Lenman, *The Jacobite Risings in Britain 1689–1746* (London 1980); B. Lenman, *The Jacobite Clans of the Great Glen* (London 1984).

CHAPTER 15 TRADE AND INDUSTRY IN THE SIXTEENTH AND SEVENTEENTH CENTURIES

The best general background studies remain S.G.E. Lythe, *The Economy of Scotland in its European Setting 1550–1625* (Edinburgh 1963) and T.C. Smout, *Scottish Trade on the Eve of Union, 1660–1707* (Edinburgh 1963), but see T.M. Devine and S.G.E. Lythe, The economy of Scotland under James VI: a revision article, *SHR*, 50, 1971, 91–106. The economic side of the Union of 1603 is considered in B. Galloway, *The Union of England and Scotland 1603–8* (Edinburgh 1986). The mid-seventeenth-century crisis and the Cromwellian occupation is covered by D. Stevenson, *The Scottish Revolution 1637–44* (Newton Abbot 1973), D. Stevenson, *Revolution and Counter-Revolution in Scotland 1644–51* (London 1977). F. Dow, *Cromwellian Scotland 1651–60* (Edinburgh 1979) considers the economy at a low point as does T.M. Devine, the Cromwellian union and the Scottish burghs: the case of Aberdeen and Glasgow 1652–60, in J. Butt (ed.), *Scottish Themes* (Edinburgh, 1976), pp. 1–16. G. Marshall, *Presbyteries and Profits* analyses the later seventeenth-century manufactory movement. The merchant communities in Scottish burghs in the late seventeenth and early eighteenth century are analysed in T.M. Devine, The Scottish merchant community 1680–1740, in R.H. Campbell and A.S. Skinner (eds), *The Origins and Nature of the Scottish Enlightenment* (Edinburgh 1982), pp. 26–41 and The merchant class of the larger Scottish towns in the seventeenth and early eighteenth centuries, in G. Gordon and B. Dicks (eds), *Scottish Urban History* (Aberdeen 1983), pp. 92–111. Particular industries are covered by I. Donnachie, *A History of the Brewing Industry in Scotland* (Edinburgh 1979); C. Gulvin, *The Scottish Hosiery and Knitwear Industry 1680–1980* (Edinburgh 1984); A.G. Thomson, *The Paper Industry in Scotland 1590–1861* (Edinburgh 1974); C.A. Whatley,

The Scottish Salt Industry 1570–1850 (Aberdeen 1987). Figures for Scottish coal output in D.U. Nef, *The Rise of the British Coal Industry*, 2 vols (London 1932) are now considered dubious. Internal trade in the seventeenth century is considered by I.D. Whyte, *Agriculture and Society in Seventeenth-Century Scotland* and D. Woodward, A comparative study of the Irish and Scottish livestock trades in the seventeenth century, in L.M. Cullen and T.C. Smout (eds), *Comparative Aspects of Scottish and Irish Economic and Social History* (Edinburgh 1977), pp. 147–64. For the Northern Isles see H.D. Smith, *Shetland Life and Trade 1550–1914* (Edinburgh 1984). For economic conditions in the later seventeenth century see R.H. Campbell, Stair's Scotland: the economic and social background, *Juridical Review*, 1981, 110–27.

CHAPTER 16 THE UNION OF 1707 AND ITS IMPACT: THE SCOTTISH ECONOMY IN THE FIRST HALF OF THE EIGHTEENTH CENTURY

The debate over the background to, and nature of, the Union continues. For an overview see R. Mitchison, Lordship to Patronage. Scotland 1603–1745 (London 1983). T.C. Smout's view is discussed in T.C. Smout, *Scottish Trade on the Eve of Union 1660–1707* (Edinburgh 1963) and T.C. Smout, *A History of the Scottish People* (London 1969). For opposition to Smout's economic interpretation see W. Ferguson, *Scotland's relations with England. A Survey to 1707* (Edinburgh 1977) and P.W.J. Riley, *The Union of Scotland and England* (Manchester 1978). More recently C.A. Whatley has entered the fray: Salt, coal and the Union of 1707: a revision article, *SHR*, 66, 1987, 26–45 and Economic causes and consequences of the Union of 1707: a survey, *SHR*, 68, 1989, 150–81. For early eighteenth-century economic development see: A.J. Durie, *The Scottish Linen Industry in the Eighteenth Century* (Edinburgh 1979); C. Gulvin, The Union and the Scottish woollen industry 1707–60, *SHR*, 50, 1971, 121–37; T.M. Devine, *The Tobacco Lords* (Edinburgh 1975); The colonial trades and industrial investment in Scotland c1700–1815, *Economic History Review*, 29, 1976, 1–13. The development of banking is covered by S.G. Checkland, *Scottish Banking: A History 1695–1975* (Glasgow 1975) and C.W. Munn, *The Scottish Provincial Banking Companies 1747–1861* (Edinburgh 1981).

CHAPTER 17 TOWARDS IMPROVEMENT AND ENLIGHTENMENT

The volume of literature on the Scottish Enlightenment is vast. For the later seventeenth century see H. Ouston, York in Edinburgh: James VII and the patronage of learning in Scotland 1679–1688, in J. Dwyer, R.A. Mason and A. Murdoch (eds), *New Perspectives on the Politics and Culture of Early-Modern*

Scotland (Edinburgh 1985), pp. 133–55 and J. Rendall, *The Origins of the Scottish Enlightenment* (London 1978). Recent major surveys of the Enlightenment with extensive bibliographies include: A. Chitnis, *The Scottish Enlightenment: A Social History* (London 1976); R.H. Campbell and A. Skinner, *The Origins and Nature of the Scottish Enlightenment* (Edinburgh 1982); D. Daiches, P. Jones and J. Jones, *A Hotbed of Genius. The Scottish Enlightenment 1730–90* (Edinburgh 1986); R.B. Sher, *Church and University in the Scottish Enlightenment* (Princeton 1985). The critical bibliography in Sher's book is the best starting place for further reading. C. Camic, *Experience and Enlightenment* (London 1983) presents a detailed survey of the childhood and backgrounds of some of the main figures. R.L. Emerson, Scotland's universities in the eighteenth century 1690–1800, *Studies on Voltaire and the Eighteenth Century*, 167, 1977, 453–74 looks at the educational background. D. Allan, *Virtue, Learning and the Scottish Enlightenment* (Edinburgh 1993) is the latest major contribution to the debate.

CONCLUSION SCOTLAND c1750: TOWARDS IMPROVEMENT AND INDUSTRIALISATION

Scotland's economic and social development in the mid- and later eighteenth centuries is traced in R.H. Campbell, *Scotland Since 1707. The Rise of an Industrial Society* (Edinburgh 1985) and T.M. Devine and R. Mitchison (eds), *People and Society in Scotland, Vol. I 1760–1830* (Edinburgh 1988). B. Lenman, *Integration, Enlightenment and Industrialisation: Scotland 1746–1832* (London 1981) provides a good summary of political conditions in mid-eighteenth-century Scotland. T.C. Smout, Where had the Scottish economy got to by the third quarter of the eighteenth century?, in I. Hont and M. Ignatieff (eds), *Wealth and Virtue* (Cambridge 1983), pp. 45–72, is a key essay. For the social and economic background to the Jacobite movement see B. Lenman, *The Jacobite Risings in Britain 1689–1746* (London 1980).

INDEX